Writing Mexican History

Writing Mexican History

Eric Van Young

STANFORD UNIVERSITY PRESS
STANFORD, CALIFORNIA

Stanford University Press
Stanford, California

©2012 by the Board of Trustees of the Leland Stanford Junior University.
All rights reserved.

This book has been published with the assistance of the Associate Vice-Chancellor for Research Affairs at the University of California, San Diego.

No part of this book may be reproduced or transmitted in any form or by any means, electronic or mechanical, including photocopying and recording, or in any information storage or retrieval system without the prior written permission of Stanford University Press.

Library of Congress Cataloging-in-Publication Data
Van Young, Eric, author.
Writing Mexican history / Eric Van Young.
pages cm
Includes bibliographical references and index.
ISBN 978-0-8047-6860-3 (cloth : alk. paper) --
ISBN 978-0-8047-6861-0 (pbk. : alk. paper)
1. Mexico--Historiography. I. Title.
F1224.V36 2012
972--dc23
2011037537

Typeset by Bruce Lundquist in 10/12 Sabon

Dedicated to the late Paul Vanderwood—
Te extrañamos mucho, Pablo, amigo queridísimo

Contents

Acknowledgments ix

Introduction 1

PART I: THE HISTORIOGRAPHY OF RURAL MEXICO AND LATIN AMERICA
1. Waves and Ripples:
Studies of the Mexican Hacienda since 1980   21
2. Rural Latin America:
The Colonial Period and Nineteenth Century   53

PART II: THE HISTORIOGRAPHY OF COLONIAL MEXICO
AND THE ERA OF INDEPENDENCE
3. Two Decades of Anglophone Writing on Colonial Mexico:
Continuity and Change since 1980   83
4. No Human Power to Impede the Impenetrable Order of Providence:
The Historiography of Mexican Independence   127

PART III: THEORY AND METHODOLOGY
5. Doing Regional History:
A Theoretical Discussion and Some Mexican Cases   167
6. The Cuautla Lazarus:
Reading Texts on Popular Collective Action   199

PART IV: ECONOMIC HISTORY AND CULTURAL HISTORY
7. The New Cultural History Comes to Old Mexico   223

Bibliography 265
Index 315

Acknowledgments

The republication of one's own essays in a volume such as this is inherently an act of hubris, but in doing so I have had a number of facilitators to whom I accrued large debts. It is a pleasure to acknowledge these debts here. The idea for such an anthology first arose in conversations with Dr. Sergio Cañedo Gamboa, then Secretario Académico and *profesor-investigador* in the Colegio de San Luis Potosí, a distinguished Mexican institution of advanced studies, and with his colleague, Dr. Juan Carlos Ruiz Guadalajara, *profesor-investigador* of the same institution, conversations that eventuated in the publication of a much longer but overlapping set of my essays in Spanish in 2010, *Economía, política y cultura en la historia de México. Ensayos historiográficos, metodológicos y teóricos de tres décadas* (San Luis Potosí: El Colegio de San Luis Potosí/El Colegio de Michoacán/El Colegio de la Frontera Norte, 2010). I am grateful to both Sergio and Juan Carlos not only for their patience and support in this project, but also for indirectly stimulating the writing of the introduction, which bears some resemblance to the introductory pages of this volume, and which helped me gain some altitude over my own previous work in order to see its shape and direction. When in a fit of hubris I approached Norris Pope, director of Scholarly Publishing at Stanford University Press, about the possibility of doing a revised but overlapping collection of my essays in a single volume for an English-reading public, rather than laugh at my proposal he expressed keen interest in the project and encouraged it at every step. The anonymous reviewers for the Press (who turned out to be not so anonymous), Margaret Chowning and Gilbert Joseph, provided perceptive and very helpful comments for revisions to writing, approach, and structure, most of which I acted upon, some of which I declined to make, but all of which were useful. A friend and highly skilled editor who helped me whip the entire collection into shape wishes not to be named, following his own deeply held professional standards, but he will recognize himself when he reads these pages.

One of the essays in this volume, Chapter 4, has not appeared in print before, but I would nonetheless like to acknowledge John Coatsworth for commissioning it as a conference paper, and William Roger Louis, founding director of the National History Center, for sponsoring the event with the Center's imprimatur. Several of the essays have been significantly revised, especially Chapters 5 and 7, each of which represents a synthesis of two previously published pieces. Chapter 1 originally appeared as "Introduction to the Twenty-fifth Anniversary Edition" of Eric Van Young, *Hacienda and Market in Eighteenth-Century Mexico: The Rural Economy of the Guadalajara Region, 1675–1820* (Lanham, MD: Rowman and Littlefield, 2006), pp. xxi–l, and is republished here by permission. Chapter 2 is an excerpt from "Rural History," in José C. Moya, ed., *Oxford Handbook of Latin American History* (2010), pp. 309–41, included here by permission of Oxford University Press, Inc. Chapter 3 originally appeared as the journal article, "Two Decades of Anglophone Historical Writing on Colonial Mexico: Continuity and Change since 1980," *Mexican Studies/Estudios Mexicanos* 20:2 (Summer 2004), pp. 275–326, and is copyright (c) by the University of California Institute for Mexico and the United States, and the Universidad Nacional Autónoma de México, and published by the University of California Press, by whose permission it is republished here. Chapter 5 was published in part as the article "Doing Regional History: Methodological and Theoretical Considerations," *Conference of Latin Americanist Geographers Yearbook* 20 (1994), pp. 21–34, and appears here by permission of Dr. David J. Robinson, executive director of the Conference of Latin Americanist Geographers; additional material in this chapter is drawn from "Introduction: Are Regions Good to Think?" in Eric Van Young, ed., *Mexico's Regions: Comparative History and Development* (La Jolla: Center for U.S.-Mexican Studies, University of California, San Diego, 1992), pp. 1–36; thank you to the Center for U.S.-Mexican Studies for allowing the use of this excerpt. Chapter 6 was published as "The Cuautla Lazarus: Double Subjectives in Reading Texts on Popular Collective Action," *Colonial Latin American Review* 2:1 (1993), pp. 3–26, and appears in this volume by permission of the publisher, Taylor and Francis, http://www.informaworld.com. Much of Chapter 7 originally formed the article "The 'New Cultural History' Comes to Old Mexico," *Hispanic American Historical Review* 79 (1999), pp. 211–48, copyright 1999 Duke University Press, all rights reserved, reprinted by permission of the publisher; additional material in this chapter comes from "El lugar de encuentro entre la historia cultural y la historia económica," in Daniel Barragán Trejo and José Rafael Martínez Gómez, eds., *Relaciones intra e interregionales en el occidente de México. Memorias [del] VI Coloquio Internacional de Occidentalistas* (Guadalajara: Universidad de Guadalajara, 2009), pp. 15–39.

Writing Mexican History

Introduction

The essays in this volume—the earliest dating back about thirty years, the most recent with the ink barely dry—are both artifacts of change in the discipline over those three decades, and signposts I have left along the road of my own individual development as a historian.[1] The route, however, has not been an entirely random one. My scholarly energies have been occupied since 2000 in researching and writing a biography of the early nineteenth-century Mexican statesman, entrepreneur, and historian Lucas Alamán (on whom more in a moment). On one level the logic of how this inquiry grew out of my previous research is fairly clear. At the suggestion of the eminent Mexican historian Enrique Florescano, my interest in Mexican rural history came to be focused on the colonial Guadalajara region for doctoral study. Where the interest itself had originated, I confess, is a mystery to me. While working on that project, my archival encounter with prolonged insurgent activity during 1810–1821 in the Lake Chapala basin, to the south of Guadalajara, especially among Indian villages, led me to a study of popular groups in the Mexican independence movement more generally. Finally, my reading of Alamán's multivolume, magisterial, and deeply opinionated work on independence opened to an interest in the author and the way his political career was entwined with

---

1. This introductory essay is a somewhat more developed but heavily overlapping version of my introduction to Eric Van Young, *Economía, política y cultura en la historia de México: Ensayos historiográficos, metodológicos y teóricos de tres décadas* (San Luis Potosí: Colegio de San Luis Potosí/Colegio de la Frontera Norte/Colegio de Michoacán, 2010). I would like to acknowledge highly useful comments on several aspects of the collection from Margaret Chowning and Gil Joseph, who read the manuscript for Stanford University Press; Norris Pope at the Press for entertaining the notion that such a volume might be of value; and a generous subvention to aid in publication authorized by Arthur Ellis, vice-chancellor for Research, University of California, San Diego, and help in obtaining it from John Marino, my colleague and sometime chair in the Department of History at UC San Diego. Acknowledgment of permission from various journals and presses for republication of the articles and chapters appears at the beginning of each essay.

the new nation whose movement for separation from the metropolis I had just studied and he had chronicled. There is another level in the logic of this progression no less clear to me, if perhaps less obvious to readers of my work, which follows a trajectory from economic history, to social and cultural history, to biography. This tracks a growing interest in what I would call "interiority"; that is, in people's interior lives, especially their emotional and experiential processes, whether in groups or as individuals. This virtual obsession (for such it has become) was not on my horizon when I opted to study the Guadalajara region and the logic of regionality more generally, but emerged more and more clearly as I puzzled over how to interpret the actions and symbolic understandings of popular insurgents in my research on Mexican independence. I had moved, therefore, from the relatively impersonal, large-scale processes of economic history to the more intimate, often hidden dimension of culture and the dynamics of social groups in the context of collective political violence, albeit also on a large scale. Any reader familiar with my book on the popular sectors in the independence movement, *The Other Rebellion: Popular Violence, Ideology and the Struggle for Mexican Independence, 1810–1821* (Stanford, 2001), will notice the attention I devote there to forms of internal mental life, psychopathology, collective manias, and even psychoanalytic approaches to history. From this cluster of interests I was drawn to a history of Mexican psychiatry from the late colonial period to 1930 or so, a study for which I began research but in which I never advanced beyond the publication of a single essay on the theme.[2] Although biography as a form of writing history still remains quite *retro* in North American academia, it seemed to offer another route to the same sort of interiority I had hoped to explore in charting the delusional worlds of the mentally ill, but within the framework of political culture rather than psychopathology and the social intervention of state institutions in the lives of the mad. While the first two stages of this evolution are represented by the essays in this volume, the third is only hinted at and awaits the completion of my project on Lucas Alamán to be fully realized. My readers will perhaps indulge me, then, as I begin with a few thoughts on Alamán.

LETTERS AND LIVES

The age of electronic media and the personal computer has for most of us eclipsed the art, habit, and pleasure of writing letters on paper. The widespread practice in the Western world of corresponding in written

---

2. Van Young (2001b); republished in an expanded version as Van Young (2005).

form depended upon the advent of inexpensive paper and writing implements, the spread of literacy, the establishment of relatively reliable state-sponsored postal systems, and the development of international commerce and banking arrangements requiring detailed, timely, and confidential correspondence. During the last several centuries, the transmission of information in letters has served a variety of purposes. Especially for common people of some education, letters have facilitated the pursuit of love, the nourishing of friendship, the acquisition of wealth, and the exchange of scientific ideas and information. For states and powerful political actors the sending and receiving of letters have also underwritten the integration of polities, the administration of justice, the collection of taxes, and the advance of political, military, and colonial projects.

For biographers and historians letters of all sorts (and, since at least the eighteenth century, newspapers) have proved to be one of the primary sources for reconstructing the past, and for the study of historical actors both humble and famous. Particularly within a cultural tradition deeply and intensely literate but little given to the publication of memoirs or autobiographies, such as that of the Spanish-speaking world, the survival of letters on paper is for the historian an essential point of entry into the private lives of public people.[3] I have been especially struck with this in recent years as I have advanced through the archival phase of a biography of Lucas Alamán—polymath, political thinker, statesman, avatar of import substitution industrialization in Mexico, Panamericanist, codifier of Mexican conservatism, éminence gris behind the last dictatorship of Antonio López de Santa Anna, and arguably the greatest historian of nineteenth-century Mexico. Alamán himself observed in the early 1830s the lack of an autobiographical/memoirist tradition in the Spanish-speaking world more generally (his specific comparison was to France, but one may assume he had in mind Europe more widely), and lamented it as necessarily reducing the access of historians to the lives of past historical actors:

The historical memoirs that form such an important branch of French literature have not up to now occupied writers in our Castilian language. Nonetheless, [such writings] not only provide important historical materials, but also at times [illuminate] history itself with the knowledge of events and the secret sources that produce them. . . . A wit said that memoirs present us with heroes *en robe de chambre*; that is, how they are inside their houses, while history [writing] offers them to us wearing armor or a blonde wig. And it is not rare to find that

---

3. For a more developed discussion of the weakness of an autobiographical/memoirist tradition in the Hispanophone world, see Van Young (2002), and in the same number of the journal *Secuencia* the wide-ranging essay of Pablo Piccato (2002).

someone who appears grand in a ceremony is reduced to nothing when we see him naked.[4]

Were it not for Alamán's prolific letter writing (although relatively little of his personal, intimate correspondence seems to have survived), it would be almost impossible to reconstruct his thinking, his internal world, and his motives during a long public life.[5] Apart from the mountains of correspondence he generated during his periods as a high official in the national government, there are clusters of quite revealing letters that tell us much about the man and the mind behind the rather aloof and certainly conservative public persona, even if they fall short of intimate self-revelation. Among these are his exchanges in the early 1830s with his friend the political general Manuel Mier y Terán, in the years before Terán's suicide; his brief exchange of letters with the American historian William H. Prescott in the 1840s; and his three-decade correspondence (stretching from the mid-1820s virtually up to the day of Alamán's death in 1853) with the Duque de Terranova y Monteleone, the Neapolitan nobleman and heir to Fernando Cortés's great entailed estate, the Marquesado del Valle, for whom Alamán served as political informant, business agent, adviser, and general factotum in Mexico. Also revealing were his occasional notes to and from Carlos María de Bustamante; the letters he exchanged with informants who provided information for him as he wrote his great history of Mexican independence in the late 1840s and early 1850s; and even his half-dozen or so surviving letters to and from Antonio López de Santa Anna, especially if one reads between the lines.[6]

While he was a great writer of letters, apart from scattered notes and a few fragmentary outlines Alamán seems to have kept no diaries or working notebooks about either his political activities, his business enterprises, or his historical writing, or at least none that have survived or come to light.

---

4. Centro de Estudios de Historia de México Condumex (hereinafter Condumex), Fondo DCLXXIV, "Memorias de Don Lucas Alamán," French and italics in the original. Translations from Spanish here and elsewhere are mine.

5. The exception to this, apart from a rather formal and remarkably unrevelatory autobiographical sketch from the 1840s and the necrological essays published after his death in 1853, is the extremely interesting unfinished autobiographical fragment cited above, written during the 1830s and 1840s, that survives unpublished. There are, of course, biographical treatments of Alamán, and partial accounts of his life, thought, and public activities in many works. The last (and best) full-scale biography is that of Valadés (1938); and for a useful biographical summary, including a time line of Alamán's life, see Morán Leyva (2002).

6. Most of this correspondence is to be found in Condumex and the Archivo General de la Nación (Mexico), Ramo Hospital de Jesús. One would hardly be aware of the magisterial status of Alamán's great *Historia de México* from reading Enrique Florescano's very accessible and often acute *National Narratives in Mexico: A History* (2006), in which Alamán's work merits scarcely three sentences of discussion (pp. 310–11).

His admirer and friendly correspondent, the contemporary American historian William H. Prescott, for example, did keep such notebooks, which have been published and make for mildly interesting reading, especially where the composition of his great historical works is concerned.[7] Alamán's working methods as a historian in gathering information are illustrated in his correspondence with informants, but his larger ideas about historical processes or anything approaching what we might think of as a philosophy of history do not show up in his letters. His increasingly Olympian and rather pessimistic view of Mexico's history (and, by extension, of historical processes more generally) comes through most explicitly in some passages of his great *Historia de México* and must be extracted from that work. His view of how history writing was to be realized *as a craft*, on the other hand, is addressed in the autobiographical fragment of the 1830s that apparently formed the seed of the later published *Historia*.[8] By contrast, a number of modern historians, especially in the Francophone and Anglophone traditions, have left not only ample collections of published correspondence, but also autobiographies.[9] The more formal, self-conscious concern with producing treatises on *how to write history* seems by and large to be a modern tendency, mostly of the twentieth century, when history as a distinct academic discipline separated itself more clearly from a belle-lettristic tradition, although there are some notable earlier exceptions.

To continue with the Alamán theme for a moment, the strong influence of public circumstances—the political instability in Mexico during the decades following independence, and the war with the United States, for example—and the disappointments of his own life (the failure of several business enterprises, his long semiexile from the center of national political life, and the death of several of his children, common enough though such personal losses were at the time) seem to have tempered his earlier positive views about the significance of human agency in history. These ideas could never at best have been characterized as "optimistic," and what he may well have thought of as failures in many areas of his life and that of his country led him to the cool, rather melancholic pronouncements at the close of his *Historia de México* toward the end of his life. Take, for example, his view of the historian's task at the beginning of his autobiographical fragment, apparently written in the early 1830s. Here he began

---

7. For Prescott's memoranda to himself, mixed with diary entries, see Prescott (1961); a selection of Prescott's letters is to be found in Prescott (1970/1925).
8. Marc Bloch, *The Historian's Craft* (1992).
9. Some recent well-known examples from the Anglophone world are Schlesinger (2000) and Hobsbawm (2002); on historians' autobiographies in general, see Popkin (2005). Closer to home for readers of Mexican history is the revealing autobiographical essay of Brading (2007).

to approach the writing of political history, which occupied his attention throughout his life as a writer, almost from the point of view of a social historian, allowing much room in the course of history itself for chance, and even the play of ludic elements. Near the passage quoted above he penned some thoughts on the historian's craft that are worth quoting at some length, I think:

> Frequently the greatest events depend upon [such] small, even ridiculous causes that the gravity of history would be offended by presenting them in all their details; nonetheless, it is through these details that we come to know men. . . . And although history should make us know them in all their aspects, there are still in almost all great actions small circumstances, perhaps unfavorable to the person who figures [in those events], that the historian and the writer of tragedies try to dress with the majestic clothing with which they dress their heroes, while the memoirist and the comic poet strive to present them in the nude, and even sometimes with malignity.[10]

Alamán took up his pen again in the early 1840s to advance the memoir, a decade or so after he had begun it, but by then the work itself had mutated from a more personal account to a larger-scale, more self-consciously historical one (tellingly, from "Una memoria de mi vida" to "Una memoria de mis tiempos") and had become a sort of predraft of what some years later would come to be the *Historia de México*.[11] The earlier, almost lighthearted tone of the lines just quoted had given way to a much darker, more fatalistic vision reflected in the later sections of the "Memoria," in which Alamán wrote of

> . . . the great revolutions that have lifted from nothing those nations that have come to be lords of a great part of the world, and which give origin with their destruction to other nations that in the impenetrable order of providence have played a part in their time, suffering [in their turn] the same vicissitudes. But there is the force of circumstance, and such conjunctures of these that compel the will. . . . There are [many] examples of these verities demonstrated on every page of history. . . . And so it is that the form of the world changes ceaselessly, empires and nations succeeding each other, with no human power sufficient to impede it.[12]

---

10. "Memorias de D. Lucas Alamán."

11. The titles of the two works bear a striking similarity: that of the early 1830s and early 1840s, given to the work in 1843, is "Memorias de D. Lucas Alamán, Ministro de Relaciones exteriores e interiores de la República Megicana en diversas épocas. En las que se contiene la verdadera historia de esta República desde el año de 1808 en que comenzaron la inquietudes que condujeron a su independencia hasta el año de 1843. Escritas por el mismo"; whereas the complete title of the great published work we know by its abbreviated title of the *Historia de México* is *Historia de México desde los primeros movimientos que produjeron su independenia en el año de 1808, hasta la presente época.*

12. "Memorias de D. Lucas Alamán."

And by the time Alamán came to write the concluding passages of the *Historia* a decade later still, he famously voiced the doubt as to whether a nation called Mexico had ever existed at all, whether there were any Mexicans, and by implication whether Mexico *could* come to exist in future. The focus had narrowed here from the history of nations and revolutions in general to that of Mexico in particular, but the vision is no less dark.

THE ESSAYS

My research in recent years on the life of Lucas Alamán has stimulated me to think not only about the nature of historical sources, but also about my own career as a historian as refracted through my studies of Alamán's historical methods and writings. The modern world would not be poorer for the destruction of my particular correspondence (most of which, in any case, has for some time taken the form of electronic mail and therefore has a short half-life), or the lack of any autobiography that hubris might tempt me to write. It would have been of enormous value to our understanding of Alamán's life, the history of Mexican letters, and even to the profile of early nineteenth-century political thought in the Atlantic world, on the other hand, had he (or someone) preserved his personal correspondence in a systematic way, and even more so had he finished his autobiography.[13] The publication of the present volume of essays, however, provides me with an occasion both welcome and sobering to consider my own evolution as a historian whose life experience—not easily separable from my writing of history—was shaped by the late twentieth century, and by personal circumstance, no less than Lucas Alamán's was by the early nineteenth century and the events of his life. It is a welcome occasion because one does not often have the opportunity to commit to paper thoughts on one's relationship to one's own work in a relatively formal way that may be read by other people, however few. And it is a sobering occasion for much the same reason, since in the process of remembering and organizing such recollections, one may not only invent things, but also realize how many gaps there are in one's own account of oneself, not to mention that even putting such thoughts into print constitutes an embarrassing act of narcissism. In framing this collection of essays it might be useful for me to offer some observations on the historian's craft, at least as I have practiced it, in addition to placing the essays in the context of my own historical research on Mexico and of how the field of

---

13. Some of Alamán's political, business, and even personal correspondence is published in Aguayo Spencer (1945, vols. 10 and 12).

Mexican history has evolved over the last three decades or so. With the patient indulgence of my readers, I take the opportunity to do so now, although the emphasis is more on contextualizing the essays published here and explaining why they were written when they were, than on offering any lectures about the discipline, or offering up personal confessionals.[14]

A good place to begin such reflections, perhaps, is with an earlier volume of my essays that appeared in 1992 under the title *La crisis del orden colonial: Estructura agraria y rebeliones populares de la Nueva España, 1750–1821*, all but one of them published previously.[15] With a couple of exceptions those were all substantive rather than historiographical essays; that is, they dealt with aspects of history itself rather than the ways in which history is written by professional historians, with conceptual tools that historians employ, or with the state of historical research on Mexico. Five of the essays looked back to work I had done on the agrarian history of the Guadalajara area (see Chapter 1 in this volume), while four of them looked ahead to a book I was then writing on popular groups in the Mexican independence struggle, and came to be integrated more or less into that work, published in 2001, considerably later than I had optimistically predicted in 1992.[16] In the introduction to the 1992 collection I basically discussed the theme of the materialist interpretation of history versus a culturalist approach, and more specifically which of these might offer the most apt conceptual tools for looking at the participation of common people, mostly indigenous peasant villagers, in the struggle for Mexican independence. This foreshadowed a major concern of mine in the intervening years that forms a major thematic axis in the present volume—the promise and limits of cultural history, and the relationship of cultural to economic history. The basic question for me then, as even now, was whether subaltern participation in the decade-long insurgency that sundered New Spain from the metropolis is most convincingly described as a massive agrarian rebellion, or as a movement to assert localist and ethnic identities, and to preserve the cultural practices associated with them. According to the first scenario, agrarian rebellion would have arisen from material deprivation due to economic conditions in the Mexi-

---

14. I have made some brief autobiographical notes that address my personal background, and to some degree my development as a historian, in Van Young (2007b).

15. Van Young (1992c). Of the eleven essays in that volume, only one is reproduced here (Chapter 5; chap. 3 in the original version). All the other essays in this volume were published after 2000, except Chapter 6, "The Cuautla Lazarus" (1993) and Chapter 7, "The New Cultural History Comes to Old Mexico" (1999).

16. *The Other Rebellion: Popular Violence, Ideology, and the Mexican Struggle for Independence, 1810–1821* (Van Young 2001c); the Spanish edition appeared in Mexico as *La otra rebelión: La lucha por la independencia de México, 1810–1821* (Van Young 2006c).

can countryside: demographic pressures, land scarcity among peasants, the spread of commercialized agriculture, and falling real incomes for rural people. According to the second, an explanatory scheme in a more cultural register would take into account popular, especially indigenous, impulses to vindicate some sort of political rights, assert ethnic identity in the face of late colonial pressures toward homogenization, and defend village communities. These diminutive polities were bounded by Indianness, a distinct ritual cycle, lifestyle, and a diminished subjecthood signified under the colonial regime by ethnic prejudice, differential tax obligations, legal disabilities, and so forth.

Looking back now on the introduction to my 1992 volume of essays, it seems to me that my answer to the question I had posed was ambivalent. The ambivalence arose from a growing realization that there exists a salutary but irresolvable tension between materialist and culturalist explanatory frameworks, and between structure and agency in human history. Chapter 7 in this volume, "The New Cultural History Comes to Old Mexico" (originally published in 1999), deepened that discussion in exploring the limits and achievements of cultural history, and the dynamics of its ascendancy during the decades of the 1980s and 1990s in historical writing on colonial Mexico. A number of my colleagues and other readers found the essay to be highly tentative in its assertion of the claims of cultural history, and agnostic about its accomplishments and potential. This opinion surprised me, since I had thought at the time (and still do) that I was merely offering a number of sensible reservations about the writing of cultural history rather than expressing tepidity about its value, or voicing skepticism about whether it can be done at all. In reading this essay my readers may want to revisit the 1999 issue of the *Hispanic American Historical Review* (HAHR) in which the article first appeared along with several other contributions by accomplished historians of modern Mexico addressing the same issues.[17] Ambivalence is not necessarily symmetrical, however, and my ambivalence some years earlier, in the 1992 introductory essay, leaned somewhat toward the materialist end of the spectrum, as suggested by my citation of an anecdote putatively involving the English philosopher Bertrand Russell, an elderly woman in one of his lecture audiences, and a turtle, while the 1999 essay leans in the opposite direction.[18] The final point I was trying to make in

---

17. Specifically with relation to my book on Mexican Independence, some of the issues about cultural history as exemplified in that work are addressed in my extended exchange with Alan Knight, originally published in *Historia Mexicana* and republished in booklet form as *En torno a La otra rebelión* by El Colegio de México in the series "Miradas a la historia" (Van Young and Knight 2007).

18. Since that anecdote may not be familiar to my present readers, let me quote integrally

invoking that story at the close of my 1992 introductory essay is that however many layers of ideology, culture, mentality, or language one peels back, there must always be a layer of materiality underneath them, basically an economically determined framework of class relations. Certainly this is true in a commonsense way, since we apprehend our surroundings through our senses, which constantly remind us at the most basic level of the world's materiality. Thus our own experience demonstrates to us the barrier that materiality interposes to our understanding of history through the basic fact that people are distinct physical beings whose internal mental processes, as mediated to the world by language and act, are at best only imperfectly accessible to their fellow beings. It is a major part of the historian's job, however, to try to transcend this separateness and make sense of the disparate narratives, and the points of view they represent, which form the basis of historical accounts. This is a rather conservative position these days—that there is an actual object (an event, a person) to be apprehended at the center of historical narratives, or where a number of narratives converge—although most practicing historians seem to hold this view, or at least write history as though they do. In my 1992 introductory essay I invoked the term "culture" just three times, twice as a noun, once as an adjective, and wrote about "collective behavior" rather than culture; that is, about action rather than belief.

By the time the introductory chapter of my book on independence, *The Other Rebellion*, was written in the late 1990s, my ideas about the relationship of culture and the forces of material life to collective political violence had changed considerably, tending ever more in the direction of culture and away from traditional models emphasizing relative deprivation and class relations as the wellsprings of action. When exactly the change in my thinking occurred eludes me now. While this reorientation in my approach to writing history was of course in part impelled by the intellectual currents around me in the 1990s (the general subject of Chapters 3, 6, and 7 in this volume), it also grew out of an encounter with the archives. This recapitulated my experience of some two decades earlier, in the early 1970s, when I was beginning the research for what eventually became my first book, on the agrarian history of the Guadalajara region

---

here the paragraph in which it appears: "A well-known scientist (some say it was Bertrand Russell) once gave a public lecture on astronomy. He described how the earth orbits around the sun and how the sun, in turn, orbits around the center of a vast collection of stars called our galaxy. At the end of the lecture, a little old lady at the back of the room got up and said: 'What you have told us is rubbish. The world is really a flat plate supported on the back of a giant tortoise.' The scientist gave a superior smile, replying, 'What is the tortoise standing on?' 'You're very clever young man, very clever,' said the old lady. 'But it's turtles all the way down!'" (Hawking 1988, 1).

in the late colonial period (Chapter 1 of this volume is now the introduction to the second edition of that book). On that occasion, however, my shift had been in the opposite direction, away from social history and its larger penumbra, and toward economic history. Influenced by my reading in European rural history (especially the French historians Marc Bloch, Emmanuel Le Roy Ladurie, and Pierre Goubert, but also English scholars such as Joan Thirsk, R. H. Tawney, and others), my original ambition had been to write a social history of a regionally delimited rural society, but I found that the archives did not readily yield the sort of data I felt was required; or at least I did not have the conceptual tools to squeeze the sources in order to extract social history from them. So in a sense I fell back on economic history; Chapter 1 in this volume is in part an updated survey of the background to that shift, and Chapter 2 is one of its sequelae. As I gravitated toward economic history, moreover, I also became more aware of the debates of the time regarding dependency theory, a body of empirical studies that I have never seen as very theoretical, but simply as instantiating obvious statements about economic asymmetries between societies, and about modes of extraction of surplus value. My book about the haciendas of the Guadalajara area in the late colonial period, therefore, with its emphasis on coherence and change in regional systems of production, consumption, and exchange became a sort of antidependency case study. My writing on Mexican regions and the nature of regionality more generally, represented here by Chapter 5, grew out of this.[19]

My methodological, conceptual, and interpretive reorientation of the 1990s, as I have suggested, moved in the opposite direction, away from economic history, toward social and cultural history. The original plan for my book *The Other Rebellion*, in fact, had been to examine the popular insurgency of 1810–1821 using three regional case studies of economic change in the late colonial period—the Guadalajara, Cuernavaca, and Huasteca regions. I anticipated that such a study would support the hypothesis that the intersection of rural population growth, agricultural commercialization by large estates in response to increasing urban demand, growing land shortages in the peasant sector, falling living standards for common people, and increased taxation spurred by the Bourbon Reforms had combined to produce a situation of material deprivation in the Mexican countryside. These changes occurred within a structure of marked class and ethnic differentiation that pushed humble people into rebellious alliance with the Creole directorate of the independence movement under the covering ideology of protonationalism, a providentialist

---

19. Van Young (1992c), and my introductory essay in that volume, pp. 1–36.

narrative (the banner of the Virgin of Guadalupe), and a virulent anti-*gachupín* sentiment shared by commoners and members of the elite alike. This approach would have produced a study similar in many respects to those of John Tutino, Brian Hamnett, or more recently the Mexican scholar Carlos Herrero Bervera, among others.[20] While there is much to be said for this scheme, and while a substantial residue of it remains in *The Other Rebellion* (especially in Chapter 3), I found it wholly inadequate to explain what I was encountering in the archives. In other words, one might say that while the deprivation model of subaltern political action, and more generally a materialist interpretation of the independence movement were true, they were certainly not only true, perhaps not even primarily true, and definitely not interestingly true (to me, at least). It would have been extremely difficult if not impossible, for example, to account with reference to material conditions alone for elements of messianic thinking among popular rebels. Similarly, the political choreography of village riot during the insurgency, the forms of spatial mobility and boundaries in the participation of indigenous villagers, the nature of violence and its objects, and the very different responses to the insurgency of rural people who shared the same material conditions were not easily explained without according culture a more central role in collective political action. To marginalize such apparently anomalous speech acts and behaviors (anomalous only if one tries to extrude them through a rigid materialist grid) as forms of "false consciousness" or hegemonic cooptation would have been to discount deeply the historical actors' own versions of their reality, and thus foreclose the possibility of a much more nuanced and interesting account of Mexican independence. It would be possible, I suppose, to dismiss the belief of the Lazarus of Cuautla (see Chapter 6 in this volume) that he could be raised from the dead by Father Morelos and his miraculous child as a sort of inconvenient excrescence of his relationship to the means of production; but it would relegate to the dustbin of history his own view of how otherworldly and mundane forces were related to each other, substituting our version for his, and in the process impoverishing our understanding of the ways common people understood their world. Then, too, I found there to be little evidence that ordinary people had material conditions in mind when they took up arms, little indication that they consistently attacked their masters as economic oppressors, and little sign of a program to remedy agrarian grievances or redress imbalances of wealth. All this turned me in the direction of a

---

20. Tutino (1986), Hamnett (1985), and Herrero Bervera (2001); and see Chapter 4 in this volume for a survey of Independence historiography and the way it has changed over the last several decades.

cultural interpretation of popular rebellion, especially among rural indigenous people, and I even went so far as to place cultural factors—issues of identity, community, ethnicity, and religious sensibility—ahead of material ones, thus reversing the normally presumed direction of causal arrows from the material to the cultural, depicting them instead as moving from the cultural to the material.[21]

The change in my own thinking about the wellsprings of collective action would not be especially interesting were it not for the fact that it exemplifies larger shifts in the practice of history during the last thirty years or so, at least among Anglophone historians. Many of the essays republished here constitute an exploration of this theme, of the shift from more materialist to more culturalist approaches, within a historiographic framework. The arc of this trend in the way Mexican and Latin American history more generally has been approached in the United States (and to some extent in Mexico, although less robustly even now) can be followed beginning with my essay of 1979, "Recent Anglophone History" (not included in this volume), in which I suggested that the older forms of political and institutional history that dominated the middle decades of the twentieth century had given way to economic and social history, a shift I traced in the changing vocabulary of historical work. Where once the titles of monographs and of articles in the *Hispanic American Historical Review*, for example, spoke of *boundaries, treaties, parties, wars,* and so forth, by the late 1960s they were likely to feature such terms as *socioeconomic, stratification,* and *elites*. The atrophying of economic history among Anglophone scholars, with a few exceptions—although it is much stronger, indeed even thriving in Mexico today—was accompanied through the 1990s by the consolidation of cultural history, developments traced in Chapters 3, 6, and 7 in this volume.

Having temporarily abandoned economic history (I think of myself as a recovering economic historian), by the way, for the seductions of social and cultural history, and now returned to economic history with my work on economic thinker and entrepreneur Lucas Alamán, I have come to see as unfortunate the decline of economic history among Anglophone historians of Latin America, and especially of Mexico. I nonetheless issued an evangelistic call for the colonization of economic by cultural history in Chapter 7. I give two main reasons for this intellectual move. In the first place, I make the case that human beings spend so much time getting and spending that economic activities must be the sites of meaning production and expressive practices that are the major arenas of interest for

---

21. For some examples of this approach, in addition to my book on Mexican independence, see Van Young (1995b, 2009a).

cultural historians. In the second place, even with the interesting shift in interest among some economic historians to the institutional frameworks suggested by the work of Douglass North, I think it useful to explore the notion that institutions do not arise from a vacuum, but reflect the cultural substrate of a given society—religious ideas, normative values, systems of gender practice, and so on. I have since climbed down off this soap box with a partial and implicit mea culpa, however, in essays not included in this collection and in the form of private reservations about the hegemony cultural history has come to exercise over the field.[22] My own feeling these days is that cultural history in the absence of economic context is just as likely to render a distorted view of its object as is economic history (or political history, for that matter) extracted from its cultural context. There are of course practical limits to what the individual scholar can do—limits of time, documentation, theoretical preparation, personal interest, the dynamics of academic careers—that make this ecumenism a counsel of perfection. Some of my readers may find in all this navel-gazing and shilly-shallying evidence of a failure of intellectual nerve, while I prefer to think of my reservations as the product of a healthy skepticism and of a lifelong tendency to be eclectic rather than doctrinaire.

Let me return to the theme of culture. Now, it is true that not everyone means the same thing when they talk about "cultural history" as both an object of inquiry and an approach. My own definition would focus on what we might call the economy of symbolic exchange, the arenas of collective representation and discourse, and such matters as religious belief, individual and collective identity, gender relations, the forms in which belonging to a community is expressed, and other ways in which people organize their relationship to the material and human worlds around them, and endow those objects and relationships with meaning. It seems to me that "meaning" is the central category of cultural history—it is the honey in the hive, the nut in the shell, the emotional resonance of the song, the memory or analogy evoked by a smell, a touch, a sound, an image. Since meaning is therefore a relational property—it valorizes one thing by reference to another—and there may be a number of distinct meanings attached to a behavior, a belief, or a symbol, cultural history can get pretty complicated and messy in adding an entirely unseen but inferred layer of connections to any historical scene. This is even more obviously the case when a number of historical actors are involved. Take, for example, the land suit, one of the classic sorts of behavior that colonial historians use to reconstruct past realities. From a purely materialist point of view what

---

22. In addition to my essay "De razones y regiones" cited above, interested readers may consult Van Young (2003c).

is at issue when a peasant village is pitted in litigation against a private landowner or a neighboring village is encapsulated in the need for peasants to accumulate funds for subsistence, ceremonial rites, and reproduction (seed to plant the next crop); to pay their rents and taxes; and to pass on property to the next generation, however little it may be. Symbolically, however, the piece of land being fought over may "mean" more than its economic value now or in the future. The geographical location of the land—a modest *milpa* (cornfield), let us say—may have significance because of where it is in relation to a cave, a stream, an ancient tree, or some sacral site. Apart from its productive capacity, access to land itself may signify belonging to a community, a lineage, or some other social grouping. Control over a piece of property may entail strongly gendered aspects, such as the right to marry and establish an independent household, the passage from youth to adulthood, or the support for patriarchal dominance over women, other family members, or non-kin dependents. And those "meanings" are only projected by one party in the equation, and may be reflected, mirrorlike, in the unspoken or even unconscious mental realm of the contending party to the litigation.

It will be noticed that this very broad (critics might even say flaccid) definition is by no means class-specific; that is, it does not suggest that the study of cultural history need be limited to those social groups that leave written records, or are the producers and consumers of the literary artifacts of a given society. The way I myself have practiced it, the boundaries of cultural history clearly embrace social groups not inscribed in the historical record, which embraces most of the population in most societies during most of history, although one always faces the issue of limited or ambiguous sources in dealing with subaltern groups. Nor should cultural history, in my view, be limited explicitly to expressive realms of human activity such as celebratory life, religion, or ritual, but should map a huge geography including everyday life and activities not perhaps universally regarded as the territory of the "cultural."[23] By the same token, cultural history is strongly linked to local knowledges in the sense propounded so powerfully (and sometimes opaquely) by cultural anthropologists such as the late Clifford Geertz. Nor does cultural history in any way *exclude* economic life except by convention, a point I have made above and at some length in Chapter 7, in which, in particular, I try to develop the point that although the institutional approach to economic history associated with Douglass North and his followers has somewhat loosened the grip of neoclassical

---

23. I have dealt with issues of definition and delimitation in a number of essays in addition to those included in this collection, among them the conclusions of at least two volumes of essays: Van Young (1994a, 2001a).

models on economic history, it is arguable that institutions themselves are the products not only of contingent historical conditions, but also of underlying cultural templates that express pervasive social values as well as instrumentalist ideas about the frameworks of economic action.

I have alluded in passing to the differences in the way the history of Mexico is written in Mexico and in the United States, or in the wider Anglophone world, for that matter; cultural history exemplifies one of these, although it is becoming increasingly difficult to generalize about it. Another difference, at least until a few years ago, would have been the application of Marxist theory to the writing of history, which was never strongly established among Anglophone historians of Mexico in particular or Latin America more generally (although dependency theory was), while it seems to me that it flourished in Mexico. These differences, however, are not restricted to theoretical approaches. They are also very noticeable with regard to certain themes, although the treatment of the themes also takes place within prevailing models of what effective history writing looks like, and these can be very distinct in Mexico and the Anglophone world. This is the subject of Chapter 4, which deals in a necessarily abbreviated way with the Anglophone and Hispanophone historiographies of Mexican independence. The essay traces the textual and ideological genealogy of writing on the insurgency of 1810, touching on some of the great canonical works produced by nineteenth-century Mexican scholarship, moving into the twentieth century, and ending with a long section on how the trends in United States historiography in recent decades have influenced how the history of independence is written there, and in what ways this literature differs from what Mexican scholars have produced during the same period. Apart from the early pages in this introduction, discussing my work in progress on Lucas Alamán, and Chapter 6, which is essentially a methodological essay about interpreting ambiguous source texts so as not to lose their cultural importance, Chapter 4 is the only essay in the volume that deals directly with my research interest of the 1980s and 1990s, the rebellion of 1810–1821.

Let me close with a word about the ways in which the essays have, and have not, been revised from their original forms.[24] Some repetitions between the original essays—identical passages and close paraphrases—have been eliminated. There have also been some changes in titles and

---

24. Throughout this volume published works are cited social science style, with the author's last name and the date of publication in parentheses, either within the text or in the endnotes. I have done this to avoid cluttering the text unduly and to keep the length of the book within reasonable limits. Readers are encouraged to consult the unified bibliography at the end of the volume.

other minor adjustments for the sake of clarity of exposition. This still leaves two potential problems that might well crop up in any such collection of essays authored by one scholar over the span of nearly twenty-five years: the age of some of the chapters, and overlap among them. Overlap occurs primarily between the first two chapters and the last one. Chapter 1 was written during 2004–5 as a historiographical update encompassing works on the colonial, and to some degree the nineteenth-century, Mexican hacienda since the initial publication in 1981 of the book *Hacienda and Market in Eighteenth-Century Mexico*, and my 1983 article "Mexican Rural History since Chevalier: The Historiography of the Colonial Hacienda," not reprinted in this volume although it has appeared in several other venues over the years. While the historical research on the colonial landed estate was just cresting in the early 1980s and dropped off sharply in quantity over the ensuing years, a great deal of work was still to appear. There is comparatively little overlap or cross talk between Chapter 1 and the 1983 article, therefore, except for purposes of setting a framework for the newer essay. But what there is in Chapter 1, I have chosen for the most part to leave in place so as not to disrupt the continuity between what should finally be seen as "Part I" and "Part II" of the same project, much in the way that movies sometimes spawn sequels. The overlap between Chapter 1 and Chapter 2 is substantial but contained. My account of the Spanish American highland hacienda literature in Chapter 2, an essay written around 2006–7, constitutes about one-third of the text, relies substantially on Chapter 1 for that part, and is meant to provide an opening into a broader discussion of Latin American rural history parallel to extended treatments of export economies and slave-based sugar plantations. Excising the hacienda section of this chapter would be like removing one leg of a three-legged stool—the entire thing would topple over. Thus I have left that section of Chapter 2 largely as it is, not out of indolence but rather a concern for coherence and breadth. On the other hand, what was to have been Chapter 8 in this volume, an essay titled "The Meeting of Economic and Cultural History," was a sort of narrowed development of the earlier-written Chapter 7, but a conceptual extension rather than a historiographical one. The two essays were written five or six years apart, the second after further reading, and after my own deeper experience with cultural history had fermented a bit conceptually in the writing of my book *The Other Rebellion* and several essays. However, my thinking on these issues is not so profound that it needs to be preserved intact, like an ancient papyrus or a Shakespeare first edition; thus I have incorporated much of the conceptual pursuit of the points of encounter between economic and cultural history as portrayed in the erstwhile Chapter 8 into the current Chapter 7. Similarly, while I gave some thought to the possibility of publishing Chapter 5, on Mexican regions, in its original form, I finally decided to incorporate much of the material from a later essay on regionalism and regionality (Van Young 1992b). This makes for a considerably longer, more complex essay. In the end my readers will judge whether these overlaps and emendations produce synergy or just tedium.

PART I

The Historiography of Rural Mexico and Latin America

CHAPTER 1

Waves and Ripples
Studies of the Mexican Hacienda since 1980

In an astute, wide-ranging analysis of Mexico's social and economic problems published on the very eve of the Mexican Revolution of 1910, the jurist, writer, and agrarian reformer Andrés Molina Enríquez produced the somewhat gnomic, oft-quoted statement, "*La hacienda no es negocio*" (The hacienda is not a business).[1] By this he meant that the Mexican landed estate was in general not profit oriented, probably not capitalistic, and certainly not modern, but a "feudal" legacy of the Spanish colonial past. At the very moment he wrote, however, capital-intensive Mexican- and foreign-owned agricultural interests were in some regions of the country producing tropical crops for export (fiber, coffee, bananas), as well as more traditional agropastoral products (meat, wheat, maize) primarily for domestic markets. Molina Enríquez's characterization proved more accurate in some areas of the country, among them tracts of the arid north (although some large estates in this region

---

1. Andrés Molina Enríquez, *Los grandes problemas nacionales* (1909). Molina Enríquez (1865–1940) was actually imprisoned briefly by the revolutionary government of Francisco I. Madero for having launched his own radically *agrarista* rebellion under the Plan of Texcoco. His ideas were central to President Carranza's 1915 agrarian decree, and also to the famous Article 27 of Mexico's 1917 constitution, later used as the basis for the expropriation of hacienda lands and in many parts of the country the creation of *ejidos*, the collective agricultural holdings partially dismantled under the neoliberal reforms of the 1990s. On his life and thought, see Shadle (1994). A number of writers on the Mexican hacienda besides me have used Molina Enríquez as a whipping boy to dispute the older view of the feudal estate; among them are Brading (1978); Miller (1995); Nickel (1997); Langue (1998); and Chevalier (1999). I want to acknowledge my own former doctoral student, Javier Villa-Flores, of the Departments of Latin American Studies and History, University of Illinois-Chicago, for research assistance with this essay that went far beyond bibliographic compilation, and also an eleventh-hour reading of my text by Paul Vanderwood.

of Mexico produced cattle and other livestock for export and domestic consumption), the more isolated zones of the west coast, and the Indian south outside henequen-, coffee-, cacao-, vanilla-, and sugar-producing areas. In these places the insertion of the hacienda into local, regional, and international markets was much shallower, capital investment and economic rationalization were at much lower levels, and social relations of production were largely untransformed from older practices, including debt peonage. To the extent that the Mexican Revolution of 1910 was an agrarian upheaval, much modern scholarship would ascribe it to the social and economic stresses generated by growing commercialization and modernization in large-scale agriculture, while other scholars would see the Mexican countryside of that era, and the hacienda within it, as feudal and backward in much the same way that Molina Enríquez did. The apparent internal contradiction in the central institution of Mexican rural life—that in some incarnations the hacienda could look feudal and in others highly commercialized, even capitalistic—did not originate in the nineteenth or twentieth century, however, but found its origin in the colonial period. It is therefore with the colonial period, and to some degree with the nineteenth century, that one must begin to construct a genealogy of land-labor regimes in Mexican history, and the ways in which these have affected virtually all spheres of life up to the present, even as the Mexico of the twenty-first century continues becoming year by year less rural and more urban, less peasant and more industrial, less "traditional" and more "modern."

The extended scholarly debate in the 1960s, 1970s, and 1980s over the nature of the Mexican hacienda (and large landed estates elsewhere in Latin America) and the institution's place in rural society, often still framed today in terms of a capitalist versus a feudal model, deeply influenced historical writing on Mexico in general and on the colonial period in particular.[2] There emerged in this extensive literature a number of important questions, still to some degree unresolved today, about colonial land-labor regimes and the legacy they bequeathed to Mexico and the other nations of Latin America. As research advanced, for example, the hacienda began to look a lot less feudal as an agrosocial unit (that is, a place where rural people both lived and worked simultaneously) than previously imag-

---

2. A recent synthetic-interpretive treatment of Latin American history, for example, affirms the supplanting of "medieval" (that is, feudal) forms of economic organization by "capitalist" ones only in the late eighteenth century; see Voss (2002, xii). For a useful review of the feudalism versus capitalism debate as focused on the Mexican colonial hacienda, see Knight (2002b), who spends a good many pages (especially 72–83, 185–201) discussing this hoary controversy. He finds that while the ideal-typical hacienda of the colonial period may have been commercialized, it was not capitalist in any meaningful sense of the term.

ined. Nor was this a purely academic debate: there were political stakes involved, especially outside Mexico, in Latin American countries that had yet to experience anything resembling an agrarian political revolution. For if the "traditional" rural estate was capitalist (or proto-, quasi-, or even cryptocapitalist) from its inception in the sixteenth century, rather than feudal, then the emergence of a bourgeois order and the ensuing social revolution that must inevitably follow in its wake were not as distant as Marxist thinkers of radical tendency might once have feared.

Empirical studies of the colonial hacienda uncovered in the institution an economic dynamism and a social polymorphism suggesting that it was in fact sensitive to changing market and labor conditions, and to the availability of capital, rather than a fly trapped in the amber of seigneurial tradition. Even the most market-oriented haciendas in the late colonial decades often relied in part on coerced labor, however, retaining a strongly paternalistic social organization and equally paternalistic labor practices, and therefore presumably a precapitalist character. This is quite apart, of course, from sugar plantations, concentrated in the Morelos lowlands to the south of Mexico City but also scattered in pockets elsewhere throughout the colony, which relied upon a core labor force of African slaves while still producing a highly commercialized commodity for the domestic market. We are thus faced with the apparent paradox of commercial economic organization and feudal/paternalist social organization, a theoretical anomaly but a manifest historical reality. It is also necessary to keep in mind that the large landed estate did not exist alone in the colonial countryside, in a moonlike landscape devoid of other population concentrations or other types of production units. Rather, it cohabited—sometimes symbiotically, often conflictually—with small towns, semidependent or independent family holdings (often called ranchos), and most importantly with landholding indigenous communities. Certainly the terms of this conflict have increasingly been studied, from informal to litigated contention over land and other resources, through everyday forms of subaltern resistance (including some forms of criminality), to small-scale riot and rebellion, and finally widespread popular insurgency, as exemplified by the Mexican independence movement (1810–1821) and the Mexican Revolution of 1910 that followed it by exactly one century.[3]

Since the initial publication of my book on the haciendas of the Guadalajara region (Van Young 1981; revised 2006a), one of the most obvious

---

3. For a still unsurpassed discussion of the relationship of Latin American banditry to forms of peasant resistance, framed in historiographic terms, see Joseph (1992). Banditry is, however, a highly ambiguous activity, and scholars such as Paul Vanderwood (1992) have made a convincing case that bandits sought to force their way into the prevailing social regime rather than resist it.

tendencies in historical writing on colonial and nineteenth-century rural Mexico has been a shift in focus from the hacienda as an economic and social institution, which drew the attention of scholars for three decades or so, to the forms of political conflict, the technologies of power, the configuration of large regional societies, the long-term macroeconomic trends, the repertoires of social distinction (among them ethnicity and the constitution of elite family networks), and even the cultural contexts that the traditional landed estate was in large measure instrumental in shaping, and in which it therefore came to be embedded. This shift in focus was partly the result of broader positive changes in the discipline of history, among these its "anthropologization." By this I mean the bleeding over into history of concepts and questions derived from its cousin discipline—questions about symbolic systems and culture, for example, or the tendency to see powerful groups of landholding elites not only in terms of genealogies and intergenerational property transfers, but also in terms of kinship systems, kinship ideology, and elite social reproduction.[4] There were also negative changes, however, including an unfortunate decline in interest in economic history, at least in the United States.[5] As I noted in a 1983 review article about the hacienda literature, the change was also possibly due in part to the apprehension of scholars that in undertaking more studies about the traditional landed estate, especially at the level of the individual enterprise, they were tending to repeat an exercise at which they had already become adept, with the addition of each case study learning more and more about less and less (Van Young 1983).

The wave of historical studies of Mexican landed estates beginning with François Chevalier's pathbreaking 1952 work on colonial haciendas waned in the early 1980s, giving way to a hiatus in this literature that has continued until very recently.[6] While there has occurred something of a

---

4. For discussions of the theoretical and methodological issues between history and anthropology, see, for example, Hunt (1989b); Ohnuki-Tierney (1990); Axel (2002).

5. For some discussion of the interaction of these currents, especially within the context of the rise of cultural history for the colonial period, see Van Young (1999), and Chapter 7 in this volume, where I make the suggestion that cultural history should "colonize" economic history; a withering riposte to the entire cultural history project is offered by a distinguished economic historian in Haber (1999). Alan Knight (2002c) finds strengths and flaws in both approaches. For the relationship between economic and cultural history, see Van Young (2003c), and Chapter 7 in this volume. On the other hand, anthropologists do maintain something of an interest in the Mexican hacienda, as exemplified by a recent special number of the journal *Ethnohistory* (Alexander 2003) devoted to the theme "Beyond the Hacienda: Agrarian Relations and Socioeconomic Change in Rural Mesoamerica," to which I contributed a commentary (Van Young 2003a). For an overview of the changes that have occurred in the field of Mexican colonial history during the last three decades or so, see Van Young (2004b).

6. Arnold J. Bauer (1998) has made this same observation in a review article devoted to works on the history of the Mexican countryside. In his view the cycle of Mexican hacienda

resurgence of interest in agrarian structures in the pre-1910 countryside, much of it has been in the hands of anthropologists and ethnohistorians, and much of it has focused on the historical interplay of class and ethnicity rather than exclusively on the conflictual relations between haciendas and indigenous communities (for some early examples, see Wasserstrom 1983 and Schryer 1990), let alone the economic history of the haciendas themselves. Some of the impulse behind this newer approach may be traced to the internal logic of investigation, by which the more accessible sources used by an earlier generation of researchers who concentrated on the economic aspects of the great estate (account books, records of litigation, notary records) gave way to more fragmentary and difficult sources (local tax returns and census documents, parish records, and the like) or to rereadings of familiar documents in a new light (e.g., Van Young 1996). Then, too, the growing maturity of ethnohistory as a hybrid discipline (this is where the "anthropologization" of history comes through most clearly), heavily historical in method and subject but anthropological in conceptual framework (e.g., Radding 1997), has brought new sets of questions to bear on established economic, political, and sociocultural themes. Finally, the convergence of subaltern studies with ideas about the agency of common people as historical actors and shapers of their own destinies has redirected the gaze of scholars to arenas in which people formerly seen only as objects—of labor exploitation, of resource appropriation, of social domination—are reimagined as subjects: subsistence farmers, petty commodity producers, consumers, participants in markets, strugglers over local forms of power, religious celebrants, and above all as resisters, rioters, and rebels (e.g., Joseph 1992; Schroeder 1998; Ducey 2004; Guardino 2005).

The apparent ebbing by the early 1980s of the wave of hacienda studies that had surged during the preceding three decades or so by no means left the institution flopping on the sand and gasping for breath on the historiographical shore. Excellent studies were and are still being produced that focus on the great estate itself (e.g., Miller 1995), but it is difficult to call to mind any historians other than the prolific Mexican scholars Rodolfo Fernández (1994, 1999, 2003) and Gisela von Wobeser, somewhat earlier (1980, 1983, 1988, 1994), or the German historian Herbert

---

studies extended from about 1950 to the early 1980s, coming more or less to a close with the publication of Enrique Florescano's synthetic essay (1984) on the colonial hacienda. Bauer notes that the history of rural Mexico, moving away from a focus on the great landed estate, then bifurcated into two tendencies, the first looking to the internal life of the great estates, "leading to the very entrance of the worker's household where . . . the sources still do not permit us to hear the peasant voice," the other tendency reinserting politics into rural life (or vice versa) in the form of studies on peasants and landowners in the process of state formation.

Nickel (1987, 1988, 1989, 1997), who have consistently continued to produce high-quality monographs on this theme. Although Fernández's work, for example, has strong elements of regional history and the history of western Mexican elites during the colonial era, these approaches are not incompatible with economic ones, and Fernández still works basically within the parameters of economic history. Moreover, while the anthropologization of the discipline drew the attention of historians toward the symbolic and the local, the linguistic turn destabilized the written accounts on which historians had always relied (although never uncritically). The result of these two convergent tendencies was that the questions many historians began to ask during the last twenty-five years or so found no answers in the economic realm. This meant that the traditional Mexican hacienda, whose history was already reasonably well known, simply lost its compelling interest for us. When the apparently inexhaustible variation in the form and function of the hacienda at the local and regional levels was reduced to a limited number of categories or analytic variables—amount and type of land, technological regimen, productive mix, scale of capital investment, organization of labor, patterns of ownership, nature of the available markets—the question arose as to how much variation there really was, and whether the variations from ideal type were worth studying so closely.[7]

Given these trends, many of the Anglophone and Mexican scholars who made early and major contributions to the historiography of the hacienda followed very roughly similar trajectories in their research, moving from the economic history of the colonial and nineteenth-century Mexican countryside, to studies of social movements or protest, and thence to cultural or even intellectual history, in some measure abandoning the field (no pun intended) of basic economic history to pursue more elusive but fashionable themes. To cite but four examples among Anglophone historians of Mexico, this was certainly true of William B. Taylor, David A. Brading, Cheryl E. Martin, and me.[8] Leaving aside for the moment his excursions into other historical areas, we can follow Taylor's movement from his important 1972 book on haciendas and native peasants in co-

---

7. The most fruitful conceptual work in breaking the landed estates of the New World down into a limited number of component variables was done as long as fifty years ago by Eric Wolf and Sidney Mintz (1957).

8. This trajectory in the work of scholars who had made contributions to the history of the colonial countryside was not restricted to English-speaking historians working on Mexico. Steve Stern, for example, moved from an early study of indigenous society in the Peruvian highlands (which, while not exactly a study of agrarian structures, nonetheless put a good deal of emphasis on landholding and labor relations), through a stage of interest in forms of rural protest, to gender relations in late colonial Mexico, and most recently to forms of historical memory in modern Chile; see Stern (1982, 1987a, 1995, 1998).

lonial Oaxaca, to his innovative study of seven years later on forms of rural social deviance and protest, and thence to his massive investigation of priest-parishioner relations and forms of popular religious sensibility in the eighteenth century (Taylor 1972, 1979, 1996). A similar shift in theme can be seen in the work of David Brading, who followed up his classic interrelated works on silver mining and rural landholding in the Bajío region of central Mexico with a series of major studies of Mexican national identity, and most recently the intellectual and cultural history of Marian devotion and the Virgin of Guadalupe (Brading 1971, 1978, 1984b, 1985, 1991, 2001).[9] Cheryl E. Martin's scholarly trajectory marked a similar course. From her fine study of sugar production and labor systems in the Morelos sugar zone (Martin 1985), she moved in her 1996 book on late colonial Chihuahua to a more complex study of a diminutive frontier social order (Martin 1996). They are both works on local communities, but the first is single-stranded and economic in emphasis, the second multistranded and largely social and cultural in approach. Among better-known Mexican scholars the same was roughly true of Enrique Florescano, for example, whose early pathbreaking works on the economic history of the Mexican countryside were followed in subsequent years by a series of studies on collective indigenous memory, native cosmogony, and forms of Mexican national self-representation (Florescano 1969, 1971, 1994, 1997, 1998, 1999).

While a personal anecdote hardly constitutes proof of this trend, at the risk of being overconfessional let me suggest that my own experience in selecting a venue and a theme for my doctoral dissertation research in rural history demonstrates it. Around 1970 or so I was looking for a relatively uncrowded part of colonial Mexico (that is, not overpopulated with the work of other historians) in which to do my own work. I had considered the Valleys of Puebla and Cuernavaca when in a casual conversation Enrique Florescano suggested the Guadalajara area because of its rich archival sources and sparse modern historiography. Initially I had hoped to concentrate this study on social rather than economic history, but during the first stage of the research—as early as the reconnaissance phase, if you will—discovered that I had neither the obvious materials at hand for such an inquiry, nor the knowledge of how to read the primary sources that I *did* encounter for evidence of forms of domination, covert resistance, accommodation, and so forth. So in a sense I fell back on the economic history of the city and its hinterland, and of the great estates

---

9. Despite his anomalous detour into the history of popular protest in editing *Caudillo and Peasant in the Mexican Revolution* (Brading 1980), Brading never developed much of an interest in forms of popular politics or political upheaval as such. For a discussion of his trajectory as a historian, see Van Young (2007a).

there, producing the kind of single-stranded history typical of economic studies. Only later—having asked myself why this region beginning in 1810 should have produced such a long-lived rural insurgency among common and indigenous people (especially in the villages around Lake Chapala, for example), a problem only alluded to briefly in the conclusion of my book on the Guadalajara region—did I turn to social, political, and cultural themes, including popular religious sensibility, political culture, and the nature of community and ethnic identifications (Van Young 1992c, 2001c). My own doctoral students have since produced much more sophisticated work on rural society both in Mexico and elsewhere. The net result of the intersection of these shifting personal interests with larger historiographical trends is that precisely as my study of Guadalajara and its hinterland was being published, in 1981, or at least within the next couple of years, the wave of hacienda studies had already crested and was receding.

One is hard pressed to think of major studies in English on this theme that have appeared within the last decade, although I will allude to some works in Spanish by Mexican historians. Younger scholars doing their doctoral research seem not to be interested in the topic. When one does see studies of rural economy in more recent years, rather than focusing on the economic workings of rural estates as such, they are quite likely to be cast in terms of environmental history (still not very well developed), and/or the struggle over resources between powerful landowners and humble people, or the way some particular agropastoral activity fit into regional, colony-wide, or even international markets. Examples of these styles of work, respectively, are Elinor Melville's (1994) fine study of sheep culture and its environmental consequences in the Mezquital Valley of the Mexican near north, Sonya Lipsett-Rivera's (1999) work on water rights and farming in later colonial Puebla, or Jeremy Baskes's (2000) reconsideration of the cochineal (a brilliant red organic dye produced from cultivated insects) industry in Oaxaca. Then, too, sometime in the 1970s or early 1980s rural history, embracing primarily hacienda studies, began to be subsumed under the rubric of the "new regional history" in the sense that *everything* in the country outside the Valley of Mexico tended to become known as "regions" or "provinces" (often, and still today, with an implicitly dismissive connotation). The oversaturation of the central parts of the country (historiographically speaking), the increasing organization and accessibility of provincial archives, and the need to test hypotheses beyond single cases or miniregions—about the feudal nature of the colonial rural estate, for example—all contributed to this outward shift of focus. Although a technical or conceptual definition of what regions were, and how they changed over time, was hardly ever offered, many scholars confidently carved regions out for study, spaces most often organized by urban concentrations at their centers.¹⁰

My 1981 study of the Guadalajara region, therefore, for whose second edition (Van Young 2006a) the present essay was written as an introduction, needs to be situated within the historiography of rural Mexico as the product of a particular historical and autobiographical moment. I suppose many of us who studied the traditional hacienda—immersing ourselves in account books, wills and testaments, sales and rental contracts, and dusty files of litigation over landownership not infrequently running to hundreds of pages each—felt ourselves to be getting under the surface of conventional wisdoms about rural life as we looked at the actual economics of the putatively feudal agrosocial units that dominated much of the Mexican countryside in the colonial era, and even up to the early decades of the twentieth century. But these interests were by no means completely homegrown among historians of Mexico. They found antecedents and models in other historical literatures, most notably in that of medieval and early modern Europe, where both the origins of the modern state system and the transition from feudalism to capitalism focused the attention of historians importantly, if by no means exclusively, on the premodern countryside (e.g., Aston and Philpin 1987). A complete discussion of these influences lies outside the scope of this brief essay, but it is represented iconically by the composite picture adorning the cover of the 1999 reedition of François Chevalier's *La formación de los latifundios en México*, the foundational classic of the field of hacienda studies.¹¹ The image shows an old engraving of unmistakably European fortified walls, buildings, and fields (probably of late medieval vintage) partially superimposed over a modern photograph of an equally unmistakable Mexican landscape, organ cactus and all. Chevalier's own book bears a dedication to the great French historian Marc Bloch, his teacher at one point, whose work on French feudalism obviously so influenced Chevalier's work on Mexico, and therefore many subsequent studies of the Mexican great estate.¹² But the enormous and rich literature on the agrarian history of

---

10. For a discussion of how regions might usefully be defined by historians, specifically drawing upon the colonial economic historiography, see Van Young (1992a, 1992d).

11. See Chevalier (1999). Originally published under the title *La formation des grand domains au Méxique: Terre et société aux XVIe-XVIIe siécles* (1952), the book appeared in Spanish in Mexico as *La formación de los grandes latifundios en México* (1956), and was published in English as *Land and Society in Colonial Mexico: The Great Hacienda* (1966). The 1999 reedition includes a new introductory essay by Chevalier, two other essays of his published as addenda to the original monograph, and a new bibliography.

12. It is interesting to note in this regard that Chevalier's great book adopts a sort of derived medievalist framework for the development of the great landed estate in colonial

Europe furnished other exemplars widely influential on me and other scholars, among them works by the Dutch historian Bernhard Slicher Van Bath (1963), the Frenchmen Emmanuel Le Roy Ladurie (1966) and Pierre Goubert (1960), and the English economic historian R. H. Tawney (1967/1912), to mention only a few.

In my 1983 review article on the hacienda historiography, written just as my Guadalajara book was itself being published (but appearing in print two years later), I remarked that intellectual disciplines—subgenres or thematic historiographies would perhaps have been better, less grandiose terms in this case—have life cycles of their own: conceived and born, they advance through various stages of maturation, and may even fall into senescence (Van Young 1983). In that article I tried to think both diachronically and synchronically at the same time—to provide both a genealogy and a geography, in other words, of historical works on the colonial landed estate and the Mexican countryside more generally. I attempted to look not only at how the literature on the colonial Mexican hacienda and its broader rural environment had developed to that point, and how works in this field were related to each other, but also to map in extremely broad patches what its major research findings had been. Some of the approaches I suggested at the end of the article in terms of a research agenda for the future were already in evidence at the time, while some have flowered very little. It would be incorrect to say that the historical work on landed estates reached a dead end, however, since the findings of investigators in the three decades or so up to the mid-1980s continued to illuminate Mexican history specifically, and Latin American history more generally, as scholars became interested in new themes and documentary sources.

THE OUTLINES OF THE LITERATURE

If the Mexican hacienda no longer occupied the center of attention, neither was it relegated to the margins. It is the purpose of this section to outline in very broad strokes where this literature went after 1980 or so,

---

Mexico, emphasizing the politico-institutional dimensions that Marc Bloch highlighted in his masterwork *Feudal Society* (1961/1939). It is only in the new bibliography of the 1999 edition of his book that Chevalier includes Bloch's other great work on the French countryside, *French Rural History: An Essay on Its Basic Characteristics* (1966/1931; originally published before the treatise on feudalism), which deals with rural society from a more strictly economic angle, and for a later period (sixteenth through eighteenth centuries)—approaches that correspond more closely to the way the Mexican hacienda came to be treated by historians after Chevalier.

suggesting how it became partially transmuted into other sorts of historical research, and along the way to allude thematically to some of the most important findings of the historiography as a whole.[13]

Macrohistory and the Hacienda

Without the basic work done on the Mexican great landed estate in the thirty years or so up to the mid-1980s, it is difficult to imagine that a whole generation of macroeconomic studies of the colonial economy could have been produced, since that economy was so obviously supported by the twin pillars of silver mining and large-scale agricultural production. Since about 1990, approximately, a series of ambitious, important, and methodologically sophisticated works in economic history have deepened our knowledge of the eighteenth century in particular. Even when they do not say so explicitly, these studies appear to be structured around a specific teleology, the necessity of explaining Mexican independence, just as much of the historical literature on the nineteenth century is aimed at explaining why the Revolution of 1910 came along when it did, and why it took one form rather than another. In the case of independence the question would be: Why did New Spain separate itself from Old Spain, and what sorts of factors, internal and external, were most important in determining the timing and nature of the break? Furthermore, this issue has often been considered in relation to a larger question regarding both revolutions, that of why Mexican economic development had advanced in fits and starts, with periods of retrogression, rather than in a more linear fashion. Mining and the great estate were so inextricably entangled—price levels, labor requirements, backward and forward linkages of mining enterprises (that is, the weight of the mining industry as a user of inputs, and the effects of silver on the Mexican economy), and complementary patterns of capital investment were only a few of the points at which they grew into each other—that works in macroeconomic history ipso facto addressed the history of the hacienda whether or not they said so explicitly. The fundamental essays of John Coatsworth (e.g., 1990) demonstrate this, for example, setting forth a number of hypotheses about Mexican economic development within a

---

13. With several exceptions I have left out of my discussion works on the hacienda or rural history after the colonial period, works published before 1980 or so, and journal articles and book chapters. A useful bibliography of studies on the Mexican hacienda published between 1966 and 1988, embracing the nineteenth and twentieth centuries as well as the colonial period and organized by Mexican state, is the list provided by Tortolero Villaseñor (1995, 365–68); more useful still, since it takes a genuinely historiographical approach to this vast literature, is Langue (1998).

macroeconomic and institutional framework, as do a number of essays by the Spanish historian Pedro Pérez Herrero (1989, 1991, 1992a, 1992b), which brought into question the vaunted prosperity of the silver age at the close of the colonial period (see also Van Young 1986a, and the other essays in the same volume; Jacobsen and Puhle 1986).

Then starting in the decade of the 1990s a number of even larger-scale works appeared, five of which I will mention here. The five texts (Garner and Stefanou 1993; Ouweneel 1996; Ibarra Romero 2000b; Miño Grijalva 2001; Knight 2002b), one by a British scholar, two by Mexicans, and two by Americans, can all be seen at least in part as lateral extensions of hacienda studies, or at least as bird's-eye views of a colonial economy dominated in large measure by the great landed estate (and see also the slightly earlier Calderón 1988). Garner and Stefanou deal with the economic development of eighteenth-century New Spain, placing much emphasis on the mining and rural economies; Ouweneel chiefly with demographic and environmental changes during roughly the same period, and the movements of production factors and people that these provoked; Ibarra Romero with a major regional economy (centering on the western city of Guadalajara) at the very end of the colonial period, demonstrating its dynamism and close linkages with other Mexican regions; and Miño Grijalva with late colonial Mexico's urban network against the background of population growth. Alan Knight's very ambitious but nicely balanced survey of Mexican history, whose first two volumes—one on pre-Columbian Mexico, the second on the colonial period—have recently appeared, is not strictly economic history in the conventional sense of the term, but with its deeply materialist framework leans so far in that direction that for most purposes it can be taken as such. Knight even goes so far as to write that

> the hacienda ... was in fact the chief single determinant of New Spain's pattern of development. By the late eighteenth century—when mining and commerce had grown substantially—the hacienda still rivaled the peasant village as the hub of economic life; it contributed the greater part of New Spain's domestic product, outstripping the mines; and its resident communities surpassed some provincial towns not only in population but also in the "diversity of [their] social, religious, and economic functions." Apart from bullion, the bulk of goods circulating in urban markets were products of the hacienda. The hacienda thus "had the power to set the pattern according to which the rest of rural life was organized," in a society which was still overwhelmingly rural.[14]

---

14. Knight (2002b, 74); quotations are from Lindley (1983, 11, 211). It is a telling comment on the state of the literature that Knight's footnotes, insofar as the history of the colonial hacienda is concerned, are mostly based on works published up to about 1983.

These five studies have a good deal in common despite their differences. First, they all employ quantitative techniques seriously (except for Knight), although the book by Ibarra Romero about the regional economy of Guadalajara around 1800 is the most explicitly "cliometric." In their heyday the hacienda studies did the same thing, but replete as they were with tables and graphs tracing prices, inventories of estates, wages, and so forth, compared with other work by more technically trained economic historians (e.g., Coatsworth 1981; Salvucci 1987; Baskes 2000; Ibarra Romero 2000b) they were actually quite primitive in their methodologies, their statistics compiled by the authors counting on their fingers and toes. Second, the five studies all take regionalization very much into account; that is, they suggest that economic development is perhaps best studied on a regional level, rather than a colony-wide or local one, with Ibarra Romero's work again most explicit in this dimension. This was an approach shared by the most ambitious of the hacienda studies (e.g., Serrera Contreras 1977; Brading 1978; Van Young 1981), since rural estates were almost always embedded in supralocal networks of markets, labor recruitment systems, and political structures calling for investigation at the regional level. Third, the books were obviously all influenced by the economic historiography of early modern Europe, also a hallmark of the hacienda literature, since what the Europeans had called agrarian history was highly developed from at least the beginning of the twentieth century, and very suggestive about how preindustrial societies were put together. In Ouweneel's case this takes the form of an explicit dialog with ideas about "high-pressure" and "low-pressure" ecological and demographic situations as theorized by Victor Skipp, Ester Boserup, and Bernhard Slicher Van Bath, among others, but the same orientation is present in both Ibarra Romero and Miño Grijalva, and to some degree in Knight.

The Regional Context

While historians have labored to fit the hacienda into large-scale histories of the sort just discussed, they have also tried to essentialize the hacienda by generalizing its history across cases and periods, and in so doing have come to the paradoxical conclusion that beyond certain generalities applicable to all haciendas (already captured in Wolf and Mintz 1957), the institution was very much a creature of place. In other words, location in a *particular* valley, a *particular* relationship to an urban or mining-district market, a *particular* situation with regard to land, water, or labor resources, and so on, not to mention a *particular* history of ownership and management, very much determined why one estate might look so much different from another. This realization had not so much escaped earlier scholars, as it had been submerged by the powerful model of the seigneurial estate derived from François Chevalier's (1952) foundational study of colonial haciendas. To be fair to the French historian, he had been careful to distinguish between the sort of estates that took shape during the seventeenth century in the vast, semidesertic spaces of northern Mexico, and the more intensively cultivated, market-oriented ones in the center and south of the country, although other scholars were less careful in applying his findings. But when the simplified Chevalier model began to crack under the impact of Charles Gibson's (1964) pathbreaking study of the Valley of Mexico, and then sagged even further with a succession of later researches on other areas of the country where the colonial hacienda looked more different still (e.g., Barrett 1970 and Taylor 1972; for all of this see Van Young 1983), it became clear that regional specificity was required to understand all the variation. That is where my 1981 book on the Guadalajara region fits into the literature, for example, as an attempt to see how market forces, landholding patterns, demographic trends, and other factors configured a major colonial region. Somewhat later I and other scholars attempted to explore the processes of regionality from a more theoretical perspective (Van Young 1992b, 1994b; Pérez Herrero 1991), employing a combination of French cultural geography and central-place theory.

There was more at stake in placing the traditional rural estate in its regional context, however, than simply adding a nuance or two to the picture of Mexican history. And this brings us back to the debate over whether colonial haciendas were more feudal or more capitalistic, or at least more seigneurial (landlord-dominated and paternalistic, that is) or more commercialized. Regional specificity seemed to offer the key to explaining this conundrum, suggesting that the nature of regions determined the nature of haciendas, and not the other way around. Where there were readily accessible markets, for example, as near cities or mining areas, estates looked less feudal because the possibilities for profit meant that they warranted larger injections of capital, produced larger surpluses for commercial sale, and functioned more within a cash-wage nexus for labor rather than a situation of coercion. My own research on a specific historical region suggested to me that despite the still paternalistic social ethos of their estates, *hacendados* worked more or less to maximize their market positions, as rational economic actors, and I therefore hazarded the characterization of them as economically capitalist but socially seigneurial (Van Young 1983). In a tactical retreat in which he ceded some ground about the regional variability of the institution and its potential adaptivity to market conditions, in order to save the social ethos of the seigneurial regime that was so much the essence of his earlier work, Chevalier (1999) took up this formulation enthusiastically at least three times (pp. 15, 20, 60), as well as citing the great French historians Marc Bloch and Emmanuel Le Roy Ladurie to similar effect regarding late medieval manorial estates. Chevalier (1999, 38; and see also Langue 1998) went on to write that the late colonial rural world moved in two distinct "rhythms," one that of quick-stepping commercialized estates with salaried labor, the other of slow-moving "underexploited" haciendas linked to very limited markets, worked by permanently settled labor forces dominated by forms of landlord paternalism and even coercion; and that these types shook out roughly along geographic lines, north to south. In any case, sometime in the 1970s the regional study elbowed aside single-estate studies as the most common and fruitful approach to Mexican rural history and the colonial hacienda, and this has largely remained the situation until today.

A quick inventory of regional hacienda histories (or, better said, studies of colonial agrarian history focusing centrally on great estates) cannot begin to do justice to what is still a rich vein of work in economic and social history. Each cluster of such studies has its own peculiar logic, each its historiogaphical antecedents that go back a good deal further than the books mentioned here. Mexico's near north and mining areas, including the great silver cities of Guanajuato and the more northerly Zacatecas (Langue 1992), the linked agricultural hinterland of the Bajío (Rabell 1986), and such important provincial capitals as Querétaro (García Ugarte and Rivero Torres 1991; García Ugarte 1992), have continued to receive attention after the two books (and other work) in the 1970s of David Brading on mining (1971) and haciendas (1978) in the Guanajuato and Bajío areas, respectively, books that set much of the agenda for subsequent research by other people. Although they employ case studies of single landholding family clans or individual estates to illustrate certain points, these and other works take the regional context seriously, looking at the way types of economic activities, investment patterns, labor relations, marketing networks, and the like were distributed spatially, forming systems bigger than localities but smaller than the country as a whole. The trend here, frankly, has been to flesh out what we already knew, or to extend established patterns to areas not studied previously, rather than to produce any startling new conclusions. Still, some of these works have already taken, or will take, their place on any list of the most basic contributions to Mexican rural life and one of its two central features (the other being the indigenous farming village). The profoundly researched study of Frédérique Langue (1992) on eighteenth-century Zacatecas, for example, substantially bears out the relationships among mining wealth, large-scale landownership, ennoblement, and the establishment of great clan lineages already laid out by her *maître* François Chevalier and then by David Brading, but in a different environment that ultimately produced a somewhat different final configuration.

Claims to regional exceptionalism in Mexican history—that is, that all regions are different, but some more different than others, and ipso facto more interesting—are strong and often justified (but can they *all* be?). Areas distant from central mining or trading zones, and therefore off the beaten path in terms of the commercial flows of colonial life, and typically still heavily indigenous in their social makeup well into the nineteenth century and beyond, have occasioned some important studies, such as Oaxaca (Pastor 1987), Veracruz (Cambrezy and Marchal 1992), Tabasco (Ruiz Abreu 1994), and above all Yucatán (Farriss 1984; Iglesias 1984; and especially Patch 1993). On the other hand, areas more central to the economic life of the colony have also received a good deal of attention. The Puebla zone, for example, strategically situated between the Valley of Mexico and the Gulf coast, with a large indigenous population, a number of fertile grain-producing valleys, a significant non-Indian landowning presence, and even major industrial sites (i.e., the textile manufactories of the city of Puebla [Thomson 1989] and nearby areas), provided an interesting mix of population and production forms, as well as an extensive colonial documentation (tax and tithe records, land litigation, notarial registers). The Argentine economic historian Juan Carlos Garavaglia and his late collaborator Juan Carlos Grosso produced both an intensive local examination of one town in the district, Tepeaca (Garavaglia and Grosso 1994), and a broader study linking the Puebla region to the rest of the colony (Grosso and Garavaglia 1996). Other studies looked at indigenous villagers' centuries-long fight against commercial agricultural estates to keep their access to water (Lipsett-Rivera 1999), at early colonial settlement patterns (Licate 1981) and land tenure arrangements (Prem 1989), and at the rhythms of estate agricultural production over the course of the entire colonial period (Medina Rubio 1983) based on tithe records. Nearby Tlaxcala, a diminutive pre-Columbian indigenous polity famously associated out of *revanchiste* and tactical political motives with the Spanish conquest of the Aztecs, and one major site for the commercial production of *pulque* (a mild intoxicant of wide popular consumption, made from the slightly fermented juice of a variety of *agave* cactus), inspired works on its general economic history (Trautmann 1981), the regional system of haciendas in general (Ramírez Rancaño 1990), and detailed studies of specific estates (Leal and Huacuja Rountree 1982).

On the western side of the country, the region around Guadalajara—long an important administrative, commercial, and finally industrial (textile) center, as well as during certain times of its history a supplier of meat and grain to the adjacent silver mining areas and even to central Mexico—

has received sustained attention in a number of monographs focusing on the colonial rural economy and the role of the hacienda within it. Rodolfo Fernández has become the rural chronicler of the area in a sustained effort over a number of years that has produced several important monographs on great estates and the families that owned them (Fernández 1994, 1999, 2003), while Thomas Calvo has published a series of heavily empirical works on the economy of Nueva Galicia in the sixteenth and seventeenth centuries, centering on the Guadalajara region (Calvo 1989, 1992), and Richard Lindley (1983) has produced a thoughtful study of late colonial urban elites and their landholdings, a book that complements my own. The late Heriberto Moreno García (1989), most of whose work focused on the Michoacán area to the south of Lake Chapala, authored a general history of livestock estates in the Chapala basin exemplifying in many respects the typical sources, approaches, and themes of the regional hacienda literature. Using a mixture of notary records and documentation from regional and national archives on land grants, entailed estates, and the transport system, Moreno demonstrated that livestock raising in the basin lasted well into the late colonial period, having started rather later than the estate-based economies in the Guanajuato or more circumscribed Guadalajara areas. Rising urban demand, he showed, stimulated an ongoing reclamation of land and the rationalization of its use (as occurred, for example, in the Argentine pampas) extending into the Porfiriato (1876–1910), when the development of the region really hit its pace.

Finally, the heartland of the colonial and nineteenth-century sugar industry, around the Cuernavaca area in what is today the state of Morelos, has received the sustained attention of historians for most of a century. There are a number of reasons for this. After silver mining, sugar production was the greatest large-scale (if geographically dispersed) industrial complex, and at periods of its history provided an export product, a venue for technological innovation in the heavily capital-intensive refining process, and a raison d'être for the importation of tens of thousands of African slaves to work its plantations. It was also an area of endemic tension over land and water between non-Indian landowners and indigenous communities, and eventually spawned the wing of the 1910 Revolution led by Emiliano Zapata. The continuity of the industry in the region over several centuries lent itself well not only to studies of sugar plantations during the colonial era (e.g., Martin 1985; Wobeser 1988; Sánchez Santiró 2001), but also to ones that span the colonial divide (Landázuri Benítez and Vázquez Mantecón 1988; Crespo et al. 1988–1990; von Mentz et al. 1997).[15]

---

15. Work on the colonial tobacco monopoly has often delved importantly into forms of production, although these were typically on a much smaller scale—at the level, really,

In addition to the hacienda studies mentioned above, which followed in their turn several important books dealing with colonial silver mining published during the 1960s and 1970s (a subliterature that has virtually dried up), this regionalization of colonial history produced a number of what may be called multistranded works. Such studies, although they may have plucked out for close inspection one element of social or economic life—landholding patterns, labor structures, race relations, market development—nonetheless sought to contextualize these factors within larger regional frameworks rather than isolating them analytically. One fine, widely influential, but hardly unique example of this trend is historical anthropologist John Chance's (1978) book on colonial Oaxaca, which emphasized race relations, the fluidity of racial ascription over time, and the increasing weight acquired by wealth and class status in a society previously thought to be dominated by the rigid *sistema de castas* (caste system). Other examples of the genre, dating from slightly later than Chance's book, are historical geographer Michael Swann's (1982) study of settlement and demographic patterns in colonial Durango, Evelyn Hu-DeHart's (1981) ambitious but still basically structuralist study of Yaqui-Spanish interaction in northwestern Mexico up until Mexican independence, and more recently still Rik Hoekstra's (1993) study of the Valley of Puebla in the late sixteenth and early seventeenth centuries. Two outstanding recent examples are anthropologist Jonathan Amith's (2005) study of the Iguala Valley and the great Taxco silver mining district, in which historical ethnography, political economy, economic and humanist geography, and intellectual history are brought together to show how various social groups involved in the agricultural and mining economies made and unmade places through their interactions over time; and the recent dissertation of Andrew Fisher (2002) discussing economic relations, ethnic interactions, and the history of small communities over the three centuries of the colonial regime in the Balsas River Depression, much the same area treated by Amith.

Works that two decades ago, or even a decade, might have taken the form of single-stranded studies—of the great estate in the context of the agricultural economy, for example, of political structures, or of racial ascription practices—have now mutated instead into more complex narratives of localities through time. French-style *histoire totale* models were certainly of some belated and ongoing influence here, as was the totalizing microhistory of the sort promoted in Mexico by the late Luis

---

of what might be called the ranch—than sugar. Still, this industry shared some of the same characteristics as sugar production, including, at times, reliance on African slavery. See especially Deans-Smith (1992); and also Carroll (1991) and McWatters (1979).

González. Probably also influential has been the overt influence of anthropology in a particularly Geertzian, "local knowledge" register, in contrast, for example, to the broader political economy sort of model characteristic of Eric Wolf's (1983) late work. This approach emphasizes the interrelatedness of social practices and cultural meanings, the inextricability of major strands of such practices and meanings from each other and from their contexts, and the need to study these processes in concrete localities, the physical settings where people live. The "thick description" method adapted from Clifford Geertz is surely about explaining why such extrication or abstraction is not a good idea, and has always been in the repertoire of good historians even before they were told to do it by anthropologists. Recent well-executed examples of this localized, intensified total history of communities, albeit in what can still be described as a structuralist (i.e., materialist) mode, are Frank de la Teja's (1995) study of San Antonio de Béxar and Leslie Offutt's (2001) of Saltillo, as well as Cheryl Martin's (1996) work on Chihuahua, all dealing with the late eighteenth century.

General Studies, Single Estates, and Elites

The other side of the paradox mentioned above is that historians are still generalizing about great rural estates by talking about "the hacienda" as an archetypal institution. This is not altogether a misspent effort, since the standing tension between model and particularity (whether at the estate or regional levels) is a generative one. In practice this continued attention to a notional, ideal-typical hacienda often boils down to published anthologies where there appears to be an effort to treat the institution generally (often in a synthetic introduction by the editor), but where in fact the individual scholarly contributions pull in the direction of particularity and the protean nature of the great estate (e.g., Buve 1984; Jarquín Ortega et al. 1990; Ávila Palafox, Martínez Assad, and Meyer 1992; and for a later period, Moreno García 1982); or of general agrarian histories (e.g., García de León, Semo, and Gamboa Ramírez 1988). One exception to this, not coincidentally, is a single-authored work by Herbert Nickel, *Morfología social de la hacienda mexicana* (1988), which perhaps approaches closer than any other work of the last quarter-century or so the magisterial status of Chevalier's foundational study, although most of it concentrates on the nineteenth and twentieth centuries. Nickel does not dispute the essential duality of the institution—its paternalistic social ethos and its commercial economic orientation. But he does provide an evolutionary scheme for the hacienda, and the study is very effective precisely because it combines the generalizing, regional, and single-enterprise approaches, quite literally by devoting a separate section of the book to each of them, in tracing the historical development of an estate in the Puebla-Tlaxcala uplands.

Equally effective in its blend of general economic and political history with case studies based on individual estate accounts is Simon Miller's (1995) examination of central Mexican grain-producing estates, primarily in the nineteenth century, but within a conceptual framework that takes into account debates generated by the colonial historiography. Miller found in the latter part of the nineteenth century the same rationalizing landlord practices that Brading (1978) and I discovered for an earlier period, a notable tendency to innovate technologically where feasible, and the adaptability of the great rural estate. Another general treatment of the colonial hacienda published within the last thirty years is Gisela von Wobeser's (1983) study of the formative period (ca. 1550–1620), based primarily on the close observation of some six hundred maps from litigation over land titles. These portray the incremental occupation of the land and its formal titling, the increasingly close proximity of estates to Indian villages and the loss of indigenous lands to the estates, and the application of irrigation techniques. A few years later William Schell (1986) published a playful but acute long essay combining a historiographical overview of the hacienda literature as it stood at that time with an investigation into its medieval European antecedents. Schell's goal was to reconcile the Chevalier model of the seigneurial estate with the revisionist characterization of the colonial hacienda as economically rational. He deconstructed what he viewed as the mistaken application of the term *feudal* by both camps and sought to demonstrate the wide regional variation in the way the institution worked and adapted itself to changing market conditions. It is interesting to note that Schell felt (with some justification) that he could sum up the preceding three decades of investigation on the colonial hacienda at this point, and implicitly write a sort of valedictory to the passing of a major trend in historical scholarship (see also Rendón Garcini 1994; Menegus 1995).

The stream of studies on single properties or groups of colonial estates, in which the Jesuit haciendas had proved a particularly apt subject because of their integrated management and high rates of documentary survival, did not dry up entirely, although it tended to dwindle notably during the 1980s (von Wobeser 1980; Laviada 1984; Rodríguez Gómez 1984; Velásquez 1988; Gutiérrez Brockington 1989; Martínez Rosales 1991). Having reached in some ways the natural limits of what could be said about the formation and management of colonial haciendas, economic historians turned much of their attention to nineteenth- and early twentieth-century estates; some of these works have been mentioned above (and see, e.g., Rendón Garcini 1990). These haciendas functioned under different conditions—technological innovation, the advent of the railroads, growing urban markets, improved possibilities for commodity exports (e.g., Wells 1985)—and their history could tell us something more directly about national-era economic development and the rural antecedents of the 1910 Revolution. Still, there were masterful works on colonial estates produced in this mode during the period, the best of which were really longitudinal studies of single enterprises over long stretches of time. Despite its relatively diminutive length, for example, Reyna's (1991) study of the Jesuit estate San Francisco de Borja, right in the heart of today's Mexico City, relied on the standard sources of notary transactions and land titles and litigation, but also used documentation from the Mexico City *ayuntamiento* (city council) and the records of properties expropriated from the Jesuits (and subsequently sold off) by the Spanish crown when the order was expelled from the Spanish realms in 1767. This book had the particular virtues of stressing water shortages as one of the great problems of managing this intensively cultivated wheat-producing estate, and of tracing its sale in fractions as the capital city encroached upon its lands. One of the greatest of such studies was that of Heriberto Moreno García (1982) on the western Mexican Hacienda de Guaracha from its colonial origins until the postrevolutionary agrarian reforms of the twentieth century, a monograph that reconstructed not only the great estate's economic workings, but also its relations with surrounding farmers and the tone of its social life, one of the few works really to do so.

A related strand of inquiry of perennial interest to agrarian historians in particular and social historians more generally, the study of elite groups, continued to find expression in monographs after the beginning of the 1980s, and aspects of it were embedded in hacienda studies. Particularly during the colonial period, when the accumulation of wealth and the consolidation of elite family dynasties were intertwined so closely with large-scale landownership, commerce, and silver mining, elite family strategies for their own social reproduction and for the intergenerational preservation of wealth were understood to be central to the study of large rural estates. Historiographical precursors in this regard during the 1970s were Doris Ladd's (1976) study of the Mexican nobility and David Brading's (1978) work on haciendas and ranchos in the Bajío region. These were followed within a few years by John Kicza's (1983) careful work on elite families in Mexico City and their strategies to diversify their wealth by investing in haciendas and thus reduce the risk of losing everything in a commercial collapse or a mining bust. Even acknowledging the extensive archival research Kicza himself did, it seems unlikely that he could have rendered such a convincing description of elite investment strategies absent the scores of hacienda studies to support his work. Other studies of a similar nature were published in the next fifteen years or so (de la Peña 1983; Balmori, Voss, and Wortman 1984; Vargas-Lobsinger 1992; Meyer Cosío 1999). Rodolfo Fernández's numerous works on the agrarian history of the old Provincia de Ávalos, an extensive zone to the west of Guadalajara, have all dealt with patterns of landownership during the colonial period, but none so explicitly with the relationship between regional power groupings and hacienda ownership as his *Latifundios y grupos dominantes* (1994).

Haciendas and Other Production Units

After the early 1980s scholars tended to turn their attention outward from haciendas as production units or parts of production systems, and from the elite individuals and families that controlled them. They now focused increasingly on the human and economic environment in which the colonial hacienda was embedded, to some extent upon other nonindigenous agricultural production units and their owners, and even more on the indigenous communities that existed side by side with them. The conventional wisdom about the pre-Revolutionary Mexican countryside portrayed it substantially as comprised of a bipolar system in which the two major actors were haciendas and indigenous/campesino communities, the haves and have-nots. These entities rubbed together for some four centuries, sometimes in symbiotic relationship, such as described by John Tutino (1986) as prevailing between many central Mexican indigenous villages and the surrounding private estates, in which the haciendas supplied access to some land and wages, and the villagers supplied a predictable labor supply, but more often in conflict with each other. As population grew during the late colonial period, commercialization advanced, and the farming resource base remained much the same, communal villages and smallholding peasants were cumulatively and increasingly disadvantaged and the polarization therefore exacerbated.

While this picture was true, it was not only true. It is all too easy to see how the bipolar picture might have developed, less out of scholarly neglect or bias than as an outcome of the available documentation on colonial estates. The politics of vindicating the agrarian aspirations of the Mexican Revolution admittedly played a role here, encouraging historians to see that great upheaval against the background of the black legend of the traditional hacienda (e.g., McBride 1923; Tannenbaum 1933). The most accessible sources tended to emphasize current accounts, patterns of investment and the maintenance of elite family wealth, production for the market, and so forth, and to mask internal relations within estates, even for something as basic as hacienda wage labor, as well as between estates and their immediate surroundings. Furthermore, the very juridico-philosophical categories of colonial life, as enacted in Mesoamerica and elsewhere, shaped the bipolar model and reinforced it through the idea that colonial society was divided into two sectors, the republic of the Spanish and the republic of the Indians (the *dos repúblicas* of colonial discourse and policy). Although it had real enough implications in daily life, the idea of the two republics was essentially a normative/prescriptive concept (see especially Borah 1983) whose efficacy varied greatly over time and geography, and whose actual existence close to the ideal type, especially in the economic realm, there is serious reason to doubt. Some of the most interesting work recently done by historians, in fact, relates to the market participation of Indian peasants during the later colonial period (see below), which indicates that the barrier between the two republics had become quite porous.

While there is something to be said for the dichotomous model of a bipolar countryside, it needs to be shifted from the ontological to the historical register, that is, from essentialist characterizations of the pre-Revolutionary (and especially colonial) countryside to a more complex view of permutations of rural socioeconomic relations that changed over time. Other forms of property holding in the countryside besides the hacienda—before the national state took an interest in counting and taxing these, and later (through property and agrarian reform measures; e.g., Bazant 1971) in creating more of them in keeping with the goals of the Revolution of 1910—were really only observable when they became embroiled in legal squabbles with villages or large estates. One knowledgeable eighteenth-century observer of the central Mexican countryside, for example, provided an interesting if somewhat vague distinction between haciendas and ranchos in the following terms:

Haciendas, in these American realms, are country houses belonging to people of more than average means, with lands for cattle, horses, and sheep, breeding pastures, and agricultural lands on which, more or less according to the capabilities of each owner, are produced various grains and livestock. Ranchos, in these realms of the Indies, are country houses of little pomp and small value occupied by men of modest means, or the poor, who cultivate the small parcels which they own or rent according to their available resources, and on which they raise domestic animals and livestock (cited in Van Young 1981, 107).

Ranchos, in other words, were nonhaciendas, implicitly much vaguer in type and inherently less interesting, if not downright invisible. Modern scholars (e.g., Alexander 2003; and see also Barragán López 1994), however, have enjoined us not to lose sight of the other agrosocial units that inhabited the countryside at most times and places, including the indigenous elite (whose interests did not always coincide with those of the communities they led), the church, nonindigenous small farmers, and others.[16] Typological variation of agrosocial units in the traditional countryside was matched by change over time, more the rule than the stasis one sometimes sees portrayed by scholars. Tutino's (1986) idea of cycles of compression and decompression in central Mexico—compression in the eighteenth century, decompression in the early nineteenth, increasing compression in the half-century or so before the 1910 Revolution—corresponding to advancing and receding agricultural commercialization, and ipso facto to lesser or greater independence for small producers, has much to be said for it. His scheme provides a large-scale framework for integrating the colonial and postcolonial eras, and the trends in economic and political life.

Indigenous communities have over the last three decades in many ways replaced the hacienda and agrarian history in the limited sense as the central scholarly preoccupation of historians of colonial Mexico (Van Young 2004b). Indians and Indian communities were just as entangled with great rural estates in most parts of the colony as elite groups, even more so, since while elite groups might draw their wealth from activities exclusive of landownership, the vast majority of indigenous people were peasants and/or laborers living in close proximity to estates owned by nonindigenous people. Almost any ethnohistorical work worth its salt, therefore, whether relying on native-language documents or not, is likely to allude heavily to the agricultural economy of whatever region or locality is under study, and specifically to the problematic relationship between indigenous communities and neighboring haciendas (among many others, for example, see García de León 1985; García Martínez 1987; Lockhart 1992; Radding 1997; Deeds 2003). Similarly, almost any hacienda study is likely to allude to Indians as laborers, competing small-commodity producers, or rivals for land and water resources. A number of conferences and scholarly anthologies have been devoted entirely or in part to the theme of Indian-hacienda interactions (Ouweneel and Torales Pacheco 1992; Ouweneel and Miller 1990; Miño Grijalva 1991), as well as monographs concentrating on the indigenous side of the agricultural economy (e.g., Loera 1981). Two of the most convincing studies were

---

16. Several of the essays in the special number of the journal *Ethnohistory* edited by the anthropologist Rani Alexander (2003), "Beyond the Hacienda: Agrarian Relations and Socioeconomic Change in Rural Mesoamerica," speak to the issue of the complex interrelations between haciendas and a variety of smaller production units in the Mexican countryside during the colonial period and the nineteenth century, especially those by Chris Kyle (Guerrero); Murdo MacLeod (Guatemala); John K. Chance (Puebla); John Monaghan, Arthur Joyce, and Ronald Spores (Oaxaca); and Christopher M. Nichols (Yucatán).

published about twenty years ago, both, interestingly enough, on regions of the colony outside the major grain-producing and mining areas. Jiménez Pelayo's (1989) study of the rugged area in southern Zacatecas known as Los Cañones used the sources typical in such investigations, with the addition of parish archives. Among her most interesting conclusions was that *hacendados* in this zone were an ethnically heterogeneous group, as opposed to the image of the white (whether aristocratic or socially aspiring) owner more common from the central parts of the country, and that tensions over landownership were just as likely to occur among pueblos as between pueblos and large estates (see also Van Young 2001c). Bracamonte y Sosa's (1993) study of Indians and haciendas in Yucatán from the late colonial period to the mid-nineteenth century applies the idea of "tributary despotism" developed some years ago by Enrique Semo (1993/1973), meaning that forms of coercion and labor taxes, rather than a more direct interest in the acquisition and exploitation of the land, drew surpluses out of the indigenous population of Yucatán well into the late colonial period. Since processes of commodification arrived later in the peninsula, the expropriation of land from indigenous communities occurred correspondingly later in Yucatán than in most other places, beginning in about the second quarter of the nineteenth century, and coercive forms of labor reduced rural people to an overt agrarian servitude that survived longer, as well (see, for example, Wells 1985; Wells and Joseph 1996).

Credit, Prices, Markets, Labor, and Technology

No matter what their social constitution as redoubts of elite social reproduction and upward (or downward) mobility, the changing situational equilibrium between them and other production units in the countryside, or their relationships with indigenous communities, haciendas would not have been viable without some form of credit to finance their operations and facilitate capital investment, or absent some fairly well-developed markets in which to sell their products. In a perennially cash-scarce economy (a bitter irony in view of the levels of silver production sustained in the Mexican colony and the role of this money/commodity in fueling European economic development) credit was extremely important. This was even more notably the case in an economic sector in which cash income ebbed and flowed seasonally, markets could be volatile and quickly saturated, and large properties might be bought (and therefore large existing debt burdens assumed, with the potential to drag owners down into bankruptcy) with small down payments, as my own research demonstrated (Van Young 1981). Since the colonial church was the major lender to hacienda owners, the few major studies that we have exploring this source of agricultural credit are important (Greenow 1983; Sánchez Maldonado 1994; von Wobeser 1994), although most writers on the hacienda itself have at least something to say about debts on large estates and what it took to service them. Although there is still a good deal of discussion among historians about how well colonial markets functioned, over what distances (e.g., Van Young 1992a, 1994b; Ibarra Romero 2000b; Miño Grijalva 2001), and to what degree rural production units were integrated into them, prices for agricultural commodities did reflect supply and demand in the colonial marketplace, whether on a local, regional, or even colony-wide basis. Price history, on the whole, so well developed for the economic and agrarian history of Europe, has not enjoyed the prominence in the story of the Mexican hacienda and rural economy that one would have thought, with a few notable exceptions such as Florescano's (1969) early and foundational work on maize prices in the eighteenth century. The reasons for this lacuna are not entirely clear. The most important is surely the heterogeneous and fragmentary nature of price series during the colonial period for agricultural commodities and items of wide consumption more generally, which has inhibited what economic historians call serial history. This was a function, probably, of institutional practices and record keeping during the colonial regime. While this theme has not been well served in terms of the number of studies devoted to it, it has not been completely neglected, either. Some of the essays in the anthology edited by Lyman Johnson and Enrique Tandeter (1990) address price history and the methodological issues involved in doing it, while the careful reconstructions of García Acosta (1988, 1995) have filled in some of the gaps.

Where the interaction of sellers and buyers creates prices, there must be commercial circuits that structure the market and intermediaries (typically merchants) who run it. A great success in colonial economic history over the last fifteen to twenty years has been the topics of mercantile circuits within the colony, and of systems of supply for major cities, in which haciendas were inextricably involved. One of the most interesting and still pending questions about colonial markets, nonetheless, was the degree to which indigenous peasants were involved in the commercial sale of surpluses produced on their own lands. The emerging consensus seems to be that given the right conditions they could be very much engaged in petty commodity production and sale, which flies in the face of the conventional wisdom about colonial Mexican indigenous farmers. Since much of the work on markets involves the manipulation of large bodies of *alcabala* (excise tax) data, it is very labor-intensive and has sometimes been undertaken by teams of investigators working together. Given the strongly regionalized layout of New Spain, it is not surprising that such studies should focus on regional systems. We have works for the urban markets of Mexico City (Duhau 1988; Quiroz 2000), Guanajuato (Alvarado Gómez 1995), and Guadalajara (Ibarra Romero 2000), and for the regions of Puebla (Grosso and Garavaglia 1996), Michoacán (Silva Riquer 1997), Tabasco (Ruiz Abreu 1994), and Huasteca (Fagoaga Hernández 2004). Much of the pathbreaking work here has been done by Grosso and Garavaglia, and Jorge Silva Riquer, who have produced among them not only important monographs, but edited anthologies as well (Grosso and Garavaglia 1995; Silva Riquer, Grosso, and Yuste 1995; Silva Riquer and López Martínez 1998). A special corner of the colony, Oaxaca, and its chief commodified product, the organic dyestuff cochineal, have been the subject of two excellent recent books by Carlos Sánchez Silva (1998) and Jeremy Baskes (2000). Although these are not strictly studies of the colonial hacienda, they do look at rural commodity production and marketing/credit arrangements in an economic niche that in a sense competed with rural estates, at least at the margins, for labor resources. Baskes has turned on its head the black reputation of the institution of the *repartimiento*, whereby local Spanish officials in the Oaxaca uplands forced (often unneeded) goods and credit on village Indians and took payment in the form of the brilliant red dye, which was then marketed with great profits, principally in Europe. He demonstrates that coercion of native producers in the eighteenth century was minimal and difficult, that the institution proved a relatively efficient way of allocating scarce and costly capital, and that apparently extortionate price markups and rates of interest on loans to native producers constituted moderate risk premiums for Spanish traders in a volatile economic environment.

The relatively autonomous activity of indigenous commodity producers in Oaxaca and the relatively shallow penetration of the hacienda economy into that region (Taylor 1972) were not representative of most of the rest of New Spain. Whatever the situation of capital, markets, ownership patterns, or other factors in the hacienda's orbit, the great rural estate was in large measure about labor: forms of mobilizing it, forms of controlling it, forms of using it. Much of the classic debate about the colonial, nineteenth-, and twentieth-century hacienda turned on when, why, and how the institution was mostly dependent on coerced labor fixed by debt servitude and other mechanisms, or on free wage-labor and rental income from its lands, and the degree to which this mix determined whether haciendas were feudal or capitalistic (Bauer 1979). Virtually without exception, hacienda studies at whatever level—general, regional, or single-enterprise—will discuss this issue (e.g., Van Young 1981, Chapter 11), which is surprisingly hard to get at because of the scarcity of surviving internal documentation from colonial estates. African slavery on colonial plantations, on the other hand, has been reasonably well studied because slaves' value as property generated careful record keeping by their owners. Although interest in rural slavery in colonial New Spain seems to have waned (while interest in Afro-Mexican populations has waxed), some interesting studies have been made nonetheless, not surprisingly about tropical lowland Veracruz (Naveda Chávez-Hita 1987; Carroll 2001), and any work on the colonial sugar industry is likely to devote much of its space to African slaves (e.g., Sánchez Santiró 2001).

Studies of rural labor as such have grown scarce. One of the only works of the last twenty years or so to focus centrally on labor practices is Gutiérrez Brockington's (1989) study of the cattle estates in the Isthmus of Tehuantepec established by conqueror Fernando Cortés and retained in entail by his descendants until the nineteenth century. While there is a good deal on other aspects in the management of the Tehuantepec haciendas in her book, the author's research led her to conclude plausibly that continued access to independent landholdings lent local laboring people more "leverage" than they would otherwise have had, somewhat improving their position in the face of the estates' demand for workers at low wages. Another particular virtue of the work is that it deals with the seventeenth century, still largely a historiographical black hole as far as colonial Mexico is concerned. Jumping forward a century, the very interesting work of Suárez Arguello (1997) on mule transport and mule skinners in the eighteenth century has a good deal to say not only about this form of labor, which often turned out to involve small independent contractors rather than wage workers, but also about the inadequate late colonial road network (for which see Castleman 2005). In connection with her work on urban wheat milling and consumables prices, cited above, García Acosta (1989) has also produced a study on urban bakeries and their owners and laborers. While not strictly in the line of hacienda studies, her book nonetheless looks at one end of the commodity chain that was anchored at its other end by wheat-producing estates. There are a few general works or anthologies on colonial labor (von Mentz 1988, 1999; Artís Espriu et al. 1992; Nickel and Ponce Alcocer 1996), and the indefatigable Herbert Nickel has produced a trio of books on labor practices in the Puebla-Tlaxcala area (1987, 1989, 1997), mostly devoted to the nineteenth century.

The relationship between scarcity or plenitude of land and labor exercised an obvious influence on the sort of agricultural technologies applied on colonial haciendas. When land was plentiful and labor scarce, markets were likely to be limited and investment in expensive technologies to boost productivity made little sense. When labor was plentiful and land had grown scarcer, as in many areas of the country in the later decades of the colonial era, technological innovation was unnecessary because additional inputs of inexpensive labor produced appreciable marginal utilities. With some exceptions, however, our knowledge of colonial agricultural technology remains hazy. One of these exceptions is the colonial sugar industry, in which productivity increases could bring noticeably higher profits to plantation owners. We know a good deal about this industry because of careful accounting systems and the relatively high capital expenditures required to improve techniques (e.g., Scharrer Tamm 1997). While there are some more general works on agricultural technologies (Rojas 1990; Menegus and Tortolero Villaseñor 1999), aside from Michael Murphy's (1986) careful reconstruction of irrigation techniques on colonial Bajío estates much of what we have applies to the nineteenth century because the sources are more plentiful and more detailed. Not much has been written in the form of book-length studies on the environmental impacts of farming and stock raising apart from Melville (1994; see also Tortolero Villaseñor 1997 and García Martínez and González Jácome 1999). Studies of material culture sometimes contain material on agricultural techniques (Super 1988; Hoberman and Socolow 1996; Bauer 2001). The impressive work done on the nineteenth century, much of its spearheaded by Alejandro Tortolero Villaseñor, is exemplified by the same author's (1995) study on technological innovation on Mexican haciendas between 1880 and the First World War. Relying heavily on patent applications, theses from agricultural schools, travelers' accounts, land maps, consular reports, and an eclectic array of other documentation, Tortolero looks at the diffusion of technological changes on cereal estates to the southeast of Mexico City, and at one sugar estate in the Cuernavaca area. He concludes that despite the production logic imposed by an ample and inexpensive labor force, some Mexican *hacendados* of the era, particularly during the sugar boom of 1900–1910, introduced steam machinery because it was prestigious, associating the owner with modernization, but that its introduction provoked resistance among laborers.

. . . *and Resistance*

The phenomenon of resistance to technology among estate workers brings me to the larger theme of resistance against established forms of authority—whether represented by the state, local oligarchies, paternalist landlords, or village officials—by rural people more generally, an important extension or transmutation of hacienda and agrarian studies, and thus to the close of my essay. Along with ethnohistory, the study of rural rebellion and other forms of violent political intervention by common people has become for the recent study of the Mexican countryside during the colonial period and the nineteenth century what the study of the hacienda was perhaps thirty years ago, although the two genres of research are by no means mutually exclusive and are in fact closely interrelated. There were a number of circumstantial reasons why scholars began turning their attention to peasant politics and collective violence. These included (again) the influence of anthropologists such as Eric Wolf (e.g., 1966); successful early forays of historians into the field (Taylor 1979) that served as stimulus and models for others; a burgeoning and more clearly conceptual approach to nineteenth-century Mexican state formation rather than just a rambling narrative of chaotic events, and of forms of peasant protest in them (Meyer 1973; Reina Aoyama 1980; Vanderwood 1992, 1998); the advent of newer forms of social history and of what came to be called subaltern studies; and the influence upon a whole generation of United States historians of America's involvement in a stubborn war of national liberation (Vietnam) sustained largely by peasants. Just as important as these factors was the fact that, except as laborers or petty-commodity producers either in symbiosis or competition with large rural estates, common people in the orbit of the haciendas, which meant most of the Mexican rural population at any time before the agrarian reforms of the post-1920 period, were largely silent in accounts of rural life. Many of us came to believe that incidents of conflict in the countryside, episodes of rebellion, or even instances of participation in larger movements were the places to hear their voices. Yet as apparently simple a question as "Did traditional debt peonage on haciendas incline laborers to rebel?" turned out to be much more complicated than we thought, and the causal connections more difficult to establish, partly for lack of empirical data, partly for theoretical reasons. With certain notable exceptions (e.g., Hamnett 1986; Tutino 1986), many of the best studies of rural violence and politics by Anglophone historians in recent years actually bypass agrarian conditions for the most part, and ipso facto the hacienda (e.g., Mallon 1994; Rugeley 1996; Ducey 2004; Guardino 2005). There is some irony in this, since an interest in the colonial and nineteenth-century hacienda and the sort of pressures a commercializing agricultural economy placed on humble rural people was among the chief impetuses in the development of the peasants-and-politics literature. Arnold Bauer has remarked that reading studies on peasant uprisings as works in the more traditional mold of rural history is "a bit like taking *Lady Chatterley's Lover* from the point of view of game keeping (as a mischievous reviewer once did in *Field and Stream* [magazine]" (Bauer 1998). This is not the place, however, to review the modern historiography of rural resistance and rebellion in Mexico (for some attention to it, see Van Young 2004b). It shows no sign of abating as yet, and has given us a rich corpus of work with some very characteristic debates: about the relationship of collective violence to agrarian conditions, the political "imaginary" of common people (e.g., when and how they developed a recognizably national sensibility), the degree of agency subalterns may have exercised in shaping their own political destinies, and the nature of cross-ethnic and cross-class alliances in such movements.

CONCLUSION

My study of Guadalajara haciendas, for which this historiographical survey was written as an introduction, was very much an artifact of its time—of the possibilities (and limits) of what historians in general and Latin American historians in particular were doing during the decade (the 1970s) required to conceive of the project, carry out the research, and bring it to light first as a doctoral dissertation, then as a book. Notary records, for example, had just come into widespread use for the economic and social history of the colonial period when the project was conceived as a doctoral dissertation in the early 1970s. On the other hand, I was unable to find tithe records for the region to cover the eighteenth century, which in any case were being little used by Mexicanist historians at the time. This meant that it was not possible to outline overall trends or changes in patterns of production or product mix over time, at least in a statistical way. Furthermore, the book stood at something of a transition point between a number of studies of individual rural estates and a broader, regional point of view that saw haciendas as nodes of interaction and recombination of production factors within larger systems. Thus, while the project launched me into thinking about how regions are constituted over time, on which I subsequently did some work (see Chapter 5 in this volume), the information I found in the archives did not lend itself easily to the sort of social history I originally envisaged doing, or at least I could not see the possibilities of it. The book also crystallized many of the debates that had preceded it, concerning the "rationality" of hacienda management, the involvement of large mixed-production estates in more or less extensive markets (as opposed to sugar estates, for example, which had always depended upon such linkages for their viability), the nature of labor relations (chiefly debt peonage), and the stability of elite ownership of haciendas. As I have tried to show, the historiography of colonial haciendas did not so much disappear after the early 1980s as take somewhat different forms and provide one platform for other trends of investigation. Great rural estates, however, have continued to be of perennial interest to historians of Mexico. As one of the central institutions in the lives of most Mexicans through most of four centuries, along with the family, the church, and the village, they offer a key to understanding the history of the country.

CHAPTER 2

Rural Latin America
The Colonial Period and Nineteenth Century

The history of Latin America has been written on and by the land. This is not an invocation of Physiocratic dogma, and still less a piece of folkloric nostalgia—it is simply a fact. While the silver pouring from Mexico and Peru, and later the gold and diamonds of Brazil, tied the colonized areas of the New World irrevocably into the economy of the Old through the Iberian Peninsula, precious metals also integrated huge regions of Ibero-America internally (although hard cash was often scarce), oiling the wheels of commerce, greasing the palms of state officials, and stimulating all sorts of local economic activities from shoemaking to sugar refining. Until relatively recent times, certainly well into the twentieth century, most Latin Americans made their living directly or indirectly from farming (Hoberman and Socolow 1996). In late colonial Mexico, for example, estimates of the percentage of the labor force engaged in agriculture, including both people linked to the market and those producing for subsistence, would stand at approximately 85 to 90 percent. This direct dependence on the land persisted during the great export booms of the late nineteenth and early twentieth centuries, while the demand for labor thus generated induced millions of Europeans to migrate westward across the Atlantic Basin, as it had earlier driven the involuntary migration of millions of enslaved Africans. These processes profoundly transformed the human face, economies, and cultures of societies such as Brazil, Argentina, and Uruguay, and to a lesser extent Chile and other areas of South America. But by the end of the twentieth century the situation had changed radically under the impact of industrialization, urbanization, and the expansion of service sectors in the national economies of the region. The percentage of the labor force still engaged in agriculture provides a gross indicator of the change, falling in Argentina from about

14 percent in 1980 to 1 percent in 2000, and during the same period in Brazil from 41 to 24 percent, and in Mexico from 55 to 24 percent. Furthermore, ownership of the land in one form or another configured colonial and postcolonial space, and long molded the social and political identity of indigenous and peasant communities, the overall social structure, the power of elite groups, and aristocratic (and racialist) values reflected in literature, art, and social practice. Great political struggles—among them the Mexican and Cuban revolutions, and the 1994 Zapatista uprising in Chiapas—were in large measure carried forward to redress social and economic inequalities arising from the skewed distribution of land, the oppressive power of landowning groups, and the influence of foreign governments and markets mediated through the export sector. It should hardly be surprising, therefore, that scholarly writing about Latin American rural history has a long and deep tradition itself, stretching back into the nineteenth century.

A major problem with writing a historiographical survey of this literature while simultaneously conveying along very general lines some of its substantive findings lies in the way that "rural history" sprawls in so many different directions. If one were to follow the *histoire totale* approach, for instance, there would be virtually no principle of exclusion in writing about what were still until recently, after all, overwhelmingly agrarian societies. To take but one example, the Catholic Church was intimately entwined with the lives of rural people, and still is. Until sometime around the middle of the nineteenth century, in most places, rural curates bought, inherited, and owned land as private farmers employing other people, typically among their parishioners, and until liberal reforms abolished the mandatory tithe, such men had derived much of their income from it. If churchmen were regular clergy, their orders often owned vast tracts of productive land. The Jesuits were especially notable for this, but many of the other orders supported their activities in part from landed income, as well, occupying large shares of the market and struggling judicially and extrajudicially against peasant farmers for the control of resources. Furthermore, when fertility rituals and prayers were performed at the edge of peasant fields dedicated to raising crops, Christian and indigenous belief and ceremonial systems jostled each other in the process. So while this range of activities may not have been dedicated exclusively to getting a living from the land, some of it was, and the activities certainly involved rural people, and the disposition of surpluses and wealth produced by farming, thus bringing into significant overlap two spheres of life—the economic and the spiritual—often thought removed from each other, and traditionally treated that way by historians.

Chapter 2

"Rural life" can therefore embrace almost anything that takes place outside urban areas. The solution that I have adopted to avoid this sprawl—which could also embrace spatial systems, gender relations, material culture (e.g., Bauer 2001), forms of popular political mobilization, and so forth—will be to focus principally on historical writings about economic activities involving farming and the land (whether subsistence or commercial, large-scale or small, mechanized or "traditional," indigenous or European), and to work outward from there, where appropriate touching upon social, political, and cultural life. Writing in economic history has been the core of rural historiography across national traditions, and while interest in economic matters has waned among historians of Latin America (at least among Anglophone scholars) in the face of the rise of cultural history over the last two decades or so, writing on the cultural history of rural areas per se, as opposed to that of village Indians, say, or women who happened to live outside cities, has yet to wax in compensation.[1] Furthermore, to avoid lapsing into a cataloguish recitation of rural historiographies on a country-by-country basis, on the one hand, or into a strictly analytical discussion by theme that strips regional systems and localities of their historical particularities, on the other, this essay tacks back and forth between countries and themes, paying the most attention to Mexico, Argentina, Brazil, and the Andean region, and bringing in other literatures where relevant. There is ample justification for this approach since the agrarian, rural, and regional historiography of these four areas has developed quite noticeably around distinct narratives whose breadth and overlap covers much of Latin American history: that on Mexico related to the feudal/capitalist dichotomy in the rural economy, Argentina's on the pampas export sector beginning in the eighteenth century, and Brazil's around the problematics of initially slave-based sugar production, and later export booms (especially coffee, still in its early stages dependent upon the labor of African slaves) cognate to Argentina's.[2]

---

1. There are, of course, problems of sources (mostly their absence or thinness) to be reckoned with in writing the cultural history of rural life. For the relationship of cultural to economic history, and some thoughts on the decline of the latter within the context of Mexicanist historiography, see Chapters 3 and 7 in this volume, and Van Young (2003c).

2. There is also admittedly a strong (to be honest, almost exclusive) temporal emphasis on the colonial period and an extended nineteenth century—say, up to 1930 or so. In part this is because of the early modernist bias in the European agrarian history literature, which was so influential in molding the agrarian historiography of Latin America; in part because work on agrarian structures in the latter part of the twentieth century tended to shade over into policy and economic studies, and to that degree became less historical; and in part due to my own area of expertise. There is also a case to be made that the colonial agrarian historiography is richer, deeper, and more accomplished than its modern counterpart. The essay's emphasis on the economic history of production processes, in the

Historical studies of Latin American rural life have a significant prehistory going well back into the nineteenth and early twentieth centuries, much of it, not surprisingly, spurred either by a critique of plantation slavery and its social sequelae, and/or by agrarian problems, with their attendant political upheavals. To cite but one example, the Cuban writer José Antonio Saco (1875–1877) published an important early study of slavery in the 1870s, in an era when abolitionism was tightly intertwined with the island colony's belated movement for independence from Spain. In a related fashion, the run-up to the Mexican Revolution, with its building agrarian pressures and political ferment, triggered the reformist critique of the Porfirio Díaz regime by the Mexican Andrés Molina Enríquez, *Los grandes problemas nacionales* (1909). It is worth noting that Saco was a philosopher and Molina Enríquez a lawyer, that both men were involved in journalism and politics, and that their work was quite characteristic of a late nineteenth-century liberal reformist tradition with a strongly meliorist bent reflected in their views of rural society and how to transform it. By the interwar period, when Euro-Atlantic social science had already gained a strong foothold among Latin American intellectuals, a refashioned concern with slavery and race relations gave impulse to a new generation of studies with an explicitly anthropological, culturalist approach, in part inspired by the desire to suss out the origins of African cultural survivals within Latin American nations. Published within a few years of each other, for example, the Brazilian Gilberto Freyre's *The Masters and the Slaves* (1933/1946) and the Cuban Fernando Ortiz's *Cuban Counterpoint: Tobacco and Sugar* (1940/1947) sought the origins of their societies' modern social problems in an analysis of the colonial and nineteenth-century plantation complex, African slavery, and race relations.[3] Although these now-classic works and others of their ilk certainly discussed the plantation complex and its economic context, they were not studies of rural history per se, since they were more centrally concerned with viewing contemporary social problems in a historical light, and their authors were therefore prompted to formulate national metanarratives as much out of political concerns as the logic of historical inquiry.[4]

---

face of the enormous literature on that and related themes, has also meant leaving aside, except in passing, discussions of peasantries and forms of political and social resistance by subaltern groups.

3. See also Curtin (1998). A related work, published just a few years after Freyre and Ortiz, is that of the Mexican anthropologist Gonzalo Aguirre Beltrán (1946) on the African-origin population of Mexico.

4. It is interesting to note that of the more than twenty published papers from a recent academic conference devoted to Fernando Ortiz's scholarship and intellectual legacy, only a couple touch on his work as a rural historian, and those only slightly (Font and Quiroz 2005). It should be added that an important local historiographical tradition of a more

National "traditions" in rural historiography have thus developed along somewhat different trajectories during the last half-century or so, although the outlines of these literatures in some cases announced themselves quite obviously long before the 1950s. These trends were mostly nourished by some of the factors already alluded to: liberal-reformist political critiques, the need to explain revolutions with notable agrarian components, the problems presented by postemancipation race relations, local antiquarian traditions, and the maturing of social science in the region. The Brazilian scholarly literature developed principally around the northeastern sugar and central-southern coffee plantation complexes, coalescing quite understandably around issues of slavery, and the Argentine historiography around the successive waves of pampas export economy in the nineteenth and twentieth centuries. Andean writing on colonial rural history tilted somewhat toward labor systems, chiefly because of the difficulties of mobilizing indigenous people for the Spanish estate and mining sectors, and following the wide documentary trail these conflicts left in the historical record, as well as toward certain postindependence export activities (sugar on the coast, wool in the highlands). The Mexican literature, in the absence of a dominant agroexport activity, developed a fixation on the mixed-production hacienda that serviced primarily domestic markets. In addition to these endogenous considerations, many historians in Latin America, Europe, and the United States who later focused on rural history were influenced by the works of José Antonio Saco, Andrés Molina Enríquez, Gilberto Freyre, Fernando Ortiz, and others of the protorural historians, but also by those of European historians of rural life, among them Marc Bloch, Pierre Goubert, Emmanuel Le Roy Ladurie, Bernhard Slicher Van Bath, R. H. Tawney, Joan Thirsk, and many others.

---

antiquarian nature within Latin America itself added its rivulet to the headwaters of what would later become a much more cosmopolitan approach to rural history. From the late nineteenth century, in particular, every city or region of any importance was likely to count (as they still do) vocational genealogists and historians among its lawyers, physicians, engineers, school teachers, priests, and other educated professionals, often with interests in the history of local dynastic families and their landholdings. These men often produced works of real value based upon careful archival research and the painstaking reconstruction of local landholdings and political life, even if they worked within relatively restricted limits and in a style strongly narrative rather than analytic. An example of this genre of work from the area of Latin America I happen to know best is Amaya Topete (1951), a detailed reconstruction of colonial landholding patterns and the genealogy of landed magnate families in the Ameca Valley, at the western end of Lake Chapala in central western Mexico. For Chile, a similarly detailed, foundational study in agrarian history was the work on one of the country's central valleys, the Valle del Puangue, by Borde and Góngora (1956), although both the authors in this case were academics.

THE FEUDALISM/CAPITALISM DEBATE: MEXICO

If one were to single out an avatar of more modern approaches to rural history, it would be a work very closely related to the European historiography of Marc Bloch's generation, produced by one of his students: François Chevalier's *La formation des grands domaines au Méxique* (1952).[5] Chevalier's work raised the question of whether the great colonial landed estate was feudal or capitalist in spirit and practice (for Molina Enríquez's verdict from the early twentieth century, see above and Chapter 1 in this volume), but he worked out his response through attacking a mass of primary documentation rather than arguing from theoretical abstraction or upstreaming from later political events. Chevalier presented a *tableau vivant* of the feudal-looking north Mexican seigneur and the patriarchal frontier society over which he ruled, suggesting that the origin of the colonial hacienda's feudalization lay in an economic contraction led by a seventeenth-century decline in silver mining production. This contraction of market demand, he reasoned, had turned the rural estate in upon itself, reinforcing what had already been an ecologically adaptive tendency in such estates toward extensive (livestock-raising) rather than intensive (grain-producing) practices, but also allowing scope for the mentality of the "grand seigneur" imported in the cultural baggage of the Spanish conquerors.[6]

In one guise or another the argument over whether landed estates in the Iberian New World were primarily feudal or capitalist in form, or some sort of hybrid, and if capitalist, when they became so, has been the grand theme of much of the writing on rural history ever since Cheva-

---

5. The book appeared in Mexico as *La formación de los grandes latifundios en México: Tierra y sociedad en los siglos XVI y XVII* (1956), and in English as *Land and Society in Colonial Mexico: The Great Hacienda* (1966). The 1999 Mexican reedition, *La formación de los latifundios en México: Haciendas y sociedad en los siglos XVI, XVII, y XVIII* (1999), includes a new introductory essay by Chevalier reviewing the writings on the Mexican hacienda after the initial appearance of his book, along with an updated bibliography.

6. Chevalier's treatment of regional and temporal variations in the economic and social morphology (the term is that of Nickel 1988) of the hacienda was in fact more nuanced than either his critics or his admirers acknowledged, although his model for the Mexican north was applied rather promiscuously by other scholars to the rest of the country and beyond. In the 1999 edition of his book he was prepared to concede that his general model of the colonial hacienda might accommodate the notion (from Van Young 1983) that these agrosocial units were capitalist (or at least highly commercialized) economically and feudal (or at least patriarchal) socially. In his masterful study of agrarian capitalism in Peru, Jean Piel (1975) makes much the same suggestions, characterizing the functioning of the colonial hacienda as capitalist externally (allowing for the accumulation of capital resources), and precapitalist internally (insofar as its relations of production were concerned).

lier. The issue spilled over into much writing about Latin America not even centrally focused on rural history, since a broader characterization of the region's entire history with reference to whether its major economic formations were feudal or capitalist could provide the foundation of large interpretive schemes (Carmagnani 1976; Kay 1980; Schell 1986; Knight 2002b). Particularly where the colonial period—the foundational moment of Latin American agrosocial forms—was concerned, the historiographic seed planted by Chevalier's great study flowered most exuberantly during a relatively brief period, between about 1965 and 1985.[7] Latin American, European, and North American scholars have debated endlessly and robustly whether commercialized rural estates can be called capitalist, protocapitalist, precapitalist, or cryptocapitalist, whether forms of coerced labor disqualified them or could be accommodated theoretically to what remained basically a Marxian framework of understanding, whether apparently rational economic behaviors were driven by aristocratic values, and so forth.

Although it played itself out most clearly in the Mexican historiography of the colonial era and the prerailroad age, this discussion produced loud echoes in the rich Argentine literature as well, especially for the period between about 1750 and the onset of the great export booms in the mid-nineteenth century.[8] And what seemed at first a parochial debate played a significant role from the 1960s in the rise of dependency perspectives (and some theoretical oddities, such as ideas about the articulation of modes of production). Dependency theory—perhaps *perspective* is a better word than *theory*, since at this remove in time it is difficult to see what was so theoretical about it—took the form in the Mexicanist literature of works such as André Gunder Frank's extended essay (published in 1979, but written many years earlier) on the transformation of the mode of production from feudalism to an early dependent capitalism in the sixteenth century, although this approach was later to find its most florid application in studies of the nineteenth and twentieth centuries (Frank

---

7. See Chapter 1 in this volume. There have been some notable *desfases* in this general periodization. The impressive outpouring of scholarly work on the pampean rural economy and society of Argentina in the late colonial and early national periods, for example, picked up momentum only as the literature on Mexico began to wane.

8. In what follows I only scratch the surface of the rich historiography on haciendas and rural life in colonial and nineteenth-century Mexico. Among a multitude of other studies, readers may wish to consult the following: for more northerly parts of Mexico, Vargas-Lobsinger (1984), Jiménez Pelayo (1989), and Langue (1992); for the more central and southerly parts of the country Taylor (1976), Couturier (1976), Moreno García (1982, 1989), Leal and Huacuja Rountree (1982), Lindley (1983), Medina Rubio (1983), Rodríguez Gómez (1984), Murphy (1986), Rendón Garcini (1990), García Ugarte (1992), Fernández (1994, 1999, 2003), Lipsett-Rivera (1999); and for Yucatan, Patch (1993).

1967; Palm 1978; Cardoso and Pérez Brignoli 1984; Semo 1993/1973). In regions removed from the core silver mining centers of Mexico and Peru economic dynamism and social change within a dependent colonial framework were portrayed by some scholars as substantial but still amounting only to a nascent form of capitalism manqué, as in Marcello Carmagnani's (2001) detailed study of Chile between 1680 and 1830 (see also Bauer 1975). Carmagnani found that during the eighteenth century Peruvian demand for Chilean wheat transformed the agrarian economy of the sleepy colony's central valleys, in the process reinforcing landlord hegemony over a resident service tenantry (*inquilinos*) and establishing an urban hierarchy in which other cities were subordinate to Santiago, and Santiago to commercial interests in Lima and Cádiz.

The view that the colonial landed estate was a messily capitalist institution—commercialized, profit oriented, economically rational, organized internally along paternalistic lines and capable of contracting in on itself when labor and/or market conditions warranted a turn toward autarchy—had hardened into orthodoxy as studies of rural economic history reached their high-water mark in the 1970s and early 1980s. In Mexico, the economic historians Jan Bazant and Enrique Semo, among others, refined this model in research on multiple haciendas in the central parts of the country, and studies by Anglophone historians (Brading 1978; Van Young 1981) demonstrated roughly the same thing (see also Bazant 1975; Semo 1977). For the Andean area, Robert G. Keith's book (1976) on colonial estates along the Peruvian coast, and Keith A. Davies' more focused study (1984) of the Arequipa region, on the south coast of Peru, supported and expanded these findings for a different environment that nonetheless shared much with Mesoamerica, especially the presence of dense, sedentary indigenous populations in relatively close proximity to urban markets. A more theoretically sophisticated treatment was that on Peru of the French scholar Jean Piel (1975), whose study embraced the entire country from the Spanish conquest up to the mid-nineteenth century, passing majestically through the wars of independence from Spain, which he characterized in Braudelian fashion as "only a political and juridical phenomenon" subordinate to changes in the land and productive arrangements. Piel remarked that there was at the time he published his book no Peruvian equivalent of Chevalier's great work, although he himself apparently aspired to create one. In tracing the development of "agrarian capitalism" in Peru, Piel saw the incipient rationalized commercial agriculture of the colonial era blossom into a more truly capitalist agricultural regime between about 1840 (with the advent of the guano export industry and the capital it made available) and 1920, which he dubbed the period of "neolatifundism" in the central Andean region.⁹ A pair of fine studies by Nicholas Cushner—who, like Piel, called large-scale commercial farming production "agrarian capitalism"—were devoted to sugar and wine production on the north coast of Peru (1980) and the still more northerly region of Quito (1982), in what is today Ecuador, during the period 1600–1767, and a third (1983) to the colonial Río de la Plata region, today's Argentina. Cushner's studies shared both the strength and the weakness that they were based on the activities of the Jesuit order, expelled from the Spanish realms in 1767. The Jesuits' punctilious accounting practices, substantial networked capital resources, and access to the highest levels of colonial power made their records unusually continuous and therefore invaluable sources, but raised questions as to how representative their enterprises were.¹⁰ The same was true of the historical anthropologist Herman W. Konrad's (1980) dense study of a Jesuit hacienda complex in central Mexico during the same period as Cushner's work on the order's Andean estates. Konrad strongly emphasized the social ecology of the Jesuit latifundia, especially their destructive effects on nearby indigenous peasant villages, thereby painting a much less sanguine picture than Cushner of rural capitalist enterprise in the colonial heartlands, and assimilating Jesuit haciendas to what other scholars had found for secular landholdings.

Theoretical leverage for drawing these distinctions had long since been provided by an important but now curiously little-cited article by the distinguished anthropologists Eric Wolf and Sidney Mintz (1957; see also Mörner 1973). They analyzed the differences between lowland plantations (staple-producing and characterized by wage-labor systems in the twentieth century, but in many areas slave-based well into the nineteenth century) and highland haciendas (nominally free-labor, farming and/or livestock) in terms of six variables—capital, labor, land, markets, technology, and modes of social control—rather than phenomenologically, as static ideal types, thus creating a typological matrix into which New World agrosocial forms might be fitted. Of these variables it has been the nature of markets (i.e., the degree of commercialization in the countryside) and forms of labor that have proven to pack the greatest diagnostic punch. Most studies of non-export-oriented rural economy for the colonial period and the earlier nineteenth century will devote some attention to the

---

9. For an interesting and sometimes sharp polemic over the development of large-scale commercial agriculture from the colonial period to the twentieth century in Bolivia, see Larson (1998) and Jackson (1994).

10. A useful collection of original documentary sources that deals with the entrepreneurial activities of the Jesuits and other regular orders is Tovar Pinzón (1971–); and on haciendas more generally for New Granada, which would later become Colombia, see also Tovar Pinzón (1980, 1988).

way farming and livestock surpluses were moved around domestic market spaces and disposed of, and it is hardly surprising that many works on rural Mexico turn their attention to such relationships, given the centrality of agricultural commercialization in the historiography of haciendas. My own study (1981) of rural estates in the Guadalajara region of western-central Mexico in the later colonial period is one of the few to do this in detail, however, describing in terms of central-place theory a regional rural economy increasingly integrated and reconfigured by the growth of urban demand over the course of a century.[11] One of the most penetrating studies on the Mexican countryside, that of Simon Miller (1995), tackles the issue of economic modernization during the longer nineteenth century, concluding that in response to improving means of transport (the railroads) and the consolidation of domestic security, great Mexican landlords were able to produce grain profitably for distant urban markets, thus following a "Junker path" toward an economic modernization whose flowering was blocked by the eruption of the Mexican Revolution of 1910. Macroeconomic studies, primarily of the late colonial period (although for the immediate postconquest era, see the excellent work of Hassig 1985), have demonstrated how large urban concentrations, burgeoning smaller cities, and mining complexes constituted markets that could organize rural production systems economically, like magnets orienting iron filings, and over the course of time reconfigured large regions in Mexico, the Andean area, and Argentina. Such works demonstrate on the whole a marked theoretical concern with the power of central places and with regionality. The studies on the Andean area are also strongly oriented toward the analysis of spatiality, but vertically rather than horizontally. They have stressed the uneven distribution of poles of economic growth there and the importance of the famous "Andean verticality," the distribution of native subsistence activity in an archipelago of complementary population concentrations and ecological niches corresponding to the imposing Andean geography of mountain tiers interrupted by intermontane valleys (Murra 1980/1956; Assadourian 1980, 1982; Klein 1993; on Mexico, see Garner and Stefanou 1993; Ouweneel 1996; Ibarra Romero 2000b; Miño Grijalva 2001; Amith 2005; for Argentina, see Garavaglia 1983).

---

11. In a closely reasoned study of the same urban area, Ibarra Romero (2000) has argued that at the close of the colonial period the Guadalajara region was much more deeply linked to outside markets than my model of regional semiautarchy would suggest. Serrera Contreras (1977) argues much the same thing for a long-range livestock trade between this area and Mexico City for the last half-century of the colonial era. Under this discussion lurks the more theoretical issue of what regions are exactly, and how they change over time (Van Young 1992a; Pérez Herrero 1992b), a discussion with relevance well beyond the bounds of colonial Mexico; on this issue see Chapter 5 in this volume, and Van Young (1992d).

The use of unfree or semifree forms of labor has drawn most attention in the debate over the hacienda, since the more coercive end of the labor continuum was anchored in African slavery (Bauer 1979; Stern 1988). This has proven a theoretical tar baby for most students of highly commercialized, staple-producing estates, no less in Anglo-America than in the Iberian colonies, since the presence of a wage-labor market with relatively free factor mobility has long been considered the single most important desideratum for defining capitalism, especially (although not exclusively) in the Marxian tradition. Theoretical problems show up in this regard from the very first labor institutions (coexistent with African slavery) established by the Spanish in the New World to control native labor, although it must be admitted that these problems arise primarily if the observer is committed beforehand to model building rather than a more eclectic, empiricist approach.

In general, early coercive labor arrangements involving colonists and indigenous people—slavery, labor tribute, corvée service—can be conceived of as mechanisms of primitive accumulation, since they created the infrastructure (urban and rural buildings, agricultural enterprises, roads, some mining facilities, etc.) of many of the colonies. The enslavement of Indians under doubtful royal authorization, or absent such license altogether, was the motive for great controversy from Columbus's time, lasted surprisingly long in some areas (especially in peripheral regions of the Spanish New World empire, often under the nominal justification of warfare), and has received some attention from modern authors, particularly the Mexican Silvio Zavala, who pioneered the study of indigenous labor history (Zavala 1994; see also Randolph 1966; Korth 1968; Góngora 1971; Jara 1981; Sherman 1979). More important than indigenous slavery for the Spanish settlers was the institution of the encomienda, which enjoyed its heyday during the sixteenth century, although as in the case of slavery it survived in peripheral areas until quite late even after it was officially abolished at midcentury. The encomienda was imported to Spain's American realms from Old Spain, where it had served late medieval Christian monarchs and their aristocratic allies in controlling newly conquered Muslim Iberians and extracting labor from them. The institution was adapted to dominate New World Indian populations through granting the right to conqueror-settlers to collect tribute from them in the form of labor (within strict limits often observed more in the breach than the observance) and commodities in return for some wages, indoctrination in Christian belief, and protection by their Spanish overlords (*encomenderos*). Because of the delegated sovereignty, the language of vassalage in which the grants were couched, and the elements of coercion in it, the encomienda has often been painted as a feudal institution. Much of the pioneering historiography, again, was done for colonial Mexico, but scholars have looked at its history in colonial Chile, Paraguay, Colombia, Guatemala, and even Argentina (on Mexico, see Miranda 1965; Zavala 1967, 1984–, 1992/1935; Simpson 1982/1950; Himmerich y Valencia 1991; Aguirre Beltrán 1992; on Chile, see Góngora 1971; on Paraguay, see Service 1971/1954; on Colombia, see Rodríguez Baquero 1995 and Calero 1997; on Guatemala, see Kramer 1994 and Herrera 2003; and on Argentina, see Vargas 1983).

Encomienda studies have flourished most, however, for the Andean area, probably because native population there declined more slowly than in Mesoamerica under the impact of epidemic disease, the labor market was stickier, and the impact of the silver mining economy focused on Potosí (in modern-day Bolivia) was more disruptive. In the colonial-era historiography, in fact, there is an inverse relationship between Mexico and the Andean zone, the former having produced many fewer studies of the encomienda and related forms of labor mobilization, but developed an obsession with the hacienda, while the latter has been much less preoccupied with the hacienda than with the encomienda and the form of corvée labor known as *mita*. One of the best of these Andean-area studies is that of Efraín Trelles Aréstegui (1982), who traces the career of the Peruvian *conquistador-encomendero* Lucas Martínez Vegazo (1512–1567) during the middle third of the sixteenth century. Trelles Aréstegui demonstrates very clearly that the encomienda was not only a form of military parasitism, but also a fundamental mode of accumulating capital and building an early colonial economy, albeit against the backdrop of implicit state coercion and with the collaboration of members of the native ruling class who intervened as mediators in the process (see also Belaúnde Guinassi 1945; Zavala 1978; Guerrero 1991b; de la Puente Brunke 1992; Ortiz de la Tabla Ducasse 1993).[12]

Although there were technical and legal differences between them, the encomienda was in some ways similar to the widely known labor practice called *repartimiento*, a form of village-based, rotating, paid corvée labor established in some places in the sixteenth century, and which lasted in a somewhat attenuated form nearly until the end of the colonial period. The harshest form of this (known as the *mita*, a term taken over from the Incas)—a practice deeply disruptive of the complex kinship, spatial, and political forms of Andean native society, since many Indians fled their villages permanently to escape it—was employed at the great silver mining

---

12. For further studies that look at Indian slavery and encomienda within the context of other labor forms and the colonial economy more generally, see Villamarin and Villamarin (1975); and also Tord Nicolini (1981), Zavala (1988), Zavala et al. (1987).

complex at Potosí, although it also provided labor for grain cultivation, sugar production, and livestock operations elsewhere (Bakewell 1984; Simpson 1938; Guerrero 1991b). A very different institution of a similar name, variously known as the *reparto* or *repartimiento de mercancías*, was also established during the early colonial period and officially outlawed by the Bourbon administrative reforms of the late eighteenth century, although it continued to exist de facto even after that. Particularly notorious for its abusiveness in Mexico and the Andes, this was a form of extractive arrangement whereby royal officials in the countryside compelled Indian villagers to buy goods from them on credit at inflated prices, thus forcing them into the labor market for money wages (as the payment of royal tribute also did) and in the process making tidy profits for themselves and their merchant backers. Jürgen Golte's (1980; see also Moreno Cebrián 1977) study of the commercial *repartimiento* in the Andean area in the late eighteenth century suggested a direct relationship between its degree of exploitiveness and the propensity of indigenous communities to join the great wave of antiwhite and antigovernment rebellion that lashed the area in the early 1780s, and the view of most historians of the practice has at best been a very dark one. Turning this view on its head, however, the American scholar Jeremy Baskes (2000; but see also Hamnett 1971, Sánchez Silva 1998) has argued plausibly that during the late eighteenth century in the heavily Indian region of Oaxaca, in southeastern Mexico, a variant of the practice fuelled small-scale production for export of the valuable dyestuff cochineal (Spanish: *cochinilla*) very much to the benefit of the Indian producers, for whom credit for living costs and production inputs was essential. He finds that force was minimal or nonexistent, and that the high prices of goods given on credit represented a reasonable risk premium for merchant backers and the provincial officials who fronted for them.

Despite the long endurance of formally coerced labor in the Latin American countryside, at least nominally free labor existed alongside it from the beginning and grew steadily in importance. Free labor as such has received surprisingly limited scholarly attention, not because historians are not interested in it, but because sources are lacking, or at best fragmented, and at least for the modern period depend heavily upon finding account books for agricultural estates or labor recruiters, which survive only idiosyncratically. Most studies of estate complexes, regions, or export sectors touch heavily on labor, however. One of the most powerful formulations of the rise of free waged labor for areas of heavily indigenous population (Mesoamerica, the Andes) is still that of Charles Gibson (1964). He suggested that for the colonial Mexican heartland the sequence encomienda->labor *repartimiento* (corvée labor)->debt peonage occurred in response to the notorious declining demographic curve for native peoples, concomitantly increasing the difficulties for estate owners in recruiting, retaining, and controlling laborers. Gibson and other scholars (e.g., Gutiérrez Brockington 1989) have even proposed that debt peonage in colonial times depended upon the ability of workers in relatively labor-scarce environments to maximize their position by extracting credit from their employers as a wage premium. But we are still left with the puzzle of why the practice should have persisted even in areas where the population curve trended upward from the midcolonial period and the pressure to recruit labor in this fashion would presumably have abated (Van Young 1981, 1983).

The extent and even the function of debt peonage, of course, would have varied with local population trends, peasant access to subsistence lands, and other conditions.[13] In modern times forms of debt peonage overlapping with slavery have existed in rubber-producing areas, including the Putumayo region of Colombia and Peru, and in Chiapas, Tabasco, and Campeche in Mexico, as well as in Yucatán's henequen plantations. A pair of elegant studies, by Peter Klarén (1973) and Michael Gonzales (1985), have delved into labor recruiting practices (the system of *enganche*, a sort of indenture contract) on Peru's sugar-producing north coast, and another into the experience of Haitians recruited to work in the sugar industry in the Dominican Republic (Plant 1987). Still sparser than the historiography of rural labor, and a direct outgrowth of it, are works on the history of rural wages themselves, so well developed for Europe and the United States. A lamentable result of this lacuna is that while we have some fine works on the history of prices, and agricultural fluctuations and crises, especially for the colonial era, we still have very little writing on the standard-of-living debate for the mass of the Latin American rural population over time, which has proved so suggestive for the rest of the Atlantic world (Florescano 1969; Trabulse 1979; Johnson and Tandeter 1990; Romano 1993).[14]

EXPORT ECONOMIES IN FULL FLOWER: ARGENTINA

After Spanish America and Brazil achieved their independence from the metropolitan powers in the early 1820s, the successor states faced the necessity of reintegrating themselves into the world economy along rela-

---

13. For the Mexican north in the late eighteenth and early nineteenth centuries, when labor was quite scarce, see Harris (1975); and more generally Katz (1984). See also the several studies by Nickel (1987, 1988, 1989, 1997). On Latin America more broadly, consult Duncan and Rutledge (1977).

14. For some exceptions, see Van Young (1992c), and indirectly, Bauer (2001).

tively free-market lines rather than within the often stultifying mercantilist framework only just being overhauled in the last half-century or so of colonial rule (Stein and Stein 1970; Bulmer-Thomas, Coatsworth, and Cortés Conde 2006). Some of the new nations were so disrupted by the very process of sundering the colonial bond that they never regained their footing; Haiti is notoriously the western hemisphere's most extreme case of this. Others, such as Gran Colombia (which broke up into three nations) or Central America (which ended up as five), took time to recover their balance, collectively investing their energies in the consolidation of their boundaries and the establishment of their new state structures, an effort that cost all the new states dearly in greater or lesser degree, the notable exception being Brazil. Moreover, nearly everywhere (again, Brazil excepted) the costs of independence included ruined countrysides, widespread mortality, impaired or nonexistent state fiscal capacity, and disrupted trade (Halperín Donghi 1973; Prados de la Escosura and Amaral 1993; Schmit 2004). As they struggled to consolidate themselves, almost all the new states of Latin America reentered the international market through mining (silver in Mexico and Peru; and somewhat later, copper in Chile and Mexico, Guano in Peru from the 1840s) and/or agropastoral production for foreign markets. Indeed, livestock and agricultural exports tell much (though by no means all) of the history of rural Latin America for the nearly two centuries since independence was consummated. Many of the products are familiar, even mundane, but formed the basis for enormous landed and commercial wealth in the region up to the Great Depression and beyond—coffee, sugar, bananas, beef and mutton, wool, and wheat are among the best-known such commodities, along with some less familiar products such as henequen (also called sisal, a hard fiber produced in Mexico's Yucatán Peninsula)—leaving a permanent imprint on export-oriented economies.

Much of the narrative of Latin America's history in the later nineteenth and twentieth centuries can also be organized in terms of the economic distortions, opportunity costs, wealth concentration, demographic changes, and social and political stresses the export economies brought in their wake, and with the social solutions invented or adapted to deal with these problems (e.g., Topik and Wells 1998). The most common of these nostrums has been the market solution, which involves expanding export industries already in place, encouraging new ones, or engaging in import substitution industrialization, all strategies more or less covered by the discursive fig leaf that a rising tide lifts even the smallest boats. A second solution is political intervention to redress imbalances in the social distribution of wealth, either in the shape of land reform (e.g., Peru in the 1960s) or outright revolution (Mexico, Cuba, Nicaragua, etc.), which theoretically runs counter to the market solution, although in the end one of its goals may be to situate smaller commercial producers and peasants more advantageously in relation to markets. A third solution can be wrapped up in efforts to increase agricultural productivity through technological interventions (i.e., the Green Revolution). In practice none of these measures has been completely effective in the long term and they may create as unintended consequences even worse social problems than they solve. Argentina constitutes a classic case of the market solution in the form of overlapping waves of export commodities dating from the late colonial period. It serves to introduce a range of historical issues touching on export economies in Latin America more broadly, but also to illustrate the ways in which the picture of the socially reductive power of exports has been significantly complicated by recent research.[15]

As with other historiographies, that on Argentine rural life had its prehistory, too, as exemplified by now classic works such as Ricardo Levene's (1927–28) investigation into the colonial economy, Jacinto Oddone's (1975/1936) study of landholding families in Buenos Aires province, Alfredo Montoya's (1956) on the salt-beef industry, or Horacio Giberti's (1981/1954) on the Argentine livestock industry, the locus classicus of conventional wisdoms about economic development in the Río de la Plata. The much-studied sequence of overlapping pampean export booms that began in the eighteenth century—cattle hides, salt-beef, mutton and wool, wheat, and a turn back to beef again—has been portrayed as sweeping all before it, producing an enduring and highly skewed distribution of landed wealth, the top rung of which was occupied by large estancias and the landowning clans that held them; extensive proletarianization, of which both the hero and tragic victim was the gaucho; a radically dependent economic structure; and long domination of the political sphere by the export oligarchy. This has been a long-accepted vision absorbed into some influential general works on the Argentine economy, such as those of Aldo Ferrer (1967) and (to a lesser degree) Jonathan Brown (1979). Superimposed upon this picture was the need to explain the late unification of Argentina as a nation-state in even the most restricted technical sense, and behind that to account for the peculiarly unmediated relationship, generally not so overt in others of the new successor states, between large-scale landownership and political power, most impressively exemplified by the figure of Juan Manuel de Rosas,

---

15. My treatment in this section of the chapter owes much to the thematic and organizational guidance afforded by several fine historiographical essays by Argentine scholars, primarily Fradkin (1993), Garavaglia and Gelman (1995), Fradkin and Gelman (2004). Sugar as an export staple has been left aside for the moment since its intimate association with African slavery makes it more logical to deal with it in the section of the essay on Brazil.

dictator of Buenos Aires province for almost the entire period 1829–1852 (Lynch 1981; Gelman 2005).

As late as the end of the 1990s some excellent, now even classic works added much substance and nuance to this general picture, looking at a single economic sector here, a different subregion there. Among many such works have been James Scobie's (1964) somewhat earlier but still canonical economic and social history of wheat production on the pampas between 1860 and 1910, Ian Rutledge's (1987) investigation of the development of agrarian capitalism (a favorite theme of the literature) in the interior province of Jujuy, Jeremy Adelman's (1994, 1999) books on property rights, capital formation, and the pampas economy in comparative (Argentina-Canada) and Atlantic contexts (along with the older, complementary work of Carl Solberg (1987), which concentrates heavily on government policy toward the wheat industry), Samuel Amaral's (1998) study of Buenos Aires estancias from the late eighteenth century to 1870, the two-volume work of Osvaldo Barsky (2003–2005) and his collaborators on pampas livestock development up to 1900, and Hilda Sabato's (1990) book on the sheep industry in the last half of the nineteenth century. Sabato's empirically rich study echoes in its central thematic emphasis the feudalism/capitalism debate played out not only in the Mexican historiography, but also for other areas of the former colonies, as in the works of Cushner and Piel on the Andean region. In theoretical terms she places her investigation of sheep culture between what she calls, on the one hand, the "pragmatic" perspective, which traces the nineteenth-century concentration of landed property in the form of large estancias to international market forces that funneled to large landowners "Ricardian rents" from the availability of fertile soils; and, on the other hand, the "critical" perspective (what we might now call the institutional, or Northian view), in which large estates are seen to be created through public land giveaways during the early nineteenth century, and consolidated through the associated political practices.[16] While her synthetic approach leans toward a somewhat simplified picture of labor

---

16. The concentrated wealth stored up in the rich soils of the River Plate area raises the issue of how natural environments are perceived and exploited, and how they mediate human relationships. To date, the field of environmental history has not developed as one might have hoped, given the relatively early success in this vein of Dean (1987), a study of the environmental effects of the Amazon rubber boom, and his later work (1995) on the destruction of Brazil's Atlantic-litoral forests. For early colonial Mexico we have the elegant study of Melville (1994) on the sixteenth-century Mezquital Valley, in which she shows that the environmental degradation of the area even in modern times was due not to the weight of human habitation in the preconquest era, as Cook (1949) had argued, but rather to the overgrazing of sheep introduced by Spanish stockmen in the sixteenth century and the "ungulate irruption" unleashed by it.

as furnished either by foreign immigrants or natives driven off the land, it does allow Sabato to devote her attention not only to large estancias, but also to what she calls small, family-worked sheep farms whose existence was long thought incompatible with market forces and concentrated property in land. A comparison of productive types with Mexico might yield the following suggestive analogy: sheep farms/estancias = ranchos/haciendas.

The historical writing on Argentine rural life has shifted during the last fifteen or twenty years, not to abandon the era of the classic export economy beginning around 1850, and which the writers mentioned above and many others have served so well in their writings, but certainly to emphasize more strongly internal market logics, and to concentrate on an earlier period, the century embracing the years 1750–1850. The historiography began to undergo a renaissance around the mid-1980s (Garavaglia and Gelman 1995), when the wave of Mexican hacienda studies, from which the Argentine scholarship in part took inspiration, had already begun to recede from its high-water mark. This renaissance shared some of the same origins as the changes that had brought about the reorientation of the Mexican rural historiography a generation earlier: first, a revisionist reaction against an earlier orthodoxy—in the Mexican case the "feudal" model of the traditional hacienda and in the Argentine case, of the Atlantic export market; and second, a turn toward ever more granular, localized sorts of documentation—notary records, estate account books, parish records, accounts of criminal trials of rural people, and so forth. It is hard to overestimate the importance of Carlos Sempat Assadourian's (1982) work in this shift of focus. His research drew attention to the organizing power of an internal "economic space" in Spanish South America during the colonial era, centered on the great Andean silver mining complexes, primarily Potosí, in what is today Bolivia. While one might feel inclined to debate whether this relationship was any less of an export economy than the Atlantocentric one that developed starting with the production of cattle hides in the late eighteenth century, it nonetheless pushed much further back in time the history of the commercial agriculture and livestock sectors and laid the groundwork for more detailed studies of the preexport boom period, which has been the major terrain of the historiographical renaissance. The work that came along after Assadourian, of which one of the major architects has been Juan Carlos Garavaglia, is typified by Garavaglia's (1987) own essays on topics ranging from regional differentiation within the Río de la Plata area to the economics of Jesuit missions in Paraguay, Carlos Mayo's (1995) study of late colonial pampean estancias, Jorge Gelman's (1996) very detailed reconstruction of a single merchant fortune, and the interesting anthology of Raúl Fradkin and Gravaglia (2004) on the rural and commercial economy of Buenos Aires province in the 1750–1850 period, as well as a number of studies on the interior provinces of Salta and Tucumán (Mata de López 2000; López de Albornoz 2003).

These and other works in the impressive wave of the new pampas historiography have emphasized the diversity of the rural production structure and of the labor force, the importance of African slaves as workers until quite late, the little researched presence of Indians, the region's social fluidity, and so forth (Mandrini and Reguera 1993). Three of the best exemplars of the new approaches are Jorge Gelman's (1998) study of agrarian structure at the end of the colonial period in the Banda Oriental, the area that would later make up much of Uruguay; the companion study of Juan Carlos Garavaglia (1999) on the Buenos Aires countryside, to the southwest of the Río de la Plata, over a somewhat longer extension of time; and Ricardo Salvatore's (2003) investigation of rural working people in the Rosas period (but see also Slatta 1983). The books share a heavily quantitative methodology, Gelman and Garavaglia deploying numbers to trace the shape of property holding, production, and population in the countryside, Salvatore to profile rural working people—gauchos, it is fair to say—to help delineate their social and political consciousness, and to define from a subalternist perspective the parameters of their freedom as social actors. Salvatore concludes that subaltern actors enjoyed a more complex political worldview and a much greater degree of agency vis-à-vis the actions of the *rosista* state than historians had heretofore suspected, while Gelman and Garavaglia arrive at analogous conclusions about the diversity of rural society before the great export boom age, the importance of intraregional markets for agricultural products, the capacity of smaller production units to survive next to large estancias, and the complexity of rural labor arrangements. Garavaglia, in particular, provides an encyclopedic description of everything from natural resource endowment (his description of the *pampa ondulada* reminds one of Braudel describing an inland, pampean sea), to demography and household economic cycles, to agricultural and livestock technology and the movement of prices for agricultural commodities.

While Argentina has come to be seen as the poster child for the power of commodities to mediate relations among human beings (what has been called "the social life of things"; Appadurai 1986), and thereby to shape political, social, and economic practices in exporting societies, the forces in play there have not been unique to the country. Latin American rural history is replete with other examples, especially since the late eighteenth century or so. Robert Ferry (1989) has written a social and economic history of colonial Caracas and its hinterland, for example, by interweaving the genealogy of elite clan social reproduction over several generations (a theme common in the rural history literature) with the transition from a cereal-based hacienda economy to the slave-based production of cacao for export (see also Guerrero 1980; Torres Sánchez 2002). Other tropical exports, such as Mexican henequen, have generated their own separate, in some cases quite substantial, literatures, often concentrating on the role of coerced labor in the process of production for international markets, as in the work of Allen Wells (1985). The wool export sector in the Peruvian altiplano has been investigated over the span of a long nineteenth century by Nils Jacobsen (1993). To take another case, there has been some very interesting historical writing on the Amazon export boom in natural rubber between 1850 and 1920. Barbara Weinstein (1983) has stressed the coercion exerted upon rubber tappers and the resistance they offered, and Warren Dean (1987) the environmental aspects. Michael Taussig (1991) has examined the social conditions and belief systems of native laborers in another rubber-producing region, the Colombian Putumayo. More recently, Bradford Barham and Oliver Coomes (1996) have completely recast the discussion of the Amazon rubber era by posing questions and applying explanatory schema drawn from the fields of industrial organization economics and environmental anthropology, demonstrating among other findings that the structure of production was much more varied than had once been thought, primarily within an upriver/downriver geography. Moreover, their explicit starting point is to learn from a historical case something of the relationship between an export boom and distorted economic development in light of a recent return to commodity exports by a number of Latin American countries under neoliberal doctrines, a policy long eschewed in favor of import substitution industrialization.[17]

Other export booms have stimulated studies, some of them within international frameworks, some embracing a model of intense commodity commercialization within one region but at least nominally within a single polity, which somewhat complicates the notion of "export economy."

---

17. This instrumentalist view of what such studies can accomplish clearly points up the fact—perhaps too obvious to bear extended comment—that historical literatures respond to more than just an internalist logic of investigation. Garavaglia and Gelman (1995) point out, for example, that the end of the military regime in Argentina in the mid-1980s, by allowing the return of exiled scholars, paved the way for the renaissance in River Plate rural history they review. Similarly, the political and intellectual effects of the Vietnam war in the United States in part stimulated among my own generation the interest in peasant resistance movements and wars of national liberation that later came to fuller fruition under the subaltern studies banner.

Among the former may be counted the "McDonaldization" of the international trade in beef cattle in the late twentieth century, for example, from Costa Rica to the United States (Edelman 1992; and for an earlier period, Gudmundson 1983). Among the latter were the colonial tobacco industry in Spanish America and the less well known but regionally significant *yerba mate* industry in Paraguay, both important commercialized intracolonial products of long spatial reach serving large numbers of consumers. Tobacco, since its processing and distribution comprised a royal monopoly from the late eighteenth century, proved a major source of revenue for the colonial government (Garavaglia 1983; Deans-Smith 1992). One such export product whose development occasioned a huge historical literature is coffee, produced for both domestic consumption and international markets, which dominated the economies of large parts of Central America, Brazil, and Colombia from some time in the nineteenth century onward, and has been a major player in Mexico, Venezuela, Puerto Rico, and elsewhere. General economic histories of Colombia have emphasized the role of coffee production in resource allocation, the dynamics of the export sector, capital accumulation, and peasant agriculture, while more specialized investigations, regional monographs, and works in historical geography and anthropology have delved into local development, land usage patterns, the politics of export-boom successions, and forms of peasant protest (McGreevey 1971; Bergad 1983; Fajardo 1983, 1993; Roseberry 1983; Ocampo 1984; Le Grand 1986; Pérez Brignoli and Samper Kutschbach 1994; Roseberry, Gudmundson, and Samper Kutschbach 1995; Chalarca 1998; Vallecilla Gordillo 2001; Palacios 2002; Clarence-Smith and Topik 2003; Ramírez Bacca 2004; Soulodre-La France 2004). Two penetrating studies take an even longer view, Lowell Gudmundson's (1986) of Costa Rica and David McCreery's (1994) on Guatemala. Gudmundson demonstrates convincingly that before the decade of the 1840s, on the cusp of the coffee export boom, Costa Rica was hardly the idealized, egalitarian, smallholder paradise that came to comprise the mythified postcoffee national image. Rather, it was a stratified society with already obvious indices of social inequality and spatial concentration of population, an image that significantly modifies our understanding of the effects of large-scale commercial agriculture on a peasant society. For highland Guatemala, on the other hand, McCreery shows clearly that during a long nineteenth century Indian peasants were shifted by national labor recruitment laws into the coffee plantation sector, effectively subsidizing it through their low wages and creating just the sort of break with traditional rural structures that Gudmundson minimizes for Costa Rica.

TROPICAL COMMODITIES AND SLAVERY: BRAZIL

As Sidney Mintz (1986) eloquently pointed out twenty-five years ago (and other authors before him, such as Noel Deerr [1949–50]), and as daily practice in the West confirms, coffee and tea came to be associated with sugar, a tropical export commodity whose worldwide consumption (save for periods of international warfare, when supplies were disrupted but demand remained very strong) has risen uninterruptedly since the age of Columbus, and which for centuries after 1492 was overwhelmingly produced in the Americas. Until the mid-seventeenth century or so the Old World sated its sweet tooth with Brazilian production, and thereafter increasingly from the British, French, and Spanish Caribbean islands.[18] Moreover, sugar production also supported domestic consumption in the coastal Andean region (northern Peru), in northern South America, and in Mesoamerica (parts of Central America and Mexico), and does to this day. Although production on a small scale was possible, sometimes within the framework of a sharecropping arrangement or by sale of cane from small independent producers to mill owners, the economic logic of economies of scale in growing sugar cane, and even more that of the substantial capital investment needed to refine sugar from raw cane—the buildings, equipment, credit chains, and so on—pushed in the direction of large-scale production units. And almost everywhere in the Americas, up until the abolition of slavery (Mexico 1829, Peru 1854, the Spanish Caribbean 1886, Brazil 1888), sugar production was strongly associated with African slavery and the trans-Atlantic slave trade (Klein 1978, 1986, 1999; Thomas 1997; Curtin 1998). So strong was this linkage that the burgeoning field of Atlantic history becomes in my opinion much more problematic as an analytical framework after the disappearance of the trade in enslaved Africans in the nineteenth century.

In terms of the scale of African slavery there, Brazil was by a large margin the most important slavocratic society in mainland Ibero-America, although the institution left no corner of the Spanish or Portuguese empires untouched. Over the nearly four centuries between 1494 and the late 1860s, Latin America and the Caribbean received about 85 percent

---

18. For reasons of space the Caribbean region—in which peasant, plantation, and export agriculture had just as complex a history as in mainland Ibero-America, and left marks just as deep on contemporary societies—is alluded to here only in passing. Nor, for the same reason, have I delved into the social and cultural aspects of Africans in the New World, although as with the ethnohistory of Native American peoples, rural history should by all rights include them. In terms of its historiographical and bibliographical orientation, this section of my essay owes much to Reis and Klein (in press), and to Klein and Vinson (2007).

of the ten million or so Africans shipped in bondage to the New World. Of the ten million, Brazil received about 35 percent, the Caribbean islands a bit more, and mainland Spanish America perhaps 10 percent. The first African slaves arrived in the Portuguese colony in the late 1530s, a scant three decades after the chance "discovery" of the region in 1500, and the sugar industry was established about the same time, coming to thrive particularly in the northeastern zone, although it eventually spread further south. Over time Brazil's economic and political center of gravity shifted southward, too, responding to overlapping waves of export economies—gold mining, then coffee production—that shared some of the same characteristics of similar economies elsewhere; and until abolition in 1888, the labor was primarily supplied by slaves of African origin. The colonial phase of this story has been dealt with by a number of Brazilian scholars after Freyre (1946/1933), among the most theoretically informed and empirically dense works being that of Jacob Gorender (1988), who was much concerned with exploring the slave mode of production in the Marxist mold. Clearly agnostic from a theoretical point of view, but basically materialist, was Stuart B. Schwartz's (1985) admirable economic and social history of the colonial Brazilian sugar economy. Based in large measure on the intensive study of records from a single large *engenho* (Spanish: *ingenio*; a sugar estate and refining operation) in the Bahia area over a long period, Schwartz's book eclipsed at the time of its publication almost all previous studies of sugar and slavery in Brazil, establishing the baseline for subsequent work. In great detail he reconstructed the labor relations, cane-growing practices and milling technology, credit linkages, slave demography, and other aspects of the industry over more than three centuries. Among his most important interpretive findings was that slavery was so tightly woven into the fabric of Bahian society that its presence tended over time to degrade all forms of labor, free and unfree alike (see also Schwartz 1992; Bergad 1999).

Other studies of Brazilian rural slavery showed the variability of the institution across regions, periods, and economic sectors, but on the whole produced findings consistent with those for Bahia. Also working on Bahia, for example, Bert Barickman (1998) produced a fine study of the tensions and complementarities between the export economy and a local commercial sector supplying bread made from cassava flour. Where Stuart Schwartz left off his study chronologically, around 1835, the earlier study of Peter Eisenberg (1974) took up the fate of sugar in Pernambuco, a neighboring area in the Brazilian northeast, from 1840 to the eve of World War I, tracing the declining arc of the sugar economy under the impact on the international market of sugar beet production, and on labor accessibility of the abolition of slavery in 1888. Alida Metcalf's (1992) study of a sparsely settled area to the west of São Paulo, corresponding roughly to the period of Schwartz's investigation, demonstrated the enduring social inequalities that slavery and large landholdings could give rise to even in frontier settings. By the time the coffee industry kicked into high gear in about the third decade of the nineteenth century, the basic pattern of large production units, slave labor, and external markets had been established. Stanley Stein's (1976/1957) classic study of a coffee-producing area to the northwest of Rio de Janeiro (1850–1890), while it demonstrated the nonaristocratic background of the planter elite and the role that racialist ideology played in underpinning the slave labor system, also showed the ruthlessness of capitalist exploitation of both the slaves and the natural environment to optimize production within a paternalistic and patriarchal social framework. Later studies on the São Paulo region have tended to confirm these conclusions while adding rich empirical detail (see also Dean 1976, Vidal Luna and Klein 2003; and on Peru, Klarén 1973).

The findings of these and other historians have contributed to a highly polemical debate about the "cruelty continuum" that had raged among Latin Americanist scholars at least since the days of Gilberto Freyre, and which saw an even more developed, indeed hypertrophied, counterpart in the historical literature on slavery in the United States. Much of the discussion revolved around the nature of postemancipation race relations in the formerly slavocratic societies of the Americas, and about what variables might account for the putatively more tolerant and inclusive attitudes in Ibero-America as opposed to Anglo-America (Harris 1964; Degler 1986). Schwartz (1985) argued convincingly, for example, that contrary to the views of Gilberto Freyre and some other earlier students of Brazilian race relations, Brazilian slavery could be just as cruel and dehumanizing as Anglo-American or Spanish versions *when such treatment was profitable*, that slave mortality was high and natality low, and that the long Iberian experience of black Africans and the supposed mellowness of Portuguese tropical Catholicism did little if anything to palliate the condition of slaves. With the economic issues largely resolved in favor of the slave owners' cruelty and opportunism, the interest of many historians turned toward the culture of Brazilian slave society, the slave community and family, slave demography, and forms of resistance, all within what would later come to be called a subalternist perspective. As in the North American historiography, greater emphasis came to be placed upon the slaves' subjective experience of their condition. An example of such work is Katia M. de Queirós Mattoso's (1986) effort to reconstruct the slaves' experience over the entire history of the institution in Brazil, a sensitive and innovative (if not entirely convincing) study of how slaves asserted their personhood within what she calls a "contractualist" legal and customary framework vis-à-vis their masters, and of the forms of "voice" and "exit" that facilitated such an assertion. In this approach, forms of slave accommodation and resistance received a good deal of attention. But as in the Mexicanist rural historiography, a turn toward social history, subalternist approaches, and cultural history seems to have implied a significant ratcheting down of effort on the economic history of slave systems, so that the excellent study of Francisco Vidal Luna and Herbert Klein (2003) even looks a bit anachronistic, while Nancy Naro's (2000) slightly earlier book devotes relatively little space to the economics of nineteenth-century slave-worked coffee *fazendas* and a great deal to social structure and demographic trends (see also Lara 1988; Reis and Silva 1989). In some ways this is the structural equivalent of the strong current among Mexicanists toward ethnohistory, which, although it deals with native peoples who were mostly peasants, is not devoted to rural history in the traditional sense of the term.

The other great receiving area for African slaves, apart from the northern Anglo-American colonies, was of course the Caribbean area, which has an enormous historical literature on sugar and slavery. This is particularly well developed for the English islands, with a tradition stretching from Lowell Ragatz's (1971/1928), Eric Williams's (1966/1944; a kind of urtext in the field), and Richard Pares's (1968/1950) works on capitalism, the planter class, and sugar, to the later works of Orlando Patterson (1967) and Richard Dunn (1973) on the same theme, and the more strictly slave- and production-centered studies of scholars such as Elsa Goveia (1965), and Jerome Handler and Frederick Lange (1978). The Spanish islands are well represented in this sugar-and-slavery literature, as well, going back to the nineteenth century, even well before José Antonio Saco (1875–1877). Among the major modern works here are Manuel Moreno Fraginals' (2001/1964; and Piqueras 2002) monumental study of the sugar industry in Cuba, primarily from the production point of view, and Leví Marrero's (1972–) even grander and more inclusive economic history of the island from the colonial period through the second third of the nineteenth century, much of which (especially the latter volumes) is necessarily devoted to sugar and slavery. Focused more on the side of the social history of the Cuban slave community is Franklin Knight's (1970) book, while Laird Bergad's (1990) emphasizes economic aspects. For Puerto Rico, Francisco Scarano's (1984) compact revisionist study of sugar and slavery in the first half of the nineteenth century demonstrates convincingly that sugar production on the island received a major fillip with the collapse of the industry on the French sugar colony of Saint Domingue in 1791, also benefiting from the sagging productive capacity of the British islands, Spain's more open commercial policies, and the possibilities of continuing slave labor imports through an illicit trade that lasted until midcentury. Although smaller in scale than Cuban sugar plantations, those of Puerto Rico also relied for their core labor force on enslaved Africans and continued to do so in the main until abolition in 1873.

Finally, the sugar-slavery nexus in mainland Spanish America has received its share of attention (e.g., Bowser 1974; Colmenares 1980; Blanchard 1992; Aguirre 2005). One of the best studied cases, interestingly enough, although after the mid-sixteenth century or so it was not a major player in the international sugar market, is Mexico, probably in large measure because the major sugar-producing region of the country was in the State of Morelos, around Cuernavaca, to the south of Mexico City, which proved to be the locus of the peasant wing of the Revolution of 1910 led by Emiliano Zapata. Despite its lurid title (*Slaves of the White God*), Colin Palmer's (1975) study provides a good survey of the African slave trade and slavery in Mexico during the early colonial period, complementing Gonzalo Aguirre Beltrán (1946) in this respect, and there are two good studies of slavery and commercial agriculture along the Gulf coast, in the Veracruz area: Patrick Carroll's (2001) on tobacco, and Adriana Naveda Chávez-Hita's (1987) on sugar. For the Morelos area proper there are a number of fine studies dealing with the period between about 1750 and 1880. Gisela von Wobeser (1988) nominally provides an excellent overview of the colonial sugar industry, but in fact limits her study to the Cuautla-Cuernavaca area even though sugar was produced in respectable quantities, if on a smaller scale, elsewhere in Mexico (the Guadalajara area, Michoacán, Veracruz) (more generally, see Crespo 1988–1990). Beatriz Scharrer Tamm (1997) focuses on sugar technology in the later colonial period, Ernest Sánchez Santiró (2001) on social structure and mercantile activity in the sugar zone, and Gisela Landázuri Benítez and Verónica Vázquez Mantecón (1988) on the domestic political economy of the industry from 1750 to 1880. Cheryl Martin's (1985) excellent book looks primarily at the tensions between sugar haciendas and the Indian villages from which they drew much of their labor, and upon whose lands they continually encroached. It is worth noting that all these fine agrarian histories pay relatively little attention to African slavery, mostly because for much of the history of sugar production in the region slaves constituted a relatively small if extremely valuable core labor force, and free Indian peasants the majority of laborers in an industry highly seasonal in its labor requirements. One of the first students of the colonial Mexican sugar industry to make this important point, and to look more deeply into the social ecology of the Morelos haciendas, was Ward Barrett (1970), a historical geographer whose minute examination of agricultural techniques, production processes and costs, capital requirements, prices for the finished product, labor needs, and profit levels constitutes not only a brilliant X-ray of a highly industrialized commercial agricultural sector, but one of the outstanding works in Latin American economic history more generally. The sugar industry did survive the colonial period, of course, albeit with a reconstituted labor force after the abolition of African slavery in the newly independent Mexico in 1829. One of the newest books mentioned in this historiographical survey, that of Paul Hart (2005), deals insightfully with the industry up to the eve of the Revolution of 1910, showing how an increasing dependence on the wage labor of peasant villagers, overproduction of sugar in the last decades before the fall of the Porfirian regime, and the failure of sugar *hacendados* to find external markets for their products all converged to sow widespread impoverishment and political discontent in the land of Zapata. Hart's work reflects current theoretical trends in the study of Latin American historical peasantries and politics that see rural people much more as the agents of their own histories than as passive objects and production factors; but that is the theme for another essay.

In conclusion, it is difficult to predict how the study of Latin American rural history will evolve in the coming decades. A look at the works mentioned in this chapter conveys the impression that over the last twenty years or so scholarly energies devoted to sanctified research themes in the field—labor systems, the traditional hacienda, estancia, and rancho, and economic history more broadly—have flagged somewhat. Within this overall scenario, however, certain areas of research interest have waned while others have waxed. The study of colonial and nineteenth-century Mexican rural history, although not exactly moribund, took a nosedive from about the mid-1980s, particularly in its economic aspects, as archival investigation reached a point of diminishing returns and historians began to repeat the same pieties over and over again. Investigation into the same period and themes in Argentina, however, began to flourish and continues to do so. Slavery, slave societies, and the social and economic effects of the "peculiar institution" have remained areas of fascination since so much of the western hemisphere is still dealing with their legacies. Apart from the interest in filling in the rural history of certain regions (e.g., Central America) and periods (the seventeenth century), some questions in the field clearly warrant further work. Among these is the social history of life on the land up to the middle of the nineteenth century or so. This is relatively easier to do for slave-dominated areas, and much harder for free or nominally free-labor areas. Because slaves were a valuable form of property, legal records of all sorts are likely to have documented slave life, while the social relations of free but humble, generally uninscribed rural people are the soft tissue of an agrarian society that vanishes over time. Another promising theme well worth pursuing further is the environmental history of the countryside under various forms of economic exploitation—traditional peasant agriculture, undercommercialized large estates, forestry and the expansion of livestock production, and export agriculture. Life on the land in Latin America has been so very important for so many centuries (and remains so in large areas today) that it is difficult to believe that, whatever the fashions of scholarly investigation, it will not remain a theme of perennial fascination for historians and other social scientists.

PART II

The Historiography of Colonial Mexico and the Era of Independence

CHAPTER 3

Two Decades of Anglophone Writing on Colonial Mexico
Continuity and Change since 1980

> I think there is little doubt that the Oregon squall will evaporate in big words. American politicians are very good at these. I wish you were in as tranquil a state in your own domestic politics. Mexico has the elements of a great nation, but these seem to be in too disorderly a condition to allow the country any fair prospect of developing its natural resources. Yet I trust the time may come.
> —William H. Prescott in a letter to Lucas Alamán, September 28, 1846.[1]

Since William H. Prescott penned these words casually in a letter to Lucas Alamán in 1846 (the two great historians never met), there has been a tendency for Anglophone writers on Mexican history to treat Mexico as a problem: a problem in economic backwardness, a problem in politi-

---

1. W. H. Prescott to Lucas Alamán, Boston, 30 March 1846; Centro de Estudios de Historia de México Condumex, Archivo Lucas Alamán (Fondo CCLXXXVII), carpeta 17, exp. 1385. Prescott was alluding to the conflict between the United States and Britain over their respective claims to Oregon, settled by President Polk in a treaty of 1846. I would like to acknowledge that an invitation from Marshall Eakin, at that time chair of the Program Committee of the Conference on Latin American History, to give a paper on almost exactly the same theme as this chapter at the Conference on Latin American History–American Historical Association meetings in San Francisco in 2002 started me thinking about these issues and trends; in the event, to my embarrassment, the paper never materialized, so that this essay constitutes a commitment belatedly kept. Matthew O'Hara made some useful comments on an early, partial draft version of this essay. My thanks also go to Karen Lindvall-Larson, formerly Latin American Bibliographer at the University of California, San Diego's Social Sciences and Humanities (Geisel) Library, for timely assistance with bibliographical matters.

cal instability, a problem in the oscillation between radical reform and stubborn conservatism—in short, as a museum of unmodernity. What can only be seen as a patronizing attitude (tinctured with *Schadenfreude*) has been widespread among U.S. intellectuals but also deeply embedded in the collective perceptions of Americans as a whole.[2] It has, of course, been mixed with great sympathy for the political travails of a sister republic, much empathy for the struggles of common people and admiration for Mexican heroes, and an enduring attraction to what in even the most sophisticated of American eyes is seen as the cultural exoticism of the country.[3] Even when the purple prose of popular historical narratives is lightened a shade or two, the sheer sweep, grandeur, and tragedy of Mexican history are hard to deny, from the awe-inspiring religious icons of the Mexica to the great political upheavals that have racked the country—the Spanish conquest, the independence struggle, the internecine wars of the early nineteenth century, foreign intervention and national dismemberment, the epic revolution of the early twentieth century, and even the dramatic political reversals of the last dozen years or so.

The construction of alterity takes many forms, and to some degree Anglophone scholars have invented in their historical writings, albeit unconsciously, a notional (and national) Other for their own cultural and political purposes, even though the Anglophone cultural world (one thinks here of the United States, Britain, and Canada) has always been sufficiently different from that of Mexico to require little embroidery to make the point. There is more than a whiff of teleological thinking in this tendency, since in the end it seeks to explain outcomes seen as virtually predetermined: why the United States has been so successful economically, and more recently so dominant on the world stage, while Mexico has often been viewed as the theater for processes of change that were not completed, went awry, produced unintended negative consequences, or

---

2. This attitude is not limited to Mexico alone, but extends to all of Latin America and even beyond. Another factor contributing to this posture, along with those discussed below, is the "white man's burden" attitude probably also shared with British thinking (particularly in the imperial vein) toward non-European areas of the world. There is an enormous literature in several disciplines dealing with this issue, which also lies near the heart of postcolonial studies; for an interesting recent treatment, see Cannadine (2001). Moreover, the very nature of the historian's craft itself, which is just as likely to dwell on apocalyptic narratives of the human past as triumphalist ones, encourages these biographies of failure.

3. See, for example, Delpar (1992). These lines are being written virtually the same day as Edward Said's death; the ideas in Said's *Orientalism* (1978) might well be applied to the establishment of a United States academic specialization on Mexico, to the power relations that have underwritten it and the institutional arrangements that have sustained it, and to the deconstruction of Anglophone writing on Mexico over more than a century. This essay is far too short to attempt such an account.

were never initiated in the first place. Since the advent of modernization theory and its leftist doppelgänger dependency theory, this case has been put most clearly and powerfully by economic historians of neoclassical bent, although scholars working in a more forthrightly Marxist vein have also made important interventions.[4] There is nothing necessarily sinister about this intellectual process, but it has worked ideologically and historiographically to depress the perception of Mexico's historical destiny while elevating that of the United States, in particular, turning Mexico into a laboratory of corruption and failure, the United States into one of virtue and success. While there has been among some American intellectuals a tendency to see Europe as a hothouse of degeneracy because of its overripe civilization (think of Henry James's depictions of innocent Americans and corrupt Europeans, for example), Mexican society has often been seen as undercivilized, both archetypes serving roughly the same ends.

It is one of the chief contentions of this chapter, however, that as cultural history and the theoretically distinct history of common people (I will refer to this as "subaltern" history not because I particularly like the word, but because it is rhetorically easy to use, and to a lesser degree because it packs a useful density of connotation) have emerged during the last two decades as major subgenres of Anglophone historical writing on Mexico they have worked, whether consciously or not, to attenuate the sharpness of the Manichean dyads of success/failure, model/problem. Cultural history has done this by injecting a strong element of relativism into the picture, concomitantly directing the gaze of many scholars away from scalar measurements focused on explicitly or implicitly unilinear concepts of economic, political, and social development, and toward hermeneutic or interpretive inquiry in which societies are studied more in their own terms, less in regard to a grand universal narrative. Previously thought uninteresting or inaccessible, the newer objects of inquiry include collective (or even individual) mental processes; various sorts of sensibility and systems of meaning (religion, gender, ethnicity); ritual, celebration, and forms of sociability; mechanisms of the social reproduction of knowledge; and the construction of group identities—and this list does not exhaust the possibilities. There is by now a heated and fairly well-

---

4. See, in particular, Coatsworth (1990), and Haber (1997b). For an extended critique of Coatsworth, Haber, and the "new economic history" in general closely paralleling some of what is said here (but some of whose more shrill pronouncements I would not endorse), see San Miguel (2004), and the astute critique of San Miguel's essay in the same journal by Sandra Kuntz Ficker (2004). I read San Miguel's article only when much of the present essay had already been written; I thank Sandra Kuntz Ficker for bringing the article and her commentary to my attention. For a Marxist view, see Semo (1993/1973).

known ongoing scholarly debate as to whether this has been a positive or negative development for Mexican history specifically, and more broadly as to whether the practice of history in the United States as a whole lost its way at the linguistic turn.[5] Whichever view one takes of the issue, however, it is undeniable that within the last fifteen to twenty years cultural history, along with the social and subaltern history to which it is allied, and from which it is in practice often indistinguishable, has come to occupy a prominent place in Anglophone history writing on Mexico and on Latin America more generally, staking out relatively new fields for itself. Native-language-based ethnohistory, for example, is an obvious success story within limits explored briefly below, while traditional fields such as political history have been revivified with new questions.[6]

Influential and increasingly visible as it is, however, cultural history has not by any means swept all other genres or approaches off the board, nor has it dragged the field into a swamp of postmodernism, as some scholars have professed to fear. Anglophone historians of colonial Mexico are following multiple tracks: they are still writing more traditional forms of social history, neoclassically oriented economic history, prosopography, and intellectual history (although very little of it), all to very good effect. To take but one example, while it is true that economic history has been less pursued of late among Anglophone historians of the colonial period (while in Mexico it seems to be thriving), the growth in sophistication and technical adeptness of what *is* being done would surely have surprised an

---

5. The fullest airing of these issues in the Latin Americanist context occurred in the special number of the *Hispanic American Historical Review* dedicated to "Mexico's New Cultural History: ¿Una lucha libre?" (1999), with essays or critical interventions by myself, William E. French, Mary Kay Vaughan, Stephen Haber, Florencia Mallon, Susan Migden Socolow, and Claudio Lomnitz-Adler, and a useful brief introduction by Susan Deans-Smith and Gilbert M. Joseph. Alan Knight took up the cudgels in his article, "Subalterns, Signifiers, and Statistics: Perspectives on Mexican Historiography" (2002c), in which, after finding that cultural history counts among its efforts more failures than successes, he nonetheless concludes that "we do not have to choose between the pomo funny farm and the positivistic prison. There are plenty of green fields in between" (Knight 2002c, 156). The discussion as to the limits and potential of cultural history vis-à-vis more traditional but no less vital genres finds echo in much recent monographic and historiographical writing; see, for example, Matthew Restall's (2003) useful review essay on native-language-based ethnohistory in Mesoamerica. Restall characterizes this scholarship as strongly empiricist rather than unduly given to "political posturing" (Restall 2003, 126), a passing reference it would be difficult to disassociate from Stephen Haber's (1999) suggestion that "new" cultural history is the half-life product of dependency theory in decay, a redemptive project distorted by left-wing political sympathies.

6. On ethnohistory, Restall (2002); on politics, Joseph (2001). This is what I take to be the project of Joseph's interesting anthology of essays, at least in part, although none of the authors deal explicitly with writings on the colonial period.

earlier generation of practitioners.[7] On the other hand, some works that fall well within the rubric of cultural history, or perhaps of social history with a cultural component, are in fact rather traditional in some ways. Take, for instance, native-language-based ethnohistory. Although there is a wide range in the degree of interpretive freedom and the broader claims that ethnohistorians allow themselves, much of what is being done in "the new philology" is distinctly redolent of the old comparative philology of the eighteenth and nineteenth centuries, and it is difficult to imagine any method more solidly empirical than this, even though it counts phonemes rather than silver ingots, sacks of wheat, or cows. To paraphrase Mark Twain's quip about premature rumors of his death being greatly exaggerated, therefore, hysterical or dismissive denunciations of postmodernism in the field have exaggerated its influence. If by *postmodernism* one means the denaturalization (but not necessarily the dismantling) by scholars of teleologies and metanarratives such as inevitable colonial maturation, liberal progress, or the development of capitalism; close attention to the subtleties of language and symbol; and methods concomitantly emphasizing local knowledges, thick description, and multiple narratives—then yes, postmodernist influence is rampant in cultural history. But if one means the introduction of an unfetteredly radical epistemological relativism (à la Paul Feyerabend), the denial of external reality, or an indifference to the criticism of evidence on the grounds that all evidence, mediated as it is by inherently unstable language, is simply codified point of view, then the careful reader of recent historical writings on colonial Mexico will find its authors to be more modernist than postmodernist, and a remarkably conservative bunch, at that. More useful critical questions about cultural history are: Does it tell us something interesting about colonial society? Does it work as a framework of explanation? Is it susceptible to reasonable evidentiary tests? Does it advance us into realms of thought and behavior inaccessible by other means?

Subaltern history has tended in the same direction as cultural history— one might call it "the disenchantment of structural materialism"—by introducing the notion of agency into the study of common people within the colonial order. Subaltern history or the study of the condition of postcoloniality are not necessarily the same as cultural history, although they may go together and are often conflated: subaltern history does not necessarily focus on culture, nor must cultural history focus on common

---

7. Several historians offer essays on the economic historiography of Mexico in the colonial and national periods, under the overall editorship of Antonio Ibarra Romero (2003b), in a special number of *Historia Mexicana* dedicated to the field (and to the memory of the late Ruggiero Romano). Especially notable of late has been the activity of the Asociación Mexicana de Historia Económica.

people. There is no inherent reason why cultural history should be limited to subaltern groups or to postcolonial societies—cultural understandings do not atrophy as one's disposable income rises, although they may become less folkloric; nor are the construction and imputation of meaning monopolies of proletarians, the socially marginalized, or the decolonized. It is through this mistaken but widely credited association that misapprehensions about cultural history as a redemptive political project may well have arisen.[8] On the other hand, where forms of popular resistance do not necessarily emerge into the public record (as they do, for example, in cases of deviance, riot, and rebellion), the cultural lens, turned on subaltern social practices with a view toward deciphering how common people negotiated their lives within the colonial arrangement and understood the world around them, naturally tends to focus on expressive forms such as religious life. The overall effect of the interest in popular agency is to have made subalterns—women, indigenous people, slaves, the mentally deviant, the poor, the socially marginalized; most of Mexican colonial society at any given moment, in other words—appear more resilient, and the colonial order more porous, more a matter of negotiation, of "adaptive resistance" (in Steve Stern's terminology), and even of self-cooptation.[9]

There are a number of factors responsible for this downward shift in the historian's gaze. One of them is the demonstration effect of early modern European historiography: many of us are still looking for our own Menocchio (Ginzburg 1980). Another is our working our way down the food-chain of sources, expectably, from the prescriptive, normative, institutional, high-political, and canonical cultural texts (although these are also being read and reread with different eyes now) to what a scant scholarly generation or so ago was considered archival dross—records of litigation and criminal accusations, for example, or the testaments of common people. A third is the influence of theoretical and/or comparative scholarship from other disciplines, such as political scientist James C. Scott's (1990) work on resistance. This recent emphasis on subaltern agency does not mean that colonialists are constructing a new White Legend of colonial society, a narrative of self-deluded colonial rulers and crafty colonized natives carrying on life by their own disguised rules under the complacent but stupid gaze of their oppressors, but rather that they are painting a more nuanced picture of what formerly looked uniformly grim and monochromatic.

---

8. For an insightful (if at times rather shrill) exploration of the distinction between cultural history and the history of common people, see the book of labor historian Bryan D. Palmer (1990: xiv): "Critical theory is no substitute for historical materialism; language is not life;" and for a defense of cultural history (albeit not an uncritical one), Bonnell and Hunt (1999).

9. Stern (1987b, 3–25).

Taking into account some of these changes, the goal of this chapter is to map the scholarly geography of Anglophone writing on the history of colonial Mexico over the last twenty-five years or so, years that correspond to the life of the journal *Mexican Studies/Estudios Mexicanos*, for which it was originally commissioned.[10] But within this broad rubric there are certain limits. Despite some emphasis on cultural and subaltern history as growing subgenres, it is not my intention to produce another installment in the continuing discussion over the nature and value of these categories; this chapter is therefore meant to be analytical and descriptive, not polemical and prescriptive. The colonial historiography has changed notably since the 1970s or so, a change marked, for example, by a perceptible decline in economic history, the emergence of the concept of political culture, and the application of anthropological conceptual frameworks. In large measure this change has been due to the impact of the early modern historiography of Europe, as noted above, to which historical writing on colonial Mexico is linked not only by the influential models of French Annaliste and post-Annaliste writing, but also by several substantive affinities in early modern Atlantic World history itself—monarchical structures of government, aristocratic types of social power, a widely prevalent worldview strongly religious in tone, a preindustrial economic life, the enduring presence of peasantries.[11] It even makes a good deal of sense to treat as a single unit the 1750–1850 period, which overlaps the traditional divide between the colonial and national eras while leaving the earlier centuries of colonial rule behind. This is one of the most interesting trends in the reconfiguration of Anglophone historical studies on Mexico, especially where a narrative structure linked to the biography of an institution, or contained by a relatively homogeneous body of documentation, makes the spanning of late colonial and early republican eras possible or even imposes it, as for example in Silvia Arrom's (2000) book on the history of the Mexico City Poor House, or Brian Connaughton's (2003) on clerical

---

10. While this essay is not meant to be celebratory of the journal, it should be noted that *Mexican Studies/Estudios Mexicanos* has done much to foster the interdisciplinary study of Mexico in the United States (although not colonial history in particular), as have a number of academic centers dedicated to Mexican studies, among them those in the University of California system as a whole (the University of California Consortium on Mexico and the United States [UC MEXUS], headquartered at the University of California, Riverside), the University of California campuses in San Diego, Los Angeles, and Irvine, the University of Chicago, and the University of Texas-Austin, among others. In the interest of full disclosure I should note that I have for many years served on the UC MEXUS editorial board of the journal, and for several as its chair.

11. For a recent restatement of some of these trans-Atlantic affinities in the early modern period, see Knight (2002b).

thinking and political change in Guadalajara, respectively.¹² Despite the logic of this approach, however, my essay strays relatively little across the colonial/national divide, and then only allusively, since it proved too ambitious to cover in a limited space recent writing about the first two generations or so after the gaining of independence in addition to all of the colonial period.¹³ On the other hand, I have found it useful to discuss some works not authored by Anglophone historians, and in some cases made available in English only relatively recently, but which have either been widely influential or which exemplify certain trends worth attending to. Examples here would be Juan Pedro Viqueira Albán's (1999) work on

---

12. An older example, dating from the very beginning of the historiographic era I am examining here, would be David A. Brading's *Haciendas and Ranchos in the Mexican Bajío: León, 1700–1860* (1978). Regarding the issue of periodization, another recent example of the overlapping framework, on a smaller scale, at least temporally, is Warren (2001), an accomplished study of popular politics; and at the other end of the spectrum, the hugely ambitious, theoretically sophisticated work of Carlos A. Forment, *Democracy in Latin America, 1760–1900* (2003). While in the cases of both Warren and Forment colonial political culture is integral to their stories, the colonial period really serves more as a prolegomenon or baseline than a full partner in their narratives. As a practical matter, a full "Age of Revolution" periodization is most likely to be employed in anthologies of scholarly essays in which almost all the authors write in a monographic mode on *either* the colonial *or* national eras and the editor or commentator attempts synoptically to place the temporally bounded essays within the larger framework. For two examples, see Rodríguez O. (1994) and Uribe-Urán (2001); my own essay in the latter volume (Van Young 2001a) reviews some of the issues. Judging from anecdotal evidence, the deployment of this "swing" periodization by graduate students working in late colonial and early national Latin American history would appear to be increasingly common. An even broader framework, although still thematic rather than synoptic (as a textbook or survey would be), is that of the recent volume edited by Reina Aoyama and Servín (2002).

13. For a wide-ranging and astute overview of historical writing on Mexico by both Mexicans and foreigners, see Florescano (2002), who is more concerned with depicting broad changes in how Mexicans (among them historians) have viewed their own history over time, than with the detailed investigation of changes in approach and methodology, the use of new sources, the emergence of new interpretive models, and so forth. Regarding the period under review here, from about 1980 on, Florescano takes a very dim view of how professional writing of history has (or has not) developed in Mexico itself: "In the time between 1980 and about 2000, instead of a progressive improvement in the methods that brought the cultivation of history to such a high point, there is noticeable a decline in the level of professional history writing, an alarming deterioration of institutions, failures in the formation of teachers and researchers, and a loss of the intellectual vigor that motivated the establishment of those [same] centers" (Florescano 2002, 445). He particularly faults Mexican historians for the fragmentation and over-specialization of history as a discipline, and for the incapacity of the field to "offer to the nation a history of itself" (p. 449). In a sense Florescano is describing precisely what has happened in Anglophone writing on Mexican history, as well, under the influence of the pervasive localization of the discipline and the drawing back from grand narrative projects and strategies, except that he sees European and North American historians as being more reflective and critical regarding changes in the discipline.

Bourbon reformers and stubborn forms of popular street culture in late colonial Mexico City, or Serge Gruzinski's (1989, 1993, 2001) on religion and the indigenous *imaginaire* in the wake of the conquest.[14] Needless to say, an essay of this length cannot possibly include everything, and even some interesting themes and key works have necessarily been left aside or only mentioned in passing. Some readers will surely find certain discussions unduly swollen (that on economic history, for example), others unduly compressed (on ethnohistory), still others strangely absent (the growing Anglophone literature on Mexican independence).[15]

SOME GENERAL TRENDS IN THE ANGLOPHONE HISTORICAL LITERATURE ON COLONIAL MEXICO

To start with (and at some risk, perhaps, of quantifying the obvious), it may prove useful to sketch in some general tendencies in the literature we are reviewing by resorting to a few statistical indicators about what is being published in English on colonial Mexico in some of the foremost scholarly journals in the field, and about what young scholars are writing in their doctoral dissertations as they train to be professional practitioners of the historian's craft.[16] A similar but more limited exercise I

---

14. Because of space considerations this essay deals primarily with books, leaving aside almost entirely journal articles and chapters in scholarly anthologies.

15. There are contradictory logics as to whether to include the English-language literature on Mexican independence in an essay such as this one—i.e., independence was the end of the colonial period, or it was the beginning of the national period (it was both, of course). I have opted to leave it aside in this chapter for lack of space, but deal with it in some detail in Chapter 4. Modern Anglophone work on the theme can be traced back at least to Hamill, *The Hidalgo Revolt* (1966), continued with Anna (1978), and saw the publication of two key works in the mid-1980s, Hamnett (1986) and Tutino (1986). As academic entrepreneurs of the highest efficacy, Jaime E. Rodríguez O. and Christon I. Archer have encouraged this work through the editing of anthologies and authoring of review articles, including Rodríguez O. (1989, 1994) and Archer (2000, 2003); and Rodríguez O.'s (1998) masterful broad history of Spanish American independence. More recently Anglophone historians of this period have begun to turn in the direction of the social history of the independence struggle, popular politics, and political culture as reflected and shaped by the outcomes of the insurgency against Spain, but this tendency has yet to advance very far; see especially Guardino (1996), Warren (2001), and Van Young (2001c).

16. I am aware, of course, that a number of caveats are to be kept in mind about such a procedure. Editors of journals, for example, may be following their own biases in what they solicit or accept for publication, rather than reflecting in as neutral a way as possible the prevailing interests in a given field. Moreover, a different (perhaps wider) canvass of professional journals might produce different findings, as might changes in the categories used in identifying articles or dissertations with certain trends. Nonetheless, such a counting exercise is likely to prove valid *grosso modo* for arriving at broad trends.

carried out in a review article (Van Young 1985) over twenty-five years ago categorized in very broad strokes all the articles on the social and economic history of Mexico and Central America in the period 1750–1850 published from 1960 to 1985 in the *Hispanic American Historical Review*.[17] This analysis indicated that counted by quinquennia there had been a "takeoff" in the number of articles published starting around 1970 (representing a doubling over the quinquennium 1960–1964, and remaining steady through quinquennium 1980–1984). Of greater importance, perhaps, was a notable change in the language of article titles, especially from the late 1960s or so, with pre-1960 key words such as boundary, treaty, party, war, and so forth, giving way increasingly to a more self-consciously social scientific vocabulary likely to include terms such as socioeconomic, stratification, factors, and elite. I also found that the late eighteenth century was beginning to receive greater attention than the early nineteenth, although I noted that if the domain had been expanded to include political themes, including the wars of independence, this imbalance would have been redressed to some degree.

More recently I carried out a survey of the 477 substantive articles in the *HAHR* (excluding other types of pieces, as for example published interviews with some of the field's senior figures) that appeared between 1970 and 2001, embracing not just Mexico or the colonial era, of course, but all of Latin America throughout the region's history. The object of this exercise was to see what the trend had been with regard to economic history as opposed to other genres. Aggregated by five-year periods, and smoothing out certain anomalies, the figures suggest that whereas during the earlier quinquennia the proportion of essays on economic history tended to stand fairly steady at between 30 and 40 percent, beginning around 1990 it had dropped to about half that level, 15 to 20 percent, and has remained there for nearly fifteen years.[18] Reverting just to colonial Mexico yet again, for purposes of this chapter I revisited all the articles published in the *HAHR* between 1976 and 2003, inclusive.[19] Of the 423 articles that appeared during these nearly three decades, fifty (in-

---

17. I included a number of caveats there about categorization criteria, coverage, and so forth. For an even broader and still valuable survey of the colonial Spanish American historiography up to the early 1980s see Keen (1985).

18. Articles on Mexico were not culled out for separate treatment, but there is no reason to think that the trend would not hold for these, as well. In an article in the same issue of the journal *Historia Mexicana* as my own, Antonio Ibarra Romero (2003b) noted that a new wave of economic history was gathering force among Mexican scholars themselves during the same decade, even as economic history seemed to be waning somewhat in the United States.

19. The ten issues (containing thirty-eight articles) published during the period 2001–May 2003 represent half a quinquennium, during which there would normally be twenty

cluding long interviews with senior historians in the field) dealt with colonial Mexico. This amounts to about 12 percent of the total (with little variation among the quinquennia 1976–1980, 1981–1985, 1986–1990, 1991–1995, 1996–2000, and the first ten issues of quinquennium 2001–2005), making this perhaps the best represented subspecialty in the field, hardly surprising given its venerable tradition and the pattern of graduate training in the United States.[20] Furthermore, the same trend noticeable in the analysis regarding the place of economic history within the overall profile of Latin American history is present in the historiography of colonial Mexico, at least as represented by what appears in the *HAHR*, and with roughly the same chronology: a drop-off in frequency of articles on economic history since about 1990. Themes represented with greater regularity in the last dozen years include politics and political culture, forms of religious sensibility, and ethnohistory and indigenous peoples, with an accompanying change in vocabulary. Other journals, other tastes: an analysis of some other major academic venues produces some results that are similar to these, and some that differ. A rapid perusal of the *Journal of Latin American Studies* issues during the decade of the 1990s reveals that very little was published on colonial Latin America in general, and concomitantly few contributions on colonial Mexico. This is, of course, a multidisciplinary journal (like the *Latin American Research Review* and *Mexican Studies/Estudios Mexicanos*) in which work on economic history, primarily of the nineteenth and twentieth centuries, remains particularly strong and well represented. On the other hand, historical journals in the United States such as *The Americas* reflect trends similar to those analyzed for the *Hispanic American Historical Review*. The U.S. journal in which the cultural history trend is most pronounced is the *Colonial Latin American Review*, established nearly twenty years ago, dedicated exclusively to the colonial period, and oriented strongly toward literature, cultural studies, and anthropology.

While acknowledging that the data sets discussed here overlap but were not constructed according to quite the same criteria, it is still possible to suggest some tentative characterizations of the Anglophone historical literature on colonial Mexico over the last two or three decades, set against the historiography on Mexico as a whole. First, beginning sometime in the late 1960s, our vocabulary became less traditionally narrative, descriptive, and political, and increasingly sociological and

---

issues of the journal (there was a double issue during these years, combining August and November 2001); data were compiled from the online journals database J-Stor.

20. It is interesting to note that the *total* number of articles per quinquennium declined steadily from ninety-three in 1981–1985 to sixty-four in 1996–2000, a drop accounted for (as any reader of the journal will attest) by the increasing length of contributions.

anthropological. About twenty years later it shifted again, into a still more anthropological register this time, with growing overtones of cultural studies, postcolonial studies, gender and women's studies, and ethnohistory. Second, along with this trend in approach, conceptualization, and vocabulary, the late eighteenth century and the early nineteenth (I have elsewhere referred to the period 1750–1850 as "Brading's Century"; Van Young 2007a) attracted a good deal of attention as opposed to the earlier colonial period and the three decades between the Mexican-American War and the advent of Porfirio Diaz. Lately this interest has perhaps drifted both forward, into the 1821–1876 period, and backward again into the early colonial era, thus reprising studies of an earlier era, with the seventeenth century still constituting something of a black hole, historiographically speaking). Finally, economic history ebbed somewhat after 1990 or so, giving way to social and cultural history, at least in the pages of the *HAHR*, although this can be seen in other journals, as well.[21]

An analysis of the doctoral dissertations on colonial Mexican history completed at U.S. universities since the mid-1970s or so bears out these findings quite closely.[22] This analysis warrants at least brief attention,

---

21. A highly visible form of scholarly recognition within the field of Latin American history itself, the Bolton-Johnson Prize (formerly the Herbert E. Bolton Memorial Prize) of the Conference on Latin American History, would appear to highlight the centrality of Mexican colonial history generally, and within it the increasing dominance over recent years of social and cultural history more specifically. Of the fifty winners or honorable mention awardees of the prize during the twenty-four years 1980–2003, sixteen dealt with colonial Mexico. This represents nearly 32 percent of the total, or almost three times the percentage represented by articles on colonial Mexico published in the *Hispanic American Historical Review* during a roughly comparable period, and slightly more than the 26 percent of the prizes (23/88) garnered by writers on colonial Mexico over the life of the prize since 1966. This indicates that historians of colonial Mexico are carrying the palm more frequently in recent years. Of these twenty-three prizewinning works eight have focused on economic history, but only two of these were published after about 1990—Melville's *A Plague of Sheep* (1994), winner in 1995, and Deans-Smith's *Bureaucrats, Planters, and Workers* (1992), honorable mention in 1993, a work arguably as much social as economic history—and six between 1965 and 1980. I thank Professor Tom Holloway, past CLAH Executive Secretary, for furnishing this information on short notice.

22. The information is drawn from a computer search of University Microfilms International's "Digital Dissertations" database. A search using keywords *colonial* and *Mexico* produced a list of 415 dissertations in several disciplines (with theses in literature perhaps even more numerous than those in history), the earliest from 1940 (Woodrow W. Borah's UC Berkeley dissertation, "Silk-Raising in Colonial Mexico"), and the most recent from 2003. Of these, I was able to determine that 112 citations pertain to historical treatments, the overwhelming majority of them earning their doctorates in history. There is also represented a scattering (fourteen) of theses historical in approach but originating in other disciplines—historical anthropology, historical geography, history of science, economics,

Chapter 3   95

since today's dissertations are tomorrow's first scholarly monographs, and the trends to be discerned in theme and approach say a good deal about how historians in the field are being trained and choosing their initial research subjects.[23] To begin with, as I have noted above, there has been a second shift in vocabulary as indicated by dissertation titles, which presumably reflect the themes and approaches of the articles and books that grow out of the theses. Whereas in the late 1960s one saw the increasing frequency of a more hard-edged social science language, since the late 1980s we are more likely to see words such as *identity (identities), culture(s), power, personhood, manhood, gender, sexuality, race/ethnicity,* and so forth, along with descriptors or compound forms such as *negotiated (negotiating), cultural politics,* and *social construction.* The most common among these are probably *culture* and *identity.* Furthermore, since these terms are common to several disciplines, and since cultural historians have turned more and more to the close exegesis of written (if not necessarily high cultural) texts in their research, if one

---

U.S. history, and so on. Since several of these have been influential among historians in the more restricted sense of the term, have become part of the historiographical landscape, or represent notable trends in the field of colonial Mexican studies, I have felt it justified to include them in this discussion. Among these are Cañizares-Esguerra (2001; history of science, University of Wisconsin-Madison, 1995); Lewis (2003; anthropology, University of Chicago, 1993); Melville (1994; anthropology, University of Chicago, 1983); and Konrad (1980; anthropology, University of Chicago, 1975). The list includes dissertations substantially devoted to the colonial period, even if their subject matter lies partially outside it; works on northern New Spain, including New Mexico, were included, while those on colonial Florida were excluded. For reasons not entirely clear to me (sloppiness? distinct agreements between UMI and different institutions? indexing criteria not captured by my search strategy?) the list appears far from complete; my own 1978 UC Berkeley dissertation is omitted, for example. Furthermore, the coverage seems most complete for the years since 1980 or so, spottier for the decades preceding.

23. It is interesting to note where these dissertations have been produced. Not surprisingly, of the 112 theses on my list, thirteen were done at the University of California, Los Angeles, and a dozen at Tulane University. These two institutions are followed by Columbia University and the University of California, Berkeley, each with seven theses; the University of Wisconsin-Madison and the University of California, San Diego, each with five; and by a group comprising the University of Arizona, the University of Chicago, and the University of New Mexico, each with four. Institutions that have produced two or three dissertations on colonial Mexican history include Emory University, Northern Arizona University, the University of Pennsylvania, Stanford University, Duke University, the University of California-Santa Barbara, Princeton University, the State University of New York-Stony Brook, the University of Minnesota, the University of North Carolina-Chapel Hill, Syracuse University (all in historical geography), the Catholic University of America, and the University of Texas-Austin. Twenty other institutions have each produced one dissertation. This rough breakdown does not include distribution over time, in which there is a good deal of variation for any given institution.

were to go by the titles alone it would be easy to mistake dissertations in history for those from other fields, especially literature.[24]

As reflected in this newer vocabulary, old themes have been reconfigured into cultural history and new themes introduced. If one aggregates into a group of expansive categories the dissertations produced during the five years 1999–2003, for example, one sees that of the twenty-six works, the themes of religion/religious sensibility and identity/ethnicity run neck and neck with seven theses each; economic history boasts four; health/medicine, gender, and institutional/political history each have two; and political culture, one.[25] Extending this categorization back to 1980 or so to embrace the twenty-five years up to 2005 or so confirms this general tendency. Although it is difficult to squeeze out an unambiguous trend, it is clear enough that economic history, with its ten or so dissertations in the quinquennium 1979–1983 and half as many during 1984–1988, has declined in overall weight, at least in the United States. In the meantime, religion/religious sensibility, with one or two theses in each of the four quinquennia 1979–1998, has picked up momentum in the last few years along with studies of identity/ethnicity, while studies of gender make a strong showing but are perhaps better represented in the field of modern Mexican history. Older, more developed, and still fruitful genres of study such as economic and political history (the latter in a restricted sense of the term) have slipped a notch or two, then, but not yet to the margins of the colonial historiography, where they would nestle with forms now almost completely out of fashion, such as biography and the more traditional history of institutions like religious orders or the organs of colonial government. On the other hand, recent works in a more cultural vein have revisited the records of colonial institutions and turned them to noninstitutional uses.[26]

---

24. For example, Felicia Smith-Kleiner's 2003 dissertation in literature from New York University, "The Re/formation of the Female Body: Gender, Law, and Culture in Colonial New England and New Spain," might well be taken for a dissertation in history, while Doris M. Namala's 2002 history thesis from UCLA, "Chimalpahin in His Time: An Analysis of the Writings of a Nahua Annalist of Seventeenth-Century Mexico Concerning His own Lifetime" or Nora Jaffary's 2000 history dissertation from Columbia University, "Deviant Orthodoxy: A Social and Cultural History of Ilusos and Alumbrados in Colonial Mexico" might be thought works in literary scholarship.

25. Creating these categories involved some compression. For example, when a dissertation seemed to me to embrace both gender and religious sensibility, I assigned it either to one or the other rubric depending upon my knowledge of the work in question or my impression of its primary emphasis. The absence of a thesis in ethnohistory from the quinquennium 1999–2003 is an oddity, since this has always been a strongly represented category.

26. This is one of the central points made in the review article of O'Hara (2001).

Chapter 3

THE EMERGING GEOGRAPHY OF
COLONIAL MEXICAN HISTORY

The general currents sketched above have carved out new features in the Anglophone historiographic landscape of colonial Mexico while leaving some formerly prominent landmarks, if not high and dry, then at least isolated and exposed to erosion. On the other hand, while certain tendencies in the historical literature would appear temporarily exhausted, what were before distinct genres have become "blurred," to borrow Clifford Geertz's (1983b) expression, producing works definitely hybrid in that they are not easily pigeonholed into exclusive categories such as "institutional history," "economic history," "demographic history," and so forth.[27] Some of these changes have been sudden and would scarcely have been imaginable twenty or twenty-five years ago, while others have been incremental and amount more to the increasing sophistication of familiar genres. The rest of my essay offers some examples of veins that have played out, others that we are still working, and still others only recently discovered, or if previously known, only within the last few years beginning to yield high-quality work, in some cases quite abundant.

The Decline of Hacienda Studies

One striking example of how a historiographic field formerly central to the development of Anglophone writing on colonial Mexico has languished is that of hacienda studies (Chapters 1 and 2 above), once so numerous that designating this subgenre as a fairly distinct field of "studies" seems not at all unjustified. The extended scholarly debate in the 1960s, 1970s, and early 1980s over the nature of the Mexican hacienda (against a background of large landed estates elsewhere in Latin America, and in medieval and early modern Europe) and the institution's place in rural society, often still framed even today in terms of competing "capitalist" and "feudal" models, deeply influenced Mexican historiography in general and that of the colonial period in particular.[28] While some studies in

---

27. There are a number of possible ways of tracing in the colonial historiography the changes I have mentioned: by contrasting pairs of works, by looking at entire subliteratures, by examining individual scholarly careers, and so forth. I have opted for a combination of all these, but for the sake of creating several broad categories I have admittedly pushed many works into a historiographical Procrustean bed.

28. A relatively recent synthetic/interpretive treatment of Latin American history affirms the supplanting of "medieval" (i.e., feudal) forms of economic organization by "capitalist" ones only in the late eighteenth century; see Voss (2002). Knight (2002b), on the other hand, spends a good many pages (pp. 72–83, 185–201) discussing this once-heated

English shared in the dependency paradigm so influential from the 1960s, such as André Gunder Frank's (1979) small but closely reasoned book on early colonial agriculture (which actually looked rather antique even as it became available in English some years after its initial publication), most work by North American or British scholars—books by William Taylor (1972), Charles Harris (1975), David Brading (1978), Herman Konrad (1980), myself (Van Young 1981), Richard Lindley (1983), and others—followed on the assumptions of neoclassical models.[29] Up until the early 1980s scarcely a year passed without the appearance of one or more such books and a host of articles, but this current of scholarship seems to have shrunk to a trickle (or a "ripple," as in the title of Chapter 1) during the rest of the decade and then virtually dried up. Toward the end of this wave one still saw excellent studies being produced, such as Cheryl Martin's (1985) study of the colonial Morelos sugar industry, but Lolita Gutiérrez Brockington's (1989) book on the seventeenth-century *haciendas marquesanas* of the Cortés estate in Tehuantepec was already somewhat isolated when it appeared in 1989, as was Patrick Carroll's (2001/1991) study of free and enslaved blacks (and the forms of rural economic units on which they labored) in colonial Veracruz, while Robert Patch's (1993) excellent work on Yucatán was really an outlier of this literature.

One is hard-pressed to think of major studies in English on this theme that have appeared within the last decade, and younger scholars these days (those doing their doctoral research) seem not to be interested in the topic. When one does see studies of rural economy in more recent years, rather than focusing on the economic workings of rural estates as such they are quite likely to be cast in terms of environmental history and/or the struggle over resources between powerful landowners and humble people, as with Melville's (1994) work on sheep culture and its environmental consequences in the Mezquital Valley, or Sonya Lipsett-Rivera's (1999) on water rights and farming in late colonial Puebla, respectively.[30] While the decline in this subfield is obvious, the reasons for it are less clear. Among them must surely be counted the advent of other approaches to the history of the colonial countryside, such as the history of rural resistance, peasant uprisings, and political movements. For example, John

---

controversy. He concludes that while the notional ideal-typical hacienda may have been commercialized it was not capitalistic in any meaningful sense of the term, but certainly that forms of landholding were the single most important factor shaping Mexican colonial society. For a review article assessing the state of play in the field of hacienda studies as it stood about 1982 or so, see Van Young (1983); and for a slightly later review (playfully eccentric but useful), see Schell (1986).

29. For a withering, but not misplaced, attack on dependency theory, see Haber (1997b).
30. See also Murphy (1986), which partakes of both.

Tutino's (1986) bold and widely influential study of peasant politics over the course of Mexican history dedicates more than half its substantial length and much of its most original archival findings to the late colonial period and Mexican independence. But Tutino's primary object is to illuminate agrarian pressures and the resulting collective political violence rather than the workings of colonial grain-producing haciendas as such, while his doctoral dissertation (Tutino 1976), more in the traditional mold of a 1970s regional agrarian study, and much like my own in this respect, remains as yet unpublished. Then, too, although the empirical findings of hacienda studies demonstrated the polymorphousness of the landed estate in colonial Mexico, they tended to keep well within certain parameters, showing less and less variation from one work to the next, so that over the course of a scholarly generation the genre lost the attraction of novelty. Finally, many of the Anglophone (and even Mexican) scholars who made contributions to the historiography of the hacienda followed roughly similar trajectories in their research, moving from the economic history of the colonial and nineteenth-century Mexican countryside, to studies of social movements or protest, and then to cultural or even intellectual history, thus in some measure abandoning the field (no pun intended) of basic economic history to pursue more elusive themes. To cite but three examples, this has certainly been the case of William Taylor, David Brading, and myself, and among prominent Mexican scholars of Enrique Florescano.

Some time in the 1970s or early 1980s, as the reach of the colonial historiography broadened and deepened, rural history, primarily embracing hacienda studies, began to be subsumed under the rubric of the "new regional history" in the sense that *every* large area in the country outside the Valley of Mexico tends to be known as a "region" or "province," often with a heavily dismissive connotation. The oversaturation of the central parts of the country, historiographically speaking, along with the increasing organization and accessibility of provincial archives, and the need to test hypotheses—about the "feudal" nature of the colonial rural estate, for example—all contributed to this outward shift of focus.[31] Although

---

31. While a personal anecdote hardly constitutes proof of this trend, my own experience in selecting a venue for my dissertation research in rural history exemplifies these tendencies at work. Around 1970 or so I was looking for a relatively uncrowded part of colonial Mexico (historiographically speaking) in which to do my own work, and had considered the Valleys of Puebla and Cuernavaca, when in a casual conversation Enrique Florescano suggested the Guadalajara area because of its rich and well-organized archival resources, and its scant modern historiography. My initial ambition had been to write a social history of rural society there, but finding I did not have the conceptual tools for such a project I fell back on the economic history of the city and its hinterland (no disrespect intended to the guild of economic historians), and of the great estates there, producing the sort of single-stranded regional history discussed below. My own doctoral students have since produced

a technical or conceptual definition of what regions were, and how they changed over time, was hardly ever offered, many scholars confidently carved regions out for study, often centering on urban areas.[32] In addition to the hacienda studies mentioned above, which followed in their turn several important books dealing with colonial silver mining published in the 1960s and 1970s (another subliterature that has virtually dried up), this regionalization of colonial history produced a number of what may be called single-stranded works that plucked out of wider contexts for close inspection certain aspects of social or economic life. One fine, widely influential, but hardly unique example of such a study is historical anthropologist John Chance's (1978) work on colonial Oaxaca, which emphasized race relations, the fluidity of racial ascription over time, and the increasing weight acquired by wealth and class status in a society previously thought to be dominated by the rigid *sistema de castas*.[33] Other representatives of the genre, dating from slightly later than Chance's book, are historical geographer Michael Swann's (1982) study of settlement and demographic patterns in colonial Durango, Evelyn Hu-DeHart's (1981) ambitious but still basically structuralist study of Yaqui-Spanish interaction up until Mexican independence, and Rik Hoekstra's (1993) study of the Valley of Puebla in the late sixteenth and early seventeenth centuries.

Works that three decades ago, or even two, might have taken the form of single-stranded histories—of political structures, for example, or elite groups, or of racial ascription practices, such as Chance's—have now instead mutated into more complex narratives of localities through long time periods, although work in the older style is still very much being done, as well. French-style *histoire totale* models were certainly of some belated and ongoing influence here, as was the totalizing microhistory of the sort promoted in Mexico by the late Luis González. Probably also influential, even where authors might shrug their shoulders at the suggestion, if not actively disavow it, has been the overt influence of anthropology in a particularly Geertzian, "local knowledge" register, in contrast,

---

much more sophisticated work on rural society both in Mexico and elsewhere. Another influence in this outward pressure in rural, regional, or provincial history was the hugely important work of François Chevalier, although much of what he had written in fact dealt with the Mexican north. In a recent revision of his own work (1999) in the light of more recent studies of rural history, Chevalier himself has acknowledged that his study of the colonial hacienda offered a somewhat abstract, generalized model that needed to be confirmed or disconfirmed by regional case studies.

32. For a discussion of how regions might usefully be defined, specifically drawing upon the colonial economic history literature, see Chapter 5 in this volume; Van Young (1992d), and several of the other essays in that volume.

33. Chance's book can profitably be read in conjunction with Murphy and Stepick (1993).

for example, to the broader political-economy sort of model characteristic of Eric Wolf's (1983) late work. This approach emphasizes the interrelatedness of social practices and cultural meanings, the inextricability of major strands of such practices and meanings from their context (the "thick description" method is surely about explaining why such extrication or abstraction is not a good idea, and has always been in the repertoire of good historians), and the need to study these processes in concrete localities, the physical settings where people live. Recent well-executed examples (both published within the last decade) of this localized, intensified total history of communities, albeit in what can still be described as a structuralist mode, are Frank de la Teja's (1995) study of San Antonio de Béxar and Leslie Offutt's (1993) of Saltillo, both in the eighteenth century. Yet another is Cheryl Martin's (1996) fine study on eighteenth-century Chihuahua. Given the breadth of her study within a limited venue, what Martin seems in fact to intend by *governance* is perhaps better conveyed by a more expansive term, such as Michel Foucault's *governmentality*, which embraces power relationships in many spheres of life and the way these dispose people to establish and live with structures of authority and legitimacy, in this case specifically the relationship among ethnicity, social hierarchy, and political subordination. Martin weaves together not only forms of livelihood, including mining, ranching, and labor relations, but also the symbolic presence of the frontier, elements of public ritual practice, and ideas about honor, race, and gender. In doing so she creates a multistranded cultural history and is able to make suggestive comparisons about how Chihuahua was similar to, and different from, society in central Mexico, the template upon which many of its essential social categories were modeled. This concern with culture is characteristic of many recent studies of provincial society, and shows up in the postindependence period, as well. Martin's own trajectory as a scholar in fact reflects the sort of shift suggested here, from her earlier study (Martin 1985) on sugar production and labor systems in the Morelos sugar zone, to a more complex study of a diminutive frontier social order: they are both works on local communities, but one is single-stranded and economic in emphasis, the second multistranded and largely social and cultural.

Economic History

Many works in colonial economic history are as much respecters of place as the multistranded regional or local history just mentioned, which itself found one of its important sources in economic studies of the hacienda. To embrace effectively all the variables and production factors at play in a given economic activity, sector, or locality, economic historians typically delimit the venues of their work while often making broader claims for the *processes* they describe as characteristic of a larger class of phenomena. There are some exceptions to this in the form of large synoptic works that are nonetheless based partially upon strong archival research, and which attempt to paint a picture of the economy of New Spain as a whole, typically in the late colonial period. The two most obvious examples of recent years are Richard Garner and Spiro Stefanou's (1993) ambitious study of economic growth in the eighteenth century and Arij Ouweneel's (1996) very interesting, quirky, and unfortunately little-cited study of central Mexico during roughly the same era. Although both works are heavily quantitative, neither is obtrusively econometric; Garner and Stefanou's is more interested in deploying mathematical models of explanation, Ouweneel's in interpreting his data in the light of ecological and demographic frameworks derived from European agrarian history and theories developed to make sense of it. Both authors find that the silver-based late colonial economy of New Spain was in some ways running to stay in place and was poised by 1800 (if not earlier) to undergo a crisis, a point of view a good deal different from that prevailing twenty-five or thirty years ago, and one that expresses the darker view of the late colonial period generally held nowadays.[34] Most "big" histories of colonial Mexico, indeed, or histories of the country more generally, tend to be economic and political in emphasis even where their central theme is not economic history per se. One would have thought, for example, that the debate as to whether colonial Mexico was a feudal or capitalist society had lost much of its heat by now (the discussion as it stood in the early 1990s is glossed well in the English-language preface to Semo's *History of Capitalism in Mexico* [1993/1973]). But Alan Knight's (2002b) confident and highly readable recent synoptic history of Mexico, cast firmly in a political economy vein, dusts it off to good effect and concludes that although the late colonial economy displayed a high degree of commercialization, it was a long way from being capitalist in both its modes of production and social relations.[35]

While not numerous, narrower monographic works in economic history have spanned a broad range of approaches and have made for some of the most interesting contributions to the colonial historiography since

---

34. For a closely reasoned defense of late colonial Mexico as prosperous and economically dynamic, see Rodríguez O. (1980); and for a discussion of these issues see various chapters in Van Young (1992c), mentioned here by virtue of its Anglophone authorship. Also worthy of note is the scholarly anthology by Jacobsen and Puhle (1986), although the individual essays are monographic rather than comparative.

35. In addition to Knight, see for example Hamnett (1999); but for exceptions, some of the essays in Lomnitz-Adler(2001), and most of the colonial chapters in Meyer and Beezley (2000).

the early 1980s, even while they take into account the subtleties of place. Anthropologist Ross Hassig's (1985) elegant study of exchange and transportation systems in the Valley of Mexico in the wake of the Spanish conquest knits together considerations of the nature of the Aztec and Spanish colonial states, native population decline, and reconfigured market networks to conclude that the sixteenth century actually saw a substantial involution in productivity and organization, a sort of conquest-induced entropy. Nor have the genre-bending and -crossing potentialities of labor history (is it economic, social, political, cultural, or all of these?) gone unrealized, as in the anachronistically celebratory study of mining labor and protest in Real del Monte by Doris Ladd (1989), for example, or the detailed and eloquent work of Susan Deans-Smith (1992) on the colonial tobacco monopoly and manufactory in the late colonial period. Economic sectors, activities, or regional economies earlier treated from a strictly institutional point of view have come in for revisionist attention that uses econometric techniques to explain their internal dynamics, the logic of their operation, and their macroeconomic context, albeit in some cases with a reconfigured attention to institutions in the mode inspired by the work of Douglass North. One may detect here, at least in part, a turn inward and downward analogous to that taking place with cultural history. Two outstanding examples are Richard Salvucci's (1987) work on textile mills throughout the colonial period, and Jeremy Baskes's (2000) study of the cochineal industry in late colonial Oaxaca.[36] The more technically mathematical of the two monographs, Salvucci's book concludes that the *obrajes* were capitalist enterprises, of a sort, albeit existing within a context of imperfect markets and resource allocation, coerced labor, and a hostile postindependence international environment in which they simply could not compete, and that they therefore failed to form the basis for a lasting capitalist transformation. There could not be a more telling indication of what the sophisticated mode of economic history has brought to the field over the last couple of decades than the contrast between Jeremy Baskes' book and Brian Hamnett's (1971) foundational and still valuable 1971 study of the Oaxacan cochineal trade. While both works are heav-

36. For a highly specialized study of a subsector of the colonial mining economy, also quite circumscribed by place, see Barrett (1987). Except as it enters into macroeconomic descriptions or figures peripherally as economic background, by the way (e.g., respectively in Richard Garner and Spiro Stefanou's book or that of Cheryl Martin 1985), the colonial silver mining sector seems virtually to have dropped out of the picture for Anglophone historians since the pathbreaking studies of scholars such as David A. Brading (1971) and Peter J. Bakewell (1971). It is telling that one of the most recent contributions on the theme (albeit not by an Anglophone historian) is a collection of readings from classic works: Herrera Canales (1998). Yet another study that teeters fruitfully between economic and institutional history, although not in an explicitly Northian mold, is Greenow (1983).

ily institutional in their frameworks (that is, they emphasize the effects of ongoing, sometimes codified economic and political arrangements such as forms of state regulation), Baskes's study is much more deeply immersed in the details of how the cochineal trade actually worked, and less with the prescriptive and normative aspects of institutions as such. Granted, the objects of the two studies were different, as clearly expressed or implied in their titles: Hamnett's was to look at the notorious *repartimiento* and the cochineal industry in the context of the Bourbon Reforms, while Baskes wanted to look at the microeconomics of production as mediating relations among Spanish officials, entrepreneurs, and native people. In a highly revisionist move, Baskes has turned the arrangement of the *repartimiento* on its head, demonstrating that coercion of native producers was minimal and difficult, that the institution proved a relatively efficient way of allocating scarce and expensive capital, and that apparently extortionate price markups and rates of interest on loans to native producers constituted risk premiums for Spanish traders in a volatile economic environment.

Allied to economic history because of their strongly materialist-empiricist interests and methods are works in historical demography, historical geography, and environmental history (bundled together here, despite their heterogeneity, for lack of space). These have followed with remarkable fidelity the channels carved out early on by the work of the Berkeley historical demographers (Lesley B. Simpson, Woodrow W. Borah, Sherburne F. Cook) and historical geographers (Carl Sauer, Sherburne Cook). The 1970s saw publication of Cook's and Borah's *Essays in Population History* (1974–1980), its last volume appearing only in 1980, and in the year following a little-cited but valuable study of the historical geography of the sixteenth-century Valley of Puebla by Jack Licate (1981). A decade later followed the demographic studies of northwestern New Spain by Daniel Reff (1991), and a long probative exercise on the Cook-Borah disease-catastrophe model for the Valley of Mexico by historical geographer Thomas Whitmore (1992). The latter work, in particular, brought the technical capacity of computers to bear upon the perennial discussion of postconquest native population collapse in manipulating large data sets and for statistical simulation. Whitmore provided substantial vindication for the more apocalyptic views of the Berkeley school of historical demographers that Old World diseases induced an indigenous population drop of something like 90 percent over the course of the first century or so after the Europeans' arrival. Environmental history looked to be coming on strong with the publication of Elinor Melville's (1994) study of the Mezquital Valley, and with Michael C. Meyer's (1984) work of a decade earlier on water in what he called the Hispanic southwest (the old Boltonian Borderlands), but has stalled for reasons that are not clear—perhaps because of the intensive site-specific fieldwork required to carry it out, or because of the expertise in ecology and biology needed to do it convincingly. Melville's compelling study found stimulation in the earlier work of Sherburne Cook (1949), and concluded that the environmental degradation of the Mezquital obvious as early as the later sixteenth century was produced by Spanish overgrazing of sheep rather than by a late preconquest human population surge, as Cook had postulated, the third in a series showing a periodicity of about four hundred years. Reff's work on northwestern New Spain produced analogous conclusions with regard to native population decline. While Meyer's work is heavily legal and institutional in emphasis, Melville's can without too much effort be assimilated at least partially to a cultural model in which the invading Europeans made choices not always dictated by an obvious rationality. As for the demographic work, it is worth noting that it has transcended materialist history and made its way into almost all scholarship on native peoples and ethnohistory, even the most avowedly cultural of it. Early on Charles Gibson (1964) drew extensively upon the Cook-Borah-Simpson studies, although he did not have the entire corpus of work available to him when he wrote. James Lockhart's (1992) now well-known stage model of central Mexican native language change, for example, can be mapped onto the familiar demographic curve for the Valley of Mexico quite neatly, and even onto Lesley B. Simpson's (1949) still earlier monograph on land use in central Mexico in the sixteenth century. Still more recently, and in a more explicitly cultural register, we have the superb hybrid 1996 work—is it art history, cartographic history, historical geography, cultural history?—of Barbara Mundy (1996) on native spatiotemporal representations as exemplified in the seventy or so maps submitted with the *relaciones geográficas* of the late sixteenth century mandated by the Spanish metropolitan authorities.[37]

Elites, Commoners, Race, Class, and Gender

Among the strongest works in colonial history published through the first decade or more of the period under review here were those lying at the intersection of economic and social history, corresponding to the study of elite groups and elite individuals, much of it focusing on the colonial capital, and some of it overlapping temporally in interesting ways the late colonial and early national periods. While this had always been a prominent tradition in the colonial historiography, in my inventory (Van Young

---

37. Absolutely indispensable to a generation of researchers on colonial Mexico have been a trio of works in historical geography by Peter Gerhard (1972, 1979, 1982), works of truly deep scholarship arranged in the form of geographic dictionaries.

1985) of Anglophone historical writing on Mexico and Central America in the "Age of Revolution" I was able to point to the "socialization of elite studies" characteristic of the period, of which the avatar was David Brading's *Miners and Merchants* (1971). Overlapping with the wave of hacienda studies, and drawing its impulse from much the same sources—early modern European models such as Lawrence Stone's (1965) work; the use of notary, intestate, and litigation records; and the localization of colonial social power in groups of merchants, miners, and large landowners—these studies appeared regularly from the late 1970s through the early 1990s. Nestled among fine works such as Doris Ladd's (1976) study of the Mexican nobility, Charles Nunn's (1979) on foreigners in Mexico City in the early Bourbon period, Linda Arnold's (1988) interesting book on bureaucrats in Mexico City in the late eighteenth and early nineteenth centuries, Robert Himmerich y Valencia's (1991) prosopography of sixteenth-century encomenderos, and Jackie Booker's (1993) study of Veracruz merchants in the late colonial–early national period, two of the most interesting and influential of these books have been Louisa S. Hoberman's (1991) on seventeenth-century merchants in the capital and John Kicza's (1983) on colonial entrepreneurs in late colonial Mexico City.[38] Hoberman's book has the great virtue of dealing centrally with the seventeenth century, still very much a historiographical black hole, and of looking at actual capital flows in commerce and at the relationship of the colonial state to merchants' dealings, as well as with the social history of the group. Kicza's book has proved foundational and of enduring interest, since along with earlier work by Brading he sketched out patterns of career mobility, marriage alliance, and strategies for the preservation of family wealth among elite merchants, entrepreneurs, and landowners.

Perhaps these historians of colonial elites did their work too well, since this rich vein of study seems to have played itself out by the early 1990s, much as hacienda studies had done a decade earlier, to be succeeded by the downward drift of colonial historians' gaze to the popular classes, in keeping with what has happened in other national historiographies. One of the more widely influential and floridly culturalist examples of social history in this genre is Juan Pedro Viqueira Albán's (1999) engrossing study of popular recreations, social control, and Bourbon modernization efforts in Mexico City, a book that glitters with a distinctly Gallic élan despite its birth as a thesis in Mexico. Viqueira Albán's work raises one of the major

---

38. Biography as a significant genre of Anglophone historical writing on colonial Mexico has virtually disappeared, although it may come back in future as cultural history. For a very recent exemplar, no less fastidiously researched and eloquent for being something of an anomaly in a historiographical landscape virtually deforested of biographies, see Couturier (2003) on the great mining magnate, the Conde de Regla.

methodological difficulties faced by historians of subaltern groups (and culture, especially popular culture), which is the thinness of the sources on people who typically do not enter the written record except in general descriptive statements, or when they bump up against the state and thus generate criminal documentation. What we have yet to see much of, at least in the form of monographs, are studies that take up where Viqueira Albán has left off, either in expanding on his account, deepening it, or extending it outside Mexico City, the venue for most of the works just mentioned. Yet what Viqueira Albán has done, along with the authors of the colonial chapters (and the work as a whole in a conceptual way) in the influential anthology on public ritual in Mexico edited by Beezley, Martin, and French (1994), is to describe the teeming ritual and celebratory life of the lower classes in the colonial period, to construe it as resistance to the hegemonic claims and modernization projects of the colonial regime, and in the process to lighten colonial life a shade or two and complicate it by introducing notions of subaltern agency. Considered as a whole this is one of the two most notable new trends in Anglophone historical writing on colonial Mexico over the last twenty years or so, the other being the emergence of ethnohistory, which overlaps subaltern history in obvious ways.

In keeping with this decentering of established modes of historical inquiry, and the turn of many historians toward the social margins for their subjects, the conceptual cluster of class, race, and gender that has so transformed the landscape of United States historical writing more generally has also had considerable influence on the Anglophone historiography on colonial Mexico. Aside from the profusion of ethnohistorical works (given separate treatment below), however, the trend has not progressed as far as one might have thought. Of this trinity class has tended to recede from the picture somewhat since it appeared so prominently in the title of John Chance's (1978) book on Oaxaca thirty years ago, although it still remains a strong ghostly presence at the banquet, mostly in the form of the idea of racial or ethnic drift in relation to economic position.[39] The issue of race itself as a determinant of social being appears at its starkest in the case of African slaves and the fate of Afro-Mestizo populations. In

---

39. On the eruption of the social margins into the center of historians' concerns in the United States history writing, which has an obvious parallel in the emergence of postcolonial studies, see Appleby, Hunt, and Jacob (1994). It is telling about the state of play in the debate about race and class in colonial Mexico—did race determine class position, or *vice versa*; and of what did *casta* position consist?—that the terms of the debate seem to have been set by the early 1980s. For example, a recent brief account of the issue by Vinson (2001, 4, 240) mostly cites historical works authored before the mid-1980s. For a prolonged discussion of why class analysis, and models of revolution based upon it, do not work well in explaining the advent and processes of the Mexican independence movement because of the prominence of ethnic conflict, see Van Young (2001c, 1–39, 495–523).

relative terms colonial Mexico was not a major slavocratic society, which probably explains why Colin Palmer's (1975) study of blacks in the midcolonial period was succeeded by only a very few major works on African slavery and free people of color during the last three decades or so, including Gerald Cardoso's (1983) unconvincing comparative work on Veracruz and Pernambuco up to 1680, and Patrick Carroll's (2001) deeply documented study on colonial Veracruz. Apart from these focused works, where there were slaves (virtually everywhere in New Spain) or free laborers of African background, they are mentioned in passing, sometimes in considerable detail (e.g., in Cheryl Martin's 1985 work on colonial Morelos), but always as part of a larger picture. More recent works on African-origin populations in the colonial period have been concerned less with slavery than with the apparently more fashionable issues of ethnic identity and consciousness, ethnic blending, social mobility, and so forth. These include Ben Vinson's (2001) finely realized study of free-colored militia units, centering primarily on the eighteenth century, and Herman Bennett's (2003) book on an emerging Afro-Creole consciousness in the midcolonial era.[40] For the late seventeenth and early eighteenth centuries we have for the *sistema de castas* more broadly the suggestive work of R. Douglas Cope (1994) on Mexico City, which also emphasizes the fluidity of racial categorizations and the considerable degree of agency of common people in turning the caste system to their own purposes, and in forming patronage alliances with their white "superiors" that allowed them to temper the grosser disadvantages of ethnic ascription.[41]

The third member of the trinity is gender, and although works on women, gender, and the family can be treated as separate historiographical categories, they are deeply interrelated and are combined here for purposes of concision. The most widely known pioneering work in this field was the book on women in Mexico City by Silvia Arrom (1985), preceded by the articles and dissertations of other scholars, most notably Asunción Lavrin (e.g., 1989), and included here by virtue of its being at least half dedicated to the colonial era. Relying upon a variety of strongly institutional sources, Arrom tempered the dichotomous view of colonial women as either well-off, considerably autonomous widows in control of substantial property, or submissive wives within a heavily patriarchal social order, to show difference across life cycle, class, and ethnic group. Although women's status changed for the better in some respects with the advent of Mexican na-

---

40. For a thorough study of the problematics of ethnic identity in the Balsas River Depression of colonial Mexico, including the self-reinvention of free people of color as Indians, see Fisher (2002).

41. See also Valdés (1978), Bacigalupo (1981), and Boyer (1997).

tionhood, a cult of the domestic sphere and something resembling the "republican motherhood" so characteristic of the newly independent United States came to subvert the improvement in status promised by nationhood and liberalism. Less sanguine still in its view of women's freedom to exercise choices about their lives in the late colonial period, in this case the election of marriage partners, was Patricia Seed's (1988) book, which took the discussion further into the realm of cultural history with its discussion of racial ideas, concepts of honor, and the theology of marriage, as did Richard Boyer's (1995) interesting study of colonial bigamy cases, family formation, and forms of community social control. While none of these three major pathbreaking books bore particularly on the system of gender relations, sexuality, women, or the family among indigenous groups, the anthology *Indian Women of Early Mexico* (1997), edited by Schroeder, Wood, and Haskett, has gone a notable distance in opening up questions of rural and native women's participation in community and political life, as actors within the family, and as property holders. Laura Lewis's (2003) study has taken us even further along this path, not only demonstrating the hybridity of theme we might expect from a historical anthropologist, but also a turn toward the multistranded approach—religious practice (albeit heterodox), ethnic identity, and gender, all rendered through "thick description"—that relates the work to the local total histories mentioned above. Finally, Steve Stern's (1995) extremely thoughtful and wide-ranging book on gender relations in the late colonial period, the system of what he refers to as "gender rights," and the projection of ideas about gender into the political realm in the postcolonial era makes an admirable contribution to this burgeoning literature. Stern delves more deeply than most other authors into the actual gender system in which the women whose lives and deaths he evokes were enmeshed. He demonstrates how male notions of honor, claims upon women for sexual, child-rearing, and domestic services, and the inclination of women to protect themselves if those claims crossed accepted boundaries into excessive male violence, were mediated by family relationships, public opinion, and women's social networks. From the methodological point of view, Stern provides in his book a fine object lesson in how to read often ambiguous criminal records (in this case, of violence against women) to maximum effect. It is worthy of note, however, that Stern's analysis is framed more in terms of a subalternist than a cultural history approach, making it clearer than in some other studies what the difference is between the two frameworks.[42]

42. On the subject of European gendered representations in the conquest of New World native peoples, see the idiosyncratic but suggestive book of Trexler (1995); and for two worthwhile recent works by literary scholars that straddle history and literature, see the autobiography of the colonial nun María de San José, edited by Meyers and Powell (1999), and

Resistance and Rebellion

To return to studies of popular culture and resistance per se exemplified by the work of Viqueira Albán, it is but a short step narratively (if a longer one theoretically) from descriptions of street and ceremonial life as defining a sphere of stubborn popular culture, to the studies of resistance by common people that, construed in their broadest meaning, can encompass everything from ethnohistory, to works on the native imaginary and collective memory, to religious practice, and certainly the background and processes of Mexican independence. Such an analytic move does make of resistance much too plastic a category, and therefore a dull instrument, so that the first three categories of work mentioned, each broad enough in itself, will come in for separate treatment below. There has been a small but interesting literature by Anglophone historians over the last two decades, however, on the institutional integuments of colonial life. These have followed less the pattern of works on the formal structures of church and state that formed much of the early basis of colonial Mexican studies, and have focused more on the legal arrangements of social control within a context of persistent and invidious ethnic distinction, wide social inequality, and recurrent stress between metropolis and colony. A pioneering work in this respect was the book of William Taylor (1979) on drinking, homicide, and rebellion in the later colonial period. Here he demonstrated through a comparative approach the social embeddedness and normative limits of both drinking behaviors and homicide among village Mexicans, as well as the "bargaining by riot" that went on when an always outnumbered colonial officialdom often gave ground to villagers' political and economic grievances in seeking to suppress local uprisings. The means by which state-indigenous interaction was kept within juridical boundaries, and by which Indians at the same time learned to manipulate the colonial system to defend their interests, were detailed in Woodrow Borah's (1983) magisterial study of the General Indian Court, a line of research he claimed to have inherited from Lesley B. Simpson. Two pivotal studies of the colonial legal system, both emphasizing culture, appeared in 1995, one on the Mexican north by Charles Cutter (1995), in which he demonstrated the existence of a prevailing legal culture much less arbitrary and crude than we had thought, the other by Susan Kellogg (1995) on the adaptation of central Mexican indigenous people to European legal norms and practices in the two centuries after the conquest. Cognate to Taylor's work on village deviance

---

Sampson Vera Tudela (2000). For an appreciation of the relationship between history and anthropology, so evident in much of the newer work on colonial Mexico, see Axel (2002).

and homicide, and to an earlier, strongly institutional study by Colin MacLachlan (1974) of the famous rural constabulary, the Acordada, was the book on crime and the system of criminal procedure in Mexico City in the eighteenth century by Gabriel Haslip-Viera (1999), in which the author specifically disavowed the idea of street crime as resistance and assimilated it more to a safety-valve model, seeing it therefore as a mechanism for the maintenance of social order. Finally, Silvia Arrom (2000) has traced in great detail, in the fashion of a European social and institutional historian, the fate of a failed Bourbon experiment in social welfare (and, it goes without saying, social control) in the form of the Mexico City Poor House, demonstrating how the stubborn culture of private charity and begging—that is, the informal practices and values organizing these activities—circumvented state efforts to corral the capital's poor and after the coming of independence turned the institution itself into an increasingly impecunious orphanage.[43]

Full-court colonial resistance movements, primarily in the form of native uprisings, have attracted a good deal of attention from English-speaking historians in the last twenty years or so, and are likely to continue to do so because of their dramatic nature, the often abundant documentation generated by them, and the window they open onto indigenous life and European-indigenous relations not only during periods of armed confrontation, but also during "normal" times. In a classificatory exercise such as this the difficulty arises of separating works on resistance from those in ethnohistory, the division ultimately being somewhat arbitrary, particularly outside the central areas of Spanish colonial domination. The genealogy of many such studies can probably be traced, whether consciously or not, to the U.S. experience with a stubborn peasant war of national liberation in Vietnam, as well as to a long tradition of studies of popular political disturbances and revolutions in American and Western European historiography, and in the historiography of Mexico, both colonial and modern. Because this body of historical literature is relatively cohesive, often addressing the same issues and working with or against a body of common theoretical and comparative works, many introductions to the books in the field cover the literature well (e.g., Schroeder 1998; Deeds 2003), so I will not belabor it here.[44] Studies of this nature include portraits of quite prolonged conquest and frontier situations, such as those in the Sierra Zapoteca of Oaxaca by John Chance (1989), the Maya area of southeastern Yucatán up to about 1700 by

---

43. On urban crime in Mexico City see also the unpublished doctoral thesis of Scardaville (1977). Another well-done institutional history of the late colonial era is Chandler (1991).

44. For a somewhat more extended discussion of the theoretical and comparative aspects of resistance, rebellion, and insurrection among rural people, see Van Young (2001c, 1–36).

Grant Jones (1989), the more compressed history of the early sixteenth-century conquest of the Tarascans by J. Benedict Warren (1985), and more recently colonial Nueva Vizcaya (embracing parts of modern-day Sinaloa, Durango, and Chihuahua) over some 250 years by Susan Deeds (2003), in which stress between indigenous groups and European invaders was endemic over hundreds of years, and the best that could be hoped for on the part of the colonists was a sort of armed and uneasy truce.

Works on Indian resistance movements as such (the N here is admittedly small) have tended to bifurcate into northern and southern branches because of the location of the episodes themselves and the patterns of colonial acculturation and exploitation that brought them forth. But it is interesting to note that the northern studies of resistance are often embedded in broader ethnohistorical treatments, such as those of Susan Deeds (2003), Evelyn Hu-DeHart (1981), and Cynthia Radding (1997), since no northern indigenous groups generated the sort of large-scale movements seen in the Mexican southeast. An exception to this is Roberto Salmerón's (1991) book on Indian revolts in northern New Spain, a relatively short treatment of a large subject in which half the work is devoted to a survey of frontier development and half to the actual uprisings themselves. For the central regions of the country we have the highly suggestive essays of Serge Gruzinski's *Man-Gods in the Mexican Highlands* (1989), which use official inquiries into idolatry cases to study the careers of four indigenous messianic figures spanning more than two centuries. Although Gruzinski himself might well characterize these episodes as instances of the *assertion* of Indian power based upon the recurrent theme of the Mesoamerican man-god, rather than as cases of *resistance* to the colonial order, it is undeniable that absent aggressive European evangelization and the subordination of indigenous people these messianic figures could hardly have arisen. For the southeast we have two absorbing studies of indigenous resistance movements, Kevin Gosner's (1992) on the Tzeltal Rebellion of the early eighteenth century, and more recently Robert Patch's (2002) on several eighteenth-century Maya revolts in Yucatán and Guatemala. The Mexican southeast (with essays by Ronald Spores, Kevin Gosner, and Robert Patch) also dominates the five monographic essays (the remaining two are by Susan Deeds on Nueva Vizcaya and Christon Archer on Lake Chapala, in modern Jalisco) in the excellent anthology on native rebellion edited by Susan Schroeder (1998), which includes an acute short introduction by her and a thoughtful afterword by Murdo MacLeod. While there is a certain amount of hand-wringing by the authors of these fine studies about the need to emphasize cultural aspects more strongly—in this case, for example, the actual theology and cosmology of native rebellious ideology—most of them (with the exception of Gruzinski) work within a materialist framework, giving actual belief systems relatively short shrift. Aside from personal predilection and theoretical inclination on the part of the authors, the reasons for this are not far to seek, chief among them the problem of sources. By contrast, Paul Vanderwood's (1998) study of the Tomóchic episode in Chihuahua in the early 1890s (admittedly lying nearly a century beyond our period) offers a convincing reconstruction of the ideology of religiously inspired millenarian rebels while stinting neither the social, political, nor economic developments providing the immediate backdrop of the episode.[45]

Religion and Evangelization

The sharpening realization on the part of historians of native resistance movements that a broad range of collective behaviors was strongly religious in character, even where the actual ideation of such movements and their leaders may lie just beyond our reach, has been paralleled by a larger trend in the literature. Although Robert Ricard (1966/1933) offered his account of the evangelization of Mexican native peoples in the 1930s, it has recently become clear that religion cannot be isolated in the colonial project, but informed most areas of life, particularly the relations between conquerors and conquered. Much of the middle ground (to use Richard White's [1991] apt phrase) between native peoples and Europeans on which contact, mixing, adaptation, and the genesis of new cultural understandings and practices took place was delimited by the porous borders of religious sensibility, and the increasing focus on this theme has within the period since the early 1980s generated a great many studies on religious institutions, religious belief, and evangelization. Since most of the objects of the church's evangelization effort were Indians, and since colonial native society became infused in virtually every corner with Catholic belief, practice, and idioms, it is extremely difficult to separate the strands of the history of colonial religious institutions, native conversion, changes in indigenous ways of thinking, and ethnohistory. The easiest works to categorize here would be those keeping most closely to what I have been calling institutional lines, in this case the formal structures of the church, its normative practices, the career patterns of its agents, and so forth. The first decade of our review period, in fact, saw the publication of two fundamental works in this genre, although they became increasingly rare thereafter: John Schwaller's (1987) study of church finances in the

---

45. The books by Gosner and Patch can profitably be read along with those of Rugeley (1996, 2001) on the Yucatec Maya.

three generations after the conquest, and his extremely valuable work (1987) on the ecclesiastical hierarchy and career patterns two years later. While individual biographies of famous churchmen were fairly common earlier on—e.g., Lillian E. Fisher (1955) on Manuel Abad y Queipo, or Fintan B. Warren (1963) on Vasco de Quiroga—if not as common as those of high secular officials, they faded out of the picture after the early 1980s, with the possible exception of Stafford Poole's (1987) book on the sixteenth-century archbishop Pedro Moya de Contreras. Nearly a decade later, in close proximity to each other, were published works of a strongly institutional character by David Brading (1994) on the diocese of Michoacán in the second half of the eighteenth century, and William Taylor's (1996) magnificent work on secular parish priests in the eighteenth century. Yet both books far transcended institutional studies, especially Taylor's. Brading's book not only built upon several decades of his research on the Bajío region, forming what the author himself characterized as the third in a trilogy on the area (after *Miners and Merchants* [1971] and *Haciendas and Ranchos* [1978]), but also provided a full profile of the Western church, including in its treatment the effects of the Bourbon Reforms, the regular orders, and the episcopal hierarchy. In some ways echoing Schwaller's earlier research on church career patterns, Taylor's study delved profoundly into issues of popular piety, the volatile priest-parishioner relations that formed the main point of contact in many areas between indigenous villagers and the structures of colonial society, issues of social control in the countryside, and the background of the clerical participation in the independence movement. Difficult to categorize readily, but partaking partly of the institutional history of the late colonial church (policy and prescription, especially in the area of burial reform), partly of the history of ideas (the advent of Jansenist influences in Mexican Catholic theology and religious practice), and partly of the history of the late Bourbon modernization project (public hygiene and *buen policía*), is Pamela Voekel's (2002) bold and suggestive book in the cultural vein, *Alone Before God*. While some parts of this work hold up to scrutiny less well than others, it does suggest an imaginative and intriguing link between the advent of liberalism in the early republican decades, and what Voekel sees in the later eighteenth century as a turn away from Baroque piety, and toward the interiorization and individualization of religious belief among late colonial Mexican elite groups under the impact of Bourbon rationality and Jansenist discourse. A cousin of Viqueira Albán's work on popular cultural forms during the same period, and related more closely to studies of the history of early modern European piety and modernization than to most of what has been done for colonial Spanish America, Voekel's book could not be more different from the works of Ricard and Taylor, although they inhabit the same world of religious discourse and practice. Insightful as the book is, it also exemplifies the ways in which good cultural history is sometimes less well realized as social history.[46]

My brief account of the outward and downward move of William Taylor's work from church institutional structures to priest-parishioner relations brings us immediately into contact with the evangelization process and popular (some would prefer the term "local") religion, most of it among indigenous people. In one corner of this terrain we have the growth in the last fifteen years or so of a small cottage industry on the cult of the Virgin of Guadalupe, given a special piquancy by controversies surrounding the canonization of Juan Diego by the Pope in Mexico City in 2002. First to appear (preceded by a decade by Jacques Lafaye's (1976) work on Guadalupe and Mexican national consciousness) was Stafford Poole's (1995) eloquent and authoritative account of the devotion up to nearly the end of the colonial era, which dated its initial propagation from the mid-seventeenth century and located it socially at first among Mexican Creoles rather than Indians. This was followed some years later by a careful edition and translation of Luis Laso de la Vega's 1649 Nahuatl account of the apparition, the *Huey tlamahuiçoltica* (also known by its first words, *Nican mopuhua*), authored by Lisa Sousa, Stafford Poole, and James Lockhart (1998). David Brading's (2001) dense and fascinating history of the devotion is a tour de force of intellectual genealogy, intertextual detective work, and sensitive readings of Marian theology. Brading agreed on many points with Poole's treatment, but emphasized Nahuatl accounts less and Creole accounts more, carrying the complex story of a burgeoning national devotion into the late twentieth century. As his book on the diocese of Michoacán forms the third work in a trilogy on the Bajío, although the three studies were executed from different points of view and each stands on its own vis-à-vis a discrete subliterature, so Brading's *Mexican Phoenix* forms part of a trilogy on Creole patriotism and Mexican national consciousness with his *Origins of Mexican Nationalism* (1985) and *The First America* (1991), on the whole perhaps the most influential body of work on colonial Mexico by any Anglophone scholar other than James Lockhart. It is worth noting, however, that concerned as they are with textual exegesis, questions of authenticity, and Marian theology, among other

---

46. For a recent, thoughtful review article on several works on the colonial church, among them Taylor's, see O'Hara (2001). Slightly off to one side of these institutional and postinstitutional studies of the church is the very important study of High Church ideology by Connaughton (2003), which deals primarily with the post-1821 period, although it has much to say about the late colonial years.

questions, neither Poole's study nor Brading's pays more than scant attention to the popular reception of the Guadalupe cult, or the ideological uses to which Marian devotion was put by common people in an ethnically stratified society. With the exception of a few works discussed below, in fact, this descent into the affective and ideational world of colonial popular religion has not been successfully achieved, primarily due to the same problem we have with resistance movements and ideologies—the lack of sufficient sources to get us there.[47]

So closely imbricated were the processes of conquest, evangelization, and the contacts between native people and Europeans that a large, innovative, and often speculative historical literature, lying at the intersection of studies of religiosity and ethnohistory, has developed within little more than fifteen years. The relative recency of these works, together with the inherently elusive nature of their subject matter, provides a strong hint that they fall almost exclusively into the cultural history register. Among the earliest of them was Louise Burkhart's (1989) important study of the categorical slippages between Christian message and Nahua understanding in the early decades following the conquest, followed by the same author's works on Nahua religious drama (1996) and her contribution to the prehistory of the Guadalupe devotion (2001). Another avatar of this wave of studies was Inga Clendinnen's (1987) captivating book on the conquest of the Yucatecan Maya, a prolonged episode during which the sheer nervousness and violence of the Spanish invasion itself provide the backdrop for a brilliant treatment by Clendinnen of the projection by Europeans of their fears onto the natives, the latter's evasion and resilience, and the invaders' savage reaction to what they regarded as a betrayal when native converts reverted to their old ways. For all its virtues, based as it is substantially on published European sources or on native accounts filtered through the Europeans or influenced by them, Clendinnen's book exemplifies some of the problems with this sort of historical undertaking in the absence of a relatively large and substantially unmediated corpus of indig-

---

47. The mention of Brading's *The First America* prompts me to comment that the history of ideas in the traditional sense has not much occupied the attention of Anglophone historians of colonial Mexico in the last two decades or so, although many historians discuss political, religious, and other ideas as part of other projects. Aside from Brading, a brilliant exception to this assertion is Jorge Cañizares-Esguerra's (2001) work on the science of history writing in the Atlantic World, *How to Write the History of the New World*. The same neglect (or perhaps better said, failure to thrive) has been true of the history of science and medicine among Anglophone scholars (Paula De Vos, personal communication). Judging by the upsurge in the number of recent doctoral dissertations dealing with some aspect of the history of medicine in Latin America, this weakness is likely to be remedied in the coming decade or so. The only monograph I have been able to identify is that of Hernández Sáenz (1997).

enous testimonies. Nearby Chiapas provides the scene for Amos Megged's (1996) study of Franciscan and Dominican efforts to evangelize the Tzeltal Indians under the sign of the Counter-Reformation and Tridentine reforms between about 1550 and 1680, touching upon the now familiar but almost infinitely varied themes of the translatability of Christian doctrine, native recalcitrance and backsliding, and the adaptation to native purposes of colonialist institutions such as the religious confraternity. These slippages along cultural fault lines and the unanticipated consequences of introducing Christian belief during evangelization furnish the raw material for two fascinating studies, the first by Fernando Cervantes (1994) on diabolism among the natives of New Spain, the second by Pete Sigal (2000) on changes in Yucatecan Maya thinking about sexuality. Both bear the hallmarks of the most intense sort of cultural history that we have yet to see: density of argument, allusion, and theory; penetration into realms of native consciousness and collective psychology in a somewhat speculative vein; close attention to high theology, intertextuality, and forms of representation; and a notable tendency, because of the nature of the documentation, to emphasize the thinking of elite groups. Cervantes's study, in particular, weaves together elements of European theological disputation such as the Franciscan critique of Thomism, native belief systems, European representations of native culture, and the practices of early colonial evangelization. He finds that the central Mexican natives adopted a belief in the Devil, which the friars had introduced in order to claim Indians for the Christian universe, in order to preserve monistic notions of the creator-destroyer divinities in their own traditional belief systems. Later in the colonial period the Devil was on his way to being reduced in European theology to a sort of trickster figure, but the natives were stuck with him well beyond the end of colonialism. Finally, two recent works on evangelization in early colonial Michoacán demonstrate the variety of approaches in the field even at this late date. One of them, Bernardino Vérastique's *Michoacán and Eden* (2000), is a sort of earnest, conventional throwback centering on the life of Bishop Vasco de Quiroga. The second, James Krippner-Martínez's *Rereading the Conquest* (2000), is a much bolder and more ambitious work. Based almost exclusively on the critical exegesis of four major early colonial texts, the book is devoted to deconstructing the way in which the history of early colonial Michoacán has been remembered in history writing, from the death of the Tarascan *cazonci* at the hands of Nuño de Guzmán to the virtual canonization of Vasco de Quiroga by writers over the last two centuries or so. Interesting as it is, it is a form of cultural history that indicates how very different the genre can be from subaltern history, and that more closely resembles intellectual history with an attitude.

The text-centered nature of Krippner-Martínez's work leads our attention quite naturally to a special little cache of studies that are almost entirely text centered but broader in approach, and which all deal with what we may call, following Serge Gruzinski, the "colonization of the native imaginary" (my own preferred translation of the original French term *imaginaire* would be something like "cultural template"). All these works share an interest in the way Christianity was received and adapted by Mesoamerican native peoples, and thus devote a good deal of energy to the evangelization process, but they also embrace the reconfiguration of indigenous mythologies, forms of nonreligious representation, the encroachment of European practices of reading and writing, native historical memory, and so forth. And although they typically deploy very eclectic sorts of evidence, from European religious treatises and historical accounts, historical chronicles in alphabetic renderings by native authors in either their native tongues or Spanish, and native codices, to Inquisition testimony, maps, and other types of archival evidence, they are very abstracted from mundane social practices and realities, and are meant to be so, since they work on the assumption that the mental changes are antecedent to the social instantiation of them. These authors make a convincing case that native ways of remembering, thinking, and even perceiving were colonized just as profoundly as native lands, labor relations, political structures, ritual behaviors, and social arrangements.

The earliest of these works, and the least affected by the theoretical considerations of the linguistic turn, was Enrique Florescano's (1994) very suggestive *Memory, Myth, and Time in Mexico*, which the author has followed with a number of other book-length studies concerning the symbology of Mexican nationalism, native mythological figures, and the system of Nahua pre-Columbian religious belief. Beginning with Nahua concepts of time and space, and always keeping at the center of his vision the practices of native historical remembering as shaped by the Aztec, colonial, and national states, Florescano takes the story of native concepts of the past through the colonial period to the independence era and the emergence of a Mexican patriotism cobbled together from elements of indigenous mythology, European linear histories, and burgeoning nationalist imagining. There followed in close proximity Serge Gruzinski's *The Conquest of Mexico* (1993; published in French some years after the Spanish edition of Florescano's book), a quite intellectually stunning work which in emphasizing discontinuity in native forms of collective memory, the devaluation of native oral and pictorial modes of representation, and the aggressive propagation of European Christianity to supplant indigenous belief systems, presented a much less sanguine picture of native cultural forms under colonial rule. Published in France just two years after the original publication of *The Conquest of Mexico*, Gruzinski's *Images at War* (2001) is a more modest, less substantiated, yet more speculative work that nonetheless packs a powerful interpretive punch and continues in many ways where the previous book left off. Here Gruzinski traces the history of the implantation of images—primarily religious ones, including church frescoes, pictures of La Guadalupana, illustrations in the famous *títulos primordiales*, religious sculptures, and so on—by the Europeans into indigenous culture, arriving along the way at the cult(ure) of the Baroque image where his discussion converges interestingly with that of David Brading in his book on the Virgin of Guadalupe. A playful if not entirely convincing coda takes the story through the twentieth century, through the flickering images of Televisa and Ridley Scott's 1982 film *Blade Runner*, where the apocalyptic icons of an ever more dystopic Los Angeles dominate a landscape of postmodern cultural hybridity. And just a few years beyond the 1990 book by Gruzinski we saw the publication of Walter Mignolo's dense and very impressive *Darker Side of the Renaissance* (1995), in which the importation and imposition of European writing systems on native cultures in Spanish America (Mexico is the central case examined), and the control they came to exert over forms of representation—religious, historical, even cartographic—take center stage still more explicitly than in Florescano's or Gruzinski's books. It is not clear if we may expect to see more such large-scale interpretive works from other authors in the near future. In some ways recent books like those of Pamela Voekel and James Krippner-Martínez, although each very original in its own right, are probative explorations of the lines of inquiry in cultural and intellectual history laid out by the works of Brading (in *The First America*), Florescano, Gruzinski, and Mignolo in the early 1990s.

Ethnohistory

Finally, there is little question that the works in ethnohistory produced at a quite steady pace over the last two decades comprise the single largest and most coherent subgenre in the Anglophone historiography of colonial Mexico. Since the Nahuatl-, Maya-, and Mixtec-based works, in particular, share such a distinct identity, they have been glossed a good deal already in methodological and review articles (most recently by Restall 2003), and I will not linger over them here as much as their importance warrants.[48] Although much recent work in ethnohistory relies on native-

---

48. Restall (2003) provides an excellent if somewhat reverential overview of the literature, and his treatment there does much of what I would have written here had he not published his article. He does make a series of useful distinctions between the New Philol-

language sources, not all of it does for the simple reason that native-language sources may be missing, as with the northern indigenous peoples who never produced alphabetic writing in their own tongues. Certainly a kinship exists between ethnohistory in a general sense and the subaltern history to which it may be assimilated by its focus on colonial indigenous people (subalterns ipso facto), even if their methods are distinct. Its relationship to works at the further reaches of cultural history is a bit more tenuous, again on the grounds of method, since in purely substantive terms its findings about native peoples after the European conquest lend themselves readily to appropriation by scholars studying the slippages of meaning and understanding within colonial society. Some of ethnohistory's best recent works and most adept practitioners, on the one hand, are quite resolutely structuralist in their approach, while on the other hand, those ethnohistorians who work in the well-established native-language-based tradition keep within remarkably conservative boundaries. Impressive as it is, much of the native-language-based investigation tends to be linguistically self-referential and therefore ultimately descriptive, relying upon the accumulation of details about linguistic analysis and change to provide some insight into native society and thinking. One limiting condition here is the sources, a problem with social and cultural history in general noted here throughout, and which in the case of native-language-based ethnohistory has now been pushed down a level into native society. Here the documentary sources are still largely, although by no means exclusively, the written records of native elites, as they have tended to be in the social and cultural history of colonial society more widely, which depends upon documents for the most part generated by the colonial state, by the literate, and by the superordinate social sphere. Nonetheless, ethnohistory as a whole has magnificently redressed the imbalance in our reconstruction of colonial Mexican society, a foreshortened vision conditioned by our having seen indigenous people as the objects rather than the subjects of their own history.

Two extremely significant works, published within a year of each other, can stand as the modern progenitors of colonial Mexican ethnohistory. These are Edward H. Spicer's *Cycles of Conquest* (1963) and Charles Gibson's *The Aztecs under Spanish Rule* (1964), focusing respectively on what we might call the Greater Mexican North, the American Southwest, or the Borderlands (depending upon one's point of view),

---

ogy and ethnohistory more generally, as well as drawing connections between this native-language-based work and cultural and social history, and providing a scheme of three stages in which the work was produced, beginning in 1976. In addition to Restall, see several chapters in Lockhart (1991b), and the introductory essay by MacLeod (2000).

and the Valley of Mexico, or Nahua-speaking lands. As with studies of native resistance movements, then, ethnohistory has tended broadly to bifurcate into two branches: a northern branch, much less developed in quantitative terms but with distinguished exemplars of the genre, and a southern branch (in fact, central, with southeastern spurs) with a great many more works, dominated by the native-language-based studies (in Nahuatl, Zapotec/Mixtec, and the Maya group) strongly associated with James Lockhart, his collaborators, and his students. The northern ethnohistories tend for obvious reasons to blur into studies of the colonial mission regime, the social conditions peculiar to the long history of the Spanish frontier (about which David Weber, [e.g., 1992] has written so compellingly), the complex history of Mexican/United States interaction, and the harsh ecology of the northern Mexican steppe-lands, mountain ranges, and river valleys. An environmental history or ecological approach makes a good deal of sense in this area of the world, since the environment obtrudes itself so obviously into cultural formations and patterns of historical change, while ethnohistorians of the more congenial central and southeastern Mexican lands rarely mention it at all. Two recent distinguished books on this northern macroregion are Cynthia Radding's *Wandering Peoples* (1997) and Susan Deeds's *Defiance and Deference* (2003), preceded and accompanied by a host of interesting works by Mexican scholars and other Anglophone investigators (e.g., Sheridan 1999). Radding's work on the Sonoran highland indigenous groups in the late colonial and early national periods—their interactions with missionaries, the changes in their economic life, their coping strategies and ethnic identities in the face of relentless pressure from ranchers, miners, settlers, and military intrusions—takes a strongly ecological perspective but is too sophisticated to be reductive. Focusing on several indigenous groups further south and southeast, and on the comparative history of their survival through the colonial era, Deeds's book is cognizant of the environmental constraints within which Indian cultures and economies developed and interacted with the encroaching colonists, but if skeptical of some of the claims of cultural history, is nonetheless more tilted toward the cultural history of the native peoples she studies.

At least in terms of the number of monographs produced by Anglophone scholars, the central/southern branch in colonial ethnohistory has been the most impressively productive, and arguably the most methodologically innovative because of its heavy reliance on native-language documents and the linguistic skills required to use them. Many of the authors of these works have found themselves in implicit or explicit dialog with Charles Gibson's foundational work on central Mexican

Nahua speakers, and even their titles reflect this (e.g., Farriss [1984] and Lockhart [1992]). The first major monographic study in this genre took some time to materialize after the publication of Gibson's *Aztecs*, and then dealt with Yucatán rather than the Nahua lands. Following upon the heels of a host of anthropologists, archaeologists, and other sorts of scholars who had already studied the Maya (e.g., Bricker 1981), Nancy Farriss's *Maya Society under Colonial Rule* (1984) realized a Gibsonian study for the Yucatec Maya some two decades after the publication of Gibson's monumental work. Structuralist as most of the work is (Farriss acknowledges as her inspirations Gibson, of course, but also Eric Wolf, little cited now by ethnohistorians of cultural inclination, an indication that our understanding of what "culture" means has swung in a different direction), however, Farriss devoted several chapters to native religious belief and cosmology under the impact of the Spanish presence, something one sees little of in Gibson's work. A dozen years further on, and we have Matthew Restall's (1997) impressive native-language-based study of the Yucatec Maya with "culture" in the title and a good deal of the text devoted not only to gender, sexuality, and religious thinking, but also nearly a hundred pages to language phenomena. Even more insistent on the primacy of language is Kevin Terraciano's (2001) prizewinning volume on the colonial Mixtecs of Oaxaca. After devoting nearly a third of its ample length explicitly to Mixtec writing and language, Terraciano takes the reader through a series of chapters encompassing community structure; social relations; forms of native rulership; patterns of land use, ownership, and conflict; religious thinking; and ideas about ethnicity. Nearly all of this is viewed through the lens of native terminologies and concepts as they survived into the colonial period and were progressively modified by the introduction of Spanish language and lifeways. With meticulous scholarship, unimpeachable expertise in the native-language materials, and an uninflected Gibsonian voice that itself helps to establish his authority, Terraciano's work is about as far from the indeterminacies and sometimes overheated readings of the linguistic turn as any materialist-structuralist history.[49]

---

49. As Restall (2003) points out in his valuable historiographical essay on the "New Philology," it has become common practice among the Nahuatlatos (an affectionate designation for those historians of a younger generation working in native-language sources, particularly in Náhuatl) to publish collections of native-language texts, often in the original with translations. Restall's contribution here has been significant, and includes his *Life and Death in a Maya Community* (1995), really more of a monograph in some ways than a simple collection of native testaments. For a valuable collection of analyses and methodological statements by some of the field's most visible practitioners, see the anthology by Kellogg and Restall (1998).

The most obvious flowering of this subgenre of ethnohistory is represented by a half-dozen or so monographs published for the most part during the last twenty years, dealing with the Nahua lands of central Mexico. Although some of these works nominally extend past the middle or so of the seventeenth century to embrace the late colonial period, they tend to concentrate on the first 150 years of colonial life, corresponding to the first two stages of native language transformation (1519–ca. 1550, 1550–1650) famously delineated for central Mexico by James Lockhart, which the authors seem to find richest in linguistic transformation and most important for acculturation processes. Within a few years of Farriss's book on the Maya the first of these works was published, S. L. Cline's (1986) study on Culhuacán in the last two decades of the sixteenth century, based substantially on native testaments, preceded two years earlier by the documentary collection edited by her and Miguel León-Portilla, *The Testaments of Culhuacán* (1984), and followed after some years by her transcription, translation, and analysis of an early postconquest Nahuatl-language census, *The Book of Tributes* (1993). There followed in rapid succession Susan Schroeder's deep analysis of the Chalco and Amecameca chronicler Chimalpahin (1991) and Robert Haskett's (1991) study of surviving and adapted native forms of governance in the Cuernavaca area, especially for the later colonial period, and a few years later Rebecca Horn's (1997) eminently Gibsonian study of early colonial political and economic structures in Coyoacán. It is a tribute to these and other works by Nahuatlato historians (and to their *maitre* James Lockhart) that they are not cookie-cutter copies of each other, but rather move toward different goals through similar approaches. Cline's book focuses on matters of native piety, family, and gender, for example, Schroeder's on a detailed reconstruction of the political structure of Chalco through a fascinating exegesis of the thinking of a sophisticated native chronicler and micropatriot. Robert Haskett concentrates almost entirely on indigenous political structures within what survived of an important preconquest city-state to the south of what became Mexico City, and Rebecca Horn's book looks at the traditional themes of taxation, labor systems, landholding, Spanish-owned haciendas, and market relationships—traditional in the sense that she seems more concerned to "establish the objective state of things" than native mind-sets as revealed in political thinking, piety, or ideas about gender.[50] These fine studies all share a documentary base in native-language sources (supplemented by

---

50. The quoted phrase is drawn from Schroeder (1991, 112), where she contrasts her own approach to the Chalco chronicler's work with the more materialist frameworks of other scholars.

the same sorts of Spanish-language official documents that nonethnohistorians rely upon), an intense interest in the native political form of the *altepetl*, and a fundamental belief that native agency within the colonial regime can be demonstrated through their common approach.[51]

In the meantime, during the 1980s James Lockhart had been producing with collaborators a series of volumes of transcribed Nahuatl documents with commentaries, and also essays of his own, as he would continue to do during the rest of the 1990s and beyond, after the publication of his magnum opus, the magnificent *Nahuas after the Conquest* (1992). The structure of this book seems almost to provide a pretext for a long, technically adept treatment of culture change as manifest through the developmental stages of colonial Nahuatl language. Beginning with a dense chapter on Nahua political organization and terminology centering on the *altepetl* (roughly a native ethnic city-state) and its fate through the midcolonial period, Lockhart moves downward to household organization, then outward to social differentiation, economic life, and religious practice, finally turning to language phenomena, which occupies nearly half the text. Lockhart has gone to some pains to indicate that his own work and that of many of his students, aside from language change, focuses centrally on the *altepetl* and the modular-rotational forms of native political organization following from it, as well as upon the interplay of cultural change and considerable continuity in central Mexican native society under Spanish domination, and also that these themes were at the core of Gibson's *Aztecs under Spanish Rule*, absent only the term *altepetl* itself.[52] While there are undeniable affinities between the work of Lockhart and Gibson on these points, the language-based approach of the former and the heavily materialist emphasis of the latter—on labor systems, landholding, farming, and so forth—could hardly be more different. Gibson did set much of the agenda for colonial Mexican ethnohistorians and other scholars, it is true, directing their attention toward the lives of indigenous people, but it is hardly surprising that these chapters on Valley of Mexico economic (and to some extent political) life, rather than references to language or his work on Aztec political entities, seem to have been the most influential in the broader field. And there is also some irony in the fact that the most intensely language-centered project to have arisen in the Anglophone historiography on colonial Mexico during the last three decades seems hardly to have taken the linguistic turn at all in the sense in which cultural history is ordinarily conceived today (and sometimes shrilly criticized), but instead hangs in an empiricist space

---

51. See also Anderson and Schroeder (1997–).
52. See, particularly, Lockhart (1991a) on Gibson.

somewhere between economic determinism and the speculative imputation of changes in native mental templates from religious or political practices imposed by the conquerors.[53]

CONCLUSION

The way Anglophone historians approach the history of colonial Mexico since 1980 or so has changed, but the changes have been incremental, not sudden; this is a social science and humanistic endeavor, after all, and not quantum mechanics. Some formerly strong currents have dried up or gone into a historiographical hiatus (hacienda studies, biography); others, even though they were already in evidence by the early 1980s, have come on very strong (ethnohistory, studies of resistance); and the field as a whole has perceptibly tipped away from structuralist-materialist approaches toward cultural ones. The turn in the direction of cultural history cannot be explained exclusively by reference to internal developments in the area of Mexican studies or history; that is, to discoveries of new sorts of documentation, the arrival of new methods on the scene, the internal logic of the work being done, or the influence of a single towering scholarly figure or school. If it could be so explained, Mexican historians of colonial Mexico would probably be following the same trend, and with a few exceptions they are not. In fact, one worrisome trend lies in the increasing divergence of the two national historiographies—the Mexican still committed to fairly traditional (although still compelling) questions, methods, and materialist paradigms, while at least a part of the American scholarship is apparently flying off into the empyrean. It is in the United States community of Mexicanist scholars where the great bulk of this Anglophone work has been and will continue to be done, and it is the intellectual environment of North American scholarship—the impact of cultural anthropology upon history, the emergence of postcolonial studies, the influence of European historiographical models, the linguistic turn in general—that has shaped the product of our labors. A judgment as to whether these are salutary or noxious influences is partly a matter of taste, and partly a matter of the explanatory power that the new styles bring to the questions they are seeking to answer, and the very nature of those questions.

---

53. See also Kartunnen and Lockhart (1976); Lockhart, Berdan, and Anderson (1986); and Lockhart (1992, 2000, 2001a, 2001b).

CHAPTER 4

No Human Power to Impede the Impenetrable Order of Providence
The Historiography of Mexican Independence

Toward the end of his life, just following Mexico's defeat in the war with the United States (1846–1848), the great Mexican conservative statesman and historian Lucas Alamán wrote of the Mexican Independence movement and the subsequent fate of his country:

> In seeing in so few years the immense loss of territory [entailed by Mexico's defeat in the war with the United States]; the ruin of public finances . . . , the annihilation of a flourishing and valiant army . . . , and above all the complete extinction of public spirit, which has brought with it the disappearance of all idea of a national character; and finding in Mexico no Mexicans, contemplating a nation that has arrived from infancy to decrepitude without enjoying more than a glimmer of the happiness of youth, nor given any other signs of life than violent convulsions, it would seem that we have reason to recognize with the great Bolívar that Independence has been purchased at the cost of everything Spanish America possesses. . . . These dreadful outcomes have given reason to discuss if Independence has been a good or an evil.[1]

While acknowledging at several points in his history of the insurgency in his labyrinthine and coolly Olympian prose that Mexican independence

---

1. Lucas Alamán (1968/1849, 5:566ff); the first part of this chapter's title is drawn from the same passage in the *Historia de Méjico*; all translations from Spanish are mine, unless otherwise noted. Lucas Alamán (1792–1853) was several times minister of interior and exterior relations after Mexico gained its independence from Spain in 1821, functioned for thirty years as the preeminent ideologue of the Mexican conservatives, worked tirelessly to industrialize Mexico (while enjoying only limited success as an entrepreneur himself), and was arguably the greatest Mexican historian of the nineteenth century. Simón Bolívar, the liberator of much of Spanish South America, developed a famously gloomy view of political life in the new republics, remarking that in trying to implant republican institutions he had "ploughed the sea." I owe thanks to John Coatsworth, Andrew Fisher, and Tom Passananti for useful suggestions to improve this chapter. The first part of the chapter title is a paraphrase of Alamán from the same passage.

was probably inevitable, Alamán nonetheless exalted the Spanish colonial period as a time of good government, prosperity, and social order, lamenting the unrestrained civil and military violence unleashed by Father Miguel Hidalgo's rebellion, and bemoaning the state of the new nation after the first quarter-century of its life.

Alamán's slightly older contemporary Carlos María de Bustamante—journalist, historian, editor, and congressional deputy—authored another early history of the independence movement that laid the foundations of much subsequent writing by Mexican historians about the period. This history may actually have been more influential than Alamán's magisterial work in molding nineteenth-century opinion among general readers. Those who penned historical works after these two often tended to mine Bustamante for facts while setting up as a straw man Alamán's conservative interpretation and famous Hispanophilism, against which they almost always reacted negatively. With his rhetorical flights, florid, overheated prose, and reluctance to offer contemplative, sociological speculation, Bustamante was no less ardent a nationalist than Alamán, but arrived at very different conclusions about what Independence meant. He condemned the Spanish colonial regime root and branch as an unjust usurpation of the legitimate indigenous states (the Aztecs and others) whose heritage the insurgency had vindicated, and from whose ruins independent Mexico was to rise, phoenixlike. In his account of the carnage visited upon the Spaniards who had taken refuge in the fortified granary, the Alhóndiga de Granaditas, in the silver mining city of Guanajuato, overrun by Father Miguel Hidalgo's insurgent army in late September 1810, Bustamante invoked the shades of the Spanish conquerors of the sixteenth century and their Indian victims, now in some measure avenged by the insurgents:

[I] imagined that I saw among those cadavers and [still] twitching limbs the spirits of Cortés, of Alvarado and of Pizarro staggering with terror while contemplating them, and of weeping America throwing herself on them, saying with a terrible voice "Of what are you so horrified seeing these victims? Have you forgotten the cruel massacres you carried out three centuries ago in Tabasco, in Cholula, in the great temple of Mexico City, in Cuernavaca? . . . Do you perhaps not know that in the scales of the great [Creator of All Things] all these crimes were weighed, and that He reserved His vengeance for my crushed and enslaved sons, after three centuries?"

And just to drive the point home unequivocally, Bustamante added a stanza of poetry condemning the conquistadores:

In this way their unjust crimes
Will be punished, one by one
Blood with blood, and tears, in the end, with tears.[2]

    2. Carlos María de Bustamante (1961/1823, 1:39). Pedro de Alvarado was second in importance only to Fernando Cortés in the conquest of Mexico and Central America, while

Alamán, on the other hand, describing the same events, to which he was virtually an eyewitness, drew from them an entirely different lesson. He wrote of the staunch bravery of the defenders ("A worthy example for Mexican soldiers!"), the frenzied, bloodthirsty assault by the "confused mob" of Indian attackers impelled to atrocities against the besieged Spaniards by their stupidity ("Such is the ignorance of the hoi polloi [*vulgo*]!"), the brutal slaughter of scores of people "whose naked bodies were [later] found half buried in maize and money, all stained with [their] blood," and so forth.[3]

There were ideological, personal, and circumstantial reasons for the different attitudes Alamán and Bustamante struck toward the conquest, the colonial regime, and the process by which Mexico became independent from Spain, as there always are among different historians of even the same generation viewing the same events. For one thing, Alamán began his public career around 1820 as a moderate liberal, but moved quickly during his early government ministries (1823–24, 1825) to a much more conservative stance. His rightward drift continued when he dominated the central organs of power as minister again in 1830–1832, hardened for a time in his last years into an unlovely alliance with Mexican monarchists, and finally underwrote his role as architect of the last dictatorship of Antonio López de Santa Anna (1853–1855). Although Bustamante, too, grew more conservative during his long public life, moving from a position of nationalism and moderate liberalism, to one of no less nationalist centralism and moderate conservatism, he nonetheless always remained an ardent republican. Furthermore, the personalities of the two men were quite different, Alamán the more serious and introverted (perhaps even a depressive), Bustamante the ebullient optimist. Finally, Alamán wrote during and after the war with the United States, with the radical European revolutions of 1848 before his eyes and looking at a Mexico that had teetered on the brink of total failure as a state, while Bustamante (who died in 1848) produced his greatest historical work during the decade after independence was won, when there was arguably still a good deal of residual optimism among public men and intellectuals about Mexico's future.

Francisco Pizarro led the conquest of the Incas. Bustamante (1774–1848) was an active participant in the Independence movement, a prolific journalist and pamphleteer, almost continually a member of the Mexican congress until his death, and a major historian in his own right as well as an editor of older histories and chronicles. He and Alamán maintained a respectful if not cordial friendship for many years, although Alamán thought Bustamante a careless, romantic popularizer as a historian, and Bustamante even defended Alamán before Congress in 1834–35 against charges of complicity in the murder of independence hero and one-time president Vicente Guerrero.

3. Alamán (1968/1849, 1:274–78).

My task in this chapter, however, is not to discuss the many and interesting ways in which historians' personalities and life experiences influence their writing, but to examine some major works of history dealing with Mexican independence, both by Mexican and Anglophone scholars. I will sketch the ways in which views of these processes have changed over the last 175 years or so in light of changes in the discipline of history, and in the social and political circumstances in which Mexican history has been written. Alamán, Bustamante, José María Luis Mora, Servando Teresa de Mier, Lorenzo de Zavala, and others among a group of near contemporaries who witnessed the Mexican independence movement, and in some cases participated in it, produced the urtexts at the beginning of a long historiographical genealogy. The later nineteenth and twentieth centuries then saw a huge (if cyclical) outpouring of histories of the independence movement and biographies of its major protagonists. The accounts of these events and men elaborated by Mexican writers have remained highly positive over time, but the interpretation of the meaning of Mexican independence has changed in subtle ways, and the sources and methods of research on the period have mutated to reflect the political and other preoccupations of succeeding generations of historians. This is no less true of the much smaller but influential body of work on Mexican independence by Anglophone scholars, but without the complications of constructing a patriotic history. It is instructive to compare the two literatures on Mexican independence, rather than integrating them thematically, since the characteristics of each emerge more clearly than if they are treated as a single historiography.

Furthermore, in the immediate wake of the insurgency most Mexican writers tended to disconnect their evaluation of the rebellion from their views of what the new country had become after its birth, or what they hoped it would become, rather than analyzing the independence movement as an inevitable outcome of the three centuries of colonial rule preceding it. In other words, historians mostly saw the long decade 1808–1821 as a beginning rather than an ending point, as a more or less discrete occurrence rather than as a moment in a long historical arc. This was ever more the case as time passed and the postinsurgency history of Mexico followed an increasingly zigzag trajectory that needed to be accounted for. The troubled history of the country up through the first two-thirds or so of the nineteenth century could hardly be attributed to the event that gave it birth, but must be laid to other factors—individual corruption, inappropriate or failed institutions, political incapacity linked to the ethnic composition of the country, and so forth. Few among the pantheon of heroic figures who initiated and directed the movement for independence survived much beyond it, if they did at all, although there were some exceptions, among them Guadalupe Victoria and a few secondary figures such as the brothers López Rayón. Almost none of them left memoirs, wrote their own histories of events, or became notable public intellectuals, in contrast to some of the great heroes of Anglo-American independence. Some of the secondary Mexican figures today look more like thugs than liberators, in fact (the Villagrán family, for example, or Pedro Moreno, Rafael Iriarte, Francisco Osorno, and Agustín Marroquín), and some of them—most notably Agustín de Iturbide—are still objects of controversy. George Washington may have had his critics, but he died of natural causes, not lead poisoning as Iturbide did. The meaning of independence in the broader sense therefore hung on the paradox of a massive, violent political episode that could be criticized at the margins, perhaps, but not in its essence, and an outcome that never quite realized the hopes of the protagonists, the closest observers of the events, or their heirs. The notable exception to this tendency, as in much else, was Lucas Alamán, the bad boy among Mexico's great historians, who was ideologically wedded to the positive aspects of the colonial regime, although perhaps not as reflexively as the conventional view of him suggests.[4] He found no difficulty at all in acknowledging that a violent and bloody (and ugly, in his eyes) birth process had produced a handicapped offspring.

THE URTEXTS

Let me begin my account of the Mexican historical writing on independence by revisiting briefly the issues raised by the works of Alamán and Bustamante, and then making some general remarks to frame my subsequent discussion. In her account of early politics and history writing in the young American republic, Joanne Freeman has noted: "As both Republicans and Federalists realized, the party that won this literary debate would claim the soul of the republic; by shaping popular conceptions of the nation's founding, they would have a long-reaching influence on later events. History was personal, immediate, and politically significant; in fact, history *was* politics" (Freeman 2001, 277). In the same vein Enrique Florescano, one of the most durable, ubiquitous, productive, and astute of contemporary Mexican historians, has noted that the historical works of the generation of Alamán and Bustamante were "distinctly partisan and polemical": "In these cases, historical writing, instead of being limited to the reconstruction of the past, overlapped into the struggles that divided political actors in the present and was turned into another

---

4. In the early twentieth century the positivist ideologue Francisco Bulnes, who differed with Alamán about the virtues of Catholicism but agreed with him on much else, assumed a similarly critical position in his writings.

arena of the ideological conflict of the moment . . . [as] a weapon to destroy the opposing political faction . . . [This was] a historiography obsessed with political change" (Florescano 2002, 360). A number of these early foundational works were products of political exile, in fact, either government- or self-imposed, with all the nostalgia, vituperation, and desire for self-vindication that can be inherent in the writings of public figures banished from their homelands. Certainly this was true of three of the most important histories of the period, those of Fray Servando Teresa de Mier (1813/1920), Lorenzo de Zavala (1831–32), and José María Luis Mora (1836), and might well be said of the origins of Lucas Alamán's work (1849–1852).[5]

Interest in independence and the decades immediately following waxed in the early decades of the nineteenth century because the events of 1808–1821 were still fresh in the memory of the nation and of Mexican intellectuals, and many of the participants were still alive. Furthermore, the events of the Reform (1855–1862), the French Intervention (1862–1867), and Revolution (1910–1920) still lay in the future, so that during the first thirty years or so of Mexico's nationhood the independence movement became in many ways the country's link to an Atlantic republican tradition, to the French Revolution, and thence to modernity. Discussions by this first generation of Mexican historians of independence turned not so much on whether the insurgent priests Miguel Hidalgo or José María Morelos were heroes, for example, which was early acknowledged by most writers (even Alamán was guardedly positive about Morelos, although he had little use for the person or revolutionary excesses of Hidalgo) and soon hardened into orthodoxy, although some figures' reputations, as I have noted above of Agustín de Iturbide, were more ambiguous and volatile.[6] It was more a matter of arguing over what independence meant as the beginning point of a trajectory of state and nation building, and of whether the early history of the new nation fulfilled or traduced the

---

5. When he was accused of taking a central role in the killing of President Vicente Guerrero, Alamán went into hiding in Mexico City for about eighteen months—internal exile, in other words—during which time he started to write a tell-all personal memoir-*cum*-history of the young Mexican republic, which appears to be the origin of his later historical works and which certainly foreshadows some of the methodological and interpretive issues aired there. This book was never completed and the long fragment remains unpublished, to my knowledge. Especially useful in preparing this part of my essay have been a number of recent works on Mexican historiography, among them Guedea (1997) (especially the essays on Mier by Yael Bitrán Goren and on Zavala by Teresa Lozano Armendares), Lynch (1999), Florescano (2002), Terán (2004), Ortiz Monasterio (2004), and Guedea and Ávila (in press).

6. See, for example, the interesting account of the changing fortunes of Iturbide in national celebrations of Independence day in Beezley and Lorey (2001).

legacy of independence. Most observers of the decade-long insurgency—men as far apart in their political convictions as the ultraconservative Alamán and the ultraliberal Lorenzo de Zavala—could agree on its tragically destructive effects, but differed as to the solutions they implicitly or explicitly argued in their work for the infant nation's ills. But there was a more elusive issue at stake, as well, having to do not so much with *what* historians remembered in their works as with *how* they remembered it, and therefore how history—particularly the history of the nation—was to be written. A romantic nationalist strain (exemplified by Bustamante's writing) led in one direction, a more Rankean (*avant la lettre*), objectivist strain (advocated but less than fully achieved by Lorenzo de Zavala) in another. Historical styles did not congeal permanently with these approaches, of course, so that positivism, Marxism, and other influences were to make themselves felt in the later nineteenth and twentieth centuries. But the historical writing of the period can be seen not only as a burgeoning debate about how historical thinking was to be done, but also as a sort of long policy discussion in which writers were constructing as much a history of the future as of the past.

Alamán and Bustamante were not the first writers to offer early and influential accounts of the independence movement, of course. The brilliant and picaresque Dominican, Fray José Servando Teresa de Mier Noriega y Guerra (1763–1827), who spent much of his adult life in monastic reclusion, prison, or escaping from them, authored his *Historia de la revolución de Nueva España* while in exile in London in 1813 (for a recent intellectual biography, see Domínguez Michael 2004; Brading 1985). Mier's history was based upon heterogeneous sources, including Alexander von Humboldt's near-contemporary account of the Mexican colony, Spanish law codes, and personal correspondence. A history of an insurgency still in its early stages in 1813, and whose outcome was unforeseeable, the book began as a highly polemical work defending the actions of Mexican Viceroy Iturrigaray and his Creole allies in their attempts to convoke a congress within New Spain (attempts thwarted by a loyalist countercoup) in response to the usurpation of the Spanish throne by Napoleon in 1808 and the crisis of political legitimacy this spawned in both Spain and its New World possessions. Mier was the first writer to suggest that independence was justified on the basis of a pact between the Spanish crown and the original conquerors of New Spain and their heirs, in which the former enjoyed inalienable dominion over what was thought of as an American kingdom politically coequal with Castile, while the latter enjoyed preference in political office and a certain degree of autonomy in arranging their public affairs. Fray Servando constructed a complicated double genealogy in which the Spanish descendants of the original conquistadores had been allowed by the crown to oppress both Creole and indigenous inhabitants, thus rupturing the compact. He also defended Spanish America against the calumnies of notorious European writers such as De Pauw, Robertson, Buffon, and Raynal about the inferiority of New World nature and peoples to those of the Old World, extolling the accomplishments of pre-Columbian civilizations and their role in creating Mexican identity. Mier wrote in a tone of highly injured and emotional nationalism, ardently advocating the virtues of republicanism and broad citizenship. But he nonetheless believed that the majority of the Mexican population *as they stood in his time* were too ignorant and unprepared to exercise the responsibilities of a republican democracy, and that the Creole elite, with whom he identified strongly, should wield power in the new nation. Fray Servando's history was much cited by subsequent historians of independence, including Lucas Alamán (with whom he long maintained a friendship despite their differing political views), who wrote of Mier's book: "This work, apart from everything that is the child of circumstance and which results from the partisan spirit that prevailed at the moment [it was created], is written with elegance and constructed with much artifice, [and] will always be appreciated for the multitude of data it contains and for the talent with which the author treats his themes" (Alamán 1968 1:52).

Following in the footsteps of Mier's hypertrophied political pamphletry, both linked with the early nineteenth-century liberal view of independence and both the authors of important histories of the struggle, came Father José María Luis Mora (1794–1850), often identified as the founder of Mexican liberalism, and his somewhat older (by six years) contemporary Lorenzo de Zavala. Educated as a priest and lawyer, Mora came from a wealthy family ruined by the insurgency, and enjoyed a long and active public career as journalist, educator, and political figure, at the height of which he served as a chief adviser in the short-lived liberal regime of Valentín Gómez Farías in 1833–34. Following his self-imposed exile from Mexico he was to live the rest of his life in Paris, where in order to alleviate his own poverty he undertook to publish his three-volume *México y sus revoluciones* (1836), on which he had been working since the late 1820s. Mora's work was never completed, embracing only the period up to 1812, but his virulently anticlerical views emerged clearly enough (this was to be a major theme of his career as a public figure, journalist, and writer), as well as his disdain for the country's indigenous population and its heritage, the very element Bustamante exalted as the basis of national identity. Indeed, he disdained Bustamante's romantic nationalism and the patriotism espoused by him and Mier. Like other early writers on independence, even those most sympathetic to it, Mora was appalled by the social violence unleashed by Miguel Hidalgo's uprising (his own brother passed into the insurgent ranks and was killed as a combatant), the religious-messianic character of Hidalgo as a leader, and the lack of a clear programmatic agenda in the movement. With Alamán, he lauded Fernando Cortés as the progenitor of Spanish Mexico and was less negative about colonial institutions than Zavala, but much more critical than Alamán. Like other liberal historians of the time who applauded the fact of Mexican independence while condemning the manner of its achievement (although he, like Alamán, praised the political and military skills of Morelos), Mora thought the decade of insurgency "pernicious and destructive" for the country, albeit necessary. He welcomed Iturbide's triumph while acknowledging that as emperor he had turned toward dictatorship.

Much further to the left than the putative founder of Mexican liberalism, or even most other contemporary public men, Lorenzo de Zavala was at various times during a turbulent public life a collaborator of Agustín de Iturbide and Vicente Guerrero, a deputy in the Spanish Cortes and the Mexican national congress, governor of the State of Mexico, cofounder of York-Rite Masonry (and a great friend of the controversial American envoy of the early 1820s, Joel R. Poinsett), minister of the treasury, ambassador to France, vice-president of the short-lived Texas Republic and himself a major landowner there, and an indefatigable writer and combat journalist. He began composing and quickly completed his *Ensayo histórico de las revoluciones de México, desde 1808 hasta 1830* (2 vols., 1831–32) while in exile in 1831 during a period in which an Alamán ministry dominated the national government. Substantively, Zavala saw history in general as the story of the search for liberty, much admired U.S. political institutions, and expressed the view that liberty itself would transform the Mexican people. The history of his country he believed had begun in 1808, preceded by a long colonial sleep of obscurantism and oppression. But unlike Bustamante, whose romantic nationalism he found laughable and whom he openly derided as a fabulist lacking in common sense or the critical criteria for writing history (the latter a view shared by Alamán; and see Brading 1991, 648ff), he did not exalt the positive heritage of the native societies, nor find in them the bases of a national identity. As with many engaged politicians of the time who turned their hands to historical works, Zavala ironically railed against the spirit of party prevailing in the work of other historians while himself writing to further his own liberal ideas and attack the ideas of his opponents. Still, he was more conscious than most of the subjective nature of virtually all the primary sources that underlay historical accounts and made something of a fetish of objectivity. Wrote Zavala, "I must relate the facts [of history] as they occurred, and present events naked of the color given to them by passions and the spirit of faction."[7] He achieved very little objectivity himself, however, often sacrificing empirical detail to the moral imperatives of narrating the history of the independence wars as a struggle for liberty. Describing the events of the insurgency as convulsive and gratuitously violent owing to the ineptitude of the leaders, like other writers among his contemporaries for whom he may stand proxy he nonetheless posited an essentially tragic vision of the initial stages of the movement. Thus Father Hidalgo might still be salvaged as a hero whose hubris led him to unleash forces he could not control. Starting as something of an optimist about the prospects for Mexico, by the years before his death in 1836 Zavala, like Simón Bolívar, had grown increasingly disheartened at the political ineptitude, lack of civic spirit, and ignorance of his countrymen, thus following an arc of disillusionment similar to that of his political archenemy Alamán.

The mantle of the great nationalist mythologizers fell next upon Carlos María de Bustamante, an ardent admirer of Mier's, as I have mentioned above, who extended the older man's claims about Mexico's indigenous heritage even further. In orotund nationalist rhetoric he portrayed his insurgent heroes as liberators of the heirs of the Aztecs, who had been enslaved by the colonial regime, in the process painting the Aztec rulers as models of good governance and exemplars of a New World Augustan age. By the time Lucas Alamán came to create his own magisterial history some twenty-five years later, the differences between the two historians (and indeed, between two more broadly interpretive points of view) had jelled quite clearly. With the benefit of hindsight and of his own central role in Mexican politics over three decades, however, Alamán dealt more explicitly than Bustamante with the issue vital to most writers of the period: Why had the recently independent Mexico enjoyed so little success politically or economically, and in particular why had the country been victimized so easily by its powerful sister republic to the north? Alamán constructed a historical narrative of failure that had begun with the rejection of the Spanish heritage by misguided insurgent chieftains who led a class war. From this fundamental mistake, he reasoned, followed the internal anarchy and weakness of the post-1821 period, the political experimentation with radical foreign ideas ill suited to Mexican realities (here the influence on his thinking of Edmund Burke was strong and explicit), and the tampering with traditional religion that produced the debacle of 1847. For Alamán, in other words, there had been not too much Spain in Mexico, but too little.

---

7. *Ensayo histórico*, 1:156–57, quoted in Teresa Lozano Armendares (1997), p. 225. My remarks on Zavala owe a good deal to Lozano Armendares's fine essay on him.

THE HISTORIOGRAPHY OF THE
POST-REFORMA AND PORFIRIAN PERIODS

After this generation passed from the scene, interest in the independence period as a distinct theme on the part of historians remained in evidence, but waned somewhat as the rebellion was metabolized into the process of nation-state construction from the Reform (1854–1867) onward, as part of a Whiggish narrative of liberalism and republicanism. Later nineteenth-century Liberal historians and intellectuals such as Ignacio Ramírez (1818–1879) and Ignacio Manuel Altamirano (1834–1893) led the same sort of hectic public lives as the earlier generation of Mier, Mora, Zavala, Bustamante, and Alamán, crossing back and forth between journalistic and belle-lettristic traditions as older writers had done. They assimilated independence to Reform and resistance to the French Intervention (1863–1867), by and large rejecting the indigenous heritage trumpeted by Bustamante and Mier and tracing the genealogy of the Mexican nation to an Atlantic republican tradition whose avatar was the French Revolution.[8] By the late nineteenth century it was almost impossible among liberal writers to pry apart ideologically the strands of French Revolution, independence, Reform, and resistance to the usurping Empire of Maximilian. During the Porfiriato (1876–1911), Porfirio Díaz assumed the mantles of both Miguel Hidalgo and the heroic figure of the Reform, Benito Juárez, an identification whose apotheosis was made word in the great multivolume history of Mexico published nearly midway through Díaz's regime, Vicente Riva Palacio's *México a través de los siglos* (1887–89). This was a monument to an inspired belle-lettristic amateurism, since there were no professionally trained historians in Mexico in the late nineteenth and early twentieth centuries owing to the lack of institutions to educate them in the craft. Typically the writers on historical themes of this period were gentleman scholars, antiquarians, and some public men (Riva Palacio himself fit this pattern), whereas the earlier generation of historians of independence had almost all been par-

---

8. My treatment of the post-Reforma historiography is quite telescoped because of space considerations. But it is worth noting that after midcentury a regionalist historiography flourished, and continues to do so into the present century, mostly focused on the histories of the individual Mexican states, or even localities, and permeated by the celebratory tone of *historia patria*. One product of this tradition particularly interesting for the history of Mexican independence is the six-volume, nearly six thousand–page-long collection of independence-era documents, *Colección de documentos para la Guerra de Independencia de México* (1968/1880), compiled and published by Juan E. Hernández y Dávalos, who originally dedicated his efforts in history writing to the state of Jalisco; on Hernández y Dávalos, see Ilhui Pacheco Chávez (1997).

ticipants in, or witnesses to, the insurgency itself or the political struggles of the early republic.

The great high-Porfirian synthesis of Mexican history, Vicente Riva Palacio's *México a través de los siglos,* represented historiographically what Carleton Beals (1932) once called the "queer frock-coated abortion" of the era's official ideology, a blend of positivism and liberalism.[9] More charitably, Enrique Florescano has characterized the work in the following manner:

> It had the virtue of integrating pasts considered enemies in a discourse that united pre-Hispanic antiquity with the viceroyalty, and both with the War of Independence, the first years of the Republic and the Reform. If the liberals of the first era, such as José María Luis Mora, had rejected the pre-Hispanic and colonial pasts, and Lucas Alamán, the head of the conservative party, had only accepted the Spanish heritage, *México a través de los siglos* for the first time extended a bridge of conciliation between the conflictive present and the various pasts of the country. (Florescano 2002, 353)

With its lush production values and over two thousand illustrations, many commissioned especially for the work by Riva Palacio, readers were drawn into a massive iconography of the nation that instilled patriotism through the eyes while explaining the history of the country in terms of the immutable laws of social evolution. Himself an important political and military figure, Riva Palacio's impeccable credentials included being the son of a major liberal statesman on his father's side and the grandson of the martyred independence hero Vicente Guerrero on his mother's.

Despite its espousal of historical objectivity, the five volumes were clearly dedicated to the vindication of republicanism and more-or-less liberal values. Lucas Alamán was in fact the target of much of its argument, especially of the volume on independence commissioned by Riva Palacio from the journalist, lawyer, sometime government bureaucrat, and eventual Supreme Court justice and senator, Julio Zarate. With its bombastic language, feigned objectivity, and ancient mythological comparisons with the heroes of independence, Zarate's book was essentially an anti-Alamaniad. Mining most heavily for its material the writings of Mora, Zavala, and Bustamante, Zarate's work nonetheless cited the great conservative historian more than any other single source while insisting at every turn upon Alamán's inexactitude and the malevolence of his judgments. Although he was not unsympathetic to the bravery and other virtues of the Spanish conquerors of the Aztecs, Zarate's was a "mestizo vision" of Mexican national identity (Ortiz Monasterio 2004, 246) whose origins

---

9. My treatment of Riva Palacio and his great collaborative works rests in part on the fine book of José Ortiz Monasterio (2004).

lay in the emergence of mixed-blood leaders in the independence struggle. True, the insurgency of 1810 might have its dark side, but it was still the necessary and positively valenced birth episode of the Mexican republic: "The royalist regime fell, and Mexico then enters on the tempestuous life of [all] young and free peoples, and begins to march down the glorious and difficult path of independent nations. It brings to its new existence the mistakes and defects inherited from its conquerors, but has inherited also their high virtues, and they will be enough to maintain its independence" (Zarate xiii, as quoted in Ortiz Monasterio 2004, 246).[10]

In large measure history had changed from being a weapon of overt political combat deployed by liberals against conservatives, therefore, into an instrument for consolidating a national consensus around the "liberal" Porfirian state. Then, with the Revolution of 1910, the figure of revolutionary, reformer, and president Francisco I. Madero came to be assimilated to those of Hidalgo and Juárez. Following the end of the armed revolution, beginning in the 1920s, interest by historians in the independence period waxed again as the postrevolutionary regime sought legitimacy in a refurbished republican tradition. The insurgency initiated by Hidalgo was absorbed into a narrative in which the modern mestizo nation had emerged from the dark night of colonialism with the independence struggle. Emblematic of the fate of independence narratives at the hands of historical revisionists over the last century or so is the figure of Father Miguel Hidalgo y Costilla himself. Historian Marta Terán has noted that the huge literature on Hidalgo has been overtaken during the last several decades by other sorts of independence studies more broadly. Furthermore, there is now less a "mono-Hidalgo"—a larger-than-life figure in the pantheon of the *historia de bronce* (bronze history); than a "poli-Hidalgo"—a liberal version, a positivist version, a Marxist version, and so forth. There has even been a certain amount of playful but respectful debunking of the curate of Dolores in modern historical novels (e.g., Ibargüengoitia 1982; Meyer 1989; Villalpando César 2000). Overall, however, Hidalgo has remained a highly positive, even sacralized figure, having been nuanced and humanized rather than fatally ridiculed and undermined.[11] The controversies swirling around his figure involve whether

---

10. About a decade after the publication of Riva Palacio's work came a masterful synthesis of its arguments by the writer, public intellectual, and educator (founder of the Universidad Nacional Autónoma de México) Justo Sierra Méndez, eventually published as *Evolución política del pueblo mexicano* (1940), which placed independence along the bumpy evolutionary trajectory defined by Sierra's liberal-positivist ideology.

11. Terán points out that we do not even have an authentic life-image of the priest, although representations of him have tended to converge to something like the description offered by Lucas Alamán (who knew him). Judging by the iconography displayed on the

he envisioned independence for Mexico or something short of it; his role in instigating, passively approving, or being swept along by the violence of the movement he unleashed; the genuineness of the recantation he made before his execution by the royalists in July 1811; whether he really had any sort of agrarian reform program in mind for rural Mexico; why he did not capture, or at least besiege, Mexico City when he had the opportunity in late 1810; whether his ideological stance was more influenced by Enlightenment thinking or a more traditional Catholic and particularly Spanish political framework, and so forth.

MEXICAN SCHOLARSHIP OF THE LATER TWENTIETH CENTURY (A BRIEF ACCOUNT)

The ludic deconstruction of Father Miguel Hidalgo y Costilla, and especially the last question—about the intellectual roots of his rhetoric and actions—point in the direction of a more serious reevaluation of the ideological elements in the Mexican independence drama, starting with the curate of Dolores and rippling outward to encompass the very meaning of emancipation and the state- and nation-building processes it kicked off. Here the divergence between Hispanophone and Anglophone historiographies emerges clearly: many of the Mexican historians of Mexican independence still privilege the realm of political thought, more in keeping with a frankly idealist and (high) text-based tradition, while the English speakers have moved into the most granular, archive-based peasant and subaltern studies, economic history, and the analysis of social structures, more in line with British and North American social history. So much is this the case that in a recent essay, one of the most accomplished of the younger Mexican historians of the era, Alfredo Ávila, could write that "the processes of Hispanic American independence are a theme for political history" whose social and economic aspects "may not be related in a direct fashion to emancipation [from Spain]."[12] In keeping with this central

---

cover of Terán and Páez (2004), some artists have felt he looked a bit like the vampire in Murnau's *Nosferatu*.

12. Ávila (2004). This entire approach, which dominates much of the recent work on Spanish American and Mexican independence by Mexican historians, seems predicated on the large theoretical assumption (seldom questioned by the authors) of the autonomy of the political realm. But aside from its symbolic resonances—that is, what politics says about other aspects of society, such as social class, ideas of community, the gender system, and so forth—political processes cannot just be *about themselves*; they must be about *something*, especially since they configure forms of state power, power whose end is surely to accomplish something other than politics itself.

concern, if many later nineteenth-century Liberal historians assimilated independence to the French Revolution, a major development in Mexican historical writing on the period since the 1950s has been the disentanglement of French Revolutionary ideology (and Enlightenment influences more generally) from the grand narrative of independence (for a different account, see Maniquis, Martí, and Pérez 1989), but mostly within a framework of high politics, constitutionalism, and the birth of liberalism, and so forth, rather than social history. There have been, however, some other tendencies in evidence in recent work, including studies of Hispanic political culture (e.g., the late François-Xavier Guerra's influential work [1993]), electoral behavior under the aegis of the 1812 Constitution of Cádiz (Antonio Annino, for example), and more socially and locally oriented studies of political participation at the midelite level and below it (e.g., Virginia Guedea, Marta Terán, Juan Ortiz Escamilla, Carlos Herrero Bervera, and others, all discussed below).

It seems fair to date the important revisionist current in interpreting the intellectual framework of the insurgency from the work of the philosopher Luis Villoro (1953; revised repeatedly until 1983).[13] In his study of ideological processes in what he called the independence "revolution," Villoro introduced (or reintroduced, or developed) three major aspects of the insurgency. First and most important, he stressed the Christian, as opposed to the liberal Enlightenment, roots of Miguel Hidalgo's thought, placing his ideas within a specifically Spanish legal-political tradition, both while he was an educational reformer in his earlier career and later as an insurgent leader. Second, Villoro insisted that the events of 1810 were inexplicable without reference to the broader Spanish world's political crisis of 1808, an argument taken up and expanded by Ernesto de la Torre Villar (1964, 1982) in his studies of the insurgency's political processes and the constitution making that accompanied them. While earlier writers (e.g., Alamán) had acknowledged this, Villoro and those who came after him laid the groundwork for studies of an imperial political crisis beginning in 1808 (or even earlier, depending upon the author) that played itself out in different ways in the different "kingdoms" of which the Spanish monarchy was composed. Third, Villoro emphasized horizontal, or class, conflicts within the society of New Spain, rather than vertical ones between peninsular-born Spaniards and Mexican-born Creoles, even if his "classes" look more like ancien régime estates than the classes of a more orthodox Marxist social anatomy.[14] The major pro-

---

13. My treatment of the older generation of Mexican independence historians, from Villoro on, owes a good deal to the guidance offered in Guedea and Avila (in press).

14. One of the odder flowerings of Marxist thought as applied to Mexican independence was the work of the Soviet historian M. S. Alperovich (1967), based exclusively on printed

tagonists in Villoro's version were the middle-class professionals—above all, lawyers—who supported independence, while the mass of the population functioned as a sort of underpainting upon which the main action was sketched. Other major scholars have carried forward this line of inquiry, two of the best known (Lemoine Villicaña 1965; Herrejón Peredo 1984, 1985) focusing their energies not on Hidalgo, but on his capable sometime lieutenant José María Morelos y Pavón, and working within a distinctly nationalist framework. Taken together these studies, although they certainly gave Father Hidalgo and the other early insurgent leaders their due, effected the salutary blurring of the origins of independence between the insurgency itself and other political processes, although the emphasis was still on the political realm.

Notwithstanding its relatively recent publication, the generously scaled study of the late French scholar François-Xavier Guerra (whose work exists only in a Spanish edition published in Mexico) has been influential in reframing much of the discussion of Mexican independence as one case of a more general political process within a wider Spanish world, and along a more extended temporal trajectory. Influenced strongly by the sort of post-Annaliste French historical tendency in which he came to maturity as a scholar (but having been trained more in the Annales tradition himself), and especially by the work of François Furet, a historian of the French Revolution, Guerra's *Modernidad e independencias* (1993) concentrated on the disintegration of the Spanish monarchy and the development of forms of modern political sensibility. In his scenario, metropolitan Spain is the avatar of political modernity, the American kingdoms (rather than "colonies") the redoubt of forms of traditional corporate conservatism, and the entering wedge the Bourbon Reforms of an enlightened absolutist state—rational, bureaucratic, efficient, dirigiste, and so forth. This interpretation goes even further toward displacing from center stage the movements led by Hidalgo, Morelos, and other insurgent priests, provincial toughs, and pettifogging lawyers, viewing them almost as mistakes, but ones that nonetheless provided a breach for the consolidation of independence when a legitimacy vacuum opened in the Spanish world in 1808. Guerra saw the incipient processes of political modernization carried forward in the New World, further-

---

sources (with the exception of some Russian foreign ministry documents). Although he claimed to make "the Mexican people" the central actor in the story of an aborted proletarian revolution that abolished a feudal regime without constructing viable institutions in its place, Alperovich in fact made a great many a priori assumptions about popular motives and aspirations that led him astray. It was no accident that the first items listed in his "Fuentes y bibliografía" section, even ahead of archival documents, were the works of Engels and Marx.

more, through the spread of Benedict Anderson's (1991) "print capitalism," the politicization of people through print media that allowed them to imagine an incipient national community. This facilitated the diffusion of political debate and knowledge through large sectors of the population even outside cities, and the opening at least of a truncated public sphere whose precocious beginnings in the late eighteenth and nineteenth centuries were elaborated upon even more lovingly by the Argentine historical sociologist Carlos Forment (2003). Placing as it did such emphasis on the realm of high politics and monarchy-wide political culture, Guerra's volume of essays (for such it was) was preceded, accompanied, and followed by fundamental and detailed research into constitution making, parliamentary and electoral behaviors, and the reception of the 1812 Spanish Constitution in the Spanish colonies by Nettie Lee Benson (1966, 1992), the Italian scholar Antonio Annino (e.g., 1995a, 1995b), the Spanish historian (and historian of Spain) Manuel Chust Calero (e.g., 2001, and several coedited anthologies), Alfredo Ávila (2002), and other very adept historians. Similar ideological struggles took place within the intellectual elite of the Mexican Catholic Church, always the handmaiden of the Spanish colonial regime and therefore tied to it in a particularly symbiotic fashion. The attempt at least among the upper clergy to accommodate political modernity in some way has been analyzed through the discursive analysis of sermons by Brian Connaughton (2003) and Carlos Herrejón (2003); at a biographical level this has been done for a major insurgent churchman from Oaxaca by Ana Carolina Ibarra (1996).

This heady mix of the history of ideas, the genealogies of modernity, and political culture has been leavened within the last decade or so by works of other Mexican historians that tend to reduce the scale of inquiry, not so much to dispute the formulations of Guerra and others by dismantling them at the microhistorical level, but to confirm them within regional and local frameworks. To a social historian such as myself, these are among the most interesting studies to have been produced on Mexican independence in recent years. Although some of them still hew to the line of political history, albeit within more limited spaces, they provide a good deal of insight into the ways in which provincial elites, common people, and even indigenous villagers lived the independence process and thought about politics. Among the best of these studies are those of Moisés Guzmán Pérez on the insurgent government of Father Miguel Hidalgo in Valladolid (today Morelia) (1996) and the rump rebel congress of Zitácuaro (1994); José Antonio Serrano Ortega's (2001) on political processes in the key central Mexican state (and silver mining center) of Guanajuato; Juan Ortiz Escamilla's (1997) research on the response of indigenous villages to the military realities of the protracted insurgency (1810–1821) itself; Carlos Herrero Bervera's (2001) microhistorical study of the social composition of insurgent forces in three provincial "case studies" and the great Mexican capital; and Claudia Guarisco's (2003) book on the changing political sensibilities of Indian communities in the Valley of Mexico. Guarisco demonstrates, in ways similar to the work of U.S. scholars Peter Guardino and Michael Ducey, the acquisition of new political idioms and burgeoning ideas of citizenship among the most humble people in the colony and new nation. Interestingly, there has been a series of shorter works published by the economic historian Antonio Ibarra Romero (1995, 2000a, 2002, 2003a) that cast much light on the popular political culture and tradition of dissidence that has, as we shall see in the next sections, drawn the attention more of Anglophone than Mexican historians. Although not himself an "insurgentologist," Ibarra Romero's studies have dealt subtly with themes dear to the hearts of those who are: patterns of rumor and the projection of political conspiracies, crime and dissidence, and the relationship of the private lives of common people with political turmoil. Finally, the doyenne of Mexican historians producing this sort of socially tinted political history is Virginia Guedea. She works like a social historian in the sense that she takes the social location of historical actors seriously, stays at a level of very fine granularity in terms of her research, and is not reluctant to deploy the detailed data she rummages from archives. In a series of fine works Guedea has investigated Mexico City's famous secret society of Los Guadalupes (1992), which organized proinsurgency propaganda, spied on royalist defenses, and provided material aid to the rebels; worked up a virtual *Who's Who* of insurgent leaders (1995); and given us a detailed study of a key area of insurgent-royalist military conflict, the Llanos de Apan (1996), during the height of the armed rebellion (1810–1816).[15]

---

15. It is interesting to speculate whether the professionalization of Mexican historians, and with it the transition from the older belle-lettristic dominance of public intellectuals, litterateurs, journalists-turned-historians, and provincial amateurs that prevailed in the writing of the country's history well into the twentieth century disposed historical scholars to be more "objective" about Mexican history, less prone to the acting out or vindication of political programs and nationalist myth making in the pages of their books. Today many professional academic historians receive their advanced graduate training outside the country (primarily in France, Britain, or the United States), or from one of a limited number of elite degree-granting institutions within Mexico (such as El Colegio de México, the National Autonomous University, and various research centers). Enrique Florescano, in fact, has suggested that history as an academic discipline in Mexico has become *over*professionalized, creating a "distorted" version of the country's history at odds with the needs of its nationalist psyche and collective memory (Florescano 2006, esp. 366ff).

Chapter 4   145

ANGLOPHONE HISTORIOGRAPHY:
THE FIRST GENERATION

Anglophone scholarship on the Mexican independence movement presents a quite different profile from that authored by Mexican historians, although there is some hint of a rapprochement in recent years. The work of United States Mexicanists has shifted over the last decades to an approach more in keeping with recent styles of social and cultural history, although work in this new tendency has not yet been plentiful. American and British scholarship has responded to some extent to intellectual and political trends external to the discipline of history itself. Among these has been the rise of interest in Latin American studies in general (and in Mexico in particular) in academic settings, partially under the impulse of U.S. government funding of area studies centers after 1960 or so. The growth of peasant studies, influenced by academic and policy concerns about Third World economic development, and the response of a generation of scholars to America's Vietnam experience and what it said about colonialism, national liberation movements, decolonization, and postcolonialism have also had their impact. The major changes, however, have occurred in response to trends internal to history as a discipline, including the consolidation of economic history, the recession of biography as a genre of scholarly writing (but not as a form of history writing for educated lay readers), and the refinement of social and the advent of cultural history. Along with these trends have come the revalorization of politics and ideological productions as discursive frameworks that not only organize social competition and conflict, but also betray deeper social meanings (a point of some convergence with what Hispanophone historians have been doing), and the development of subaltern studies.

Anglophone historians have long had an intense interest in the history of Mexico, perhaps more so than in any other country of Latin America. In academic settings in Britain, Canada, Australia, and the United States, if colleges and universities have any historian of Latin America at all (which most do), they are likely to have a Mexicanist, then after that possibly a Brazilianist or an Andeanist.[16] It is fair to say that this interest

16. Short of going over lists of history faculty in all British, Canadian, American, and Australian institutions of higher learning and adding up the numbers, there is no way to test this assertion statistically. As a first approximation, however, I added up the numbers of all the lists of regional and thematic groupings into which the members of the Conference on Latin American History, the largest professional association of Latin American historians in the United States, are distributed. Mexico presents by far the largest list, with 303 of 783 total members. Since there are over 1,300 names on the lists, one must assume that there is a good deal of double and even triple counting. Still, the dominance of the Mexican his-

found its wellsprings and much of its continuing impulse in imperial(ist) concerns and ideologies dating from the nineteenth-century scramble among Western European powers for hegemony over the fragments of the Spanish and Portuguese empires, in some cases in the hope of territorial acquisition, and in later concerns with stable environments for commercial markets and foreign investment. In the case of the United States it has also been tinted with the concerns of ideological affinity for one of our "sister republics," and by intellectual, national security, and economic interests in the fate of Mexico's protracted and dramatic state- and nation-building processes. This engagement has bred an enormous but uneven literature whose prehistory goes back as far as the eighteenth century in the case of the British, then to a host of English-speaking travelers in the decades following independence. In the case of the North Americans, this interest can be traced back to writers of the early and mid-nineteenth century (e.g., W. H. Prescott, H. H. Bancroft, and others, and somewhat further afield, even Washington Irving), and there were some important early personal memoirs dealing with Mexican independence itself (e.g., Joel R. Poinsett 1824). While the history of the conquest of Mexico has been an enduring theme among Anglophone historians, and that of the colonial period a major focus of interest, during the twentieth century U.S. historians have been more captivated by the Mexican Revolution and its political implications, with the British following suit in this. In more recent decades scholars on both sides of the Atlantic have become increasingly occupied with the nineteenth century, most especially the apparently chaotic but traditionally understudied period between independence and Porfiriato (ca. 1821–1876), including the early republican period, the Reform, and the French Intervention and its aftermath.

The Mexican independence movement obviously formed a watershed between the colonial period and the republican era, but what sort of watershed it was can still be debated. It has never been clear (*pace* my remarks above on early nineteenth-century Mexican writers) whether the decade 1810–1821 constitutes the end of the colonial regime or the beginning of the modern era, or how its internal dynamics illuminate endings and beginnings. As a social process itself, the Mexican struggle for independence is really very murky in many respects. Nor did its authors—the priests, military men, and rural chieftains who were the most visible political actors—have the intellectual background, the time, the inclination (apparently), or the longevity to produce works of political

---

tory field (as compared with 203 for the Andean area, 134 for Brazil, and so forth) is quite obvious. The numbers were compiled from the Conference on Latin American History *Membership Directory*, 2004.

thought parallel to those growing out of, or antecedent to, other major modern political upheavals. Until comparatively recent years the same was true of the chaotic, violence-ridden politics of the early republican period (1821–1867). The process of Mexican independence has proved the object of some attention by Anglophone historians over recent decades, but to a limited degree. One has the impression, in fact, that the history of the independence movement is a tar baby that few scholars have wished to embrace.

Let me cite but one prominent example of an Anglophone historian whose work illustrates these problems. Although our understanding of the late colonial and early national periods would be greatly impoverished without the writings of the British scholar David A. Brading, one of the most accomplished historians of Mexico, Anglophone or Hispanophone, he has worked *around* the Mexican independence movement rather than addressing it squarely (Van Young 2007a). One of his seminal contributions to Mexican historiography has been as the chief architect of the "Age of Revolution" periodization in which the century 1750–1850 is taken, if not as a unit, then certainly as a long stretch whose continuities and changes are best seen as mutually defining phases. Brading's writings have made what previously seemed an all but impermeable barrier between colony and nation rather porous for certain purposes. In a trilogy of works (Brading 1985, 1991, 2001) he has developed the powerful idea of Creole patriotism, essentially a class ideology with loud nationalist overtones that could never form the basis of inclusive nationalism, and which proved substantially incompatible with nineteenth-century liberalism. The central issue in much of Brading's work is how Spanish American thinkers, in the process of Creole self-fashioning, saw themselves in relation to the Old World, to the native peoples of the New World, and to the large historical meaning of the entire imperial/colonial enterprise. He has portrayed early nineteenth-century ideologues such as Fray Servando Teresa de Mier and Carlos María de Bustamante as champions of a Catholic republicanism and insurgent Creole nationalism poised midway between radical anticlericalism and the Hispanic conservatism articulated most notably by Lucas Alamán. Brading has aptly compared Mier and Bustamante to the Slavophiles of prerevolutionary Russia. But in his grand mapping of intellectual genealogies, the independence struggle appears mainly as a nursery for ideologies seeded in the Bourbon half of the "Age of Revolution" and flowering in the national half. Echoing what Brading has done, some of the most interesting recent work that does deal with the insurgency, especially in terms of political culture, treats it as a bridge or transition between the late colonial period and early republican Mexico rather than as an object of central importance in and of itself (although for a contrary view, see Taylor 1985).

Judging by what has been published, there is still more interest in the preinsurgency period and the political sequelae of independence than in the independence movement itself, considered narrowly as stretching between 1808 and 1821. The interest in the early republican period, particularly from the point of view of politics, ideology, and civil strife—the fascination with federalism, for example—was a theme of deep interest for Mexican scholars long before the Anglophones turned their attention to it relatively recently. Political life in the young republic, mostly concentrating on "high politics," the activities and ideological discourse of elites, formal institutional and electoral politics, and so forth, has thus been well served by the work of such Anglophone writers as Brading, Timothy Anna (1990, 1998), Linda Arnold (1988), Nettie Lee Benson (1966), Michael Costeloe (1986, 1993), Stanley Green (1987), Charles Hale (1968), Jaime E. Rodriguez O. (1989, 1994, 1998, whom, although he writes and publishes in both English and Spanish, I have for purposes of this essay considered an Anglophone historian), and Richard Warren (2001), among others.

With few exceptions, the newer trends in social and cultural history have bypassed the era of the independence wars themselves in favor of ostensibly "sexier" themes, such as religious sensibility, ethnic relations, the history of the family, women, and gender, public ritual and celebratory life, and so forth (e.g., Beezley, Martin, and French 1994, and Chapter 3 in this volume). The reasons for the failure by Anglophone scholars, with few exceptions, to apply new approaches to a theme of traditional attraction for historians of Mexico are not entirely clear. Perhaps it is because Anglophone writers have felt that with the Spanish imperial crisis anatomized, the biographies of many of the great figures written, and the political and military history in large measure mapped out, there is little interesting ground left to explore in the period of the independence wars themselves; in other words, that we already know it all. What this boils down to is an implicit assertion by historians of the independence process that only politics in the narrower sense (and in the public realm, at that, which I have discussed briefly above) was what really mattered in the period. Thus if social history is simply history with the politics left out, as the English historian George Trevelyan quipped many years ago, then putting politics to one side in a primarily political process leaves little for the social or cultural historian to do. Nor has the concept of political culture, encompassing the fundamental substratum of thinking about public life (even below the most local-level processes), the basic rules of the game (about the legitimacy of violence, for example), what people expect to gain from political participation (the allotment of social goods, including nonmaterial ones), and what politics *means* to people (about place and history, for instance, or about gender roles), made a successful jump to work on the period, for the most part (with some exceptions noted below). By its perceived nature, therefore, the independence struggle has lent itself to the tradition of heroic biography and political narrative still so much a part of the Anglophone approach to the history of Mexico, and of Latin America more generally, until sometime in the 1960s (Van Young 1985), so that the social and cultural history already very fashionable among English-speaking historians of Europe and the United States were slow to make their appearance.

A second source of the Anglophone neglect of Mexican independence may have been the conflict's absence from the large-scale works of comparative historical sociology that have often stimulated questions, at least in a diffuse sort of way, about periods, themes, or events; examples would be the works of Barrington Moore, Jr. (1966), Theda Skocpol (1979), Jack Goldstone (1991), and Sidney Tarrow (1994), to mention only a few. There were two reasons for this exclusion, as I noted in my own book on Mexican independence (Van Young 2001c). The first is that the former Ibero-American colonies were long marginalized from Atlantic-world thinking about processes of state formation and nation building. Their history was regarded more as an effect than a cause, since the historical narrative of modernity was thought to have unfolded outward from the Euro-Atlantic center (à la world-systems theory) rather than inward from the periphery. Studies of social and political processes in the core were therefore privileged over those in the fringes. A second reason is that most classical theories of political struggle and social upheaval, even when they are not explicitly Marxist, derive their explanatory power from models of class conflict that can be applied only incompletely and with some difficulty to the ethnically and culturally divided colonial societies of Spanish America. Still, there is enough English-language historical writing on Mexican independence, considered in its more restricted sense, to form a solid and visible cluster or point of crystallization in what British and U.S. scholars have written on Mexico during the period 1750–1850. Furthermore, social and cultural history as styles of inquiry and interpretation have not been uninfluential in Anglophone writing on Mexican independence over the last three or four decades, even if much of this scholarship is actually concerned more with the "socialization of politics," or at most with political culture, than with social actors, subaltern agency, or forms of symbolic expression.

To begin at the most general level, there have been a substantial number of synoptic histories of the Latin American independence movements published by Anglophone historians since 1960 or so, including (but hardly limited to) those by Peggy Liss (1983), John Lynch (1986), Richard Graham (1994), Jay Kinsbruner (1994), Lester Langley (1996), and most recently Jaime E. Rodríguez O. (1998), all of which take the Mexican case into account seriously. Indeed, that one can speak of Mexico's independence movement as a "case" at all—that is, as one exemplar of a larger class of phenomena with which it shares certain similarities but also differs in important respects—may be one of the major contrasts between English-language writing on the period and the enormous and rich body of scholarship produced by Mexican historians over nearly two centuries. Yet it is quite striking how little attention has been paid to this great political upheaval, which took place at the very dawn of the era of the nation-state, by theory builders who have devoted themselves to trying to understand processes of revolutionary change in the early modern and modern world, or of state and nation building.[17] In addition to the two factors mentioned already, part of the reason for this neglect may be the thinness of the fundamental historiography on Mexican independence itself, in terms of the basic social, economic, and even cultural themes and research that might lend themselves to synthesis and interpretation by the more sociologically minded scholar.

Anglophone interest in Mexican independence was first represented by biographies of the lives of the great heroes of the movement, among them W. S. Robertson's on Agustín de Iturbide (1952), John A. Caruso's collective portrait (1954), Hugh M. Hamill, Jr.'s on Miguel Hidalgo y Costilla (1966), and Wilbert H. Timmons's on José María Morelos (1970), as well as a group of mostly still unpublished biographies of independence-era figures who later came to prominence in republican politics, done as doctoral dissertations during the 1930s, 1940s, and 1950s at the University of Texas at Austin (and among more recent studies see, for example, Vincent 2001). But by the 1960s and 1970s the reaction against the biographical tradition in North American academic history pushed the approach of those historians working on Mexico more into the channels of social history as mapped out by European historians. The best of the older biographies, Hugh Hamill's (1966) work on Father Miguel Hidalgo's rebellion, is less a biography, actually, than an eclectic work combining intellectual, social, and political history to examine a relatively brief but pivotal historical moment, and has proved foundational in the Anglophone historiography of independence. It traces the career of the parish priest who initiated the independence struggle by heading a salon

---

17. For a discussion of why this may be so, see Van Young (2001c, 1–36). One obvious exception has been Benedict Anderson, whose seminal work *Imagined Communities* (1991) discusses Mexican and Spanish American independence at some length, importing them to the very center of modern nation-building processes, but whose treatment seems misguided in many ways (for critiques of Anderson, see Lomnitz-Adler 2001; Van Young 2006b).

conspiracy and then a massive, armed proletarian uprising against the Spanish colonial regime in New Spain between September 1810 and the spring of the following year, when he was captured, tried, defrocked, and executed. The study still warrants a deep reading, and exemplifies the transition between the older biographical tradition and the newer social history tendency. With his deep empiricism, resolute resistance to comparisons or sociological generalizing about revolutions (perhaps a reaction to reading too much Crane Brinton [1965] as a lad), and his slant in favor of biography and the chances of historical accident, Hamill essentially portrayed Father Miguel Hidalgo as a naive bungler who let an abortive social revolution by discontented, humble brown people overwhelm his ambitions for independence and political enfranchisement for Creole (white) Mexicans. Despite its liberal undertones, in fact, Hamill's interpretation of Mexican independence bears a strong resemblance to Lucas Alamán's, although some of Hamill's conclusions—for example, that Indian peasants were "too ignorant and disorganized to present a solid front" (p. 218), or that a strong impulse toward total independence was present in the movement from its very inception—have been disputed or even overturned.

A few years after Hamill, Timothy Anna (1978) provided the first thorough modern treatment of the fall of the colonial regime on a temporally broad canvas covering the entire decade of the Mexican insurgency, albeit focused almost exclusively on Mexico City. In this sense it was the inverse of Hamill's study, since it avowedly focused on the response of the royalist regime to Hidalgo's uprising, from top downward and center outward, asserting that the popular insurgency had already been amply studied (which it had not, as the recent works glossed below amply demonstrate). Anna's was one of the first works to make use of an extremely wide gamut of primary sources, including military and political records generated by the colonial authorities in Mexico City, collected in the Mexican national archive, the Archivo General de la Nación; documents from the municipal authorities of the capital, housed in a separate archive; and correspondence and other records from the Spanish archives in Madrid.[18]

18. Using similar sources, plus a large collection of contemporary newspapers, travelers' accounts, records of congressional debates, and the work of historians such as Alamán, Bustamante, and Mier, Anna was subsequently to produce an important pair of books (1990, 1998) on the young republic, the first on the career of Agustín de Iturbide, royalist officer turned "liberator" of Mexico and then first (short-lived) Emperor, and the second on national politics in the period 1821–1835. An unpublished essay by Michael Burke (1980) foreshadowed much of this later work with its emphasis on the social composition of the popular insurgency and its imaginative use of criminal records from the Ramo Criminal of the Archivo General de la Nación, but was never expanded upon by its author, to my knowledge.

He dealt with the issue of why the Spanish colonial regime in Mexico imploded so quickly between about 1816 and 1821, suggesting that the struggle for independence was not so much won by the insurgent coalitions as lost by the royalist regime because, for various reasons, it let its authority be fatally compromised in imposing its wartime measures. In Anna's view Mexican independence was neither the outcome of a revolutionary impulse on the part of Hidalgo and other insurgent chieftains, nor a counterrevolutionary one on the part of a frightened Creole elite reacting violently to the revival in 1820 of the liberal Spanish constitution of 1812, but a compromise solution preserving elements of liberalism within a monarchical framework. At about the same time Christon Archer, in his *The Army in Bourbon Mexico* (1977), described both the military culture of the late colonial period, and the careers of many of the Spanish officers who nearly defeated the movement and subsequently came to play roles in the political life of the new republic after 1821.

The 1970s and 1980s saw the advent in American and British historical writing on Mexico of a new regional history, heavily economic in emphasis, which had always been practiced among Mexican historians themselves, one shrunken subgenre of which reached its apotheosis and codification as "microhistory" in the work of Luis González (1968). This pushed research on Mexican independence in a new direction and was to eventuate in what we might call the provincialization, localization, and eventually the subalternization of work on collective political violence in general and the independence movement in particular.[19] Mexico seemed to many of us to be made up until quite late into its national history of an ill-integrated patchwork of localities and regions, which could explain why economic development, national consolidation, and a nationalist sensibility came so late to the country, and which brought into question large explanatory frameworks predicated on a more or less unified national space, political culture, market, and so forth.

Heavily influenced by this trend, following soon after Anna and in part as a reaction to his *chilango*-centric approach (*chilango* is a slang and slightly deprecatory term for a native of Mexico City), came Brian Hamnett's very smart *Roots of Insurgency* (1986), in many respects the intellectual forerunner of much that came after it in the study of resistance, rebellion, and revolution. Much broader in scale than the work of Hamill or Anna, Hamnett's book embraced the entire period 1750–1824, tracing the long-term origins and the course of the Mexican insurgency in several regions outside the capital, principally Puebla, Guadalajara,

---

19. On regionality and regional studies in Mexico, see Van Young (1992d), and Chapter 5 in this volume.

Michoacán, and Guanajuato. Wrote Hamnett himself in his Conclusion (p. 206): "Traditional histories of the Independence movements have focussed [sic] largely on the national dimension and have dealt considerably with both ideology and Creole alienation. The approach adopted in this present study has been regional and local." Although in his treatment of causation for collective behavior Hamnett never actually advanced much beyond a fairly simple model of deprivation theory, he did acknowledge at least in passing that other factors probably played a role in fueling popular insurgency. In this regard he stressed among other themes status loss, threats to the identity of small rural communities, agricultural commercialization, the breakdown of conflict-resolution mechanisms, and very localized grievances of long-simmering nature. The crisis of Spanish imperial legitimacy that reached a head in 1808 opened an opportunity for local elites to coalesce around themselves fairly frail and temporary cross-class and cross-ethnic alliances in which local impulses were translated into colony-wide forces that eventually toppled the royalist regime, only to fall back again with independence into a Hobbesian chaos of small-scale conflicts and grievances. In this important study one began to see the explicit emergence of a theme that has occupied much of the attention of Anglophone historians of independence since Hamnett: the independence movement(s) as peasant rebellions and popular insurgencies. Furthermore, a theoretical framework for the empirical findings, only hinted at in Anna's study in a few allusions to Max Weber (not actually cited in the bibliography) or Carl Friedrich, became in Hamnett interesting if still embryonic discussions of such phenomena as the mobilizing potential of the Virgin of Guadalupe (based on the ideas of the anthropologist Victor Turner), Eric Hobsbawm's work on social banditry, or theorists of counterinsurgency in modern guerrilla warfare.

John Tutino's thoughtful and highly theoretical intervention, *From Insurrection to Revolution in Mexico* (1986), constitutes a transitional link between an older, politics-centered narrative and a newer revisionist trend, even though it was published in the same year as Hamnett's book (and, incidentally, as Alan Knight's monumental study *The Mexican Revolution* [1986]). Tutino's work was more overtly theoretical in its attack and grander in its ambitions than Hamnett's, since it embraced two hundred years of rural rebellion in Mexico, from the mid-eighteenth century to 1940, although the longest, most empirically original, and best-developed part, in my view, relates to the era of independence. He relied on Barrington Moore (the Moore of 1978's *Injustice* rather than of the better known *Social Origins of Dictatorship and Democracy* [1966]) for a discussion of how authority and legitimacy were maintained or eroded between provincial elites and peasants, prompting concerted action here, local jacqueries there. Theda Skocpol (1979) made an appearance in Tutino's discussion of intraelite rivalries and political crisis, and Eric Wolf (1966, 1969)—whose formulations he critiqued, but whose lead he nonetheless followed—regarding the disruptive effects of agrarian capitalism in the countryside. The book sets up an interesting sociological matrix of four factors whose covarying configurations at different places and times accounted for the forms, intensity, and duration of peasant protest, and the effects that such rural collective action might have on national-level politics. The four factors are, first, material conditions—basically whether peasants were economically prosperous or poor, or something in between; second, autonomy—the degree to which rural people, as individuals or in communities, controlled their own fates (or thought they did); third, security—the predictability of their incomes and capacity to meet subsistence needs; and, fourth, mobility—peasants' possibilities for moving around to escape bad conditions, find work, exploit new lands, and so forth. The independent variable for Tutino is what he has called "agrarian compression," the cyclical advance and retreat of agricultural commercialization and the stresses this exerted on peasant communities, mediated by the four factors I have just outlined.

Despite all the high-concept sociologizing, therefore, the independence struggle was for Tutino no less a peasant rebellion than for Hamnett, induced by much the same pressures on labor, land, subsistence, community structure, and leadership capacity among villages that Hamnett identified for the late colonial period. Furthermore, Tutino's analysis shared several elements with Hamnett's. He identified the imperial crisis of 1808 as a triggering mechanism for popular protest, and intraelite competition as the essential weak spot in the structure of social and political control through which the magma of rural uprising erupted. One sees in both works, moreover, an emphasis on regional specificity (primarily the Bajío, but also Guadalajara, the Sierra Gorda, the Morelos lowlands, San Luis Potosí, and some other areas) as both an analytic tool and an explanatory framework for the failure of popular protest to coalesce ideologically into an agrarian reform program. But whereas Hamnett's emphasis (a natural outgrowth, one suspects, of his earlier writing on political questions in the Spanish Empire) was on the Mexican regions' attempt to pull away from the center, which was to show up after the achievement of independence as the struggle over federalism, and on insurgent and counterinsurgent warfare, Tutino's was on peasantness and on constructing a reasonable model of rural insurrection in broader theoretical terms. Hamnett's work was in a general way more historicist, Tutino's more sociological, with the attendant advantages and disadvantages of specifying and generalizing, respectively.

Chapter 4

THE SUBALTERNS ARRIVE

Having moved downward and outward in focus, from biography and the high politics of the metropolis or the colonial capital to peasants and regions, the most recent works devoted all or in large part to the Mexican independence struggle have added yet another layer, that of subaltern politics, as well as at least a nominal interest in culture. Here the object has been to explore, within the obvious (and not-so-obvious) limits of the available documentation (e.g., Chapter 6 in this volume), the collective and subjective experience of common people, mostly peasants, as political actors rather than objectified members of an economic category being acted *upon*. The basically structuralist approach of Hamnett, Tutino, and others (e.g., Knight 2002b, 283–331) is still there, but has been diluted rather than camouflaged by much attention to subaltern politics. There has also been a move away from the immediacies and contingencies of *histoire evenementielle*, whether embodied in heroic biography or even in broader studies, such as Hamill's and Anna's, and toward a long-term history of popular political practice and consciousness in keeping with the thumbnail definition of political culture I offered above, themes substantially alien to earlier works. Temporal frameworks have expanded so that the 1750–1850 period is taken in earnest, and the decade of the insurgency located as a blip, albeit a huge one, on a long trajectory of rural politics in which repertoires of coping mechanisms, peasant protest, and collective violence develop over generations. And it is with this approach that the figures of rural common people, most often airbrushed out of the *historia de bronce* or depicted merely as background to the main action, are painted back into the history of Mexican independence, emerging as the bearers of political traditions and agendas of their own that sometimes put them into alliance with elite nation builders, but very often into conflict with them.

Two recent books by Peter Guardino and another by Michael Ducey (both trained, not coincidentally, at the University of Chicago), all fine studies, exemplify these trends and likely foreshadow the tone of future works on peasant politics generally, and the Mexican independence struggle specifically. Primarily interested in illuminating the chaotic politics of early republican Mexico, both authors found they could not understand the peasantry's role in processes of nation making if they did not begin with the political forces unleashed by the independence struggle. Guardino's (1996) study of peasant disturbances in the state of Guerrero during the first half of the nineteenth century devotes only about forty pages directly to the period of the rebellion against Spain. His account actually fills in a good deal of the late colonial background of the region, however, and therefore qualifies as taking the 1750–1850 period in earnest. In so doing he lays down the main lines of his argument for the entire period. Specifically offering a critique of historical sociologists and anthropologists who have portrayed peasants as backward looking and reactive, or as natural anarchists, Guardino stresses peasant agency and engagement with politics on the national stage. He mostly discounts agrarian pressures as a motive for peasant participation in violence against the colonial regime in alliance with local elites, stressing instead the theme of political autonomy at the municipal level as a shared political agenda between humble rural people and their leaders. His argument substantially boils down to making the well-taken point that peasants exercised agency in politics; that is, that they made conscious choices aimed at maximizing their positions. Their putatively parochial vision extended to the national state, in Guardino's view, as a means to ensure traditional or even expanded forms of local autonomy.[20] In a second book (2005), on the state of Oaxaca, Guardino shifts the weight of the investigation to the late colonial period and the wars of independence, incorporating a comparison of popular politics, both rural and urban, within the state over the course of a century. Here the concern is more explicitly with political culture, so that collective violence recedes into the background somewhat. Center stage is occupied by the transformative power of new forms of political discourse, subaltern citizenship, and the window onto republican practices opened by the brief application at the local level of the liberal Spanish constitution of 1812, albeit still within an ethnically divided society.[21]

Michael Ducey's book (2004) bears considerable similarity to Guardino's two studies, but changes the venue to look at subaltern politics in the fascinating region known as the Huasteca, which embraces parts of the modern states of Veracruz, San Luis Potosí, Mexico, and Hidalgo, stretching from the tropical lowlands of the Gulf coast to the colder uplands of the central Mexican plateau. Like Guardino, Ducey is fully steeped in theoretical discussions about peasant agency, rural class alliances, and

20. Other relatively recent Anglophone studies that stress peasant agency and the engagement with, and influence upon, national politics by humble rural people include Mallon (1994), and Wells and Joseph (1996) for Mexico, and for Peru, Thurner (1997), Walker (1999), and Méndez (2005). It should also be noted that a major influence on many of these studies, although in some instances not explicitly cited, has been Benedict Anderson's (revised 1991) highly influential work, *Imagined Communities*; see note 4 above. The discussion of the works of Guardino and Ducey is based in part on recent reviews I have written of these books for scholarly journals.

21. For a critique of this position that minimizes the transformative power of the famous 1812 Constitution of Cádiz, and emphasizes instead the continuities in the political culture and repertoire of collective political violence in indigenous villages, see Van Young (2009a).

the problematics of nation building. He examines village riots in the region as responses to the "second colonization" imposed by the Bourbon Reforms of the period after about 1760, a series of fiscal, political, and economic measures concocted in ad hoc fashion in Spain to shore up the creaky structures of colonial domination and extract more revenues from the colonies. Ducey outlines the ways in which the prolonged guerrilla struggle during the decade 1810–1821 eroded old patterns of elite domination, introduced new idioms of politics and citizenship, and allowed for the emergence of new political entrepreneurs. Particularly careful to portray the local power struggles and odd cross-class alliances that prevent facile characterizations of postcolonial developments, he goes beyond 1821 to describe cycles of republican-era rural political violence, especially in 1836–1839 and during the so-called Caste War of the Huasteca, 1845–1850, which became entangled in unforeseen ways with the American invasion of the region during the Mexican-American War. Ducey concludes that, much as local peasant political actors may have taken into account the national scene, they did so as a means to achieve local ends: "The peasant utopia was based on the village, and when the peasants imagined the nation, they dreamed of creating a nation of pueblos" (p. 174).[22]

My own study of the popular sectors of the Mexican independence struggle (Van Young 2001c) takes culture, in works like Hamnett's and Tutino's a residual category of analysis that does not do much work, even more seriously, descending to a level of finer granularity in its use of primary sources (one recent critic finding it so granular in this respect that the narrative line is said to disappear almost completely: see Knight 2004, with a response in Van Young 2004a). One of the chief empirical contri-

---

22. A very valuable study paralleling in many ways the work of Guardino and Ducey (from a youngish scholar also trained at the University of Chicago), and complementing Timothy Anna's study of the royal government in the capital, is Richard Warren's *Vagrants and Citizens* (2001), which deals with popular politics in Mexico City during the insurgent decade and the first ten years of republican life. The book deals primarily with electoral behavior in municipal elections under the Spanish Constitution of 1812 and the first federal constitution in Mexico, the charter of 1824. Warren demonstrates that such elections were not necessarily just fig leafs, fictions invented to legitimate oligarchic rule within empty republican forms, but actually voiced the political inclinations of humble urban folk, just as public ceremonies intended as performative expressions of state power in fact provided occasions for popular groups to subvert allegiances to the prevailing regime, whether royal or republican. I have not devoted to Warren's book the attention it deserves in my main text because of lack of space. It should also be noted that a number of recent scholarly anthologies, some of them growing out of conferences, are devoted all or in part to the theme of Spanish American or Mexican independence. Among these (not an exhaustive list, to be sure) are Rodríguez O. (1989, 1992, 1994), Lynch (1994), McFarlane and Posada-Carbó (1999), Archer (2000, 2003), Uribe-Urán (2001), Thurner and Guerrero (2003), Cahill and Tovías (2006), and Doyle and Pamplona (2006).

butions of the work is the social profile of popular insurgents presented, in which statistical correlations are drawn among a series of variables, including age, civil status, occupation, and most importantly ethnicity, explaining in part a variable propensity to engage in specific patterns of collective political violence during the decade 1810–1821. Contrary to the conventional wisdom about the ethnic makeup of the insurgency, for example, the findings reveal that most of the rebels were indigenous people rather than mestizos, which runs against much of the still current national mythology about the independence movement. Peasant agency within the context of subaltern politics is still there, but it explicitly faces *away* from the politics of state and nation building, and resolutely *toward* the preservation of personal and collective identities linked to the maintenance of village communities as largely autonomous entities; in other words, it did not employ idioms of nationalism, or even protonationalism. Furthermore, the causal model for political action rests strongly upon a notion of culture as expressed in community integrity in the political and celebratory domains, and is less concerned with access to land within a materialist framework, which is what one still sees in the more recent Anglophone studies glossed above. Among other casualties of my findings are the accepted ideas that independence was substantially the outcome of a cross-ethnic, cross-class alliance iconically represented by the figure of the Virgin of Guadalupe; that peasant rebels acted only when mobilized by local or regional insurgent chieftains (*cabecillas*); that parish priests somehow "whipped up" proinsurgency sentiment among common people of color in the countryside; and that violence was consciously directed against native-born Spaniards in an instrumentalist rather than scapegoating fashion. In my study the faint outlines of common people and their political agendas are imported to the center of the story, filled in as robustly as possible, and foregrounded. This complicates considerably the rather Whiggish interpretation that because independence from Spain was finally achieved, it was what most ordinary people strove for.

Finally, we are seeing the revalorization of high politics at the level of the Spanish Atlantic world during the Napoleonic period embodied largely in the work of Jaime E. Rodríguez O. and a group of like-minded scholars and sometime collaborators, primarily in Mexico and Spain, among them Alfredo Ávila, Manuel Chust Calero, Virginia Guedea, Roberto Breña, and Antonio Annino (and see also Forment 2003; Adelman 2006). This trend parallels the subalternization and localization of politics on the ground in the Mexican insurgency. These tendencies are linked through the notion that common people in Spanish America knew and cared a good deal about efforts to reform the empire ("the monarchy" is favored in many of these works over "the empire," and "kingdoms" over "colonies" to describe the American components of the Spanish monarchy) in the late eighteenth century, and especially after 1808. They lived in an informationally saturated environment despite their limited literacy (see, e.g., Guerra 1993), this account asserts, and the brief enactment of local and empire-wide voting rights under the Spanish constitution of 1812 both politicized common people and provided a venue for the expression of their burgeoning sense of citizenship. Rodríguez O. has developed the argument in a number of works that insofar as Mexico was concerned, the initial political impulse of Creole leaders both in the country and as representatives at the Spanish parliaments during the period was to attain autonomy within a reformed imperial structure, not to strike out for independence. This program was legally and ideologically buttressed by long-established notions in Spanish political philosophy and practice of residual popular sovereignty, and the idea that the Spanish realms in the Americas were not in fact colonies but kingdoms coequal with the ancient units of the Spanish monarchy, to which the rights of Spanish citizens applied. On this view the Mexican insurgency was not at first an anticolonial war of national liberation, since Mexico was technically not a colony, and edged in the direction of independence only when autonomist reformers failed to prevail in overhauling the imperial political arrangement and the Bourbon monarch, Fernando VII, proved completely unconciliatory and rigid after his restoration in 1814.[23] The difference between this work and older studies about intraimperial politics during the crisis of the monarchy (Anna 1983; Hamnett 1985; Costeloe 1986) is that some of the scholars in this group have extended their attention not only to the mechanics and legalities of the Spanish empire, but to political culture and local politics, as well, although what one could call high politics still holds pride of place.[24]

---

23. In my reactionary fashion I tend to employ the term *empire* on the assumption that if something looks like a duck, walks like a duck, and quacks like a duck, it is a duck. Certainly there were important technical and political differences implied in the status of the overseas Iberian lands as kingdoms within a universal Spanish monarchy, but to my eye it is often (not always) analytically useful to refer to the New World polities as *imperial domains*.

24. Parallel to this development, the Anglophone historiography also saw the publication (mostly by North Americans, but also in some works by Europeans published in English) of a series of important, large-scale works in economic history—Coatsworth (1990), Jacobsen and Puhle (1986), Garner and Stefanou (1993), Ouweneel (1996)—clearly aimed at explaining, in part, the reasons for the fall of the colonial regime and the apparent structural weakness that plagued the new nation, and therefore bearing strongly but indirectly on the independence movement. Yet other Anglophone scholars have worked on the Mexican church up to, during, and after the 1810–1821 period (e.g., Brading 1994; Farriss 1968; Connaughton 2003; Taylor 1996), some on specific social groups within the population (e.g., Ladd 1976), and still others on the comparative aspects of Mexican and Anglo-

160   *Part II*

CONCLUSION

My necessarily brief overview of Mexican historians' views on their country's independence struggle bears out the truism that revolutions, especially when they give birth to new states, eventually generate their own mythologies, many of them embodied in officialist historical accounts; in the case of Mexico this has been called the *historia de bronce* (bronze history, from the use of bronze in casting statues of national heroes). New ruling groups need to make these large-scale social and political upheavals seem natural, heroic, legitimate, and just, while common people must make sense out of their experiences of internal war, social dislocation, and death. Postrevolutionary social institutions and practices—schools and curricula, most obviously, but also the mobilization of armies, the creation of public art, ceremonial occasions, symbolic expressions such as flags, the discourse of the political class, and so forth—collaborate to set the stamp of inevitability on the violent disappearance of the old regime and the emergence of the new. Great public convulsions inscribed in chaotic events, collective action, blood, and words are then reproduced generation after generation by guardians of the public memory, including politicians, teachers, writers, artists, and historians. Especially since the emergence of modern revolutionary nationalism in the late eighteenth-century Atlantic world, these social and political semiconfabulations have become tied to the fate of the great invented tribes we call nation-states. But while revolutionary mythologies create social memories of high specific gravity, they also tend to blur or efface others altogether, so that the act of creative remembering implies selective forgetting, as well. Political roads not taken are erased from the maps of officialist history, dissenting voices from the time silenced, inconvenient social groups airbrushed out of the picture or their actions reconfigured to conform to a less messy, heroic scenario. Thus the teleology of revolution comes to explain how and why the existing postrevolutionary reality came to be the only one possible, why it did not follow some other course, and how the present regime carries forward the revolutionary tradition.

Even critical social science study of revolutionary upheaval by historians and other scholars after the fact may be pressed into the service of what can be called "outcomism." This emphasis on outcomes would take the form, for example, of the apparently unimpeachable proposition that because nearly all of the Spanish American colonies had become inde-

---

American independence movements (e.g., Countryman and Deans-Smith 1983; Langley 1996) or among Spanish American liberation struggles (Domínguez 1980; Forment 2003; Adelman 2006).

pendent nation-states by the third decade of the nineteenth century, the winning of independence and the establishment of republican regimes in its wake were therefore the necessary outcomes of the struggles against Spanish dominion. It would follow from this that all social groups swept up in the struggle on the rebellious side were striving for that result; but this was not necessarily the case. To frame an analogy, simply because any number of people are going up the same escalator at Nordstrom's, and may even get off on the same floor, does not mean they are all headed toward the lingerie section, or home wares, rather than to the photography salon or the gift-wrapping counter. Revolutions are likely to be extremely complex events in which different groups of people, to say nothing of different individuals, engage in collective political violence for different reasons, nation making not necessarily foremost among them. One of the most promising trends in the recent historiography of Mexican independence, in evidence among both Hispanophone and Anglophone scholars, but having rather distinct disciplinary genealogies, is to question the pieties of the *historia de bronce* by foregrounding the role of humble people, examining what can be called political culture, and reopening questions about high politics, constitution making, and representative institutions. This certainly represents a change in the way the period has been treated over the long haul, and is a product of both the internal logic of research and of shifts in emphasis in the discipline.

The Anglophone historiography on Mexican independence does not demonstrate the somewhat thermometer-like relationship to contemporary public life and discourse that one finds in works produced by Mexicans themselves, at least up until the last two decades or so. Anglophone scholars are much more distanced from the changes in the political weather and cultural landscape that have impelled Mexican historians to reinterpret their own history in dialog with the times in which they write, albeit within fairly narrow limits. To invoke a homely colloquial expression, Anglophone historians have no dog in that fight, so that the impulse to unscramble its complications in terms of the political genealogies of present-day party alignments or policies, which has so motivated Mexican historians for two centuries, has not materialized among most American and British scholars. This is hardly surprising, and would hold true for all national historiographies when the writings of natives and foreigners are compared. If one were to look at the last century of writing by U.S. historians on the American Revolution and the early republic, for example, the swings from conservative, to liberal, to Marxist, and back again would be quite striking (think only of the corkscrewed trajectory from Henry Adams, to Charles Beard, to Gary Nash, and to Gordon Wood, among a host of others), as would the influence of the methodological and theoretical changes within the discipline of history itself. Another sign of this distancing is that recent U.S. writing on Mexican independence (substantial but hardly abundant), and on political upheaval in Mexican history more broadly (of which there is getting to be a good deal), tends to be more theoretical (or at least conceptual) in tone than its Mexican counterpart. One reason for this, I would suggest, is that for work on a relatively obscure corner of world history (or so it is thought by most mainstream historians in this country) to earn legitimacy in the North American academy, it must situate itself in relation to larger conceptual and/or comparative debates to which it may be seen to make a contribution. The Anglophone historians of Mexico have become adept at this, whether in regard to peasants, subaltern groups more generally, nation-building processes, political culture, or other issues that touch on Mexican independence and the construction of the new nation. While this repertoire of ideas has much explanatory power in itself, its deployment should therefore be viewed as a discursive strategy often having little if any resonance among Mexican historians, since they do not need to justify writing about the country's history. The result, as I have noted of Mexican and Anglophone historiography on colonial Mexico more generally (see Chapter 3 in this volume), is a significant gap between what the two communities of scholars are doing, and a truncation or muting of the dialog that would benefit both groups, although there are some signs that this is beginning to change.

The most fruitful approach to the continuing reevaluation of Mexican independence would probably include at least three elements. First, we need to define a sufficiently extended historical trajectory along which to place the events of 1808–1821 so that continuity and change can be delineated more clearly amidst the fog of dramatic twists and turns. My own candidate for such a periodization, and increasingly that of other historians of the later colonial and early national eras, embraces the century 1750–1850 (e.g., Van Young 1985, 2001a; Uribe-Urán 2001). Second, scholars of the period should adopt, in the words of John Coatsworth, "a cheerful eclecticism that endorses multiple, layered narratives of independence, its meaning, and its impact" (Coatsworth, personal communication). Methodologically, this would imply neither abandoning the archive for the reading room, nor the reading room for the archive. It would also entail application of the comparative method, not only in widening the vision of independence processes in Mexico to encompass a broader Spanish world in political crisis, as many Hispanophone historians of ideas and political culture have done, but also in employing the cross-case comparisons more typical of North American scholarship, even if this method has still not often been applied to this specific theme. Finally,

Hispanophone and Anglophone historians should enter into dialog with each other more, something that Jaime E. Rodríguez O., for example, a perfectly bicultural scholar who has made his way in the corridors of both academic worlds, has been urging for a number of years. This would mean that North Americans, in particular, earn the right not to be seen by their Mexican colleagues as arrogant carpetbaggers, and that the empirically rich, culturally informed, and intellectually distinct Mexican scholarship not be disdained by North Americans as insufficiently theorized in a very particular Durkheimian-Weberian social science tradition. The advent of the bicentennial decade of Mexican independence in 2010 (or 2008 if one prefers) has offered just such an opportunity for deepening and widening dialog, not just among professional historians, but among their respective reading publics, as well.

PART III

Theory and Methodology

CHAPTER 5

Doing Regional History
A Theoretical Discussion and Some Mexican Cases

In describing the geography of central Mexico to the Emperor Charles V, Fernando Cortés is said to have taken up a sheet of parchment, crumpled it in his hand, and thrown it down upon a table, telling his monarch that the country looked like "*un papel arrugado*" (a wrinkled piece of paper), a trope probably as recognizable to the newly subjugated indigenous people of Mesoamerica as it still is to us today. The varied and difficult topography of the country still strikes us forcefully after many millennia of continuous human occupation, even though its asperities have been softened somewhat by the modern technologies of transportation and communication, and the penetration of human settlement virtually to every corner of the republic. The comparatively large distances from one end of the country to the other (especially during the colonial period and the early nineteenth century, when Mexico reached its greatest extension) have compounded its physical characteristics to produce an enormously complex arrangement of climatological zones, microecologies, subcultures, and local histories. This luxuriant and confusing variety has played a central role in the evolution of Mexico's history and in the consciousness of Mexicans as portrayed in their politics, art, social thinking, and *mentalidad*.

One major form this looming geohistorical consciousness has taken in Mexican history, historiography, and national identity is a strong regional differentiation within the country. If one reads very far in the literature of recent decades on Mexican regional history, however, one quickly discovers an interesting fact: regions are like love—they are difficult to describe, but we know them when we see them. Why the lack of systematic definitions of a concept that has become so central to historical work on Mexico and Latin America as a whole, when scholars have long entrenched themselves so deeply over such theoretical constructs as feudalism, dependency, social class, race, and gender? The reason is clear enough. Most of us already think we know what a region is: it is the area we are studying at the moment. In practice this most often boils down to a city or town with a space around it—for example, the Puebla region, the Guadalajara region; while others are designated by some more general term not linked to a specific urban concentration—the Bajío, the Huasteca, the northwest, the Morelos sugar zone, and so on. This common usage has an implicit structure of categories that I will address at least obliquely below. The basic point is that with these simple mental images of polarized and nonpolarized space we already have the definitional elements of the concept of region, largely borrowed from central-place theory as developed by economic geographers. Yet apart from such a priori formulations we generally do not waste much time trying to clarify what we mean when we talk about geohistorical regions.[1] Thus we find ourselves as historians in the peculiar but not unfamiliar position of op-

---

1. Many—in fact *most*—works dealing with Mexican regional history do not specify what they mean by *region*, but rely on a kind of descriptive impasto to arrive at a set of limits. Allen Wells (1985), for example, in his classic work on the henequen industry, treats Yucatán as a single region, without attempting any conceptual justification for such a definition. This leads in turn into some apparent difficulties in dealing with what he must term intraregional economic differentiation (northwest versus southeast), but which in fact look more like interregional differentiation. Claude Morin (1979), in his empirically dense and stimulating work on Michoacán in the eighteenth century, acknowledges (p. 175) that the concept of region may mean something more to an economist than to a sociologist or geographer. He then opts to study his region as defined by political-administrative boundaries, which leads him into difficulties similar to those that beset Wells. In another recent study, Mark Wasserman (1984) employs the word *region* in one form or another twenty-one times in his first four pages, but defines the term (not wholly convincingly) as being congruent with the political borders of Chihuahua State. Joseph Love (1978), on the other hand, develops for Brazil an interesting treatment of regions based on what he calls uniform and nodal regions (i.e., formal and functional regions, respectively). Ultimately, he lays most stress (as one would expect of a political historian) on regions as parts of subnational political units, bouncing off each other like billiard balls, as opposed to their internal structures. For similar examples on a smaller scale, see Bernstein (1967) and Luis González (1982). In fairness to González, it should be noted that the late great historian demonstrated a long-standing interest in the "microhistory" of what he called *"terruños,"* or localities, rather than in larger entities or systems. On the other hand, González (1973, 37) acknowledged the relationship of local (regional) history to considerations of spatial structure when he wrote: "In critical history the basic [element] is time . . . In local history space is very important." On all these aspects, see Van Young (1981, 3–5; 1983, 5–61; 1984; 1992d). In U.S. historiography *region* is often replaced by *section*, and *regionalism* by *sectionalism*. Historian Richard White makes the point that U.S. history textbooks tend to allow a central role for regions and regionalism in their treatments of the period up to about 1900, then let them "begin to fade like disappearing ink" (White 1992, 1). I have substantially expanded this chapter from the original 1985 conference paper and subsequent published versions. Some of the new mate-

erationalizing a complex concept before defining it. But regions are hypotheses to be proven, and when we write regional history we should be attempting to do just that rather than describe already existing entities.

Despite this theoretical haziness, however, we see regions in Mexico everywhere we look, and in fact the geohistorical region and regionalism are central to the Mexican experience. This must mean that the concept has considerable utility for us. In fact, in the memorable phrase of Claude Lévy-Strauss, regions are "good to think." My method in this essay is to play with the idea of region in a hopefully useful way, to approach a definition of it, and to deal with some of its implications for the way we locate ourselves in space, time, and the social order. To illustrate my points I will make some allusive but concrete references and comparisons to empirical examples drawn from the literature on geohistorical regions in Mexico, and conclude with some thoughts on the implications of strong regionalization for the country's history more generally.

REGIONALITY

The concept of region in its most useful form, it seems to me, is essentially a spatialization of an economic relationship.[2] A very simple (if admittedly tautological) working definition would be a geographic space with a boundary to set it off, the boundary determined by the effective reach of some system whose parts interact more with each other than with outside systems. On the one hand, the boundary need not be impermeable, nor on the other is it necessarily congruent with the more familiar and easily identifiable political or administrative divisions, or even with topographical features.[3] Simple as this definition is, why is it even necessary to specify what we mean by regions before we undertake to describe them, instead of just bumping along intuitively? I would suggest

---

rial originated in a rethinking (although not a radical revision) of the original argument and empirical cases, and some has been incorporated from Van Young (1992b).

2. This point of view is not altogether congenial to traditional economic theory. It was implicitly assumed that spatial resistance did not enter into equilibrium models of the economy, in which "everything ... is in effect compressed to a point," creating a "dimensionless habitat" in the words of Walter Isard (1956, 25). For a general theoretical and historical introduction to location theory and central-place theory, beginning with von Thünen (1966/1826) in the early nineteenth century, which underlies much of this chapter, see Isard (1956, 1–23) and Berry (1967, 59–73), and more particularly the well-known essay of Carol Smith (1976b). For a stimulating interdisciplinary synthesis owing much to the anthropological point of view, see Guillermo de la Peña (1981a).

3. Ciro F. Cardoso (1982) has made this point in a short article distinguished by flashes of clarity and insight alternating with puzzlingly opaque passages.

that there are three reasons. First, if we do not establish some theoretical a priori definitions, we may end up explaining the wrong social phenomena with reference to regions; that is, if we do not know what a region is ahead of time, it is hard to get much analytical leverage from the concept of region. For example, certain economic phenomena notable in Mexican history may have more to do with the reductionist tendencies of extraregional or even extranational forces than with the internal characteristics of regions in and of themselves (e.g., Moreno Toscano and Florescano 1977). Moreover, the lack of a sufficiently rigorous definition (or perhaps better said, a definite set of questions) regarding regions may have led to a certain confusion between region*ality*, the quality of being a region, and region*alism*, the self-conscious identification—cultural, political, and sentimental—that large groups of people develop over time with certain spaces.[4] Second, comparisons built around the concept of regionality become problematic if we do not know more or less clearly what variables we are comparing, or if the ones we pick—location of production functions, marketing structures, resource endowment—are not comparable across large spaces. Finally, regionality itself is a dynamic concept whose study can tell us much about fundamental types of social change over time in defined spaces; if we have no model of what comprises a region, how are we to deal convincingly with change other than in a descriptive manner? To sum up with the words of Walter Isard (1975, 12), the developer of the hybrid discipline of regional science: "How can you start collecting information for a regional study when you have not discussed the concept of a city or a region? You are putting the cart before the horse."

Why, particularly with regard to Mexico, are regions good to think? Many reasons could be adduced, but two in particular suggest themselves strongly, one of an empirical/historical nature, the other of a theoretical nature. In the historical case, regions seem to correspond in some way to natural horizons of reference, to natural empirical categories for locating ourselves in space that probably have not changed much since preindustrial times; that is, the actual space itself (its size) may have altered, but probably the idea has not. Pierre Goubert (1971) has made the point that in the prerailway age most Europeans lived their lives within the precinct of a parish, generally comprised of a small town and the surrounding district—an area traversed in a day's walk or ride, probably from ten to thirty miles in diameter. He goes on to note that such people would have considered themselves foremost as citizens of a locality, and then as

---

4. This conceptual problem seems to lie at the heart of the studies of Bernstein and González, and possibly also of the otherwise masterful synthesis of Carr (1973); see also Lomnitz-Adler (1992).

subjects of a king.[5] While Goubert does not provide a technical definition of what a region is, his main point nonetheless holds for rural people in traditional Mexican society, especially beyond the level of the village or hamlet. Migration patterns, for example, tend to confirm this, at least for the era before readily accessible mass transportation. The major sending areas for rural migrants to late-colonial Antequera, Guanajuato, and Guadalajara were primarily within the hinterlands of these regional capitals (see, respectively, Chance 1978; Brading 1971; Van Young 1981; Cook 1970). In the theoretical case, regional analysis helps to resolve the tension between generalization and particularization. Among modern students of Latin America the anthropologist Robert Redfield was among the first to try to bridge the gap between local, small communities and national-level societies by construction of his "folk-urban continuum" (Redfield 1960, 1968). On the theoretical level, regional analysis can do for spatial systems what Redfield tried to do for cultural ones—reconcile the microperspective with the macroperspective.[6] To quote another anthropologist, Carol Smith (1976a, 4), whose work contributed a good deal to my present analysis: "With other approaches, generalization requires one to assume that what is true of a part is roughly true of the whole or that what is true of the whole is also true of the parts. Regional analysis can build system variability into its model of explanation, so that generalization is neither far-fetched nor banal."

Moreover, the regional framework also accommodates several approaches to the concrete study of what goes on in such a space over time, among them the finalist, the instrumentalist, and the processualist. In the finalist approach, we look at regions and their histories—the Bajío or

---

5. Cardoso (1982, 4–5, 8) takes issue strongly with Goubert's analysis, insisting on the impossibility of applying to the New World models of space and population developed for the Old World, since colonial Latin America was marked by "social and economic mobility, by immigrations, by population transplantation, by the moving frontiers of various types"— but not on a mundane, day-to-day basis, one should observe. Goubert (1971, 115–16) speaks generally in a deprecating tone of local/regional history, calling the enormous outpouring of antiquarian local history in nineteenth-century France "petit bourgeois social science," adding that in this historiographical genre "History becomes a game where the guiltless amateurs of local history provide others with materials they find useful." In Mexico, by extension, consigning a place to the limbo of being a "region" may convey a barely masked pejorative connotation, a sort of spatialized alterity originating in the *chilango* perspective, as in the phrase *"Fuera de México, todo es Chauhtitlán,"* which roughly translates to "Outside Mexico City, every place is a godforsaken village." González (1982, 31–36), on the other hand, speaks fondly of the local historiographical tradition and its nonprofessional practitioners. Those of us who have toiled in the historical vineyards of *la provincia* in Mexico have much cause to be grateful to the numerous *licenciados, médicos, arquitectos,* and *ingenieros* who have chronicled their towns or states since the nineteenth century.

6. On Redfield, see also de la Peña (1981a).

the Huasteca, for example—because they are interesting in and of themselves. The instrumentalist approach—describing what happens in region X at time Y in relation to processes of a similar order in another region—can tell us what is happening in the nation as a whole, as a superregional system. The processualist approach is more akin to a social laboratory, in which things that happen within a region or between regions are seen to be worth attention as generalizable, transhistorical social processes; examples would be the formation of transportation and marketing networks, central-place hierarchies, linguistic and cultural differentiation, and so forth. There is nothing to prevent us, of course, from working on all these levels simultaneously, and indeed many of the best regional studies by historians and other scholars do precisely this, even though their methodological agenda may be more implicit than explicit (e.g., Brading 1978; Martin 1985; García Martínez 1987; Pastor 1987).

A huge literature exists in several languages exploring the virtues of the regional theoretical framework (see, for example, Gilbert 1988); and for Mexico, regionally based studies across several disciplines abound. At this point, therefore, it might be useful to raise some issues that tend to cast constructive doubt on the utility and appropriateness of the regional approach, to caution us in our attempts to see large slices of historical reality in this way, or at least to nuance the rather reductionist applications to which we might be tempted by simple models of regionality. The first is the elusiveness of regions; the second their historicity; and the third the possibility—indeed the *necessity*—of bringing other analytic viewpoints to bear on the problem of regional spaces other than central-place theory, the more inclusive pseudodiscipline of regional science, or other models of regional identity, structure, and process.[7]

The very plasticity of the regional concept makes it a slippery intellectual technology despite its apparent concreteness, a characteristic it shares with other key modern concepts in the human sciences, such as power, class, capitalism, and so forth. One modern authority has said flatly that "the delimitation of regions is not an easy task" (Richardson 1978, 17). Definitions are so difficult that regional economists, for instance, are

---

7. These do not exhaust the problems of conceptualizing Mexican regions along the lines of central-place theory. Another problem is that classical central-place theory, upon which regional analysis is explicitly built, requires a large number of ceteris paribus assumptions—the even distribution of population across an unbounded isotropic plane, perfect economic rationality of consumers, and so on—that are in reality seldom met (Berry 1967; Smith 1975). In this connection it is surely no accident that much of the work of prominent economic geographers and other regionalists has been devoted to substantially homogeneous environments (in Berry's case [e.g., 1967], the U.S. Midwest, most notably southwestern Iowa).

often relieved when they must deal with established politico-administrative entities as though they were the same as regions, because policy considerations or the nature of the data so dictate. A number of economic historians and other regionalists have pointed to the miltivocality of the concept of region. Among them is Pedro Pérez Herrero, who notes that regions can be "natural, historical, economic, linguistic, cultural, ethnic, censal, military, religious, fiscal, educational," not to mention the issue of the levels involved in regional analysis, from Latin America as a whole down to the single municipality (Pérez Herrero 1990, 1). Thus the multivocality of the regional concept is in a very real sense an artifact of the discourse in which we are engaged; if the discourse is deconstructed, what happens to the region it has created? Historian Ignacio del Río (1989, 27) has put this eloquently: "Regions are formed and disappear according to the theoretical principle being followed. We acknowledge that they themselves are dynamic realities, but it is the case that regions change according to what we are studying: it would appear that, as if they were magical objects, we also create them or make them disappear." On the other hand, as with any investigation, when we look at regions we are bound by the data as well as by a priori theoretical assumptions. From this point of view, regions often appear to be artifacts of statistics, themselves in turn the residue of a political discourse. We habitually refer to political and administrative entities—in the case of Mexico, for example, colonial intendancies or modern states—as coterminous with regional economic systems, when they may not be at all. But to do otherwise would be like trying to lift ourselves off the ground in our own chairs. The terms of the debate are given before the discussion begins, the empirical reality so strongly defined by antecedent political decisions that it is nearly impossible to revise it along alternative lines.

The elusiveness of regions remains clear even when we have made a choice of definitional strategy, since the boundaries of a given region may become so blurred or ragged as to disappear entirely, leaving only a center of gravity. This may be represented as the problem of contiguity occasionally discussed by geographers and other regionalists. Certainly the classical conceptualizations of region allow for geographical spaces not structured around central places, as when we speak of formal or homogeneous regions as opposed to nodal or functional systems.[8] The case is made below,

---

8. A formal region would be one in which places or features within a regional boundary—farms or other production units, let us say, or geographic properties—share a phenomenological similarity, producing a largely homogeneous environment in which the parts resemble each other but are not necessarily systematically interrelated. A functional region, on the other hand, would be characterized by internal differentiation and interdependence of its component parts, as exemplified by a central-place system.

however, that it is social embeddedness and the dimension of time, in addition to geographic or phenomenological criteria, that define regions most meaningfully for the purposes of historians, so that homogeneous or formal regions are spaces of low "regionalness." The homogeneous or formal model, in fact, virtually implies spacelessness, since it depends upon reference to homogeneous criteria (pure geography, per capita income, other social indicators, etc.) as opposed to internal differentiation and the friction of distance. Furthermore, the neoclassical models often associated with the macroeconomics of homogeneous regions posit conditions such as perfect mobility of commodities and factors, free and instantaneous information flows, and zero transportation costs (Richardson 1978, 19–21). If the reach of a regional system is gravitational rather than formal in this way, however, it becomes fairly clear that all places need not be part of regions, nor do regions need to be contiguous with each other. Might it then be more useful to think of regions as polarized spaces, constituted by cores and peripheries (Grigg 1967, 470–78)?

The elusiveness of regions embraces not only the spatial domain, but the temporal as well. Let us begin by granting two assumptions: that things called regions have somewhere existed in the history of Mexico and are not simply—or not purely—artifacts of agendaed observation (C. Stern 1973, 15–16); and that change over time is essential to their constitution. Another way of putting this second statement is that while synchronic analysis gives you a space, diachronic analysis gives you a region. Here we should turn briefly, then, to the issue of historicity in two senses: first, whether as a real quality of historical space regionality may be time-bounded; and second, whether regions subjectively exist "in history" at all—that is, whether they have any historical reality for the people who live in them.

As for the first point, a number of scholars have noted the possibility that regions are time-bounded; that is, that the appropriateness of the regional construct as a descriptive or analytical category may vary over time in the same space. Concretely this might mean, for example, that certain areas of northern Mexico began as homogeneous or formal regions (regions of low "regionalness" in our terms), evolving later into regions well defined by internal structures, subsequently to be absorbed into some sort of macroregional systems. The historian Pierre Vilar, for example, has pointed to the particular appropriateness of the regional concept for the study of precapitalist societies (Vilar 1976).

Certainly the way the regional historiography on Mexico has evolved strongly suggests that this has been our view. For example, regional studies of the Mexican colonial period have been shaped strongly by European historiography, grafted onto a strong tradition of Mexican local and antiquarian history (exemplified in different generations by the histories of Mexican states by such scholars as Pérez Verdía [1951] and Almada [1952, 1955]). A major formative influence here, via the *Annales* school, was the French cultural geography of the early part of the twentieth century, championed by Paul Vidal de la Blache, with a large admixture of English local history. Here the emphasis was on the *genre de vie* distinguishing each *pays*, distinct cultural areas that mostly corresponded to rural, nonindustrialized parts of France. The geographer David Grigg has characterized this as "a method of analysis suited to localized, agrarian societies [which] has been markedly less successful in dealing with modern industrial societies" (Grigg 1967, 465). Historical studies of regions per se have tended to dominate much of recent colonial Mexican historiography, giving way for the twentieth century (bypassing the nineteenth, as in so much else) to three sorts of studies less about regions themselves than about what goes on inside them: (1) political studies of regional caudillo politics, elite networks, or popular movements (e.g., Falcón 1984; Wasserman 1984; Salamini 1978; Jacobs 1982; Benjamin and Wasserman 1990); (2) large-scale economic regionalizations (e.g., Bassols Batalla 1967, 1979, 1984; Bataillon 1982); and (3) social indicator studies (e.g., Wilkie 1967; C. Stern 1973). For the modern period, it seems to me, regions have come to be seen as problems—as the ossified remains unearthed by archaeologists of the state—whereas for the early modern period they are often seen not only as descriptions of spatial systems, but also as building blocks of economic development. Part of the reason for this, of course, is also that with the nationalization of distribution—that is, the growth of a national market—regional lines *do* become blurred, and lines of commercial exchange in some sense outrun those of production, making of the region a sort of choke point in national development.

As for the second point, it would certainly seem to be the case that cultural attitudes about such fundamental orienting axes of our lives as sexuality, time, and the material world, despite a degree of transhistorical, biological fixity, are enormously plastic cross-culturally and within a single culture over time (Spiro 1982; Thompson 1967; Richards 1990; Van Young 1992b). That this is also the case with our sense of place, in its broadest meaning, has been pointed out by the historical geographer David Robinson, among others. Our reference points, our ideas of community and the "natural" horizon of perception and actions, the spaces we conceive to be the natural ambit of our lives, even probably our sense of our own bodies in space—all these are culturally determined and may therefore change with time and circumstance. Robinson (1989, 167) suggests that interurban rivalry was a potent political and economic force in eighteenth-century Spanish America, and should be read as an indicator of people's strong identification with place. It should be noted, however, that the place being identified with is a city, not a region. We have just noted that the region in general as an analytical construct, and particular regions individually, may be bounded historically from the observer's point of view. But what about regions as a subjective experience? Have they ever existed or exerted strong pulls on people's minds and hearts? Or is regionalism in this affective sense simply out of fashion in most of the modern world, along with belief in monarchical forms of government, hysteria in the psychopathological sense, and the other cognitive detritus of bygone mentalities?

The case can be made without too much of a stretch that regions do not really exist as historical or cultural subjects, but only as objects. Localities and nations, ethnicities, families, tribes, and corporate groupings—these all exist as subjects, as the markers of conscious self-identity among people, but not regions. Under certain circumstances—in the history of Mexico, for instance—regions may be seen in some sense as alliances of localities against supralocal centers with claims to hegemonic authority. This would especially be true among the elite family networks that tended to dominate regions (Robinson 1989, 167). But in a broader social framework they are weak in their claims to affective loyalty as compared to experienced or "imagined" communities, localities, or nations (Anderson 1991). People can be loyal to landscapes, villages, structures of authority, even ideas, but less likely to systems or depersonalized abstractions. Who is loyal to a region but a geographer? Who weeps over it, poetizes it, is ready to die for it? We are faced here with the interesting contradiction of a concept with considerable analytical vitality but a problematic historical existence, at least in the sense that it may never have existed except as the reification of abstract analysis. But at least since the time of Marx, class has *also* taken on subjective reality for people as a political instrumentality—has been appropriated, in the insight of E. P. Thompson (1963), through a process of historical struggle and autodefinition—whereas region remains an abstract notion.

Before moving on to a brief, suggestive discussion of Mexican regionality as such, I want to close these general remarks with a further answer to the question "Are regions good to think?" the answer being "Yes, but one needs to think about other things, too." There are, of course, a number of ways of thinking about space or about regions. Among these (but not limited to them) are the cultural ecology tradition associated with the work of Carl Sauer (e.g., 1963), regional science (e.g., Isard 1956, 1975), the Marxist or political economy approach (e.g., Salinas and Moulaert 1983; Markusen 1987), and the humanist tendency, or what we might call "moral topography" in the Thompsonian sense (Tuan 1974, 1977;

Relph 1976, 1981; Buttimer and Seamon 1980; Entrikin 1991; Lefebvre 1991). The regional science approach, most obviously associated with central-place theory, has been attacked from both political economy and humanist perspectives. The moral topographers, as I understand it, would probably make the case that materiality is antecedent to spatial relations, that the distribution of people and things in space has first and foremost a semiotic and symbolic value, and that therefore to separate out space as an independent variable is highly artificial and even counterproductive for an understanding of the way people operate (Gore 1984, 11ff).

More relevant for purposes of the present discussion are the criticisms of regional science theory by the political economists. They would insist that mode of production and the resultant social relations are antecedent to spatial constructs like regions, which themselves are no more than the loci of class struggle and other processes growing out of a given mode (e.g., Roberts 1992). In this view, the modified neoclassical economic modeling of central-place theory and its offshoots, which after all stress the costs of moving commodities, people, or information between places, are incompatible with the political economy approach (Moulaert 1983, 16; Salinas and Moulaert 1983); the more so, it would seem, with the advent and development of capitalism. This debate resonates with that over the emphasis on circulation versus mode of production in dependency and world-systems theory. Now, it is true, on the one hand, that the social relations determining the spatial organization of a region may transcend the territorial limits of the region itself (Moreno Toscano and Florescano 1977; Florescano 1979; Moulaert and Salinas 1983; Assadourian 1982). It might also be noted that the word *region*—from the Latin *regere*—carries the sense of ruling, commanding, or directing, an etymology Michel Foucault underlined when he wrote, "The region of the geographers is the military region." (Gore 1984, xiv). This implies politically directed force and, behind it, the power of control over the means of production. On the other hand, since people even in theoretically natural, limited, and nonmonetized economies are always exchanging things, and since capitalism is a relative newcomer to the world scene, the question arises as to whether regionality as defined by systems of exchange is relatively independent of the mode of production. This is a conundrum I cannot resolve here, but it is desirable to take into account both the friction of distance *and* the prevailing mode (or modes) of production in analyzing regionality. After all, without production there can be no exchange, and without exchange, no spatialized relationships (e.g., Pérez Herrero 1990).

Can regional analysis, then, really accomplish all that its more ardent proponents would claim for it? Certainly such an approach to historical structure and change has certain problems or limits even over and above the caveats I have just suggested. One of these is that classical central-place theory, upon which regional analysis is built, requires a large number of ceteris paribus assumptions—the even distribution of population across an unbounded isotropic plane, perfect economic rationality of consumers, and so on—that are in reality seldom met, certainly under Mexican conditions (Berry 1967; Smith 1975).[9] Another conceptual problem is to determine the next higher level to which regions relate—the larger matrix into which they fit: is it a metaregion, a nation-state, the world system, or what? In practice defining this upper limit to the hierarchy is a good deal more difficult than defining the lower one, which is likely to be a city, town, or village. Finally, with its inevitable emphasis on economic elements, spatial relationships, and certain types of social interactions, regional analysis may leave aside other important aspects of structure and change, such as ethnicity and ethnic conflict, for example.[10] Notwithstanding these problems, the regional approach has proven itself of enormous value in numerous studies, and should continue to do so in the future. The regional focus provides a point of convergence for two central themes of historical analysis in Mexico and Latin America—city and countryside.

Looked at from a certain perspective, the internal structure of a region also constitutes a matrix for the convergence of physical and social space.[11] As theoretical concepts, regional and social class systems demonstrate a notable parallelism. The concept of region essentially spatializes economic relationships, and the concept of social class does roughly the same thing, substituting the metaphor of social space (as when we speak of social distance or social mobility) for that of the actual distances of physical space. In addition, regional and class systems share at least three other common, interrelated characteristics. They demonstrate differentiation—that is to say, functional differences among their component parts or groups. They demonstrate hierarchy—that is to say, asymmetrical power relationships within the system. In the case of class systems this is obvious in the unequal distribution of wealth, status, and political power, but it also occurs in regional systems, of course, in the form of settlement hierarchies. Finally, they display the characteristic of articulation—that is

---

9. In this connection it is surely no accident that much of Berry's classic book is devoted to a detailed geographical-historical analysis of the central-place system of southwestern Iowa.

10. This is not necessarily the case, however. Chance's work (1978), though not explicitly cast in a location theory framework, nonetheless clearly establishes the role of spatial elements in the changing ethnosocial composition of the Oaxaca region and the city of Antequera; see also the theoretical remarks of Smith (1976c, passim).

11. For a series of stimulating studies on this theme see volume 2 (1976a) of Carol A. Smith's work on regional analysis, especially the general introductory essays by the editor herself and Stephen M. Olsen; see also de la Peña (1981a, 76ff).

to say, some kind of predictable, ongoing interaction among the elements that constitute the system.[12] Beyond what may be regarded as fortuitous similarities, however, the regional and class modes of analysis intersect in meaningful ways, so that one may speak of social structures peculiar to certain types of regions for certain explicit theoretical reasons. The relationship between geographical space and social structure in Mexican history, in fact, is one of two major issues that I particularly want to address in the rest of this chapter. To do this, I will first develop briefly a dualistic typology of historical Mexican regions, and then in concluding make a few empirical observations linking certain elements of that typology to the peculiarities of Mexican economic and social development up through the end of the nineteenth century.

Let me interject a word here about the temporal range of the cases discussed. Since I am by training and in my earlier scholarly work a colonialist, many of the empirical examples in this essay are drawn from the colonial period, and I have also drawn on the works of historians (Pierre Goubert, for example) who have written on early modern Europe. Before Mexico entered the railway age in the last third or so of the nineteenth century (Grunstein 1994; Kuntz Ficker 1995; Kuntz Ficker and Riguzzi 1996; Kuntz Ficker and Connolly 1999), however, many of the infrastructural constraints (primarily on transportation networks) affecting territorial integration and economic development that prevailed in the colonial era would have carried over into the first half-century or so (ca. 1821–1875) of the national period. Roads were notoriously bad and transportation costs correspondingly high, often prohibitive, although some late viceregal investments to improve this situation were realized (Castleman 2005). With the growth of the railway system state capacity also grew enormously, extending the reach not only of production and commerce (Coatsworth 1981), but also of policing powers and political control (Vanderwood 1992). Many of my conclusions, therefore, are just as applicable to the prerailroad Mexico of the era before Porfirio Diaz as to the colonial centuries. Interestingly, the advent of the Spanish may actually have caused a retrogression in the economic integration of the sixteenth-century Valley of Mexico as

---

12. With regard to this last point, one is prompted to comment that the strong tendency to regionalism in Mexican history (as also in many other developing countries), and a concomitantly overdeveloped regionality, if one may call it that, are frequently symptoms of disarticulated economies. In much the same way, the lack of a strong class structure and its typical replacement by caste, estate, or other strongly segmented structures may be seen as a symptom of weak social articulation. Looked at from this perspective, much of the Mexican historical experience has been a struggle to replace the regional definition of society with a class definition, although theoretically the two concepts are not mutually exclusive.

preconquest transportation and marketing systems were reconfigured by the conquerors (Hassig 1985). In any case, railroads changed the game fundamentally, so that a great deal of caution must be exercised in applying my conceptual discussion of regions and regionality much beyond the late nineteenth-century cases I discuss (Yucatán, for example). By the same token, much of the theoretical writing I invoke is based on modern case studies by geographers, economists, and anthropologists, and must be applied with caution to Mexico before the late nineteenth century, lest we stumble into anachronism. Still, many of the same fundamental issues were in play across the railroad divide—the political versus economic definition of regions, the influence of export versus domestic markets in shaping regional systems, the application of phenomenological versus functional criteria of definition, and the relative costs imposed by the friction of distance.

COOKING UP REGIONS: PRESSURE COOKERS AND FUNNELS

Regional economies and societies in general, and in Mexico in particular, are likely to be quite different from one another depending on whether they are linked to internal or external markets, or to put it in terms of regional analysis, whether the central place in the region is inside of it or outside of it. This is not the paradox it seems at first. As I have already suggested, some regions may be seen to center on cities, and display a more or less symmetrically structured urban hierarchy within themselves and a concomitant internal division of labor. Other regions may be described as groupings or clusters of production units or firms linked to an outside market in a qualitatively similar manner, and in which regionality is defined less by economic complementarity than by a sort of phenomenological similarity. As it happens, this admittedly oversimplifying dichotomy corresponds to the functional and formal definitions of regions as developed primarily by geographers.[13] Graphic metaphors for these two very different forms of region would be a pressure cooker and a funnel, respectively. The distinction I am making between pressure cooker and funnel types also corresponds in a general way to character-

---

13. In the words of Carol A. Smith (1976a, 6): "Regions can be defined formally or functionally, the former placing emphasis on the homogeneity of some element within a territory, the latter placing emphasis on systems of functional relations within an integrated territorial system." Claude Bataillon (1982) makes much the same distinction, placing special emphasis on the presence of cities or central places in functional regions.

istic regional marketing systems designated by central-place theorists as solar and dendritic types, respectively.[14] On the basis of this typology, I would further suggest the hypothesis that the complexity of regional social structures and the nature of class relations is likely to be strongly influenced by the internal spatial and settlement arrangements of the two types. In the pressure cooker model, characterized by a relatively complex and hierarchically polarized internal space, we are more likely to see over time a proliferation and complication of internal structures. These would occur, for example, in landlord-peasant relationships, in credit usages, in marketing and commercial arrangements, in the social role of mediating groups, and in class relations. In the funnel model, characterized by a relatively low degree of internal spatial polarization, we are likely to see a simplification and homogenization of internal economic and social relationships, and a concomitantly sharper differentiation between social classes. In other words, I am suggesting that there is an inverse relationship between spatial and social polarization, or to put it in yet another fashion, that complexity produces complexity and simplicity, simplicity. Lest it be objected that I am reinventing the wheel, I readily admit that the dual typology itself is hardly novel, and echoes the accepted distinction between nonexporting and exporting regions. The point I am trying to make, however, is that the presence or absence of a dominant export activity has interrelated spatial and social implications for the host region, something often overlooked by historians working on Latin America.[15]

14. I first attempted to develop the pressure cooker/funnel typology in Van Young (1979, 1984). On the definition of solar and dendritic marketing systems, see Smith (1976a, 1977).

15. For a generally interesting and wide-ranging collection of essays concerning the development of agrarian capitalism in general and export economies in particular in Latin America, see Duncan and Rutledge (1977); many of these essays, particularly the concluding one by Magnus Mörner, touch on the issues raised in this chapter. The pure forms suggested by the pressure cooker/funnel dichotomy exist only in the laboratory of the mind, of course, and in practice actual historical situations are not as simple as the models suggest. In the case of the exporting, or funnel, regions, for example, intraregional subsistence and commercialized food economies may be linked to the export sector, thus compromising the "simple" funnel model. An instance of this would be the slave and nonslave food and livestock-production sector associated with the sugar economy in colonial and nineteenth-century Brazil; see Schwartz (1985), Stein (1976/1957), and Furtado (1965). On the other hand, regions which are apparently instances of the pressure cooker model, and which seem to be undergoing some kind of autochthonous development, may be linked at least weakly or indirectly to dynamic external economies or economic sectors. For example, the opening up of northwestern Mexico and the dynamism of the (export-oriented) silver mining economy of western Mexico seem to have had much to do with the economic development of the Guadalajara region in the late colonial period; see Van Young (1981, 142, passim).

Before looking at some illustrative cases of regional types and discussing their implications, we need to take a step backward for a moment to the basic concept of region in order to clarify a central assumption. Since regions are properly defined by the range of some kind of system internal to them, and since human societies are typically constituted by a large number of different kinds of mutually affecting systems, what is the system of choice for defining regions? One can readily call to mind several that might be candidates, including the facts of physical geography itself, the distribution and type of economic production, political structure, and exchange or market relationships. It is this last system—the structure of exchange, or markets—that lies at the heart of central-place theory, which in turn provides the basis for most of the recent theoretical work on regional analysis.[16] Central-place theory has been defined, in fact, as the theory of the location, size, nature, and spacing of clusters of market activity. Geographer Brian Berry (1967, 1) has put this very clearly: "It is in the system of *exchange*, through the process of *distribution*, that the supplies of producers and the demands of consumers are brought together. In this sense, the interconnections of the exchange network are the strands that hold society together"[17]—and that hold regions together, one might add. It is to market relationships, then, that we should look if we would understand the nature of geohistorical regions.

---

16. The determining influence of space and transport costs on economic production is the main theme of classical location theory, most of which derives from the work of Johann Heinrich von Thünen (1966/1826). For an interesting application of von Thünen's ideas to Mexico, see Ursula Ewald (1977). Among geographers, Claude Bataillon (1982, 204), after an eloquent and insightful critique of the theory of natural (i.e. geographical) regions in Mexico, seems to emphasize the production function as the major defining variable of regionalization. This same emphasis would appear to underlie the discussion of urban "scale" and the "productive strength of [a given city's] sphere of influence" in Hardoy and Aranovich (1978).

17. To quote Smith yet again (1976c, 312): "Surplus is a product of exchange, not a fact of production, for its level depends upon the means used to extract it, not just the means used to produce it." Market relationships as the central structuring principle of regions are particularly appropriate to preindustrial or substantially preindustrial peasant societies, even where important forms of nonpeasant production exist. Their appropriateness to regional analysis in industrialized societies, where production relations tend to assume a dominant position, is an open question; on this point, see Smith (1975, 96). As will be seen below, and as is fairly obvious on an empirical level, production and marketing systems are in reality difficult to separate, since often the type of production is antecedent to the type of marketing system. For a powerfully argued contrasting view, emphasizing structures of production rather than of exchange in the definition of regions, see Roberts (1992, 231): "Yet what bound people to a region, willingly or otherwise, was their common dependence on particular forms of production." Roberts provides in his essay a macrohistorical interpretation of the place of regions in Mexico, as do other chapters in the same volume (Liverman and Cravey 1992; Pérez Herrero 1992b; Monsiváis 1992).

One of the peculiarities of Mexico's historical development is that, aside from the perennial presence of mineral exports, primarily in the form of silver and petroleum, the country has never found itself in the grip of the monocultural export cycles one has come to associate with most of Latin America at one moment or another. Examples of these boom-and-bust cycles would be first sugar and then coffee in Brazil; guano and then sugar in Peru; cattle, sheep, and wheat in Argentina, and so on.[18] Few instances of the funnel or dendritic region are found in Mexico's history, therefore, and certainly none that occupied such a central role in the economic development of the country as a whole as the ones referred to above. Two cases that do illustrate aspects of the funnel/dendritic type, however, are the sugar economy of the Morelos area extending into the nineteenth century, and the development of the henequen industry in nineteenth-century Yucatán. It is precisely the infrequency of such unbalanced export-dominated regions that makes the pressure cooker/solar regional type relatively frequent in Mexico, and the two cases of this I wish to discuss briefly are the Guadalajara region and parts of the colonial bishopric of Michoacán.[19]

What one expects to see in regions structured along dendritic lines of internal organization is an orientation toward the outside for purposes of marketing a single export staple—thus the funnel metaphor. This would certainly be the case in the sugar-producing zone of the Morelos lowlands during the colonial period, and even more markedly so in the nineteenth century with the considerable expansion of the industry's productive capacity, the advent of the railroad, and the growth of the national domestic market. One would also expect to see the atrophy of internal marketing linkages; the squashing of the regional urban hierarchy into extreme nonlognormality—that is, the dominance of one entrepôt city and/or an external metropolis in flows of goods into and out of the region; a high degree of property concentration; and simplification of the social stratification system. As to the breaking down of internal commercial linkages, some of the colonial towns of the area, such as Yautepec and Cuautla, certainly look like the nodal points in a dendritic system centering on Mexico City

---

18. There is, of course, an enormous body of historiography on these economic cycles and the related social and political effects of staple exports, including most general and case studies along the lines of dependency theory. A particularly good collection of essays covering most of Latin America in the postindependence period is that edited by Duncan and Rutledge (1977).

19. The discussion of colonial and postcolonial Morelos is based substantially on Martin (1985) and de la Peña (1981b). The material on Yucatán is drawn from Patch (1985), Strickon (1965), and Wells (1985). The discussion of the colonial Guadalajara region is based entirely on Van Young (1981), that of colonial Michoacán on Morin (1979).

(de la Peña 1981b, 25–26).[20] Since the sugar produced in the region could not possibly be consumed locally, either in the colonial or postcolonial periods, Mexico City served as the major market and therefore as the regional primate city, showing an extremely high degree of primacy.[21] All writers on the history of the Morelos export zone have pointed to the tendency for property in the sugar-producing areas to concentrate over time due to the possible economies of scale that such concentration offered, among other factors.[22] Finally, both de la Peña (1981b) and Martin (1985) point to the social simplification of rural areas under the impact of sugar: that is, its homogenizing effects, specifically the tendency for small producers and middling groups to be wiped out. Martin writes especially of the resurgence and proliferation of small producers in the former export zone when large-scale sugar production receded from the late seventeenth century until about 1760.[23]

---

20. See also the remarks on this characteristic of dendritic regional systems in Smith (1977, 133–38). Compare also the analysis of Appleby (1976) speaking of the wool-exporting zones of highland Peru in the modern era: "The more land concentrated in fewer hands, the fewer the merchants necessary to serve producers, the more local merchants will be by-passed for larger mercantile houses in higher-level centers, and, consequently, the greater the degree of primacy exhibited in the export area."

21. On the Mexico City market for Morelos sugar, see the interesting article of Crespo (1984a). Crespo's figures (p. 204) indicate that between 1893 and 1911, only about 4 percent of Mexico's total sugar production was exported on the average, ranging from a low of virtually no exports in 1899/1900, to a high of 8 percent a decade later. Much the largest part of sugar production during the colonial period was destined as well for internal consumption within the central part of the viceroyalty itself, chiefly in the Mexico City market; on this point see von Wobeser (1984). Sugar exports from colonial Mexico to Europe were generally (though not always) unprofitable because of high transport costs compared with Caribbean and Brazilian producers; see Van Young (1970). On nonlognormality as a measure of urban primacy, see McGreevey (1971b). Lognormality means that a city's population size is related to its rank in an urban hierarchy—that is, the second city is half the size of the first, the third is one-third the size of the first, etc. McGreevey's figures (p. 121, Table 2) indicate that of the capitals of eight Latin American countries included in his data (Argentina, Brazil, Chile, Colombia, Cuba, Mexico, Peru, and Venezuela), Mexico City demonstrates the earliest and most notable degree of urban primacy (i.e., nonlognormality).

22. See also Barrett (1970), Warman (1981), Womack (1969), and several of the essays in Crespo (1984b).

23. De la Peña (1981b, 29–37) discusses the social heterogeneity and accompanying diversified economy in the highland areas of the Morelos zone in the colonial period, particularly in Tlayacapan and some other pueblos, and goes on to describe the reductive effects on this region of the nineteenth-century expansion of sugar in the lowlands (pp. 66–68). Martin (1985, 124–55) similarly describes the simplifying effects of the revival of sugar production on the "remarkable social variety" that had developed in the lowland sugar region up to the middle of the eighteenth century, concluding that sugar culture and its related economic arrangements explain the lack of "symbiosis" characteristic between large production units and peasants in other areas of central Mexico (pp. 215–16). For an

Perhaps an even clearer case of the funnel, or dendritic, region, is that of northern Yucatán under the impact of henequen export development in the nineteenth and early twentieth centuries. The Yucatecan henequen boom is an interesting case because, unlike the colonial and nineteenth-century Morelos sugar zone, where the staple product was present from nearly the beginning of the colonial era, in Yucatán the industry of the classic export boom period was created ex nihilo and had a relatively short cycle. Before henequen took hold in the latter half of the nineteenth century, the peninsula was quintessentially peripheral—a genuine economic backwater. In an excellent article and other work, Patch (1985) has described the dynamics of the colonial economy in terms strikingly similar to the rest of New Spain. The basic elements here were Indian demographic recovery, land pressure, large rural estates, local urban livestock and grain markets, and so forth: in short, a pressure-cooker situation, or several of them existing concurrently, constituting a number of small regional complexes.[24] Slightly later, what might have been an export cycle elsewhere took the form in Yucatán, in Howard Cline's (1947–48: 79) phrase, of an "episode." This was the development of the sugar industry along the southeastern frontier during the period 1750–1850. Despite the overwhelming orientation of this sector toward production for an internal peninsular market, one begins already to see the effects of the internal logic of economies of scale, and the advent of the harsh labor regime prefiguring that of henequen (Wells 1985, 24).[25] While it would be an exaggeration to say that the situation of the peninsula changed radically overnight with the arrival and rapid growth of the henequen industry after midcentury, it

---

analysis of even more radical homogenization and social simplification under the impact of sugar culture on Peru's north coast, see Klarén (1973), who describes increasing land concentration, the destruction of a class of prosperous independent small farmers, the disruption of the urban commercial structure by the intrusion of sugar plantations into local exchange relations, and the emergence of a rural proletariat vulnerable to social dislocation and anomie. On the lack of socially mediating groups and the development of social "anomie," compare De la Peña (1981b, 66–68, passim).

24. Patch (1985, 48–49) stresses in concluding the internal causes of change in the colonial economy, primarily population growth, and suggests that only with henequen did the peninsular economy reorient itself toward the outside. Strickon (1965, 44) points out that the exiguous export earnings of Yucatán in the early nineteenth century derived from the extensive livestock economy in the form of beef and other animal products marketed in Cuba. Farriss (1984) has described the social adaptations of Indian society to the colonial economic regime. For some interesting comparisons with early colonial Central America, see MacLeod (1973).

25. Strickon (1965, 50) states that in the late 1830s the plantation zone produced sufficient sugar to export from the peninsula. Wells (1985) goes on to say that even with a "sub-regional" division of labor, total peninsular exports, including sugar, were minor compared to the total value of subsistence production (i.e., the traditional maize-centered agriculture).

is nonetheless true that the fiber industry changed the economic structure of Yucatán and with it the internal structure of Yucatecan regions. Fiber production in the northwest of the peninsula, chiefly organized along lines of large, highly capitalized estates, quadrupled during the 1870s, with a predictable effect on the overall size and organization of the labor force. By 1900 about 75 percent of the officially calculated acreage of Yucatán was devoted to henequen culture, and a half to three-quarters of the peninsula's rural population lived on plantations (Strickon 1965, 55–56). Not surprisingly, the rural Indian population of the henequen-producing region became heavily proletarianized and the village communities weakened. The region appears to have undergone the social skewing and simplification of class structure that the funnel/dendritic model would predict.[26] Furthermore, unlike the traditional mixed-production haciendas of the prehenequen age, the plantations made no attempt at self-sufficiency. This meant that a complementary maize economy grew up in the old southeastern frontier zone to feed the food-deficit henequen region, a development that forestalled a diversified recovery in the old sugar zone.[27] Finally, one would expect to see under the impact of such changes a simplification and homogenization in the regional commercial and marketing arrangements. To quote Smith (1977, 138): "[B]ecause the production system is highly concentrated, the distribution system is highly concentrated. And because the market for the region's surplus is external, there is no need for a well-articulated rural marketing system."[28]

26. Wells (1985, 9, 153ff, 184; Strickon 1965, 57). Wells observes (p. 184): "The co-optation of village ejidos by *henequeneros* in the northwest throughout the Porfiriato had impaired what had once been a healthy peasantry and had isolated the hacienda community from its institutional base, the communal village." He concludes (p. 184) that: "Unlike the north of Mexico, Yucatán lacked a sizable middle class capable of joining with disgruntled *hacendados* to lead the revolution. Henequen's legacy was a plantation society with a class structure similar to the sugar societies of the Caribbean"; on the political implications of this for the period leading up to the Mexican Revolution of 1910, and the Revolution in Yucatán, see Wells and Joseph (1996).

27. Wells's (1985, 91–92, 94) apt term for this indirect effect of henequen development is "economic suction;" see also Strickon (1965, 59) and Appleby (1976, 292–93), referring specifically to Yucatán. For similar instances of interregional symbiotic dyads linking funnel-like, food-deficit exporting regions with food-supplying regions, see Smith's (1977, 100ff) remarks on western Guatemala (coffee in the lowlands, food production in the highlands) and de la Peña (1981b; sugar in the lowlands, food in the highlands). These "symbiotic dyads" throw us back onto the original question of what constitutes a region. De la Peña (1981b, 29), for example, refers to the Morelos highlands as themselves constituting a distinct region historically differentiated from the neighboring lowlands, while Wells (1985, 7–9) opts for the idea of an "intraregional dependency" within an identifiable Yucatán region composed of "dominant" and "marginal" subregions.

28. See also Appleby (1976, 294, 302–3). As far as I can tell, no thorough historical

By contrast with the funnel/dendritic regions I have just described, parts of the colonial bishopric of Michoacán and the extended hinterland of Guadalajara displayed notably the characteristics of the pressure cooker/solar regional type. Taking Michoacán as a whole, one diagnostic criterion for the lack of a strongly funnel-like, dendritic structure is the internal consumption of products such as sugar often associated elsewhere with export markets. At the close of the eighteenth century only about 25 percent of the bishopric's 170,000-*arroba* sugar production was destined for export out of the area.[29] Another characteristic of an inward-turning as opposed to an outward-turning orientation was the presence in the bishopric of periodic markets in small and middle-sized towns, and some larger cities: Zamora and Tangancícuaro on Sundays, Pátzcuaro on Fridays, Valladolid on Thursdays, and so forth.[30] The presence or absence of market periodicity in central-place systems is important, by the way, because it is an indicator of the nature and degree of intraregional urban hierarchy, of the degree of consumer choice, and of the degree of lateral linkage at lower and intermediate levels of the hierarchy. As to solar central-place systems, they are not incompatible with

---

study of the marketing structures of these two Yucatecan regions had yet been made as of the mid-1980s, so that my conclusions and those of other writers were highly tentative.

29. Morin (1979, 144). The evidence Morin deploys regarding the salt trade in another passage (p. 147) to prove the high degree of commercialization in the bishopric vis-à-vis external markets is less than convincing, since salt, even in the ancient world and even in nonmonetarized economies, was a commodity of traditional long-range trade because of its high unit/value. In other words, if anything were to be traded at all, salt would be. Of cotton production, however, the largest part was in fact exported from the bishopric (p. 145). Good as it is, owing to which it has arrived at canonical status in the literature on Mexican regional history, one of the problems with Morin's book is precisely his failure to differentiate sufficiently coherent regions within the bishopric of Michoacán, which as an entity in and of itself is virtually meaningless. The tentative statements here about regions based on Morin's work seem justified, however, on the grounds that since most of the data embrace the bishopric as a whole, and since the whole is unlikely to have exceeded the sum of its parts, his figures represent, *grosso modo*, the performance of the component regions.

30. Morin (1979, 153). For a discussion of periodicity and its importance, see the various works of Smith already cited, and various of the essays in her edited collection, *Regional Analysis*, especially that of G. William Skinner, and also Skinner (1967, 63–97). For a summary of the periodicity argument, see Hassig (1985). Smith's theoretical discussion of solar-type central-place systems, which she refers to in one article (1976c) as "administered" or "partially commercialized" marketing structures, though it establishes the essential elements for the treatment of empirical cases in Mexico, provides anything but a perfect fit. More generally, her sophisticated analysis fails to take into account: (1) interregional relationships; (2) agrarian societies/regions in which staple crop production is *not* in the hands of peasant producers (i.e., where it is dominated by haciendas and plantations); and (3) intra- and interregional differentiation over time (i.e., her analysis is static).

the existence of a certain amount of market periodicity, although they are characterized by a truncated (generally two-tiered) urban hierarchy and a marked degree of regional urban primacy. Still other signs of a pressure cooker/solar pattern appear in the form of relatively complex and widespread local marketing arrangements, and of very limited importation of foodstuffs except for high unit/value items like alcoholic beverages and cacao (Morin 1979, 145).

During the late colonial period and early nineteenth century the Guadalajara region provides an even clearer example of the pressure cooker/solar type of central-place system, or at least one better known to me. The political and administrative capital of a sprawling territory, Guadalajara certainly functioned as the regional primate city, and the urban hierarchy of its extended hinterland therefore demonstrated a predictably high degree of nonlognormality. Using the volume of commercial sales for selected towns in the Guadalajara region in 1800 as a proxy for town size, sales in the primate city were more than twenty-five times greater than its nearest rival within the region, the substantial provincial town of La Barca.[31] Furthermore, the commercial or marketing structure of the region displayed the characteristics one would more or less expect to find in a pressure cooker/solar type. Thus, despite the reductionist tendency of the commercial relationships centered on the regional primate city, country towns had at least some lateral linkages in terms of credit relationships, itinerant merchants, periodic markets, and so forth. On the other hand, intraregional specialization of production, although it existed, was limited.[32] A recasting and analysis of data developed in a statistical treatise about the middle of the nineteenth century by a local statistician-geographer reveals a large degree of homogeneity in the regional commercial network, and a squashed urban hierarchy approximating the two-tiered arrangement one would expect to find in such a regional type. Of the approximately twenty towns covered in the survey, whose commercial establishments I have classified according to the sim-

---

31. Van Young (1978, Table 11-3); the source is the Biblioteca Pública del Estado (Guadalajara), Archivo Fiscal de la Audiencia de Nueva Galicia, vol. 218; the peso values are derived from *alcabala* (sales tax) figures, not including *fincas* (real estate) and *igualas* (annual lump-sum payments), and assume a collection rate of 6 percent. By contrast with the Guadalajara region, one of the unique peculiarities of the Bajío at the same period was its less skewed urban network, which displayed a lognormal size distribution of its towns; Wibel and de la Cruz (1971); and see also Moreno Toscano (1978) and Morse (1986).

32. For a general statement of solar regional structure, see Smith (1976b, esp. 36ff). Smith lays some stress on the fact that "peasant communities in . . . [primate city] . . . hinterlands each specialize in a distinctive market commodity." In the Guadalajara region specialization certainly existed, but how one would measure its relative significance remains a moot question.

ple tripartite division retail, service, and artisan-retail, about two-thirds were small retail establishments, with the service and artisan-retail types dividing up the remainder evenly. Towns at some distance from Guadalajara in dry-farming areas with mixed economies of cereals and livestock had very high percentages of retail establishments, while the region as a whole demonstrated a relatively low degree of intraregional specialization, with strong vertical and comparatively weak lateral linkages. Small country stores, and also the larger establishments in provincial towns, dealt mostly in dry goods, food, and hardware, and tended to have limited inventories. These businesses habitually carried large numbers of very small debts on their books, many from rural Indians, secured with various *prendas* (items given as surety for credit), including guns, agricultural implements, articles of clothing, and religious objects (Van Young 1978, 519–27; and also Van Young 1982). Finally, despite the increasing agricultural commercialization, skewing of property holding, and rural proletarianization, the region sustained a remarkably complex agrarian structure including a large group of independent family farmers (*rancheros*) and a substantial scattering of rural middlemen, occupational pluralists who provided important commercial, credit, and brokerage functions in the regional economy and society.

If the pressure cooker/solar model has any predictive value for regional economies, we should expect to see three features of such systems: (1) markets of a very limited geographical range for almost everything except high value/low bulk commodities; (2) low levels of regional exports for agricultural commodities; and (3) an overall low level of commercial exchange *among* regions of this type making up a larger economic space. Taking the Guadalajara region as a case in point, these characteristics are precisely what one in fact sees around 1800 and probably much beyond. Such a conclusion in the case of the Guadalajara region takes on even more significance because this area of New Spain is typically cited, along with those of the Bajío and Michoacán, as among the most economically dynamic of late colonial New Spain (Florescano and Gil Sánchez 1974). If one analyzes the figures on regional production and commerce given in a report for the year 1803 by José Fernando de Abascal, the Intendant of Guadalajara, one sees that net exports from the intendancy were comparatively small. Of a total gross regional product of some 8,729,000 pesos, net exports amounted to 443,000 pesos, about 5 percent of the gross regional product, or approximately ten pesos per capita for the greater Guadalajara region's total population. Eliminating mining production from these figures, virtually all of which was exported from the intendancy, the figure drops to 2 percent. Furthermore, if one increases Abascal's maize production figure by 25 percent, as seems reasonable, to correct for unrecorded subsistence production of this basic commodity, the figure on exports would necessarily drop even further.[33] What one sees in this case, then,

33. Abascal's report is published in Florescano and Gil Sánchez (1977, 108–32), "Provincia de Guadalajara. Estado que demuestra los frutos . . . en el año de 1803." It is probably based on tithe records and sales tax returns. I have rearranged Abascal's figures and done some calculations of my own to derive a rough breakdown of regional production and trade on the basis of several sectors/industries of the economy (see following Table; figures are rounded to nearest thousand pesos).

Ramo (industry/ sector)	Value of total production	Total value of imports	Total value of exports	Net value of exports (i.e., exports less imports)	Net value of exports as % of production in that sector	Net value of exports as % of total production (sum of column 2)
Agriculture	3,051,000	151,000	904,000	753,000	25	9
Livestock	1,341,000	—	261,000	261,000	19	3
Industry	1,320,000	69,000	624,000	555,000	42	6
Hides/leather	407,000	128,000	199,000	71,000	17	1
Textiles	1,620,000	136,000	308,000	172,000	11	2
Mineral	990,000	12,000	884,000	872,000	88	10
	8,729,000	496,000	3,180,000	2,684,000		

Precisely what Intendant Abascal meant by the designation "Provincia de Guadalajara" is not clear, but it is probably coterminous with the intendancy, a larger unit that overlapped the Guadalajara region proper as I have tried to define it elsewhere (Van Young 1981, 11–27); my calculations are thus only a rough approximation. Furthermore, neither Abascal's figures nor my own take into account contraband into and out of the region. The intendant gives a figure for "*comercios*" under his rubric "imports" of 2,241,000 pesos, but it is clear from the totals that this is a *different* figure from the total imports specified under the categories agriculture, livestock, and so on, and must have consisted of various sorts of value-added goods, probably manufactured items. It is justifiable, therefore, to leave this figure out of the calculations when deriving net exports (gross exports less gross imports in all categories except *comercio*). Subtracting the value of "*comercio*" (2,241,000 pesos) from that of net exports (2,684,000 pesos) gives a result of 443,000 pesos, the total positive trade figure for the year. This figure was then divided by the "gross regional product" (8,729,000 pesos) to produce the positive trade balance of 5 percent of GRP, assuming a regional population of about 500,000 (possibly a bit on the conservative side); for population, see Van Young (1981, 36–37). As to regional maize production and the role of maize exports in the regional total, my calculations are very rough and ready. Abascal's report gives a total maize production for the *provincia* of 1,860,000 *fanegas* (hundredweight) in 1803, of which some 444,700 were exported (to what destination is not suggested), or about 24 percent (at 1 peso/*fanega*). With a total count of about 500,000 people, the actual amount of maize required to feed this population would have been about 1,750,000 *fanegas*, a little less than Abascal's figure. This calculation supposes an average of 4.5 persons per family, and an average annual family consumption of maize of 15.6 *fanegas*, for an average annual per capita consumption of 3.5 *fanegas*. Descriptive and quantitative data for the eighteenth and nineteenth centuries indicate maize consumption at about these levels, with adult men consuming 150–180 kgs per year, adult women and children somewhat less. (The daily half-kilo of maize should be compared to bread consumption by contemporary European laborers, who generally demanded one kilo per day). On the other hand, considerations of body

and probably those of other regions as well, is a kind of iceberg effect in which only the tip of the regional economy was drawn into a wider commercial nexus, while the enormous mass of it, to the degree that it was commercialized at all, produced, consumed, and traded on an intraregional level only. One can even envision multiple levels of economic integration embracing primary exchanges (administration and taxation); secondary exchanges (consumer durables and luxuries, and capital flows); tertiary exchanges (consumer nondurables on a commercial scale, and possibly labor mobility); and quaternary exchanges (small-scale consumer nondurables).[34] In lieu of hard evidence indicating substantial interregional trade, data on the arbitrage between regional

---

size, levels of physical activity, and caloric requirements support these general calculations insofar as consumption levels are concerned. Certain underlying assumptions are at play. Supposing an average Mexican man of the period to measure 1.63 meters in height and to weigh between 55.3 and 65.3 kilos, he would require a daily intake of 2,433 calories; an average adult woman of 1.62 meters in height and between 45.4 and 53.5 kilos in weight would require 1,850 calories daily; an average child under fifteen years of age, about 1,800 calories. The total of these caloric minima would amount to a daily family requirement of roughly 9,000 calories, or some 3,285,000 calories per year. Assuming, further, that the family in question would have obtained 75 percent of its caloric requirements from maize (an estimate perhaps on the conservative side), and observing that a kilo of maize supplies about 3,500 calories, we have an average annual "maize-cal" requirement of about 2,500,000 calories, the equivalent of 708 kilos (15.6 *fanegas*) of maize.

My calculations are based substantially on Cross (1978), and accord reasonably well with the work of Cook and Borah (1974–1980). The estimates of adult masculine consumption and the percentage of total calories derived from maize are drawn from Nickel (1984), and Coatsworth (1987). An earlier version of this chapter based its maize consumption estimate on the figures of Hassig (1985, 20–21). Various colleagues brought to my attention the fact that Hassig's figures (about twice the level of those presented here) are improbably high for reasons not altogether clear. If the corrected figure—2,220,000 fanegas—for the total regional production of maize (445,000 + 1,750,000 *fanegas*) is closer to the truth, then the quantity exported (445,000 *fanegas*) falls from 24 percent of total production to about 20 percent. Lower maize consumption on the part of wheat eaters within the province would probably have been counterbalanced by the use of maize for feeding pigs and other livestock. In this same year (1803), of a total wheat production of 54,287 *cargas,* or 3,701,386 kilograms (a *carga* equals about 68.2 kilograms), the province exported about 20,890 *cargas,* or some 38 percent. This differential in favor of wheat over maize exports makes sense, if there was an exportable surplus of wheat, since the same transport cost per unit would bring higher earnings to wheat exporters because of the much higher average price of that grain. Of the total production of livestock in 1803—1,340,558 pesos in value—approximately 20 percent (260,688 pesos) was exported, but the secular tendency in livestock exports was toward decline (Van Young 1981, 47, 70, 82). For a more detailed treatment of late-colonial rural living standards, see Van Young (1992, Chap. 2). For some comparative considerations of material life in colonial Latin America, including much attention to food consumption, see Van Young (1994c).

34. This same point has often been made; see Morse (1986, 80ff), Brading (1986), and Lockhart (1986).

markets of commodity prices such as maize or other grains is sometimes used to infer the existence of such commercial connections and the developed, wide-ranging market economy assumed to underlie them, but this argument is not altogether convincing (Lindo Fuentes 1980).[35]

REGION AND STATE IN MEXICAN HISTORY

What, finally, are the implications of such a regional structure for the society as a whole? First, it indicates a weak horizontal or spatial integration, and goes some way toward explaining the centrifugal tendencies in Mexico notable during the colonial period, and even more so after the

---

35. Lindo Fuentes's (1980) excellent article points to the high correlation among the movements of prices in several regions in New Spain based upon presently available price series for the eighteenth century. But he also admits that such apparent sympathetic movements may be due as much to the effects of fortuitous climatological or other nonmarket factors, as to the arbitraging of prices in interregional markets (p. 277). On the other hand, the pressure cooker/solar regional type would be expected to show a marked "sluggishness" or "stickiness" in price responses at best, since such systems are typically subject to nonmarket (i.e., political) constraints and are by their very nature weakly linked to other regions; on this point see Smith (1976c, 336). My own work on the Guadalajara region (1981, chaps. 3-5) indicates a relatively late market development almost totally intraregional in scope, with virtually no introduction of basic food consumption items from outside, even in times of severe crisis. Thus, inferring from a high correlation of basic commodity price movements that prices were being arbitraged in a large-scale, interregional market is like concluding that because two patients have a high temperature they are both suffering from the same disease. Morin (1979, 195-201) makes this point very clearly in noting the wide variation of prices from one locality to another within the bishopric, and the stickiness of their movement: "Other examples may confirm the existence of local markets in which prices assume an anarchic form, [which is] out of keeping with the image of a space unified by a network of exchange within which prices hardly differ except as a function of transport costs. These inequalities reveal a very defective integration, since the exchanges of one place with another do not obey the rule of cost minimization and profit maximization" (p. 196). And Morin concludes: "Despite the volume of exchange and the importance of markets, and that overall commercial activity was constantly growing, the circulation of goods [lacked] the mechanisms of a market economy" (p. 201). My conclusions about the autarchical tendencies of pressure cooker/solar-type regional economies have drawn a good deal of dissent over the years since the material in this chapter was first published. Specifically for the Guadalajara region there is the powerfully argued study of Antonio Ibarra Romero (2000b), which analyzes the Abascal report of 1803 but concludes that the region was much less autarchic economically, more porous, and more dynamic than my portrayal would suggest. Some historians (Silva Riquer, Grosso, and Yuste 1995; Silva Riquer and López Martínez 1998; Silva Riquer and Escobar Ohmstede 2000; Miño Grijalva 2001; Silva Riquer et al. 2003; Silva Riquer 2008) have found more robust trading networks among cities and regions, others a higher level of participation by indigenous producers in intra- and interregional markets.

achievement of independence in 1821. Second, the weakness of horizontal articulation would directly relate to the weakness of vertical, or sociopolitical, articulation, since it probably indicates a relatively low social division of labor. Admittedly, one is likely to find a crazy-quilt pattern here, with fields of distortion surrounding mining areas, administrative centers, and the ever-anomalous Mexico City. And third, one would expect to see such a society, in times of acute political crisis, tend to break up into its constituent parts along the preexisting lines of stress I have just been outlining. This is exactly what happened in the years following 1810, in which one can trace through the social history of rebellion the deep-running disarticulation of Mexican society all the way down to the village level.

It is not an unreasonable view that Mexico, at least until the advent of the railroad in the last quarter of the nineteenth century, demonstrated many of the characteristics of a notably regionalized, substantially disarticulated society in both the social and economic dimensions. Now, having spent a good deal of time earlier in this chapter criticizing (or, perhaps, qualifying) the central-place and regional science theory upon which this interpretation must rest, I should explain here what regionalization and disarticulation do *not* mean. They do not imply an aggregate of hermetically sealed, autarchic regional spaces, all centered on cities. The model here is rather more one of regions seen in terms of central gravitational pulls, with peripheries rather than boundaries. Regions' shapes and sizes may change over time, the forces that bring them into existence giving way to different forces that sustain them and their "regionalness" even declining or disappearing altogether, as I have suggested. Nor do regionalization and disarticulation exclude the integrating effects of backward economic linkages from certain domestic sectors (mining or railroad construction, for example), forward linkages (the oiling of commercial circuits, as in the colonial period and nineteenth century, with Mexican-produced silver), long-range trade in imported products (whether luxury items, manufactured goods of wide consumption, or capital goods), or the external orientation of some regional economies producing for supraregional or even international markets. And still less do regionalization and disarticulation preclude the differentiation of the Mexican colonial/national space along other lines than exchange relationships and productive arrangements, such as linguistic tradition, culture, or administrative identities. The question will be asked: Compared to what other areas was colonial and early national Mexico regionalized and disarticulated? Certainly it was so in comparison to much of contemporary Europe or the Anglo-American colonies and young nation, from which its economic trajectory diverged increasingly after about 1800 (Coatsworth 1990, 32). On the other hand, compared with Peru, and despite the convincingly portrayed integrative effects of the mining *arrastre* there and the existence of non-urban-centered "ethnic economies" involving long-distance trade by Indians, New Spain and early national Mexico were apparently better integrated (Assadourian 1982; Slicher Van Bath 1992).

Several lines of evidence can be cited in support of this view of the colonial and early national Mexican economy, but I would like to focus briefly on two, relating to the eighteenth century, primarily as background for some concluding remarks on the tension between state and region in Mexican history more broadly conceived. The first of these has to do with the reach of commercial circuits in general and patterns of interregional trade in particular, the second with the colony-wide social division of labor and the social structure of Mexico's elites. First, the relatively low proportion of goods of intraregional origin exported from most Mexican regions at the close of the colonial period tends to indicate their low degree of economic integration with outer regions and with the center of the country. It is necessary to acknowledge the problematic nature of trying to construct regional accounts, the analog of macroeconomic calculations concerning gross national or gross domestic product (Richardson 1978, 30–37). The case study I have developed in these pages to support this idea is that of the Guadalajara region during the late colonial decades.

Second, it seems possible to trace back at least partial responsibility for late colonial Mexico's social and urban structure to the relatively weak "national" market integration just alluded to. The hypothesis here is that each of several regions tended to have its own primate city and did not export much to the others. The implication of this weak horizontal or spatial integration of New Spain is striking. With limited opportunities existing for market development, economies of scale, or real economic growth, the weak regional integration allowed only a low degree of social division of labor, and therefore a weak class structure and vertical, or sociopolitical, articulation. The blame for this situation cannot be ascribed entirely to Spanish colonial policies, as is sometimes asserted, but certainly the Spanish state must bear its burden of responsibility. As to the weakness in class structure, recent research on Mexico City suggests that a class struggle among two or three groups clearly differentiated from each other on the basis of ownership of the means of production was unlikely because of the absence of economic preconditions necessary to such groupings. The viceregal capital (and presumably other cities as well) had a highly segmented or "cellular" type of urban social structure (González Angulo Aguirre 1983). Industrial establishments remained on the average very small (with certain very limited exceptions), so that the workplace could not serve as a locus for the development of class antagonisms. The one significant exception to this generalization, it appears, was the region of the Bajío, which possessed something approaching a true urban network at the close of the colonial period, characterized by a lognormal size distribution of its cities and a better developed class structure than the rest of the country. And it was precisely in this region that the rebellion for independence broke out in 1810, and in which urban uprising as a component of it was most notable.

If this scenario of Mexican spatial and social structure is anywhere near accurate, a number of revealing implications follow, of which I will cite only two. First, it would mean that the apparent disintegration of New Spain into its constituent regions at the beginning of the nineteenth century was a process already implicit in the organization of the colonial space at least as far back as the eighteenth century, if not earlier, and cannot be laid exclusively to the destructive effects of the independence wars themselves (Pérez Herrero 1990). And second, the effects of Mexican regionality on the country's social structure potentially tell us a good deal about the forces unleashed by the *grito* of September 1810—about the failure of political opposition or popular protest to coalesce along class lines, the rampant and violent localism of popular rebellion, and the feudalization of the independence movement as a whole (Van Young 2001c). These characteristics of the independence struggle in turn can be seen to explain much about the nature of Mexican political and economic structures in the ensuing century, up to and even beyond the Revolution of 1910.

In its most basic formulation, the problematic of space—of regional history, in this case—can be reduced to the question of energy exchanges between man and environment (e.g., Adams 1975); with the efficiency of energy transmission, whether in the form of goods and services, taxes, information, political decisions, and so forth; and with what geographers call the friction of distance. The frameworks within which these exchanges take place, whether institutionalized or ad hoc, are at the center of many of the questions that concern historians and other regionalists: market relationships, production arrangements, the structures of the state, the burgeoning of nationalism, the homogenization of culture. Yet strongly spatialized as these questions may be, we reduce our theoretical understanding of history to geographical determinism only at the risk of misapprehending what it is that drives individuals and societies forward.

If one takes the energy-exchange model and its spatial dimension seriously, interesting questions are opened up for large-scale thinking about the history of Mexico. For example, one of the constant preoccupations of students of Mexican history in this century, and of national political and cultural discourse within the country itself, is the growth of the Mexican state, particularly since the Revolution of 1910. Indeed, in the triumphalist interpretation the entire economic and political development of the nineteenth century, or Mexican history even further back, may be seen as a long and chaotic prolegomenon to the emergence of the modern postrevolutionary Mexican state (Friedmann, Gardels, and Pennink 1980). While this narrative might be characterized as simplistic or even teleological, much can be said for it. Political and military struggles over the control and constitution of the Mexican state may be viewed as attempts to construct or capture an instrumentality to reduce the friction of distance, and therefore increase the efficiency of energy extraction by the center. For example, whether members of the active political public in the nineteenth century considered themselves liberals or conservatives had a good deal to do with whether they thought the growth of markets should precede the growth of the state, or whether affairs should be the other way around. Similarly, the growth of modern Mexican nationalism—of national identity and *lo mexicano*—has had much to do with the breaking down of the many regional pointillisms through more efficient systems of transport, market mechanisms, military logistics, and media of information exchange.

Seen from this vantage point, the growth of Mexican state power since the early nineteenth century, and the impetus toward economic development that went along with it as both effect and legitimizing ideology, may be seen as a process whereby the country's strong regional structure was weakened and its weak class structure strengthened, as I have suggested above. Contemporary Marxists tend to think regionalism a force impeding the progress of history, a manifestation of conflict between the mobility of capital and the immobile nature of social reproduction (Markusen 1987), and therefore presumably also an obstacle to the unfolding of social relations of production. The process of state building has not been without its costs or setbacks, of course. Assuming for the moment a degree of congruity between colonial regions and Mexican federal states, these latter entities have tried at various times to block the emergent hegemony of the central state (Carmagnani 1983; Cerutti 1992). In the postrevolutionary period the forward progress of the central state against the forces of regional control of resources is especially well illustrated by the development of irrigation and power projects centering on Mexico's great giver basins (Barkin and King 1970; and for an earlier era, Kroeber 1985). On the ideological front, myth building and state building were essential concomitants for the rooting of nationalism and national identity beginning in the nineteenth century (Brading 1985; Robinson 1989, 169), while a Mexican national historiography was tentatively forged out of the building blocks of regional history (del Río 1989, 30–31; but for the Revolution, compare Vanderwood 1987).

The class structure of a developed capitalist system is arguably a more efficient mechanism (up to the point that it begins to suffer serious feedback effects) for extracting energy from the environment than a highly regionalized economy, with the outcome that the social groups controlling the high ground of the state, and their pet projects, are the beneficiaries of the net energy gain. Nationalism is the covering ideology for this process of increasingly efficient extraction. The question should perhaps not be why states are born and grow, but rather why regions existed and continue to do so. This problematic relationship among region, class, and state raises a number of questions for the history of Mexico. Did a strongly regionalized society like prerevolutionary Mexico have a segmented class structure? Was it a one-class society, with a dominant traditional elite and nothing much else in the way of class groupings, such as Peter Laslett (1965) suggested some years ago for preindustrial England? Or did it really comprise a number of minisocieties, each with its own class structure, joined by some trade, language, and a loose political envelope? Historians and other scholars are still grappling with these questions, and regional analysis of various sorts seems an important technique in their repertoire. In this sense, whether regions actually survive in all their vigor and multiformity or fade into historical anachronisms, they still remain good to think.

CHAPTER 6

The Cuautla Lazarus
Reading Texts on Popular Collective Action

This chapter addresses how one might approach historical texts as evidence from an insistently (though not nihilistically) skeptical point of view. In particular, it speaks to some epistemological and methodological considerations suggested by varieties of postmodernist thinking, above all the linguistic turn in the human sciences. I am interested, concretely, in thinking about the documents I have been working with for some years in writing a social history of popular collective action during the Mexican wars of independence at the beginning of the nineteenth century, including criminal trial records, judicial confessions, letters, and other sorts of texts. I should emphasize that I am not writing so much about Mexico at the beginning of the nineteenth century, as about textual analysis and the constitution and boundaries of historical knowledge in a wider sense, using the example of my own research as a point of entry into a larger discussion of possible interest to historians. Within this general program, I am particularly interested in exploring the limits of what one can say about the motivation and ideology of common people, many of them illiterate, from analyzing such documents. Although large questions of structure and agency inevitably hover in the background of any such discussion, they are not my concern here, but chiefly the hermeneutics of relating actors' categories to forms of recorded discourse and individual behaviors. My central specimen text is the short, tantalizing record of a criminal prosecution for insurgency against José Marcelino Pedro Rodríguez, whom the Spanish royalist authorities executed in 1812, and who apparently believed he could be returned to life by Father José María Morelos, the famous rebel leader. The subtext is the well-known Derridean aphorism that all interpretation is misinterpretation.

My rethinking of these issues has been triggered by the reading of three widely influential books, all of which have been stimulating (but none completely convincing): historian Simon Schama's *Dead Certainties* (1991), political scientist James Scott's *Domination and the Arts of Resistance* (1990), and a collection of essays edited by the anthropologists James Clifford and George Marcus, *Writing Culture: The Poetics and Politics of Ethnography* (1986).[1] Schama's book reconstructs, through avowedly fictionalized historical accounts, two tenuously related real-life incidents: the death of the English General James Wolf during the Battle of Quebec in the French and Indian War in 1759; and the notoriously grisly 1849 murder of George Parkman, Boston physician and man of property (the historian Francis Parkman's uncle), allegedly at the hands of Harvard chemistry professor John Webster over some debts owed Parker by Webster. Scott's book deals with the nature of resistance by subordinate groups to ostensibly hegemonic social and ideological orders. He offers a provocative model distinguishing (though not disassociating) public from private subaltern behaviors, but one that may in the last instance be excessively voluntaristic (or hyperagential, as I come to call it). The anthology of Clifford and Marcus explores the issues of authority and objectivity in ethnographic writing, offering a number of powerful critiques whose object is to crack the authoritative facade of observers' categories, expanding the space for interpretive play and incorporating the plasticity of language in a constructive way.

The essay inscribes a discussion of ideas of resistance by rural people, and of how one comes to know what the nature and locus of resistance are, within a meditation on the sources in which I was immersed for many years while studying the popular sectors in the movement for independence in Mexico. I try to situate these in turn within a contemplation of the limits of historical knowledge imposed by the instability of meaning in language, the cultural biases of external observers, and the sheer unknowability of past events. Trapped, in essence, between sociologizing

---

1. On the rethinking of ethnographic method and writing, see also Marcus and Fischer (1986). On poststructuralist thinking in literary studies, anthropology, history, and the other human sciences, see among many other works Harland (1987; a reference I owe to John Hart), Eagleton (1983), and Ellis (1989); and for a freewheeling Marxist attack on the application of linguistic approaches, Palmer (1990). A number of people who made useful comments on an earlier version of this chapter deserve my thanks, including Brooke Larson and an anonymous reviewer for the *Colonial Latin American Review*, John Coatsworth, Michael Gonzáles, Maurice Brungardt, Paul Vanderwood, Barbara Tenenbaum, Stanley Stein, and the late Enrique Tandeter (who offered sage advice that I did not take). The essay is dedicated to the memory of Michael Merritt, a prominent Chicago artist and scenic designer, college roommate, and friend who died much too young. He would have understood intuitively, I think, the point I try to make here so laboriously.

or letting historical actors have the story all their own way, I try to suggest for historians of popular collective action a mapping of interpretive space somewhere between smugness and existential paralysis, taking into account that actors' words generally mean what they say, even if not *only* what they say; and that all action—and most especially political action—has affective and cultural significance. I do not see that the puzzle of the trialogue among intended meaning, preconscious/unconscious meaning, and imputed meaning has a ready solution; there must always be a certain amount of epistemological hand-wringing associated with these issues. The prescriptions offered briefly at the end of the essay certainly do not answer the questions raised in the body of the piece, much beyond suggesting the utility of cautious "thick description" (e.g., Geertz 1973), no novelty to social historians anyway. Nor would I claim any particular insight into the body of dense critical and theoretical work I touch upon, still less any original conceptual contribution. Rather I swim along, pilot fish–like, in the subaqueous shadows of the larger, man-eating theory builders, scaring up my own set of small questions in the murky waters. My own interest in all these questions is at least as much ludically as theoretically driven (rather like that of Schama's, I suspect).

ALAS, POOR YORRICK

For those who have not read it or spoken with a friend who has read it, or who have somehow missed the saturation reviewing and feature stories on Schama's book, its author, and the death of traditional history in newspapers and literary journals on at least two continents, *Dead Certainties* is an absolutely enthralling, elegantly written, superbly intelligent (and in my opinion rather duplicitous) fictional evocation of the two episodes mentioned above. Though Schama himself is ultimately somewhat evasive about the ontological status of his two narratives, he does in an "Afterword" refer to them both as basically "historical novellas," stressing that his technique has been to "dissolve the certainties of events into the multiple possibilities of alternative narrations" (Schama 1991, 320, 322). Apparently this is meant to suggest that Schama's account of the Parkman case, in particular, has some special credibility and claim upon our attention—more than, say, a James Lee Burke or Scott Turow novel—because it *could* have transpired (crossing here the threshold from the possibilistic to the probabilistic sense of "could"). Nonetheless, his question is a perennial one for historians, but no less fundamentally interesting for that. Basically it has to do with the dividing line between fact and fiction; and by extension, for our purposes, between explicit and implicit forms of evidence, and between the baldly empirical and the subtly inferred. His answer seems to be that the line, if in fact it exists at all, is a highly porous one, and that the fictive imagining of the novelist and the factual imagining of the historian are not that far apart. The difference between what "actually happened" between Parkman and Webster, or on the Heights of Abraham during the Battle of Quebec, and what we are able to reconstruct of it as historians, depends on the multiplicity of fragmented accounts we typically have of such occurrences, and on the Rashomon-like divergences of those accounts. Beyond that, Schama seems to remind us, is the nature of textuality itself, for we are dealing with written texts here as evidence, or their refraction in the iconography of epic visual representation, as in Benjamin West's famous painting of Wolf's death, and of how written documents are produced, and what we can understand of them.

To put this in another way, there may be no acceptable way of determining which of several accounts of an event has a greater truth value than another; furthermore, there may be very severe limitations on what we are able to understand of texts produced by other hands, in other times, in other cultures.[2] In other words, these doubts spread along both synchronic and diachronic axes. If this is so, then our claim to do "scientific" history in any sense, based on the careful and "objective" exegesis of texts, is called seriously into question. Furthermore, these very claims are themselves a cultural artifact with a history, as Michel Foucault and other thinkers have suggested at once so powerfully and opaquely, and forms of knowledge themselves the outcome of power relationships. The progressive differentiation of literary and scientific discourses—of fiction from fact, of subjectivity from objectivity—over the last several centuries has often been noted. The late French theorist and critic Michel de Certeau characterized fiction as "[playing] on the stratification of meaning; [as narrating] one thing in order to tell something else; [as delineating] itself in language from which it continuously draws effects of meaning that cannot be circumscribed or checked" (1983, 182). On the other hand, some postmodern reflections on the traditional humane disciplines have pointed to the convergence of fictional and factual imagining in their very techniques of textualizing, in the sense that they never really diverged at all. Recent critiques of anthropological method, for example, have suggested

---

2. This is hardly a novel insight, I concede, and has been well chewed over by European social and cultural historians, in particular. For a cluster of observations on the limits of anthropologically informed textual interpretation, aimed directly at Robert Darnton's (1984) provocative work, and which I take closely to parallel my own, see Chartier (1988, esp. chap. 4), a reference for which I thank Brooke Larson.

that all ethnographic writing is allegorical, providing detailed descriptions of other cultures at the same time that they tell us about our own, telling us one thing in order to convey a story about another at the same time (Clifford 1986). If one substitutes history for ethnography in this formulation, one cannot go far wrong.

Taking its cue primarily from the multivocality of language, all this epistemological slipping and sliding has of course become the province of the renewed interest in language in the human sciences, its basic categories, structures, and processes. Opaque and unpalatable as this theoretical ooze sometimes seems to those outside the literary-critical or cultural studies establishments, and furthermore acknowledging that good historians have always been critical of their source-texts, we nevertheless skirt this critical ferment at our peril. My own theoretical stance is that of a quizzical and rather nervous positivist, beset on every side by doubts. An exposure to the lingual virus may leave effects almost impossible to shake, producing recurrent episodes, as with malaria or Chagas' disease. Fits of existential shaking, fevers, and sweating punctuate long periods of apparent remission, only to be set off again by encounters with particularly enigmatic texts.

From an unreconstructed positivist's point of view, the worst-case scenario would run something like this. Our intuition tells us that there is an "objective" reality under the flux of language, and that we might recover it if only we could scrape away the accretions of language itself, and the crusts of ideology. It is palpably counterintuitive, to most of us, to maintain that the events we seek to recover themselves exist only through the medium of language, that in a sense there are no antecedent "real" events separate from language, but only representations of linguistic conjunctures, an infinite regress of opposing mirrored images arching away from us to a distant vanishing point beyond our field of vision. Moreover, under such a set of assumptions language becomes more than just a medium (albeit an infinitely complex one) connecting us to the distant object, its role more than an extrinsic transmitting entity like the ether of nineteenth-century physics. It becomes the object of our inquiry itself, and the product of that inquiry not the reconstruction of a discrete thing, but a conversation with the past. But an intuition is, in a sense, a statement about the possible. Our ideas about the possible depend upon our ideas about the probable, and these are culturally determined. Thus intuition would seem almost infinitely plastic, a geographical feature of that cognitive and moral landscape many of us have come to think of as *mentalité*. Where, then, is the boundary of that country where the indeterminacy of language reigns, or is it an open frontier?

For those of us who take this epistemological critique seriously, there has occurred a radical shaking of assumptions and decentering in history and the other human sciences. One of the implications of this is that we must make space for a double subjectivity, that of our objects and that of ourselves, and for the instability of meaning along both synchronic and diachronic axes (that is, in the historical moment and in history). This space has always been the privileged realm of art, as for example in the modern novel, but in discourses seeking to arrive at "Truth" as opposed to "a truth," the attempt at adjustment could conceivably be paralyzing rather than liberating. And this is all the more the case with historians, for whom the apprehended social reality is not immediately at hand, but mediated by the written accounts of other people. Thus, while an ethnographer may arguably claim to "read" a social text—in describing a ritual, for example—the historian renders a reading of a reading, or rather a reading of a writing of a reading (viz., Chartier 1988).

THE CUAUTLA LAZARUS

The young historian-hero of Henry James's unfinished last novel remarks that "recovering the lost [past] was at all events . . . much like entering the enemy's lines to get back one's dead for burial" (James 1917, quoted in Schama 1991, 319). This is doubly and rather ironically true in the case of José Marcelino Pedro Rodríguez, an illiterate Indian man of twenty-five years old, by all odds an agricultural laborer, wounded by royalist fire and taken prisoner just outside the Mexican town of Cuautla, in the Cuernavaca sugar zone, on 23 March 1812. To refresh the memory of those readers not on close terms with the military history of the Mexican independence struggle, Cuautla was the site of a three-month-long siege during the late winter and early spring of 1812, with insurgent chieftain José María Morelos's forces bottled up inside the town, and the royalist besiegers commanded by the future Mexican viceroy Félix María Calleja.[3] Born and probably living on a local hacienda, Rodríguez had been in the town a month serving as a rifleman, and was apparently captured while foraging for food or animal fodder by night outside the siege lines. Under interrogation he gave a good deal of interesting information about conditions within the besieged town, the rebel leadership there, the composition of the insurgent forces, and so forth. The unfortunate Pedro Rodríguez was sentenced summarily to be executed the following day, Tuesday, 24 March, and in fact the sentence was carried out.

3. For a good account of the basics of the Cuautla episode, see Hamnett (1986).

But the most interesting thing about Rodríguez's case was the exchange with royalist interrogators following his formal signed statement, duly if somewhat elliptically recorded by the military scribe taking down the testimony in the rough-and-ready court martial. When royalist officers asked Rodríguez if he wanted his body returned to Cuautla after execution, he replied affirmatively, asserting that Father Morelos had with him a child who would bring him back to life (*"para que lo resucitase el niño que tiene el cura"*). Rodríguez added that he wanted to be taken back to Cuautla *"para que lo viese el cura Morelos, y viera que por su causa andan perdiendo la vida"* (so that the priest Morelos would see him, and would see that for his cause [people] are losing their lives). Slightly later, however, Rodríguez denied having said anything about being brought back from the dead, and insisting only that he had heard from some *mandones* (officials) from the town of Miacatlan that Morelos had with him in Cuautla a child capable of reviving the dead after three days, but that he himself (Rodríguez) had never believed it.[4]

Now, even a reasonably sophisticated critical reading of this text might take it at face value in the sense that the manifest content rather than the manner of the text's making and its context immediately and dramatically claims our attention. I was fascinated to encounter it, as also evidence of widespread messianic and millenarian beliefs among rural insurgents during this period, since it begins to indicate how very basic religious thinking and imagery were to ordinary people's view of the world, of politics, and of political protest and violence.[5] The Lazarus reference is the most obvious element of Pedro Rodríguez's statement.[6] This could

---

4. Nettie Lee Benson Latin American Collection, University of Texas at Austin, Hernández y Dávalos Collection, 4.71.371–83, 1812. I have quoted the Spanish original so as not to lose the flavor of the encounter.

5. To anticipate a bit my brief discussion of Scott (1990), he makes the unsurprising but nonetheless insightful suggestion (chap. 4) that the particular historical forms taken by a dominant (not hegemonic, in his view—never hegemonic) social order will call forth equally particular forms of cultural and social resistance. Standing this formulation on its head and applying it to the case of colonial Mexico, one can construe the pervasive importance of religious reference and imagery among popular insurgent groups as evidence that the most important mode of ideological domination in the colony was religious, and the most important macrosocial bonds were religious ones.

6. A number of colleagues (personal communications) have suggested to me different interpretations of Pedro Rodríguez's statement and its constituent elements. Maurice Brungardt, for example, espouses a Trinitarian interpretation, with the central figure as Christ rather than Lazarus, rightly pointing to the ideological relationship between resurrection and revolution. Paul Vanderwood suggests that the child in the grouping is the infant Jesus, Barbara Tenenbaum that it might be a religious icon rather than a person, and Donald Stevens playfully that it might have been Father Morelos's illegitimate son, Juan N. Almonte (1803–1869), or, alternatively, a famous cannon Morelos had with him, called "El Niño" (a life-giving phallic

be pursued rather interestingly to its origins, by the way, since he himself was illiterate, and since in any case there is little evidence that rural people of the time read the Bible. Most of his religious ideas would have come to him through bits of catechistic and other religious training when a child, and through the sermons of his parish priest.

The question of these lines of transmission aside, however, the evocation of Lazarus in the tomb in connection with the miraculous restorative powers of the priests who led the insurrection in its early phases is interesting for two reasons. First, it was not idiosyncratic to Pedro Rodríguez.[7] In fact, it resonates strongly with beliefs in leaders' supernatural powers characteristic of messianic movements spanning centuries and continents.[8] Nor were such beliefs limited to uneducated rustics: we know that Father Miguel Hidalgo wore an image of the Virgin of Guadalupe on his chest under his priest's cassock, though how far he believed in its efficacy as a talisman against actual bodily harm is impossible to say. Second, and perhaps even more intriguing, is the presence in Rodríguez's version of Lazarus, with himself as the resurrected man and Father Morelos presumably in the role of Jesus, of the child with the mysterious powers. In the original version of Lazarus's resurrection from the Book of John, there is no third person directly involved in Jesus' raising of the dead man. The spare account simply narrates Christ's recital of the famous "I am the resurrection and the life" speech, the rolling away of the stone from the mouth of the tomb, and the emergence of the four-day-dead Lazarus into the world of the living.[9] This passage from the Gospels, so rich for us in religious, metaphorical, and literary resonances, would be changed in fundamental ways by the addition of a third party to the picture, and not just a neutral witness at that, but a child who actually mediates Christ's miraculous intervention in the natural course of life and death. This would be tantamount to Leonardo's having added a pair of laughing cherubim or a happy face looking over the shoulder of the La Gioconda.

The interposition of the child between Lazarus/Rodríguez and Jesus/

---

symbol in this instance?—asks Stevens). Both Vanderwood and Stevens acutely point to the element of the returning culture hero almost certainly personified in the figure of Morelos, and its resonances with the preconquest religious beliefs and mythologies of Mesoamerican indigenous peoples, an argument I have made elsewhere (e.g., Van Young 1987, 1989a, 2001c). For reasons expounded in the text of this chapter, as well as for others whose discussion is precluded by space constraints, I find the Lazarus interpretation most credible.

7. Virginia Guedea, personal communication. See also the royalist political tract of Fermín de Reygadas (1811).

8. For some examples of special talismans, ointments, and so forth worn by the faithful to avert harm from the enemy's weapons, and of the miraculous resuscitative powers of religiously inspired leaders, see Vanderwood (1994) and Adas (1979).

9. John, Chapter 11, verses 1–44.

Morelos totally shifts the moral and narrative weight of the episode, not necessarily in a direction flattering to the Mexican insurgent priest. Why should Pedro Rodríguez's version have done this? One possible reason, as I have elsewhere suggested, is that Mexican parish priests of the late colonial period—Morelos, Hidalgo, and other rebel leaders among them—venerated as they may have been in some cases, fulfilled the role of mediators between their parishioners and the supernatural powers represented by God, Jesus, the Virgin, and the Saints. On the one hand, therefore, their brokerage function may have been such an inherent aspect of their personae, and their personalities so familiar, that they were able to attract little if any of the powerful affective and symbolic connection whose formation was necessary to the development of a popular messianic figure. They were middlemen pure and simple, and no significant quantum of supernatural power could adhere to them. On the other hand, priests may simply not have been expendable in the moral economy of the peasant village universe.[10] The child would seem to fulfill this sacral lacuna, but at the expense of Morelos's own sacrality.

Up to this point in my analysis of the Pedro Rodríguez episode I have mostly adhered to the manifest content of the text and to some questions and speculations generated by it. But if we look at the textuality of the document, its role in representation and at the circumstances of its making and their power to shape its meaning, it is surprisingly much harder to get anywhere because those circumstances themselves raise tough methodological and epistemological problems for which there are no easy solutions. In other words, it is not so much that we have a set of floating signifiers, as that they are anchored so firmly and narrowly in singular circumstances that their meaning is obscure or unrecoverable. Why, for example, did Rodríguez's royalist captors even ask him what disposition he wanted made of his body? In the many hundreds, perhaps thousands, of criminal trials and court martial proceedings of accused insurgents that I have seen for the period this is the only instance of such a question I have encountered. Had he said something off the record to provoke the question, were they taunting him for some reason, or was it just the casual question of a curious officer? And what of the accused's remark to the effect that he wanted Father Morelos to see that people were losing their lives in his cause? At such a remove in time and culture it is difficult to tell from the tone of his statement whether Pedro Rodríguez conceived of Morelos viewing his corpse as a fillip to the priest's flagging spirit, or

---

10. See Van Young (2001c), where this point is mentioned as part of a more extended discussion of messianic elements in the popular ideology of the period. My thinking on this issue was greatly stimulated by the work of Gruzinski (1989).

a reproof of his irresponsibility in leading a futile movement. Certainly judging by other confessions and legal statements of the time few accused insurgents actively courted martyrdom, and fewer still assumed a defiant stance in the face of royalist authorities civil or military.

Even more intriguing is the question of why Pedro Rodríguez apparently changed his mind while or after making his initial statement. By the close of the interrogation he claimed never to have said anything at all about being brought back to life, but only to have heard from some other people that Morelos had with him a miraculous child who could revive people after three days, but that he himself had never believed this. The difference between the two versions he provided in his statement, obviously, was that in the second he distanced himself from the belief, attributing it to other people instead while repositioning himself as a skeptic. Which is his "real" testimony, and is there any way of determining the authenticity of one as over against another from the text we have before us?

Furthermore, it is not as if these ambiguities could be resolved by recourse to a detailed semiotic or content analysis of what Rodríguez said and how, since the text was not constructed in such a way that we can even recover exact wording, and certainly not important nonverbal cues such as tone of voice, facial expression or body language, and so forth. This record and most others were not verbatim recordings but transcriptions by military or other notaries from what we must assume to have been notes taken during interrogations and other judicial processes, and which were fleshed out later and read to the accused for ratification or emendation. Personal narrative statement, as in "I left my village to join the insurgents," becomes displaced into the third person, as in "He testified that he left his village to join the insurgents," without any way of recovering exact language or winnowing the interjections of the transcriber or other parties from the words of the testifier. As far as I can determine, states of mind of accused insurgents or elaborations of their political or other beliefs were not of great interest to royalist authorities, but only matters of fact bearing on whether the accused had taken up arms against the colonial regime. This is a good deal different from an Inquisition procedure, for example, whether in the Old World or the New, in which the internal voices of motivation and belief of the accused were equally or even more important than events in the behavior stream, and which produced a different sort of text in consequence (Van Young 2001c; 1986b, 390, note 11).

If it is difficult to know exactly what Rodríguez said, it is that much more difficult to know what he meant. Meaning matters because it bears on interpretation and helps to prevent us from falling into the reductionism of outcomes. It is most important in the backward linkages historians typically try to forge, in providing explanations rather than predictions.

The search for meaning provides one pathway to determining the answer to the apparently simple, but in reality almost inconceivably difficult, question of why people do the things they do. And the answer may be that they do things for very different reasons than the outcomes of their actions would necessarily suggest. Acknowledging this can strip away at least part of the teleology that often flavors our explanatory schemae, and which boils down to statements that approximate the form, for example, that something called Mexican independence occurred because people wanted it to happen. Certainly *some* people may have wanted it to happen, but just as certainly this is something to be proved and explored rather than assumed and naturalized.

One final aspect of Pedro Rodríguez's testimony bears extended attention: the context of domination within which the document was produced. This discussion will lead me in turn to a brief critical consideration of James Scott's ideas on the hidden transcripts of resistance. It is manifestly the case that Pedro Rodríguez must have been under a great deal of stress while giving his statements: wounded, having just come out of a crowded town under close siege and continuous shelling, fearing for his freedom if not his life, and so forth. Then, too, there may have been a translator present, as there was in many, many cases, and/or Rodríguez may have commanded a much less than perfect spoken Spanish. Certainly he was illiterate, as his signing the final version of his confession with an "X" indicates. So this was not a neutral environment for him, or anything approaching it (if indeed any such thing can be said to exist), but a space almost certainly bristling with the symbols and artifacts of domination—scowling royalist soldiers, guns, possibly physical restraints upon him. Beyond this was the entire ideology, technology, and daily lived experience of colonial domination itself. This included ideas, which Pedro Rodríguez may even have internalized to some degree himself, about the inferiority of the Indian: that indigenous people were lazy, childlike, libidinous, unreliable, bibulous, suggestible, sunken in ignorant torpor, and savage when provoked to anger.

We know the sort of effects these conditions produced in accused insurgents in prison examinations, courts martial, criminal proceedings, and other legal venues, since there are occasional hints and fragmentary descriptions in the texts we are interrogating. One Luciano Pérez, for example, accused of insurgency and shot by the royalists about the same time as Pedro Rodríguez, when questioned aggressively "responded with his eyes downcast, his head bowed, and scraping his twisted hat between his legs."[11] Other accused men stammered, stuttered, lapsed into complete

---

11. Archivo General de la Nación (Mexico City) (hereafter, AGN), Operaciones de Guerra, vol. 15, fols. 40r–51v, 1812. Compare Victor Hugo's (1987/1862, 267, 270–71)

silence or steadfastly refused to say anything, or became ill. Insurrectionary leader Ignacio Allende developed very convincing headaches which interrupted the interrogations that eventually led to his execution in 1811. We know that people evaded, fabricated Münchausen-like excuses, and actively lied to exculpate themselves. Very few actually engaged martyrdom, even when they faced certain condemnation and death and presumably had little or nothing to lose by assuming a defiant attitude.

All this is to say hardly anything of the people who played some direct role in the making of the texts themselves—the interrogators, the notaries, the prosecuting attorneys and defense lawyers, the judges and other royalist officials, and the supernumerary players who may have witnessed all or part of such proceedings over the period of a decade. Furthermore, it is interesting to note that the very form in which interrogations were carried out and confessions taken (that is, final statements from the accused) seems quite heavily to have stressed passivity on the part of the accused. Thus a construction of action by indirection, of being in the wrong place at the wrong time purely through no fault of one's own, being forced to act against one's will, and so forth, may actually have been encouraged by the very forms of judicial procedures. Certainly this would fall under the rubric of what James Scott calls the performance of public transcripts, to which I shall allude again below. Indeed, so often did accused insurgents offer up the excuse that they were pressed by the rebels or otherwise swept up in collective violence, that we are tempted to wonder whether there was actually any rebellion at all. Speaking of one man captured after the battle of Calderón outside Guadalajara in early 1811, but implicitly addressing the self-exculpatory statements of thousands of other accused rebels, a weary crown prosecutor said: "that if all the culprits apprehended at the battle of Calderón were allowed similar justifications, and decisions as to the justice or injustice . . . [of punishing them] . . . were to be determined on that basis, . . . there would not be a single one who within a few days would fail to make such a claim."[12] Other elements framing confessions and related judicial docu-

---

moving description of the defendant Champmathieu at the bar, a simple wheelwright wrongly taken for the fugitive Jean Valjean:

He made gestures signifying denial, or else he gazed at the ceiling. He spoke with difficulty, answered with embarrassment . . . He seemed like an idiot in the presence of all these intellects . . . like a stranger in the midst of this society by whom he had been seized . . . the accused listened opened-mouthed [sic], with a sort of astonishment . . . slowly [turning] his head from right to left, and from left to right—a son of sad, mute protest . . . [and later] . . . The man, standing, and twirling a hideous cap in his hands, seemed not to hear.

12. Biblioteca Pública del Estado (Guadalajara) (hereafter, BPE), Criminal, paquete 30, exp. 3, ser. 699, 1813.

ments as texts would have been the balancing acts between due process and the glut of accusations before legal bodies; the structure in which testimony was taken down, as I have noted: in the third person, by a notary of some sort; and the frequent presence of translators whose proficiency at indigenous language we can only guess at.

If we start to look at confessions and other judicial documents as a genre of texts produced in determined historical circumstances, then, with an eye to determining the sorts of considerations that controlled their production as texts, we can identify at least two overlapping logics that may have been at work in the case of Pedro Rodríguez. There was, first, the logic of self-exculpation; that is, the need to let oneself off the hook in terms of criminal or political responsibility or punishment. Could this be what Rodríguez had in mind in virtually repudiating his radical Lazarist views? And second, there was the discursive logic. This would have embodied the culture of the legal process and of legal confession, and of what Scott (1990) has called the "public transcript" of domination and subordination, of what was *expected* to be said *by* whom and *to* whom, and the stereotypic ideas deployed in such a dialogue. The discursive logic might also have included resonances with religious confession and absolution, and the mechanism of reincorporation into the body politic.[13] But as each layer is added, the problematics of directly recovering the faint voice of Pedro Rodríguez become thicker and thicker.

Given such conditions, what sort of claims can we make for the idea of transparency, that the window through which we look upon these vanished lives "as through a glass darkly" does not in itself obscure our vision; that the tool packs none of its own weight; that the efficiency of information transmission, if you will, is nearly perfect? Direct apprehension through a transparent instrument is little more than a pious hope, especially in a cultural situation in which major groups in the population were separated off from each other by the markers of ethnic identity and language. In this context, the anthropologist Renato Rosaldo (1986) has produced a trenchant critique of Emmanuel Le Roy Ladurie's *Montaillou* (1978), an historical ethnography of rural life and the Albigensian heresy in fourteenth-century France. While it hardly cripples this magisterial work, Rosaldo's critique nonetheless raises major questions about its methodology. He points out, through an analysis of Le Roy Ladurie's treatment of his major primary source, the testimonial registers

---

13. For an interesting discussion of the implanting of the Sacrament of confession with colonial evangelization, and its role in social and ideological control, see Klor de Alva (1992). The form and tone of judicial confessions during the independence wars often suggest their sacramental counterparts. An illuminating study of similar issues in France of an earlier era is Davis (1987).

of Jacques Fournier, Bishop of Pamiers and Inquisitor, the ways in which the historian separates "the context of colonial domination from the production of ethnographic knowledge . . ." (Rosaldo 1986, 93) through the establishment of an authoritative ethnographic voice somewhat akin to the voice-over narrative in a documentary film or the omniscient narrator in a novel. This technique allows Le Roy Ladurie to ignore what Rosaldo calls the "tainting" of Bishop Fournier's registers by the "context of domination," and to naturalize them as nearly weightless, transparent conduits to a long-dead past.

If Le Roy Ladurie's oversanguine stance regarding the transparency of his sources is shared by most of us who deal with similar issues, a radical corrective has been offered by the Indian social historian Ranajit Guha (1983) in his work on rural insurgency.[14] His prescription is to turn elite discourse on its head (you will notice that we have drifted here to nonconfessional, mostly nonjudicial texts, such as military, administrative, political, or journalistic accounts), or turn it inside out, like a photographic negative. By thus taking dark for light and light for dark, Guha suggests, we may derive from the biased language of such official discourse "real" views of popular action and motivation not available in other sources. Where colonial authorities might characterize localized village rebellion in terms of "contagion," for example, Guha bids us read the term as code for "the enthusiasm and solidarity generated by an uprising among various rural groups within a region" (Guha 1983, 9). What exactly the warrant for such a radical inversion might be is not clear, since assuming a perfect correspondence between the texts of domination and popular reality, even in this cryptopositivist fashion, would seem problematic. In taking up this method we are likely to fall into a post-Foucauldian romanticism where everything protesters say is good and true, and all officials are fools. This takes us too far in the direction of empathy and further than ever away from the painful struggle toward objectivity.

The anthropologist and critic Vincent Crapanzano has remarked that "[t]he ethnographer conventionally acknowledges the provisional nature of his interpretations . . . [but not] the provisional nature of his presentations" (1986, 51). Strong resistance to this problematizing of historical or ethnographic transparency is to be expected, naturally, since we are all loathe to see the collapse of clear standards of verification (Clifford 1986, 7). In this sense the eye-rolling and snorting attendant in some circles upon discussions of the linguistic turn are similar to those one sees

---

14. I have addressed Guha's work in slightly more detail in Van Young (1990, 155–56), from which the present brief treatment is drawn. For an extensive discussion of Guha within the context of a rich treatment of banditry and other forms of rural resistance in Latin America, see Joseph (1992, 312–17).

in response to the application of psychoanalytic ideas, but not in themselves arguments against the usefulness of these intellectual technologies. One reason for resistance may be, of course, that these totalizing viewpoints affect not just the *picture*, but the frame; not just the *statement*, but the grammar.[15] Furthermore, in the case of deconstructionist thinking, the theoretical language, as it comes to historians and social scientists from literature and critical studies, is frequently so obfuscating and the studies themselves so apparently precious and removed from real-world situations, as to produce the impression that this is the province of overrefined esthetes who wouldn't know a peasant from a pipe wrench.

The concerns I am discussing (that is, with textuality and history) are particularly apposite where the project is to analyze the nature and meaning of literary texts or accounts in the traditional sense: chronicles, primitive histories, diaries, and travelers' accounts, for example, or single or multiple eyewitness accounts of individual historical incidents. Some very interesting work on early Latin America and the Encounter has been done in this mode in recent decades by a number of literary scholars, among them Todorov (1984), Adorno (1986), Hulme (1986), and Greenblatt (1991), to mention just a few. We must acknowledge, however, that while most literature is text, not all text is literature. Dealing with a collective phenomenon such as a popular uprising, in which the documents through which we access action and thought are typically treated as so much ancient detritus rather than "Texts" is quite another matter, the analytical juice we can squeeze out of one or a few cases that much more limited. In this latter sort of enterprise, then, what useful questions does the lingual perspective allow us to ask? Is it enough just to take it into account in the form of a caveat or caution? Or should it exercise a more fundamental influence in helping us formulate questions and hypotheses? I think it should and can aid in doing the latter, and I have tried to indicate some of these possibilities in my partial unpacking of Pedro Rodríguez's case. But at the very least it is a negative method that can provide some strong hints as to preferred readings of the minor texts that mean so much to social and cultural historians. This question of how to read readings brings me back, for an illustrative example, to James Scott's influential book, *Domination and the Arts of Resistance*, and to the implicit assumptions he makes regarding the interpretation of texts and the imputation of meaning and motivation from them.

---

15. Being told that one is resisting out of unconscious motives, or that one lacks the intellectual subtlety to master a corpus of ideas and cannot therefore criticize it, are not constructive arguments, either. For a blast against the deconstructionist prophets and their priests for just such procedures, see Ellis (1989, 3–17).

TRANSCRIPTS, NAIVE MONARCHISTS, POSTSCRIPT

I will not attempt to summarize here Scott's complex and suggestive study, which builds particularly on his widely influential earlier book *Weapons of the Weak* (1985). The center of Scott's argument is an impressive critique of Gramscian and post-Gramscian variants of the concept of hegemony, the idea that social orders often hold together despite the stresses and strains of class and other divisions because the dominated collaborate in their own exploitation by elites who control the technologies of power and legitimation. Basically he argues for what he calls a "paper-thin" version of this social glue, in which the discourse of power and subordination is embodied in a public transcript, and the discourse of resentment and resistance in a hidden transcript. The public transcript consists of acts as well as speech, has people paying their taxes, deferring to the powerful in various ways, and at least nominally acknowledging the ideological claims of religion and the state. The hidden transcript, on the other hand, has them telling unflattering stories about the bosses, spreading rumors, repeating folktales with admonitory punch lines, and even appropriating bits of elite political discourse that they turn upside down or otherwise consciously manipulate in the cause of subversive recitals. All these and innumerable other encrypted forms of everyday resistance are aspects, in Scott's eloquent words, of "an acrimonious dialogue that domination has driven off the immediate stage" (1990, 111).

Suggestive as Scott's argument is, it assumes on the part of oppressed groups a conscious and highly adaptive duplicity whose existence, in my view, is difficult if not impossible to prove from even the most open-ended reading of the historical texts of resistance. Such a duplicity is the corollary of an even deeper-lying assumption in Scott's work, which I will call hyperagentialism. This is the doctrine (and I think I exaggerate only slightly here for purposes of emphasis) that people basically act any way they choose given certain structural constraints on them, irrespective of the drags of culture or the unconscious; that vis-à-vis language they can decode all too well the meanings they constantly swim in or have foisted upon them; and that those meanings are so stable that they can be contested or countered as a conscious strategic act of resistance to domination. Useful as this perspective has proved as a corrective to the homologous magnitude view of rural people in traditional or transitional societies, in particular, who draw much of Scott's attention, it is perhaps overcompensatory. Ironically enough in Scott's case, this approach appears to come full circle to something akin to rational choice theory, even though it grows originally out of Scott's own moral economy model of peasant political behavior. That many historians have come to see members of subordinated or oppressed groups as historical actors in their own right is one of the most salutary trends toward change in our discipline during the last decades. One of the most important avatars of this view, which has now grown the carapace of orthodoxy, is of course E. P. Thompson (1963, 1971). But in Scott's version this open consciousness tends to reside so close to the surface of people's lives, and become so rational and so goal oriented (so hyperagential, as I have called it) that it does not allow very well for the manifestly messy and overdetermined—that is to say, multicaused—quality of people's motives and actions. Scott's discoursers of hidden transcripts seem to have sociologies but no psychologies. But here let us return to two concrete texts with an eye toward alternative readings of them, both having to do with the popular naive monarchism I have found linked to messianic expectation in the independence period, and both bearing upon the issues of interpretation raised so far in this chapter (Van Young 2001c, Chapter 18). I reserve for later brief discussion the relationship of all this to the case of the Cuautla Lazarus.

Let me briefly lay before my readers two incidents. Chronologically speaking, the second occurred in early 1811 and concerned a group of men from the village of Juchipila, in the rough country to the north of Guadalajara, in western central Mexico. The men were arrested after the climactic battle of Calderón and finally absolved of charges of insurgency by the Audiencia of Guadalajara in the summer of 1814. In attempting to prove that they were pressed into rebel service involuntarily, the accused men produced evidence that they had been among the villagers actively swearing an oath of allegiance to King Ferdinand in September 1810, just after the outbreak of the Hidalgo revolt. The actual oath itself had apparently taken place in the village plaza (the venue is unclear), with the village Indian *alcalde de primer voto* Jacinto Núñez "dressed as decently as he could afford," according to one Spanish witness, assuming the voice of all the indigenous inhabitants, and the Spanish official don José Ignacio Luciano Romero speaking for the white *vecinos* (neighbors). The two men apparently stood on a wooden platform and declared (in what order or if simultaneously is not specified) "*¡Viva, viva el Rey!*" (Long live the king!); then Núñez, at least, threw down a few coins on the platform. There was also said to be on public display in the village a likeness of the king and a sign condemning the insurrection.[16]

In point of time the first incident occurred in the fall of 1808, in the

16. BPE, Criminal, leg. 6, exp. 54, 1813; leg. 1, exp. 23, 1814. The inherent symbolism of the money is clear enough; it ran with the king's writ and bore his image. The meaning of Núñez throwing the coins down on the wooden platform is rather ambiguous, however, but probably derived from some traditional ritual usage.

village of Epazoyuca, just a few miles to the northeast of Mexico City, during a public procession. Bearing in his hands a standard with the image of the Virgin of Guadalupe, the Indian official Pablo Hilario was standing next to the indigenous governor of the village, who bore another standard with the likeness of King Ferdinand VII. When the large, ethnically mixed crowd began yelling "*¡Viva Fernando Séptimo!*" (Long live Ferdinand VII), Pablo Hilario chimed in with "*¡Viva Fernando Séptimo y mueran todos los gachupines!*" (Long live Ferdinand VII and death to all Spaniards). One Spanish witness to the incident observed that Hilario's statements was "very much like those indecorously repeated even in the public plazas."[17]

The first of these incidents, which obviously falls under the rubric of a ritualized civic expression of political loyalty and solidarity, would in Scott's reading constitute a performance from the public transcript. Let us bracket the messy question of whether some members of both ethnic moieties of the community may have subscribed to this expression while others may not have. The second incident, although also taking place in a public venue, would fall into Scott's category of an expression from the hidden transcript. His litmus test for hegemony, and therefore his theoretically driven reading of these texts, would be whether, in the course of active protest (which Pablo Hilario's "*mueran los gachupines*" [death to the Spaniards] would seem to embody) "subordinate groups still embrace the bulk of the dominant ideology" (1990, 91). For Scott, however, the juxtaposition of the naive monarchist formula upon the invocation of violent protest gives the lie to the former and emphasizes the "truth" of the latter as an expression of what Pablo Hilario and hundreds of thousands of other rural Mexicans probably felt and aspired to. Specifically relating his scheme to this sort of popular legitimism, Scott comments: "In a form of symbolic jujitsu, an apparently conservative myth counseling passivity becomes a basis for defiance and rebellion that is, in turn, publicly justified by faithful allegiance to the monarch! . . . A history of the need to dissimulate as well as long practice in the strategic use of hegemonic values are all we need to gasp the use value of naive monarchism" (1990, 98, 100). But is it? In trashing the concept of hegemony and basically positing that protesters from subordinate social groups act out of a conscious and even elaborated programmatic critique of the structures of domination, Scott seems to discount entirely the possibility that people such as Pablo Hilario or the loyal Indians of Juchipila actually believed in the doctrines associated with naive monarchism. In fact the evidence of just such texts that I have analyzed elsewhere indicates that such beliefs

17. AGN, Criminal, vol. 226, exp. 5, fols. 267r–361r, 1808.

were widespread among the rural population of late colonial Mexico, and that they were taken in great earnestness rather than put forward as pretexts or ideological noise to jam the perceptions of the dominant regime. The proof of the genuineness and vitality of these beliefs is that when rural protesters were left to their own devices—when they spoke or acted in programmatic terms, constructed their village utopias, and spun out their counterhegemonic fantasies—they very often invoked the figure of the Spanish king as protector, redeemer, and even messiah in a totally uncynical way (Van Young 2001c).

This suggests at least two observations about the concept of hegemony, by the way. The first is that hegemonies may be superimposed one upon another. In the present concrete case ideas about messianic monarchs in the late colonial period seem to have resonated with ideas left over from the pre-Columbian period, so that they blended with and reinforced each other. The second is that partial hegemonic incorporation may well coexist with counterhegemonic protest; that is to say, ideological performance based on public and hidden transcripts need not be an either/or proposition. I think a more nuanced reading of the sort of text I have been dealing with here reveals that most societies, particularly premodern ones in which the technologies of communication and domination were so rudimentarily developed, are a good deal lumpier and less homogeneous that Scott's view would allow. Such sociocultural orders would accommodate many more contradictions than one might imagine, many more living anachronisms, and perhaps partial hegemonies more circumscribed by time and space than we are wont to admit.

The alternative reading I have given these texts does not depend upon any theoretically overheated deconstructionist exegesis of them. But it does suggest that we should stick reasonably close to those texts, at least for starters, and avoid extruding them through a theoretical appliance that reduces to a sickly paste the manifestly lumpy reality we are cautiously hoping to recover. People who find themselves engaged in protest movements, furthermore, often join them for a multiplicity of reasons other than, or in addition to, political disenchantment or motives of economic grievance. My own research on the independence period shows people acting out of a volatile mix of political belief, economic deprivation, religious sentiment, family connections, friendship, peer pressure, herd instinct, sexual obsession, vengeance, curiosity, and bad judgment. All of these can be recovered from texts of the period, but disentangling or prioritizing them is extremely difficult. While I think the concept of the hidden transcript a good one, I am equally inclined to think in terms of private agendas. So, in closing, we are back to our texts again, to the instability of their meanings and the multivocality of our historical subjects.

How do these observations about Scott's work relate to the case of Pedro Rodríguez and the epistemological haze I have generated around it? Essentially they raise two closely related though rather different questions. Is actor-defined meaning recoverable from these sorts of texts; and if so, based on what assumptions? Is personal motivation recoverable, even while it may or may not overlap (but most likely does both, simultaneously) with what historians are able to construct of structural explanations for action? My own tentative answer is that we can approach actor-defined meanings more closely than we can understandings of individual motivation, though in both cases always by degrees. Between the ambiguity suggested by the Cuautla Lazarus's testimony, and the confident and credible prescription Scott offers for forms of popular resistance, lies a terrain of interpretation in which behavior and discourse owe their form to multiple influences; motivation is messy, fragmentary, and contradictory; and signs ambiguous. Pedro Rodríguez's belief in the possibility of resurrection at the hands of Morelos and the miraculous child might very well have been accompanied by strains of a naive monarchist ideology. In his thinking, naive monarchism or even messianic beliefs centered on the Spanish king would not have comprised merely a discursive screen to disguise an antiregime critique, any more than his views about resurrection would have constituted a consciously elaborated metaphor for the redemptive power of revolutionary violence.

What is one to do with all this ambiguity? It seems to me that as historians we have several possible options. One would be to yield to epistemological panic and abandon the project of writing history altogether. A second would be to continue blithely on as though none of these problems existed, which I suspect most of us will do, though it will become increasingly difficult even should the more tangled and nihilistic varieties of critical thinking pass from the scene. This also seems to me manifestly foolish, like trying to fire a cannon that one knows to be so flawed that it will blow up in one's face when the powder is ignited. A third option would be to slide into the warm, sticky, and welcoming waters of unself-conscious narrative and simply write romantic and engaged just-so stories. This is one implication, surely, of what Schama has done, and of the prescriptive recommendations of Hayden White (1987). The fourth option would be to try to incorporate in a meaningful way knowledge from a lingual project. This has value both in the positive sense, as to what we learn of cultural practice and social structure from taking textuality seriously, and the subtlety and color we can add to our accounts by listening carefully to the words of our speakers and text makers; and in the negative sense, as to what the epistemological limits of our reach are. A final option subsumes the fourth, which is that by building up our ethnographic knowledge on a variety of fronts we can make our inferences, and therefore our understandings of our subjects, more likely to be reasonable, in a probabilistic sense. We run the danger here, of course, of simply compounding error and distortion if our ethnographic tool kit is flawed to begin with, but frankly I see no alternative. Furthermore, I would offer three working caveats as a sort of background methodological program for research in social/cultural history. First, we should listen to language as affective and symbolic, not just as instrumentalist. Second, we should keep in mind that behavior and utterance are likely to be overdetermined. Third, as individuals should not be taken for the whole (fetishism), neither should otherwise credible structural inference be confused with a model of motivation.

Passing thus from criticism to prescription, and from a dogmatic inductivism to the threshold of positive theory, is difficult, the more so when the two are separated by a contradiction. For if language is at one and the same time the medium of our apprehension of past lives and the distorting lens through which they are glimpsed, why should any reading of the texts I have cited be privileged over any other? Where is the epistemological high ground here? Surely it lies on the humane scholar's traditional map of reasonableness, contextuality, and subtlety. But even where these criteria come into play the tension between language and culture-bound observation, and the pull toward "objectivity," will almost certainly remain unresolved, much as the perennial contradictions between generalization and particularization, or the material and the ideal. While the tension is frustrating, it is also generative.

PART IV

Economic History and Cultural History

CHAPTER 7

The New Cultural History Comes to Old Mexico

The human, the social question [is] always dogging the steps of the ancient contemplative person and making him, before each scene, wish really to get *into* the picture, to cross, as it were, the threshold of the frame. It never lifts, verily, this obsession of the story-seeker, however it may flutter its wings, it may bruise its breast, against surfaces either too hard or too blank. "The *manners*, the manners: where and what are they, and what have they to tell?"—that haunting curiosity, essential to the honor of his office, yet making it much of a burden, fairly buzzes about his head the more pressingly in proportion as the social mystery, the lurking human secret, seems more shy.
—Henry James, *The American Scene*

An anthropology which abdicates the search for explanatory theories of culture and society in favor of particularistic interpretations of specific cultures and societies exclusively is an anthropology whose attraction will . . . become confined to scholars whose intellectual curiosity is limited to, and whose intellectual appetite is nourished by, strange customs of exotic peoples. For the rest . . . that aim produces . . . anorexia curiosa; in a word, boredom.
—Melford Spiro, "Cultural Relativism and the Future of Anthropology"

One day while driving through a beautiful autumn countryside, a man from the city passed by an apple orchard. There a strange sight met his eyes and he slowed his car to observe it more closely. A strapping farmer dressed in overalls was staggering about the orchard, borne down under the weight of an enormous pig, which he carried in his arms. With some difficulty, the man saw, the farmer would lift the pig up to the height of the lowest fruit-bearing branch, the animal would daintily nibble an apple, and the farmer would then stagger along to another apple tree, where the process was repeated. Puzzled and fascinated by this, the man from the city stopped his car by the side of the road, hopped the wooden fence into the orchard, and pursued the farmer while he continued to stagger from tree to tree. Addressing the heavily perspiring rustic (for it was an unseasonably warm day), the man from the city asked, "Excuse me, sir. Do you mind my asking what you are doing?" The farmer answered in a friendly way, "Why no, mister, I don't mind tellin' you at all. I'm feedin' the pig his lunch." The city man considered this for a moment while following the farmer and pig to the next tree, then offered, "Well, doesn't feeding him that way waste an awful lot of time?" And the farmer replied, "Why hell, mister, time don't mean nothin' to a pig!"

OF PIGS AND PROMISCUITY

Whether the meaning of time for the pig (or more properly, for its owner) fell into a Taylorite register (time as money) or a Thompsonian one (time as culture) is impossible to tell.[1] The larger point of this homely Chayanovian parable, however, is that man the exchanger of calories with the natural environment and man the exchanger of meaning with other men are not easily separable entities, although academic disciplines and subfields of historical writing tend to cleave the two apart as though they were.[2] One of the arguments I hope to make in this essay is that cultural history and economic history (or other sorts of quantitatively based history, for that matter), though most often thought separate from each other, or even antithetical, because of epistemological, methodological, or boundary distinctions, may usefully be united to the benefit of each. This

---

1. On Frederick Winslow Taylor (1856–1915), the industrial engineer whose "time and motion studies" in American factories spawned "Taylorism" just after the turn of the twentieth century, see Kanigel (1997); see also E. P. Thompson's seminal article (1967) about the cultural stresses attendant upon the transition to a modern work regimen. Two books on time in a cultural and historical perspective that have stimulated my own thinking are Withrow (1988) and Crosby (1997).

2. The Russian agronomist A. V. Chayanov, a major theorist of peasant economic life writing primarily in the early Soviet era, suggested that traditional peasant farmers may "self-exploit" their family labor to the point of discomfort without apparent regard to obvious criteria of economic utility, for reasons based in a different rationality having to do with family and plot size, the demographic cycle, and so forth; see Chayanov (1986). For useful analyses of Chayanov's thought, see Thorner (1986) and Shanin (1986).

possibility has partially to do with the principle of overdetermination: that a single effect, such as the action of an individual, say, may have several causes, so that economic and religious motives, for example, might jostle each other in the thinking of one person; and partially with the idea that all human actions and expressions have cultural valences, or meanings. To illustrate, let us take the case of monetary wages. From a strictly economic point of view, wages may be said to reflect the relationship between the supply and demand of labor in a given market. Wages may simultaneously reflect not only value, however, but individual worth—not just decisions about leisure time, subsistence strategies, and maximization, but about culturally specific normative ideas of work, self-valuation, gender roles, the investment of time in private versus public activities, and so on. Paul Vanderwood writes of the millenarian rebels at Tomochic, in northwestern Mexico in the early 1890s, for example, that their antimodern ideology condemned doctors, priests, and money. Yet the believers awarded themselves extraordinarily high (nominal) money wages for fighting against the Porfirian government. I have found instances of the same thing amongst the insurgents of the independence period nearly a century earlier, but without the explicitly antimodernist ideological baggage (Vanderwood 1998; Van Young 2001c). What were these people thinking? Paradoxical as such an approach/avoidance to money might appear, they seem to have been saying that although the reigning powers of state and property might control the medium of economic exchange, they themselves knew their own worth and were ready to expropriate the markers of that worth by force, if necessary, in essence replacing their economic value with a moral one. I want to suggest, therefore, that cultural history should actively colonize economic relations, as it has done political systems, on the imperialist assumption that all history is cultural history. Why this is not a flaccid formulation that dilutes the conceptual precision of culture, but a salutary form of promiscuity, is one of the central points I hope to make. I shall return to these issues in the last section of this essay.

This chapter does not pretend to survey all, or even a large part, of what has been done in the cultural history of colonial Mexico.[3] The cov-

---

3. In the preparation of this essay I have found particularly suggestive several review articles (Gasco 1994; Kicza 1995; Deans-Smith 1998; Radding 1998). Several journals, among them the *Colonial Latin American Review* and *Historia y Grafía* (Universidad Iberoamericana, Mexico City), periodically publish substantive pieces and review articles that air these same issues. However, since the interdisciplinary mix of these journals tilts heavily toward what one might call postmodernist historical, anthropological, and literary studies, they tend to preach to the converted, the tone of their treatment of cultural history being more celebratory than critical; for a closer analysis, see Chapter 3 in this volume. For a general

erage is admittedly spotty, privileging projects such as ethnohistory either because I am more familiar with them, or because they encapsulate certain problems for new cultural historians or embody certain of their successes. Nor does this essay attempt to answer the large questions, such as what culture is, what cultural history is (a history of the production and reproduction of socially constituted meanings will have to do as a rough-and-ready definition), or what is "new" about the cultural history some scholars are writing for colonial Mexico. Still less does it lay out a systematic theoretical approach to what we are calling cultural history. My approach instead will be to raise a series of questions (in most cases altogether easier to ask than answer) about how cultural history is being practiced, what its goals and values are, and how it relates to other forms of historical inquiry. I place a particular emphasis on epistemological and methodological issues, many of which have arisen in the course of my own work over the last two decades or so.

My readers will perhaps permit me a few words of confessional before I undertake my task. Even aside from a self-conscious tendency to overly long methodological and theoretical prolegomena because we are not sure of our own ground, and even apart from a fascination with labyrinthine postmodern cultural studies, the genre of cultural history tends somewhat toward navel-gazing, as is often remarked even by its own advocates. The premises of cultural history are by no means self-evident or universally accepted in a discipline such as history, long dominated by materialist forms of explanation. This may be especially true in a subfield such as Latin American history, which struggled to reinvent itself after the dismantling of dependency theory as a metanarrative (Haber 1997a). It is for such reasons, for example, that I found Steve Stern's (1995) somewhat compulsive theorizing in his book on gender ideology in late colonial Mexico thoughtful rather than self-abusive (as alleged by some critics), and particularly apt given the strongly hermeneutic approach he took in his microethnographic description of women at risk from male violence and patriarchal repression. Moreover, the cultural history literature often betrays autobiographical undertones. Partly this is due to the increasing convergence of cultural history with anthropology, whence we have bleeding into our discipline examples of cryptoconfessional from eminent practitioners such as Ruth Behar (1993) and Paul Friedrich (1986). But

---

discussion of Mexicanist historiography up until about 1990, see Florescano (1991). My own present essay engages in something of a dialog with interlocutors (French 1999; Haber 1999; Vaughan 1999) represented in the issue of the *Hispanic American Historical Review* in which much of the material in the present chapter appeared; see also Haber (1997c). The latter part of this essay incorporates much of the original English version of my article, "El lugar de encuentro entre la historia cultural y la historia económica" (Van Young 2009b).

partly it just makes sense given the nature of the approach and its own coordinates in cultural studies. Whereas we once arrayed ourselves as observer and object, we now have two subjectivities warily circling each other, or even three if the maker of the source-text is distinct from the actors being described. If the observers are in the picture, in other words, their assumptions and the mode of their gaze warrant some attention.

I used to be a great deal more sanguine about the possibilities of resurrecting and understanding long-extinct worldviews and symbolic systems, until I came face-to-face in the latter stages of my own work on the Mexican popular insurgency of 1810–1821 with some apparently intractable problems. In the course of thinking through my research materials, I was increasingly drawn to culture—to the process of meaning formation, the codes by which meanings are stabilized and transmitted, and the ideas in people's minds—through the question of individual motivation for joining in collective political violence. It seemed that the internal images in people's heads forming the basis of these motives rarely had anything explicitly to do with economic grievances, or with larger, more abstractly structural representations of "interest." Seeing people's behavior as a reflex of class or market relationships, therefore, seemed reductive and out of synch with the evidence. This threw me back ever more on the representations themselves, whether of family, community, forms of earthly authority, religious cohesion, or cosmic order, as being largely at the source of collective action. It is extremely difficult to construct a wholly complete or satisfactory model of motivation on this basis, however, primarily because one cannot get close enough to the actors' thinking. Nor, on the other hand, have I been able to leave behind the economistic forms of explanation prevailing in most studies of early modern collective action, particularly among peasants. This has meant forging a complex circularity between historical-structural (that is to say, essentially materialist) explanations of collective behavior, and culturalist explanations. Many of those who delve into cultural history have followed something of the same trajectory, and may find themselves with me, having one foot on the shore and one in the boat. My imperialist project for cultural history represents an attempt to resolve this problem.

GENEALOGIES AND CHRONOLOGIES

The city man in the orchard evoked in my opening paragraph may be seen to represent (in the sense of "stand in for") an ethnographer. Nor is it an accident that my two epigraphs are drawn from the disciplines of literature and anthropology. Cultural history's near obsessive interest in the problematization of texts (in the literary sense) and in language obviously originated with poststructuralist literary studies; its ethnographoid method, and to some degree its characteristic interests in "subaltern" groups and in forms of community and identity, derives from anthropology. The linguistic turn, especially, and the putatively destructive influence of the postmodernism presumed to flow after it like boiling magma through a volcanic vent, have called forth some astute but shrill criticism from more "traditional" historians right and left (both politically and epistemologically).[4]

Whatever its genealogy and the authorities it typically invokes to anchor itself, however, the new cultural history as practiced for colonial Mexico is not in fact a radically postmodernist project, because its practitioners seem to believe in the (at least partial) knowability of past realities, and that there is a difference between the fictive imagining of the novelist and the factual imagining of the historian.[5] Postmodern weltschmerz or epistemological anarchism are therefore remarkably absent from this burgeoning literature. Nor, on the other hand, is the new cultural history the half-life product of a deteriorating dependency theory, despite the fact that some of its practitioners fashioned themselves as *dependentistas* earlier in their careers, or were so described by their critics.[6] This genealogy disavows or ignores the anthropological influences so obvious in the approach, which new cultural historians would never do. As one young historian has observed, attacks upon the new cultural history resemble a "rear-guard action against a paper tiger [or perhaps, better said, a straw man]," because of the actual care and caution with which cultural-historical methods are typically applied.[7] There is, in fact, nothing very

---

4. For right- and left-wing attacks see, respectively, Himmelfarb (1987) and Palmer (1990). For a remarkably moderate defense of the new problematic of language and subalternity, see Appleby, Hunt, and Jacob (1994), and for an extremely sophisticated but sometimes opaque airing of the central issues, Berkhofer (1995).

5. This is not a particularly porous boundary for colonialists, it seems to me, perhaps because of the traditionalist, text-anchored (in the limited sense) training most of them receive. Where one does occasionally find the more adventuresome impulse to substitute one's own subjectivity for that of the people one is studying, or at least a willingness to extrapolate from the known without bashfulness, is in more modern history; see, for example, Becker (1995). After giving a series of lectures in Spain some years ago touching on these issues, I was asked the question of what the difference is between fiction and history; my own answer: footnotes. For some discussion of this theme, see Chapter 6 in this volume; on historians and footnotes, Grafton (1997).

6. That particular teratology makes the new cultural history appear even *more* of an abortion to its critics, by the way, because dependency theory itself focused above all on matters of political economy.

7. O'Hara (1997). It does seem to be the case that the most extreme positions among proponents and critics of the new cultural history tend to be taken in methodological/theoretical debates in print (and online) rather than in the monographic literature itself; I owe

radically "decentering" to be found in a methodological/epistemological inventory of this history. Among the major features of the new cultural history would be: (1) the study of mentalities, if by this one means the perduring mental structures that motivate individual or group behaviors, and the symbolic systems people use to explain the world around them; (2) a particular, though by no means exclusive, interest in subordinate groups in history; (3) a certain turn toward inductivism in the writing of history; and (4) a highly critical stance (occasionally, however, regressing to credulity) toward sources and textual interpretation (O'Hara 1997, 2).

Given the interest of the new cultural history in what have been called subaltern groups (a point to which I return below), is there some convincing way of differentiating cultural history from social history ("history with the politics left out")? Or is the study of subalterns, within the cultural dispensation, simply a sort of fizzed-up political history transposed to another register, not very different from older revisionist styles of the social history of working people developed by E. P. Thompson and Eric Hobsbawm, among others? Social and labor history also saw themselves as redemptive projects aimed at restoring voice to historically marginalized groups passed over in canonical accounts. But there is nothing particularly uncultural, as there is nothing particularly unsocial, about plotting the history of elite groups (for excellent examples, see Ladd 1976; Kicza 1983; Schwaller 1987; Hoberman 1991). Thus it cannot be the downward drift in the gaze of cultural historians that makes cultural history cultural, but rather its particular techniques and goals. This means that not all subaltern history is necessarily cultural history, except to the degree that it attempts to deconstruct hegemonic formations that impinge on the production and reproduction of meanings and the symbols that instantiate them.[8] What differentiates subaltern history in the cultural mode from social history, then, is an attempt to use many of the same sources for different, or complementary, ends: in the one case to arrive at a history of meanings for the partially inscribed, and in the second to situate people socially, primarily with regard to considerations of social class. The cultural history of subaltern groups, however, may attempt to situate people socially within the framework of class while at the same time looking at mental/symbolic processes that may or may not be shaped by class experience, or by it alone. The conquest of Mexico did not create a peasantry, but it made of the existing one an ethnically subordinate

---

this observation to Andrew Fisher. One of the functions of critical debate and of criticism more generally, of course, is to denaturalize practice.

8. I tend to agree with Haber's (1997c) observation that seeing everyone as a subaltern in some circumstances—the king is subaltern to God as the slave is to the overseer, and so forth—empties the concept of much of its utility.

underclass. Although the power of ethnicity—of "Indianness" or caste—may indeed have been fading with time, it was still very strong by the late colonial period. Understanding subaltern cultural history primarily with relation to class position, therefore, may be something of an anachronism for colonial Mexico, during which forms of ethnic and localist identity may have been as strong or stronger than those of class.

The advent of new cultural history can be accounted for (to borrow a model from the history of science) as much by internalist as externalist explanations. The internal logic of the field of colonial Latin American, and within it colonial Mexican, historiography has been to work its way down the documentary and institutional food chain to the most fragmentary, biographical, and folkloric data, to arrive at a level where the waters are murky and large-scale explanations loom like rusted hulks on the teeming ocean floor. To understand what is going on down there has required something like a minor Kuhnian (Thomas Kuhn 1970) paradigm shift in the face of accumulating puzzles or anomalies cast up by the old metanarratives grown creaky with stress. If the regular evangelizers of central Mexico did their work so well, for example, as in the compellingly Whiggish portrayal of their project rendered by Robert Ricard (1966/1933), how did indigenous culture and lifeways survive to the extent they apparently did? If the hegemony of the colonial state lay so heavily upon the land, why was "bargaining by riot" so common between colonial rural communities and the Spanish regime, and how was there political and ideological (let alone physical) space for recurrent episodes of Indian rebellion (Taylor 1979; Katz 1988; Gruzinski 1989; Schroeder 1998; Van Young 2001c)? But the paradigm shift has been sly and incremental rather than disjunctive—more an ad hoc, somewhat compressed evolution than the jarring reconfiguration of normative practice Thomas Kuhn originally envisioned. It has produced in the new cultural history what might be called an "ironic project," in the sense that much of the new writing stresses the contradictory nature of the explicit and the covert, as in describing state "hegemonic" action and popular cultural "reception" and reappropriation of ideological elements.[9] This sense of irony, where irony is "a contradictory outcome of events as if in mockery of the promise or fitness of things," is what drives most of the colonial-era essays in the wide-ranging anthology on ritual and public life by Beezley, Martin, and French (1994), or even Stern's (1995) evocation of the colonial system of "gender right."[10]

---

9. This is surely one of the reasons for the wide influence of Scott's (1990) work, although for reasons I have tried to outline elsewhere (Chapter 6 in this volume) Scott deals less than convincingly with culture.

10. The quoted definition of irony is drawn from the *Compact Oxford English Diction-*

Finally, it may be of interest to ask of the new cultural history: How new is "new," and is the newness that of the emperor's new clothes? Well, to some extent (to paraphrase Molière) perhaps we have been speaking cultural history for a long time without being aware of it. One need not bring a particularly overheated reading to Charles Gibson's canonical *The Aztecs under Spanish Rule* (1964), for example, to see it as cultural history, or at least as laying out the elements for a *cultural* approach to the history of central Mexican indigenous peoples, nor to the work of Gonzalo Aguirre Beltrán (1946, 1953, 1963) of the 1940s through the 1960s to see it as a profound study of systems of social classification, and of the social production and reproduction of meaning. And one could surely go further and further back with such an archaeology. But as a self-conscious subgenre of historical writing on Mexico whose practitioners more or less recognize each other, and which has its own burgeoning corpus of canonical works, theoretical reference points, source and methodological predilections, and—yes—specialized argot, the new cultural history only goes back to about 1990 or slightly earlier. Take, for example, Enrique Florescano's survey of Mexican historiography, *El nuevo pasado mexicano* (1991). In his section on "Revalorización y recuperación del virreinato" (pp. 31–45), Florescano certainly cites a number of historical works that we might construe as exemplars of cultural history, but the vocabulary he employs is that of social history, even in commenting on the ethnohistorical studies of Nancy Farriss (1984) and Victoria Bricker (1981), both of whom certainly deal with the historical experience of indigenous peoples from a culturalist perspective, that is, in terms of language, ethnic identity, religious belief, and above all, systems of symbolic meaning. In the closing pages of his essay (pp. 155–56), Florescano actually mentions cultural history, although only obliquely and somewhat coyly. By contrast, his book of a few years later (1997) on ethnicity and the state in the history of Mexico's indigenous peoples is redolent of culturalist jargon and concepts.

Nor is it coincidental that two journals devoted primarily to cultural history (the Mexican journal embraces more than just the colonial period) are relative newcomers by disciplinary standards, dating from the early 1990s: the Universidad Iberomericana's *Historia y Grafía*, and the City University of New York's *Colonial Latin American Review*. The opening editorial statements of both journals stress their interdisciplinary, "revisionist," and I think implicitly culturalist agendas.[11] A glance at the

---

ary, 2nd ed. (1991, 878); complementary definitions include "a figure of speech in which the intended meaning is the opposite of that expressed by the words used," and "a condition of affairs or events opposite to what was, or might naturally be, expected."

11. Chang-Rodríguez (1992). Wrote Guillermo Zermeño (1993), editor of *Historia y*

tables of contents over the years demonstrates how this self-mandate has worked out in practice. The very first issue of *Historia y Grafía* (1993) was dedicated primarily to the work and influence of the French critic, cultural theorist, and historian Michel de Certeau. Of the two additional articles in this first issue, one treated Mexican museums, a hallmark concern of cultural historians. In succeeding years each issue was dedicated to a specific theme. For instance, number 4 (1995) was centered on "*historia e imagen*" and contained articles on the significance of the "royal body" in the French Revolution, on photography, on the interactions between Hollywood and the Mexican cinema, and selections from the work of Pierre Bourdieu and Paul Ricouer. The next issue (no. 5, 1995) backslid to haciendas and *hacendados*, while the first issue of 1996 (no. 6) continued with fairly traditional essays on "ruptures and continuities" between the eighteenth and nineteenth centuries and the second (no. 7) examined Jesuit thinking on Mexican culture and history. In the following year (1997), *Historia y Grafía* explored both the theme of "*marginados, integrados, y condenados*," embracing articles on melancholy, film, and morality (no. 8), and the theme of "bodies in history," with pieces on religion, gender, prostitution, and dance (no. 9).

Since its founding in 1992, the *Colonial Latin American Review* has quite consistently combined historical, anthropological, and literary approaches in its editorial selection policy, typically touching on issues such as mapping and representation; prophetic traditions; textuality; postcolonialism; Indian-Spanish relations; subalternity; academic culture; conqueror historiography; the intersections of race, class, and gender; and carnivals. An entire issue in 1995 (vol. 4, no. 2) was devoted to an extravaganza of historical and literary studies on Sor Juana Inés de la Cruz; and the first issue of 1996 (vol. 5, no. 1) explored "cross-cultural communication and the ambiguity of signs," which seems to say (or signify) it all. But even journals of a relatively traditional, not to say staid, bent reflect the same tendency, if in a more muted fashion. *Mexican Studies/Estudios Mexicanos*, admittedly an interdisciplinary venue and not

---

Grafía about the self-reflective (some would doubtless use a less flattering term) agenda of the journal:

Now better than ever we know that the construction of knowledge and science is fundamentally a collective [process] . . . There is a line [of inquiry] that especially interests us to encourage and promote, for whose treatment the historian has not generally encountered an adequate space: that of reflection on the meaning and function of his own practice . . . In that sense we want to look at historiography as part of a system of communication, of great complexity as much within as outside its own discursive forms . . . In this way, *historiography* is simply a form of representation of lived human and social experience (emphasis in original; in the interest of full disclosure I should mention that I have long been a member of the international editorial advisory boards of both journals).

limited to colonial history, published one article of an arguably "cultural historical" approach in 1990, and peaked with six of eleven representing this tendency in 1993, although the proportion had declined to one quarter by 1996. The *Hispanic American Historical Review* has always been somewhat more eclectic in its publication profile, interestingly enough, but across wide variations over time (4 out of 17 articles devoted to "cultural historical" themes in 1990, 7/13 in 1991, 5/14 in 1992, 4/14 in 1993, and 1/13 in 1994) it, too, has shown some inclination to drift over into the cultural realm, with about half the total articles reflecting this approach in the 1996 and 1997 volumes (5/10 and 5/11, respectively).[12]

The Emperor's clothes issue branches into two slightly different questions, one of which furnishes the agenda for most of the rest of this essay. First: Does the new cultural history only consist of a set of terms, a jargon, imported from other disciplines and other historiographies? And, if so, have its advocates simply employed this language to undergird a mild historical revisionism regarding, say, religious sensibilities, gender constructions, or the role of common people vis-à-vis the state, thus carving out a niche for themselves in the field while in the process making exaggerated claims for their approach? Is it, in other words, a sort of discursive exoskeleton for a creature whose innards are pretty undefined and squishy, or does it say something new enough to be interesting? The second question is larger and harder to answer: Has the new cultural history generated, or is it likely to generate in the future, some larger understandings about the workings of Mexican society and culture over the long term, or will it simply remain bogged down in the sort of particularistic exoticism skewered by the anthropologist Melford Spiro in my second epigraph? In brief, there are two answers to this question. On the one hand, it may be too early to tell. On the other, the utility of the approach might well come to depend precisely upon cultural historians working in the promiscuous and imperialist mode suggested at some length in what follows.

12. It goes without saying that my "statistics" rest upon an impressionistic perusal of the journals' tables of contents, not upon a careful reading of every contribution or any sort of formal content analysis; in the hands of someone else this same exercise might produce quite different results. About twenty-five years ago I conducted a similar "survey" of offerings in the *Hispanic American Historical Review* over the period 1960–1985 in Van Young (1985), but with the somewhat different objective of trying to determine when late colonial/early national studies blossomed. I concluded, at least based upon a count of *HAHR* articles, that it must have been around 1970. I also noted, however, that beginning in the early 1960s one tended to see a more sociological language in the journal, and more contributions in the area of social history. An avowedly cultural history has not so much drowned out more established forms of political, economic, intellectual, or social history as added another voice to the polyphony.

CULTURE AS TEXT AND TEXT AS CULTURE

To begin my substantive and methodological discussion proper, let me place on the table the palindromoid statement "Culture is to text as text is to culture," which must figure centrally in any project to study culture in past time (basic here is Ricouer—e.g., 1981). This takes us back to the influence of anthropological thinkers on the new cultural history, since this is basically a paraphrase of Clifford Geertz, and behind him of literary and cultural studies scholars. As an aphoristic pronouncement this reads reasonably well; as a research program for doing what we are calling new cultural history in general, and for colonial Mexico in particular, it is very treacherous. The terms of this statement, which in part encapsulates the relationship between anthropology and history, are not reversible because cultural historians are mostly asking anthropologists' questions without access to anthropologists' tools, by which I mean primarily fieldwork techniques in the ethnographic present. Victor Turner (1969, 1974) may well liken pilgrimages or initiation ceremonies to theater, for example, or Geertz (1973) and other anthropologists treat culturally expressive phenomena as texts, whether cockfights, cat massacres, or puppet shows (e.g., Darnton 1984; Beezley, Martin, and French 1994). In doing this they are themselves "reading" them as performances or narratives expressing, among other things, who the actors are and what they are saying about themselves and their worlds, while at the same time producing rendered-down or condensed versions of a larger, more chaotic, richer reality. Ethnographers, let us remember, order the ritual or other behavior as a text, superimposing their own readings over those of the actors themselves; in the process they doubly distill a "text" from the buzz of reality, and then essentialize from it. Cultural historians do the opposite, since typically they seek to resurrect the entire culture from an inscribed fragment. The two methods, then—the ethnographer's seeing "culture as text" and the cultural historian's seeing "text as culture"—work in exactly opposite ways, the one through condensation and selection, the other through expansion and rehydration. The problems here for historians in mimicking what ethnographers do consist not only in the pastness of the past, but in the textuality of the text and the narrativity of the narrative.[13] While ethnographers do a writing of their own readings, therefore, historians do a reading of a writing of a reading of a fragmented record or partial experience.

---

13. I have discussed these questions at somewhat greater length in Van Young (1994a). For some interesting observations along these same lines, and the multilayered approach the cultural historian might adopt both to construct a coherent narrative and to break open the false coherence of a narrative account, see Cohen (1997).

Chapter 7   235

The peculiarly open-ended and arbitrary nature of this procedure, absent the ethnographically present native against whose account the scholar's wilder projective liberties may be checked, is one of the reasons for the apparently flaccid methodology of which avowedly cultural historians, or those working along parallel lines and whose studies claim some cultural component, are sometimes guilty. This often raises eyebrows among nonbelievers and new culture history advocates alike. Among these distortive techniques are overinterpretation, ethnographic upstreaming, and the importation of anachronistic analytical categories or forms of experience from one temporal/cultural setting to another. All of these techniques may slingshot through the primary sources and back out again, leaving in their wake things that were not there to begin with. What goes in as "interrogation," in other words, comes out as interpretive conclusion, sometimes without hitting any vital organs or resistant material at all. As an example of overinterpretation, Inga Clendinnen's (1991) lyrical and riveting evocation of precolonial Aztec life seems to me to make claims for the existence of a society-wide Mexica culture based on exceedingly shaky extrapolations from elite-generated forms of discourse that may or may not have represented the thinking of common people.[14] To cite another example, Nathan Wachtel's (1977) classic study of conquest and early colonial-era Spanish-Andean contact, which at times embraces Mesoamerica as well as the Andean region, prominently employs the technique of ethnographic upstreaming, relying upon descriptions of modern ritual behaviors such as "Danzas de la Conquista" as an interpretive axis along which to understand the cultural content of early European-native interactions. But this method requires so many ceteris paribus assumptions about the relationship of contemporary to centuries-old practices that it immediately raises suspicions. How are we either to blot out or factor in the effects of two or three centuries of evangelization, state and nation building, and rural commercialization, or more recently the effects of modern media, civil strife, and global capitalism? Finally, let me offer as an instance of the anachronistic importation of conceptual frameworks Doris Ladd's (1989) book on eighteenth-century mine laborers in the Pachuca silver mines. In her attempt to find

---

14. The author undertakes an eloquent defense of her interpretive techniques in both her introduction and closing methodological essay. Comments Clendinnen (p. 4): "It is possible that the carrier squatting back on his heels in the marketplace waiting for hire, and watching the great lord and his entourage walk by, sustained a very different view of the workings of the world they both inhabited. I do not intend to assume so." By contrast, Clendinnen's (1987) early work on the conquest of the Yucatec Maya, an avatar of the cultural history of Spanish-indigenous contact and misapprehension, though no less bold conceptually, is much more restrained in its claims and more convincing in its conclusions.

a relatively advanced syndicalist mentality (arguably a "cultural" artifact) among the workers in the Conde de Regla's silver mines at the famous Real del Monte complex at Pachuca, Ladd continually forces the evidence to her own ends, traducing the very authentic voices of the workers she seeks to amplify. Her attempt to map onto late colonial Mexican laborers E. P. Thompson's (1963) conclusions on burgeoning English working-class mentality ignores the history of capitalism, of colonialism, and of ethnically stratified societies. That she did not find a Mexican Francis Place is little short of miraculous.

Examples of all these questionable techniques can be found in Richard Trexler's *Sex and Conquest* (1995).[15] A very widely respected historian of Renaissance Florence, Trexler has in this work of admirably dense scholarship turned to the Europeans' interpretation of the berdache of American indigenous peoples, a permanently transvested young male who lived as a woman, fulfilling traditionally female domestic and other responsibilities, and taking the passive (i.e., nonpenetrative) role in sexual activities with other males. During and after the conquest of the native American peoples, Trexler argues, the Spanish conquerors, churchmen, and chroniclers turned their ethnographic observation of the berdache to ideological advantage in "feminizing" the conquered by generalizing sodomy and associated "vices" to the entire subject population, thus laying the basis for violent repression of "unnatural" practices and for the imposition of Christianity and European rule. At first glance this is not an uninteresting argument. But whatever else may be shaping the politics of his interpretation, Trexler has certainly succumbed to the temptation to fill in the gaps in the historical record with untoward speculation, reliance upon apocryphal evidence, tortured readings of his sources, questionable ethnohistory (referring to the Aztecs and Incas, for example, as "tribal" peoples), and a reliance upon "upstreaming" and historically transcendent categories that violates the very spirit of cultural particularism that this sort of history is meant to embody. Cultural history of this sort is likely to throw as much doubt on the approach as Sigmund Freud's and William Bullitt's (1967) hatchet job on Woodrow Wilson did on psychohistory.

To return to the text-as-culture paradigm, what most often show up in the documents, as we all know, are the institutional aspects of colonial life: traces of formal structures such as property systems, judicial and administrative structures, or kinship relations; or if we are lucky, freeze-dried versions of rituals, episodes of collective action, conflict situations, and so forth. In the fluid and inclusive approach to culture that I have

---

15. On the other hand, I have personally found other work of Trexler's to be more circumspect and modest in its claims, and very suggestive; see, for example, Trexler (1984, 1988).

found most useful, these social artifacts play a major role. But culture, and therefore the object of the cultural historian's gaze, also resides in the way these things, particularly stable institutional complexes—religious thinking and political practice, for example—are connected, and the meaning that cultural practitioners impute to them through these connections. It is this "soft tissue" that is the first to go with the passage of time and the hardest to recover for the historian. It is precisely in these connections that meaning, the most important element of culture, resides, since meaning is a relational property, an understanding of one thing in terms of another: it forges the path from one system, institution, practice, or set of ideas to another. Ethnographic fieldwork, and more specifically the dialogic relationship that in the best of circumstances it presumably engenders between the observer (a culturally constituted subject) and the native practitioner (another culturally constituted subject), is in itself no guarantee of transparency in the study of a given culture; the controversy over Margaret Mead's ethnographic work or the perusal of some of Bronislaw Malinowski's field journals and letters attest to this. Nor is the question resolved whether cultural distance from the culture under observation, or cultural proximity to it, provides a better ethnographic vantage point, as the heated exchanges some time ago between Marshall Sahlins and Gananath Obeyesekere over the former's historical ethnography of the Hawaiian cultures and Captain James Cook's violent intersection with island history make plain (Sahlins 1995; Obeyesekere 1992). But in fieldwork in the ethnographic present, "native" practitioners of a culture can at least expand on the meanings of ritual behavior or spatial organization, for example, in dialogue with the ethnographer, so that the living context of a behavior or discursive element becomes much clearer (or paradoxically, more overdetermined and ambiguous) than it ever is in a document.

The greater part of what practitioners of the new cultural history are doing, and much of their historiographical success, is based upon the peculiarity that the documentary islands rising from whole continents and subcontinents of past experience are thrust to the surface of the historical record by forms of conflict or deviance that we then take as a starting point to recover "normal" life. Most of this documentation was generated by the crossing of individual biographies with public life, typically by the action of the state, in this case the colonial state. It is not too much to say that had there been no colonial state, there would now be no possibility of doing cultural history of the "newer" sort.[16] Although what

---

16. Eloquent on this conjunction of state power and the cultural and political history of popular protest are Wells and Joseph (1996, esp. 1–17); see also Joseph (1992). My own doubts regarding this possibly distorting conjunction are partially worked through in Chapter 6 in this volume.

follows is by no means an exhaustive catalogue, let me cite the work of a few scholars that I consider innovative and that ultimately depends upon the intersection of private and public life.

THE NEW CULTURAL HISTORY OF COLONIAL MEXICO: SOME EXAMPLES

The history of madness, for example—whom societies think mad, how those ideas change over time, the symptoms and content of psychopathological formations, and social and medical responses to insanity—continues to be a growth industry in North American and European historiography and a now-classic terrain for cultural historians, since it deals centrally with socially constructed meanings and their distortive mirroring in the minds of the disturbed (e.g., Porter 1987; Castel 1988; Scull 1989; Grob 1994). María Cristina Sacristán (1992, 1994) has almost single-handedly opened up the field of the history of Mexican psychiatry with a pair of books on madness and society, in the more developed and later of which she shows a clear trend toward the secularization of attitudes, both on the part of social arbiters and mad people, in the *siglo de las luces* (Enlightenment). Her work is based almost exclusively on Inquisition and criminal records that would never have come to exist had the individuals she studies not fallen into the toils of the state apparatus in some way. In relation to the church authorities and the documentation left behind by their encounter with the Mexican population, the same is true of Solange Alberro's (1988) book on the Mexican Inquisition during an extended seventeenth century; of Sergio Ortega's (1986) interesting anthology on marriage and bigamy, sexual perversity, and other acts of socially deviant sexual behavior; of Richard Boyer's (1995) lovely book on bigamy and family life; of Juan Pedro Viqueira Albán's (1987) fascinating look at public entertainments in Mexico City during the eighteenth century; and even of William Taylor's (1996) monumental study of late colonial parish clergy, much of whose basic data arose out of conflicts between curates and parishioners. Steve Stern's (1995) illuminating study of the ideas and practices of gender relations among common people in three regions of New Spain during the late colonial period depends almost exclusively for its central documentation upon criminal records, while other works on gender (one of the new cultural history's success stories) by Patricia Seed (1988), Silvia Arrom (1985), and Asunción Lavrin (1989), among others, also rest upon varieties of documentation generated by "deviance" and contention under the gaze of the state. Garden-variety deviance and crime have been interestingly treated by the late Carmen Castañeda (1989), Carlos Manuel Valdés Dávila (1995a), and Teresa Lozano Armendares (1987) on the basis primarily of local or regional criminal archives. Finally, Susan Kellogg's (1995) work on Indian litigation, resistance, and acculturation depends almost exclusively upon judicial records, as did Woodrow Borah's (1983) pre–new cultural history study of the General Indian Court, and Charles Cutter's (1995) book on the judicial culture of the Mexican north in the late colonial period.

Another great success story of the new cultural history of colonial Mexico is the continuing wave of ethnohistorical works treating indigenous groups. The documentation undergirding these studies was for the most part generated by the colonial and successor states in their efforts to control, exploit, acculturate, and punish for their recalcitrance colonized Indian peoples, and must therefore be read with many of the same caveats as texts on other characteristically "cultural" themes. Since ethnohistory is by now a venerable genre of historical writing on colonial Mexico, however, and has always been influenced by our sister discipline of anthropology, it was by no means "invented" or even significantly reshaped by the new cultural history in quite the same ways as studies of "deviance," religious sensibility, or gender, for example. Here the influence of the new cultural history has been more diffuse and incremental, but still powerful in a number of ways. For one thing, old periodizations have been called into question, to be replaced with a *longue durée* sort of approach, presumably due to the fact that cultural change is a much slower process than political change and less subject to the contingencies of political epiphenomena that typically drive periodizations (Andrien and Johnson 1994; Rodríguez O. 1994; Uribe-Urán 2001). In some cases ethnohistorical studies beginning or anchored in the colonial period edge well into the nineteenth or even the twentieth century, as exemplified most recently in the work of David Frye (1996), Cynthia Radding (1997), Pedro Bracamonte (1994), and Antonio Escobar Ohmstede (1998). In addition, under the new dispensation indigenous peoples have shifted from the position of objects, even if empathetically treated ones as in Gibson's *The Aztecs under Spanish Rule* (1964), to that of subjects, as when Frye and Radding speak of ethnic and localist identities from the actors' points of view. Still, the refiguration by new cultural historians of indigenous actors from objects to fully realized subjects has been, and is likely to remain, a difficult and incomplete one because of the sources available. This is why the occasional biographical study, even though not cut consciously in the new cultural historical mold, and even when focused on members of the indigenous elite rather than subalterns, can be so valuable in illuminating Indian culture, as with Susan Schroeder's (1991) study of the Chalco chronicler Chimalpahin.

It is probably fair to say, in fact, that as good and plentiful as the ethnohistory of colonial Mexico has become, much of it is parallel, strictly speaking, to the new cultural history rather than of it. The literature claims its culturalist credentials more from its somewhat traditional ethnographic tendencies than from any postmodernist or cultural studies genealogy, so that often it has to be *read for* the cultural meanings and symbolic exegeses one would suppose typical of the new cultural history, rather than supplying them intentionally and overtly. Unexotic as this genre of colonial history is, it can still be of impressively high quality. Among the monuments to this sort of careful ethnohistorical reconstruction are the volumes of the series *Historia de los pueblos indígenas de México*, edited by Teresa Rojas Rabiela and Mario Humberto Ruz for the Centro de Investigaciones y Estudios Superiores en Antropología Social (CIESAS) and the Instituto Nacional Indigenista, and organized (for the most part) by state within the Mexican union. Although apparently pitched to an educated general audience, most of the volumes in this collection are better than solid and some are outstanding. All bear some of the hallmarks of the new cultural history. Among the volumes are studies of Oaxaca by María de los Angeles Romero Frizzi (1996), Guerrero by Danièle Dehouve (1994), Sonora by Cynthia Radding (1995), Tabasco by Mario Humberto Ruz (1994), the greater northeast by Carlos Manuel Valdés Dávila (1995b), the Yaquis by Evelyn Hu-DeHart (1995; one of the few studies in the series that hews to ethnic rather than state lines), and Chiapas by Jan de Vos (1994).[17]

A second discernible current within the ample stream of ethnohistory can be identified with James Lockhart's (e.g., 1991b, 1992) Nahuatl-based scholarship and the work of his students, among them Sarah Cline (1986), Susan Schroeder (1991), Robert Haskett (1991), Rebecca Horn (1997), Kevin Terraciano (2001), Matthew Restall (1995, 1997), and others. This impressive, dense, and detailed work exalts the principle of reliance upon close readings of indigenous language sources. Admittedly this brings it closer into line with the new cultural history, and its virtual obsession with recovering the subaltern voice, than most exemplars of the more traditional sort of ethnohistory cited above, even if it is the voice of an indigenous elite that speaks loudest because of inevitable doc-

---

17. Other volumes in the series I understand to be forthcoming, while still others already published deal with the nineteenth century. A significant number of works on colonial ethnohistory have appeared from various regional research entities, such as the Archivo Municipal de Saltillo, directed by Carlos Manuel Valdés Ávila; see, for example, Cuello (1990), Adams (1991), and Offutt (1993). Still other works of a similar genre, typically focused on more limited geographical areas, include García Martínez (1987), Menegus Bornemann (1991), and Hoekstra (1993).

umentary biases. Nonetheless, the Lockhartian school generally eschews the new cultural historians' emphasis on "mentalities," the attempt to decode symbolic systems, the tendency to look upon cultural expressions of all kinds as texts, and the linguistic hypertrophy associated with cultural studies. In this scholarship language is extremely important, it is true, but as Lockhart himself has insisted, the axis is philology rather than power. There is an inclination among the authors to feel that the work is done when the philology is done. This accords ill with the new cultural history, which often sees language as an artifact of power, not a transparent medium. But on the whole the work of Lockhart and his students has opened the interior of colonial indigenous society in ways fundamental to any understanding of culture, while it lays reasonable claim to being the most innovative and recognizable "school" of colonial history yet to emerge.

Finally, a third tendency within colonial-era ethnohistory sits squarely within the new cultural history framework. Perhaps its best known exemplars are works dealing with "the conquest of the imaginary," as Serge Gruzinski has put it. Notable here would be studies by Gruzinski (1993), Walter Mignolo (1995), Christian Duverger (1993), Enrique Florescano (1994), Louise Burkhart (1989), Fernando Cervantes (1994), and Jeanette Peterson (1993), among others. Many of these works concentrate primarily, although by no means exclusively, on the early colonial period, the era of initial cultural contact between Europeans and indigenous peoples, and purport to deal with the colonization of forms of representation—of how people think of and talk to themselves, and to other people about themselves. The representational forms emphasized, including written and spoken language, painting and other visual media, and historical memory, are seen as venues of domination, resistance, and accommodation. Such studies tend to privilege religious thought and sensibility as the most illuminating site for revealing what colonization meant to both colonizers and colonized. Compared to the less flashy works in ethnohistory typical of the Lockhart school they are altogether of a more speculative bent, which can lead to the overinterpretation I noted in my discussion of Richard Trexler's work. Furthermore, one sometimes loses the distinction in this style of scholarship between the new cultural history and a more traditional sort of intellectual history exemplified with great eloquence and panache by David Brading's *The First America* (1991). Fernando Cervantes's (1994) fascinating study of diabolism in the sixteenth century, for example, traces one root of Indian attraction to the Christian Devil to his association by the friars with complex Mesoamerican deities utilized as a proxy for the Evil One. This created a sort of theological reflux in which the Devil became validated rather than the indigenous deities invalidated. Still, one finds Cervantes focusing primarily on high theology and its complexities rather than the *carne y hueso* of popular indigenous belief systems. This often produces a "top-down" approach to cultural history at odds with the new cultural history agenda, since high theology and other sorts of elite thought are presumed to have occupied a hegemonic status they may not in fact have enjoyed, or that at least remains to be proved.[18]

THE DIFFUSION OF CULTURAL HISTORY

The "culture as text and text as culture" palindrome—the methodological problem of recovering culture in past time from a flotsam of historical record—overlaps with another problem, the definitional one. Given the anthropological origins of the concept of culture, and even with the recent expansion of its domain and the advent of cultural history, it still retains more than a hint of the exotic, the quaint, the folkloric. We find a widespread tendency in discussions of culture not only to see it instantiated in specific events or behavioral subsets, which is understandable, but also to reify and commodify it, which is understandable but ill advised. We hear about dominant groups (paternalistic employers, for example, or the church) "using culture" as though it were a discrete substance, separable and residual.[19] This tendency to the reification and commodification of culture has multiple causes, one of which is that scholars need to study *something*, not *everything*; that is, there is an analytic imperative. In the process of yielding to this imperative we tend to filter cultural practices or complexes out of their contexts, making them

---

18. In her gloss on Stafford Poole's (1995) impressive study of the cult of the Virgin of Guadalupe, Susan Deans-Smith comments that Poole's approach "precludes his asking questions that would require deeper exploration of popular religious devotion" (Deans-Smith 1998, 265). The same observation would hold for Jacques Lafaye's (1976) canonical work on Mexican nationalism. One developing subfield related to ethnohistory to which I have only alluded, but which deserves a separate treatment of its own, is the theme of resistance and rebellion, specifically among colonial indigenous peoples. Depending upon how such studies are approached, they can tell us much about the contested meanings central to the experience of colonial domination and negotiation. See, for example, García de León (1985, esp. vol. 1); Barabas (1989); Jones (1989); Gosner (1992); and Castro (1996).

19. This seems to me implicit, for example, in Linda Curcio-Nagy's (1996) thoughtful introductory essay to a special number of *The Americas* dedicated to colonial cultural history. In her discussion of the "grand fête" (including viceregal entries and other public celebrations), Curcio-Nagy writes in a distinctly instrumentalist vein of the "functions" of large-scale spectacle. This viewpoint also seems implicit in a number of the essays in Beezley, Martin, and French (1994).

into somewhat static objects, "things" or "commodities," rather than processes woven into larger webs of meaning. Another cause is that the development of a specialization responds to the ecological imperative in our profession that each of us dominate some sort of "studies": "representation studies," "Indian studies," "Mexican Revolution studies," and so forth. A third cause is the application of Gramscian hegemony to the understanding of cultural formations, by which we understand that cultural artifacts, or clusters of ideas or practices, flow in a stream from the top of society downward.

Despite my presentation in the immediately preceding pages (and in Chapter 3) of a catalogish discussion of some of the new cultural history's characteristic themes, I believe that cultural history should not be sited in a particular venue or specific set of phenomena to be examined exclusively and in isolation, but should be seen instead as an approach, as a way of looking at things, the most important of which is socially constituted meaning, always a relational property, as I have suggested. A parade, a mass, or even a major rebellion is after all only a "window" onto society (to employ a trope that has gained perhaps too much currency); it is not the entire house. Such an event or institutionalized expression cannot be made to stand in for an entire culture: it is not a proxy for it, nor does it encapsulate it (Van Young 1994a). We ghettoize culture in this fashion only at the risk of misapprehending or overlooking the most important part of what we study. In glossing the ideas of François Furet and Robert Darnton, Lynn Hunt (1989a, 9) observes in this connection that they

> strongly warn us against developing a cultural history defined only in terms of topics of inquiry. Just as social history sometimes moved from one group to another (workers, women, children, ethnic groups, the old, the young) without developing much sense of cohesion or interaction between topics, so too a cultural history defined topically could degenerate into an endless search for new cultural practices to describe, whether carnivals, cat massacres, or impotence trials.

If people really live suspended in webs of significance they themselves construct, as Geertz (1973, 5) has written, then culture must be in many places where we cannot see it, or where it does not occur to us to look, or where it might appear as background to the central social action. It is finally more useful, I believe, to take culture and cultural practice this way, as a medium that pervades social orders and part-social orders, rather than as exotic lumps for decoding. This promiscuity, as I have called it, the idea that culture is to be found everywhere, and that the new cultural history is an approach rather than a specific set of topics, has several interesting implications. Let me explore three of these for a moment.

The first is that we might take another look at economic history as cultural history and at economic relations as the sites of generation of cultural meanings, which is still not the prevailing approach at the moment. The cultural history of colonial Mexico is most readily recoverable, as a practical matter, at those points where private lives crossed the public record, as I have suggested. Along with political rebellion, crime, and other sorts of "deviance," including religious heterodoxy, economic life has long been acknowledged as such a privileged site because the interests of even a relatively weak colonial state demanded that forms of property be recorded, regulated, and taxed. There are other reasons why the colonization of economic life by cultural history is likely to be fruitful. For one thing, the relatively underdeveloped state of civil society and the episodic reach of a Western lettered tradition in Mexico even in the late colonial period meant that documents that might have been generated by civil corporations, citizens' groups, newspapers, memoirists, letter writers, and so on, are relatively rare and therefore sources of an overtly "cultural" nature concomitantly scarce. Moreover, the low degree among rural and urban people alike of differentiation between residence and workplace in the colonial era meant that the boundary between work life and private life, between "economy" and "culture," to put it more crudely, was porous or nonexistent.[20] There are also theoretical reasons for the colonization of economic history by cultural historians, which I deal with at some length in the concluding section of this essay.

The second implication for cultural history of utilizing a more inclusive concept of culture has to do with the notion of agency, in turn a central issue in discussions of resistance and the study of subaltern groups. We would probably all agree that a good dollop of agency was a salutary ingredient in reining in the juggernaut of structuralism and putting common people, especially, back into history by making actors of them. When we ghettoize or exoticize culture in the way that I have suggested is common, however, seeing it as limited to discrete social sites or events only, we in fact facilitate what might be called the "apotheosis of agency" by adding far too many degrees of freedom to individual thinking and action. That is to say, if the cultural matrix within which dominant and subordinate groups are embedded is only a hegemonic relationship; and if the locus of hegemony is seen to be limited to multiple but discrete sites only (say,

---

20. This would be most obvious in the case of peasants, whose working and living venues were completely miscible, but I am also thinking of patterns of protoindustrialization and early industrial establishments, in which the distinction between workplace and homeplace was not a hard and fast one. On extensive "homework" in the late colonial Mexico City tobacco manufactory, see for example Deans-Smith (1992), and on protoindustrialization in the textile industry, Miño Grijalva (1990, 1993) and Ouweneel (1996).

protonationalist mythification or religious thought); and, furthermore, if subaltern agency manifests itself in consciously denying, appropriating, inverting, subverting, or otherwise rearranging the flow of readily identifiable hegemonic "quanta"; then all subalterns (as also every member of a dominant elite) are pretty much free to do what they like. Cultural "targets" are always ready at hand, standing out unambiguously in the ideational landscape and largely unsupported by other "targets" or more generalized attitudes. This conception of thinking and behavior clearly derives from rational actor theories and the microeconomic modeling from which they arose, which is rather ironic in view of the way the literature on rational actors and moral economists has developed.[21] It is thus difficult to square the apotheosis of agency, in some ways an *a*culturalist or *anti*culturalist position, with a denser, more inclusive notion of culture, so that culture is not just a sort of hobby in which historical actors engage when they are not off negotiating, resistently adapting, or expanding their spaces. The constraints represented (often unconsciously) by culture, therefore, are just as important as the degrees of freedom vouchsafed by a theory of historical agency. To take but one example, Steve Stern's (1995) portrayal of the constraints imposed upon colonial women's freedom by the prevailing patriarchalist ideology has the balance just about right. Just as history is said to be nature's way of making sure that everything does not happen all at once, culture is nature's way of making sure that all meanings are not possible simultaneously.

In exoticizing or ghettoizing culture in the way we habitually seem to do, and superimposing upon it romanticized notions of agency, we deny the sheer weight of culture in mapping the world for human beings and shaping their behavior. This comports very well with rational actor models but very ill with anything most of us see around us or in documents about the way people really behave. To take but one example, Cheryl Martin's (1996) impressive study of eighteenth-century Chihuahua is a very thoughtful, clearly written, and deeply researched work coming about as close as anything on the historiographical horizon to a community study in the new cultural history mode. But it does share the tendency of much recent work in social and cultural history to apotheosize historical agency and discount culture, so that in essence all the subalterns become rational actors. In my view this finally produces an altogether overly romanticized view of evolving society on New Spain's northern frontier, and may unjustifiably minimize some of its resemblances to central Mexico. And it is not clear why agency should generally be called into play, by the way, only in explaining subaltern resistance, or sly forms

---

21. For a sharp critique of rational choice theory, see Green and Shapiro (1994).

of adaptation, rather than in explaining why people allow themselves to be co-opted into a given social configuration or become active practitioners of prevailing cultural usages. One compelling reason may be that it is forms of resistance rather than cooperation that often show up in the documentation.

The last implication of pursuing an expansionist strategy in cultural history can be discussed very briefly; it is raised by the fine essays of Mary Kay Vaughan and William French in the issue of the *Hispanic American Historical Review* in 1999 in which the debate about the new cultural history was originally aired. I suggested at the start of this essay that politics might be colonized by the new cultural history, but in large measure it has been the other way around: the history of politics (in the more restricted sense) and of the state have captured culture. Admittedly this "statolatry," as Alan Knight (1986, 1:315, 559n386) has dubbed it, shows up more obviously in the historiography of the nineteenth and twentieth centuries than in that of the colonial period. In Vaughan and French's hands, in fact, the new cultural history appears little more than a refiguration of political history. Partly this emphasis on the Mexican state and its doings is an effect of the peculiarities of Mexican history itself; partly it is the result of the deformation introduced into both political and cultural history by Gramscian hegemony as a widely employed theoretical framework; and partly it is the consequence of the sources available to historians—the detritus of private lives and civil society bumping up against the state. This is true in large measure, although less markedly so, for colonial history, even leaving behind the enormous number of traditional studies describing the colonial regime and its workings, some of which can actually lend themselves to cultural history (e.g., Arnold 1988; Chandler 1991). Even where the colonial state is not the central object of the account, there is some tendency to project cultural phenomena or ideologies into the political realm in order to validate the enterprise of cultural history, as in Steve Stern's (1995) epilogic discussion of gender and politics, Patricia Seed's (1988) treatment of the Bourbon state, and Susan Deans-Smith's (1992) considerable attention to the colonial regime in what may profitably be seen as a study in the history of petty commodity production, gender, and the culture of labor. Thus cultural history becomes a biography of the state by other means, centrally concerned with a metanarrative of power, as opposed to questions of how people lived their lives on a daily basis, or what they believed about the world around them or about the next world, for that matter. But are political questions the only interesting ones to be asked, or political answers the only interesting resolutions? Why not elbow aside these teleologies for a more diffuse cultural history of "being Mexican"?

THE COLONIZATION OF ECONOMIC HISTORY

Space limitations preclude my entering at length here into the complex but oft-rehearsed debate between materialist and culturalist points of view, but I shall allude to it at least briefly. In expanding on Chartier (1982) and commenting on the reorientation of "fourth-generation" *Annales*-school historians toward language and the autonomous, non-reflexive nature of culture, Lynn Hunt (1989a: 7) writes:

> As Chartier claimed, "the relationship thus established is not one of dependence of the mental structures on their material determinations. The representations of the social world themselves are the constituents of social reality." Economic and social relations are not prior to or determining of cultural ones; they are themselves fields of cultural practice and cultural production—which cannot be explained deductively by reference to an extracultural dimension of experience.

The colonization of economic activity by the new cultural history rests on assumptions quite different, therefore, from the economistic ones that often prevail in studies of collective behavior and expression. These latter assumptions support the reverse colonization movement, that of culture by economy, reducing discourse, ideology, and meaning to reflexive products of economic forces. The way in which this semiotic or hermeneutic approach constitutes a counterpoise to the essentially economistic position that one still sees even in the new cultural history has been expressed eloquently by Marshall Sahlins (1976, vii–viii) in the opening pages of his *Culture and Practical Reason*, worth quoting at length:

> For some, however, it is clear that culture is precipitated from the rational activity of individuals pursuing their own best interests. This is "utilitarianism" proper; its logic is the maximization of means-ends relations. The objective utility theories are naturalistic or ecological; for them, the determinant material wisdom substantialized in cultural form is the survival of the human population or the given social order. The precise logic is adaptive advantage, or maintenance of the system within natural limits of viability. As opposed to all these genera and species of practical reason, [I propose] a reason of another kind, the symbolic or meaningful. It takes as the distinctive quality of man not that he must live in a material world, circumstance [*sic*] he shares with all organisms, but that he does so according to a meaningful scheme of his own devising, in which capacity mankind is unique. It therefore takes as the decisive quality of culture—as giving each mode of life the properties that characterize it—not that this culture must conform to material constraints but that it does so according to a definite symbolic scheme which is never the only one possible. Hence it is culture which constitutes utility.

To put it somewhat crudely, while in the economistic formulation (in Sahlins's terminology sometimes "utilitarian," sometimes "materialistic") "interest" would be antecedent to "cultural expression," in the semiotic/ hermeneutic formulation the reverse is the case—cultural ideas would be antecedent to interest, interpretation to social object.[22] This radically idealist position is so far uncommon in the new cultural history of colonial Mexico (except possibly for the above-cited works of Gruzinski and Mignolo) and may well remain so. But even if cultural historians were to shift somewhat in this direction, while avoiding going overboard into the particularistic, hermeneutic relativism that the anthropologist Melford Spiro (1986) warns against, it might produce interesting results.

I have experimented with this sort of project myself in revisiting in cultural terms some earlier work of my own on colonial land conflicts in the Guadalajara region in the late colonial period, which primarily pitted indigenous communities against nonindigenous landowners (Van Young 1981, 1996). I stood my earlier analysis on its head, that is, to look at these detailed legal records not primarily for data on economic relationships that generated social conflict, but as expressions of cultural ideas among indigenous villagers, mainly having to do with the community as a primordial locus of identity and loyalty. This does not mean that economic struggles had no real-world causes or implications for access to resources, livelihoods, market position, and so forth. But it does suggest that social conflict that at first appeared exclusively or primarily economic in origin might well have had deeper roots of a symbolic and ideational nature. In other words, people were not arguing just (or primarily) over calories, or over control of other people's calories, but also over meanings. Moreover, it means that ways of getting calories themselves generated meanings. An impressive exemplar of this sort of approach not for colonial Mexico, but for eighteenth- and nineteenth-century Europe, is David Sabean's (1990) book on rural Germany; the European historiography is replete with such works (see also Le Roy Ladurie 1966, 1978).

---

22. See, for example, the remarks of Gareth Stedman Jones (1982, 22) on the relationship of ideas and discourse to material interest: "We cannot therefore decode political language to reach a primal and material expression of interest since it is the discursive structure of political language which conceives and defines interest in the first place." Even more to the point is Marshall Sahlins's (1976, 12; emphasis in original) gloss on the anthropologist Meyer Fortes's (1967) treatment of Tallensi kinship: "Fortes does not deny the ecological constraint of the economic interests; he points them out. But he does not insist that the *social effects of practical interest—not to mention the nature of that interest—depend on the structure in place*. Again the economic logic is socially constituted." On the other hand, anthropologist William Roseberry (1989, 1–29) frames a powerful critique of Geertz and Sahlins from a historical materialist perspective, but in my view his claim that a historical political economy, after the manner of Eric Wolf's *Europe and the People Without History* (1982), ultimately provides a better explanation of the links among economic cultures, meaning, and human action is not completely convincing.

Sabean argues generally that property and the mode of its production mediated, but did not solely determine, human relationships, and that the putative contrast between a "traditional" social order based on kinship and face-to-face contact, and a "modern" one based on contractual relationships is considerably overdrawn.

For the history of colonial Mexico one finds some precedent for this cultural colonization of economic life in the history of traditional elite groups realized in the prosopographical or biographical style, even though they have not been written explicitly in the new cultural history mode, as well as in the beginnings of environmental history. In addition to the books I have already mentioned by Schwaller, Ladd, Kicza, and Hoberman, I would point to work by Charles H. Harris III (1975) on the Sánchez Navarro family, Richard Lindley (1983) on the merchant-landowner elite of late colonial Guadalajara, John Tutino (1976) on Valley of Mexico landowners, and David Brading (1971) on silver mining and landowning families, to mention just a few of the studies in this genre (and for a later era, Lomnitz and Pérez Lizaur 1987). Arij Ouweneel's (1996) book on the ecological and economic history of central Mexico in the eighteenth century is definitely attuned to cultural issues in terms of his treatment of economic paths pursued by indigenous communities, but for him cultural factors play the role more of constraints or idealized models for action than sites of meaning generation and worldview. More obviously in the new cultural history camp at the moment, interestingly enough, are works that assume an avowedly ecological perspective on regional history and ethnohistory, and in which environments are socially constructed not only by economic action, but by human perception. Although these studies are not plentiful as yet, one hopes to see more of them in future. An outstanding example of this mode of inquiry is Elinor Melville's (1994) account of environmental degradation in the Mezquital Valley under the impact of overgrazing by sheep in the early colonial period. Although her emphasis is clearly on changes in the environment—ultimately in its economic carrying capacity—she demonstrates the influence of habitual modes of environmental exploitation that were culturally determined. Even more in the cultural history style is Cynthia Radding's *Wandering Peoples* (1997), in which the author weaves together the logics of Spanish colonial penetration, indigenous resistance, and an unforgiving environment into a tapestry of encounters over time in which economic formations are clearly shown to be effects of cultural "choices" as much or more than their causes. Danièle Dehouve's (1994) study of indigenous groups in colonial Guerrero does much the same thing for a somewhat smaller venue.

Before going any further with this theme, I feel it necessary to acknowledge, at risk of caricaturing or essentializing both economic and cultural history, that there are a multitude of differences between these two approaches, and I do not wish to minimize or erase them since in these differences lies a potentially fruitful tension. Let me offer an illustration. An important tendency within cultural history, as I have mentioned, has been the introduction of the concept of agency in historical actors, above all for subaltern groups, but by no means limited to them. Very often in economic history peasants, for example, are treated from the point of view of producers, or consumers, or workers, but always as an agglomeration of units formed by productive forces or the constraints and possibilities of the market. In the case of political history peasants are often seen as a homogeneous mass (Marx's famous "homologous magnitude") manipulated (or led) by elites and other political actors. But with the advent of cultural and subaltern history we are coming to see them as the agents of their own destiny, to a certain degree, with a gamut of political options, and very often behaving in terms of a distinct form of economic rationality. This trend in the study of peasants and other common people might be called the "disenchantment of structural materialism."[23] I can anticipate an objection here from some of my readers, which is that for certain purposes it is more efficacious—in other words, it leads to better answers—to rely on methods of objectification, while for others it is more useful to enter through the door of subjectivity and agency. This is effectively the case, and because of this—because, in short, certain conceptual frameworks and sets of methods are appropriate for some questions, other frameworks and methods for other questions—it becomes easier to see that there is less of a contradiction between what have been referred to as more positivistic forms of historical inquiry and more hermeneutic ones.

Now let me pass to a more detailed discussion of the differences, commonalities, and complementarities between cultural and economic history, and by extension those between hermeneutic and quantitative approaches to the writing of history. It is by no means a simple matter to disentangle the operations of human beings as exchangers of calories with the environment, and exchangers of meanings among themselves. There are a number of sites—that is, clusters of social patterning sustained through time—at which economic and cultural history are mutually illuminating and where the boundaries between them become increasingly porous. Generally, in fact, the relationship between economic and cultural history, in

---

23. There is another problem here, of course, which results from the historian's endowing the historical actor—*any* historical actor, not just groups of common people—with too many degrees of freedom (we might call this "hyperagentialism"), thus erasing the effects of culture as a template that constrains people's actions within certain limits, just as it may enable them within others. For a discussion of this point, see Chapter 6 in this volume.

the sense of a conflict, is a nonissue; they collaborate well in looking at historical problems such as the representation of wealth and well-being, taste (Veblen), and religion (Weber). Furthermore, cultural historians need to take into account how people get and spend, since most of us invest much of our lives in these occupations. On the other hand, many questions of historical interest, such as the noneconomic motives of labor, the investment proclivities and social reproduction patterns of elite groups, and so forth, slide more and more into a cultural register as they gain distance from neoclassical models of market behavior. The central question about the relationship between cultural and economic history (or to put it another way, between quantitative/structural and hermeneutic/interpretive approaches) may not be so much about which one presents a more "accurate" or "real" picture of the world, but how far down the edifice of the social construction of reality they go, and where, if at all, they hit bedrock. A conflict may arise, it is true, when in the methodological area the claims of cultural history are subjected to the verificational criteria of the more hard-edged types of economic or quantitative history. But even here it is important to recognize that there are often steps antecedent to quantitative operations, which involve the social construction of categories of economic behavior that are not themselves reducible to artifacts of that behavior. In other words, the way we understand economic life itself depends on the construction of categories—capitalism, for instance—that are themselves the products of cultural dispositions.[24]

Let us take the case of small-scale land sales, for example, which parallels that of money wages, invoked in my opening pages. This has been one of the chief objects of interest for those scholars interested in the social and economic history of peasants, but it can also furnish a good deal of information about habits of life, peasant worldview, and so forth. In my own work on Mexican rural society I have encountered many such interactions, in which we may assume, for the moment, that peasant sellers enter freely into sales of land parcels. From the point of view of both buyer and purchaser, what is immediately at issue is the market value of the land, as well as its "use" value. But "use" value may embrace a more complicated calculation than simply what the land can produce: it may also encompass ideas about loyalty and affective bond to place, about the unseen world, about ancestry, about social standing within a village community—in other words, not just about material exchange or advantage, but about other forms of exchange and obligation, as well. We may register the transaction simply as a "sale," but this is only one dimension

---

24. See the discussion of George Lukacs, *History and Class Consciousness* (1971), in Van Young (2001c, 17–19).

of what is taking place, and at that, it is a social construction that filters out an important aspect of the behavior and may therefore distort our understanding of it.

It may be useful to pause for a moment here to reprise in expanded form the brief definition, alluded to in earlier pages, of what is meant here by *culture*. I take culture to be made up of those intergenerationally transmitted codes and symbols by which groups of people impute meanings to the world of humans, things, and forces around them, and by which they convey that information to each other; by which they understand, represent, reinforce, or contest relations of power and domination; and through which they define their own identities by the stories they tell about themselves (Van Young 2001c, 19). If this seems an excessively "mentalistic" construct, let me add that it would also include concrete behavioral practices in dealing with the world—the "correct" way to get things done, for example, and the normative understandings that underlie these. I confess that this is a very broad definition. Cultural history is the study of these ideas, meanings, and practices in the past, as economic history is the study of economic activity in the past. With such a broad definition, we might think of culture as an encompassing medium, like the ether of nineteenth-century science, in which various forms of human activity are embedded, all of which, including the most apparently mundane, have symbolic meanings for their performers. Such a plastic and inclusive definition may seem to make of culture a dull instrument of inquiry, without much of a cutting edge or any readily apparent principle of exclusion—that is, a way to distinguish cultural from noncultural. But I do not think this is true: when it comes to concrete scholarship, there is simply good cultural history and bad cultural history, just as there is good and bad serial or economic history, or a methodology that specifies the terms under discussion as opposed to one that is sloppy or overly permissive. To take up the small illustration of peasant land sales again, an economic historian might be centrally concerned with downstreaming issues of productivity and wealth; that is, with how such a transfer of productive resources affects the wealth and material well-being of a community at moment of sale + time x. A cultural historian, by contrast, might try to get at the subjective meaning for the seller of compromising or perhaps entirely severing a bond with an ancestral place through the sale of a piece of it, or that of placing himself within a new economic context by increasing his reliance on wage labor, emigrating to a city, and so forth. One very obvious difference between the two approaches, of course, is that the economic behavior can be observed and isolated as an event in the etic realm (the observable behavior stream), while the mental behavior—the noneconomic meaning of the economic event or, if one prefers, the symbolic economy of the exchange—may remain relatively inaccessible, in the emic realm (the less readily observable affective, cognitive, and symbolic stream).

If the definition of culture (and therefore of the objects of cultural history) just offered is very broad, there is also the tendency, as I have suggested, with excessively narrow or specialized definitions of culture and the cultural realm, of consigning culture to a "behavioral ghetto." Cultural history has been ghettoized less by its critics than by its own practitioners to embrace almost entirely expressive forms of behavior: religious sensibility, art, and celebratory and ritual life, for example. There are a number of reasons for this setting of borders. It allows cultural historians to develop privileged vocabularies and grammars—terms of art, if you will—and specialized methodologies, among them the close reading of texts, a great scrupulosity in the decoding of recorded spoken language, and the imputation of broad cultural style from artistic style (e.g., Gruzinski 2002). The carving out of this specialized niche, while it may ghettoize cultural historians and devotees of cultural studies, also permits them to act as the prophets or oracular interpreters of that same language. The worst excesses of postmodernism—not as an interesting epistemological posture, but as an academic practice—and of postcolonial studies are extreme examples of this, at least in the United States. There is also the influence of cultural anthropology, from which much of the impulse toward cultural history arises, as well as the avowedly hybrid form now called historical anthropology (Axel 2002). Finally, there is the generally acknowledged tendency of historians to be splitters rather than lumpers. That is, historians find that cultural manifestations occur in specific places, and thus need to be explained not only with reference to widely applicable mental templates, but also in terms of local knowledges and momentary conditions (Geertz 1983a; Sahlins 1987). The quotient of "localness" in cultural manifestations is high, in other words, and this conduces to the sort of ghettoization I have mentioned.

As I have already implied, we can say that symbolic/expressive behaviors have important, even determinative economic dimensions, since they set the parameters within which economic behaviors occur. Many questions flow from this proposition. Let us take as an example, again, the issue of wages and incomes. What is the acquisitive power of what people earn, and how do they make decisions about spending their incomes? How much leisure time do they have, what sorts of choices do they make about whether to work more or have more leisure, and how do they use the leisure time they have? Is the wealthiest man in the village also the most powerful, and does he get to march at the head of the saint's-day parade? This relationship between cultural and economic behaviors extends into the realm of what people value,[25] what they consume, the choices they make in investing their time in one sort of activity rather than another (i.e., the opportunity costs), and the returns they expect—material, symbolic, spiritual. Ideas and motives about wealth and status obeying what we might recognize as a strictly economic rationale—that status gives access to wealth, and wealth buys status, in a circular fashion—can coexist perfectly well with ideas or predispositions about religion, gender, personal and group identity, and so forth. Wages may simultaneously reflect not only the relative value of a quantum of labor, however—that is to say, its *cost*—but also notions of its *worth*, a concept of value more elusive but no less important than price. These notions of worth may not necessarily be translatable directly into terms of maximization or other economic objectives, and may include culturally specific normative ideas about work, leisure, gender and status roles, our relation to the unseen world, and so forth. Moreover, in some situations a cultural understanding is more important than the economic calculus in terms of apparently rational market behavior, or the relationship is circular rather than linear.

In order to descend from this level of abstraction into concrete historical cases of interest both to cultural and economic historians, let me illustrate the idea of overdetermination with two examples much studied by historians of Mexico and Latin America more generally. My first illustration is the field of hacienda studies, generally to be seen as a subgenre of economic history, one in which the importance of the substrate of cultural ideas, norms, and practices in explaining the performance of this institution through time is particularly vivid. The work of François Chevalier on the colonial hacienda set much of the agenda for an entire generation of such studies by linking the seigneurial ideals of medieval and late medieval manorial latifundism in Europe to the establishment of large landed estates in the Americas (Chevalier 1999; Van Young 1983). Chevalier's seminal study was somewhat misunderstood, I believe, and generalizing claims were made for it by other scholars that its own author might not have pressed so far. It is also true, however, that the studies that followed in his footsteps were in large part dedicated to substituting a more clearly economic rationale for the functioning of the colonial hacienda, one less determined by a medieval seigneurial ideal of social power, status, and political dominance for their own sakes, and more clearly dedicated to the maximization of utilities in changing market circumstances.[26] This was most often encapsulated as a contrast between feudal and capital-

---

25. Oscar Wilde famously quipped that a cynic knows the price of everything and the value of nothing.

26. For a recent review of the "feudal" versus "capitalistic" characterizations of the colonial great estate, see Knight (2002a, passim).

istic models of the institution, respectively. A purely rational economic model of the hacienda falls far short of its actual historical reality, however, since the tone of the institution was in many instances so clearly seigneurial; that is, it constituted a sort of theater of patriarchal power. The economic decisions of its governance were clearly influenced by the cultural landscape, in which considerations of social status, strongly familistic values, masculinity, and social hierarchy loomed large and may even have trumped ideas about profit maximization vis-à-vis the market. A number of historians have linked landholding patterns to the social reproduction of colonial elite families, most obviously in the foundation of the *mayorazgos* (entails) that sometimes underwrote the creation of titles of nobility. These strategies not only involved the accumulation and preservation of wealth, however, but also a strong dynastic impulse and what one can only think of as familism: a tendency to see the social order less in terms of state and civil society, for example, or even of class, than of clan (Banfield 1965). This is not to say that profits were not important in explaining the way haciendas were operated, but only that noneconomic motives might be equally or more compelling.

Another example of the interaction of economic rationality and cultural expression would be the behavior of the traditional church in Latin America.[27] The Catholic Church, in all its manifestations, was without doubt a major political and economic player at all times and places in Latin America, and remains so in many areas. But could its vast sphere of influence and its deep imbrication in nearly every aspect of life (until quite recent times) have been created or sustained without religious piety, or without a belief in its essential mediating role between humans and divine forces? One can of course understand the Church primarily in concretely economic terms. In colonial times, in particular, its enormous wealth functioned as a bank in a prebanking age, it served as a redoubt for elite groups to exercise leverage in both the market and the state, and it absorbed into a life of celibacy excess children whose marriages would otherwise have tended to disperse elite wealth through inheritance obligations, and so forth. One can even project an interesting economic model onto the thinking behind religious piety and practice, seeing believers as making spiritual investments, savings, and decisions about opportunity costs. But this would be to hollow out the moral, affective, and spiritual content of religious sensibility in an extreme way. The fact, for example, that a *juzgado de capellanías* (chaplaincy court) might redeploy wealth

---

27. I am well aware that there was no monolithic "church," just as there was no single type of hacienda, but for purposes of this discussion I have essentialized these institutions in an admittedly reductive fashion.

originating in pious bequests to secular economic activities through loans, does not obviate the fact that we have here an intertwining of spiritual and mundane economies. Are we to assume that the desire of individuals to leave endowments to chaplaincies and to pay for masses in order to see their own and their loved ones' way through Purgatory is to be discounted as a mere pretext for the disposition of economic surpluses? There is a distinction to be made between *intention* and *consequences*, of course, and in the latter case between *manifest* consequences and *latent* consequences. From this point of view, unless one adopts a crudely Marxian framework of interpretation, it would seem more reasonable to assume that piety begets accumulation, rather than the other way around, or at the very least that they stand in a dialogic or codetermining relationship to each other. Here we have advanced a step beyond overdetermination to circularity.

Beyond the ideas of overdetermination or even circularity, there is a still more radical position about the relationship of the cultural and economic realms, a macrohistorical model that embraces entire epochs in the history of the last few centuries, especially in the West and the areas most strongly influenced by it. Some thinkers have suggested that economic activities themselves are not constitutive of cultural categories—that the latter are not reducible to the former, in other words—but that cultural categories are antecedent to economic ones (e.g., Sahlins 1976). Among these thinkers are Marshall Sahlins, Georg Lukacs, and Karl Polanyi, who have suggested that historical materialism itself, as a way of understanding the world, can be historicized as a form of analysis. We might thus find historical materialism (and within it, the tendency to see culture as significantly formed by economic arrangements) to be a less than appropriate framework for understanding all historical epochs, or all societies within the same epoch. We might need to acknowledge that people living within a noncapitalist social framework have other points of reference for their beliefs and behaviors than economic ones, the logic of production, distribution, and accumulation. There are strong traces of this idea in the concept of the "articulation of modes of production" much debated among development economists, anthropologists, historians, and other scholars in the 1960s and 1970s. This argument proposed that in societies in which an incomplete or ongoing transition to capitalist forms took place, large segments of the population (most obviously peasants) were organized according to other modes of production, and that these forms demonstrated their own economic logic, even though they were articulated with the dominant mode of production (Van Young 1992c, chap. 4). In *The Great Transformation*, for example, Karl Polanyi wrote: "Economic motives per se are notoriously much less effective with most people than so-called emotional ones" (Polanyi 1957, 219). Polanyi dealt with the idea that self-regulating economic markets, as they came to exist and were apotheosized in the West, were in many ways a historical anomaly. This implies that historical metrics—ways of measuring development, growth, advance, or whatever one chooses to call it—derived from market-oriented economies are inappropriate intellectual technologies for looking at noncapitalist or even protocapitalist societies. Here let me quote again from Polanyi: "The goals for which an individual will work are socially [and, Sahlins would suggest, culturally] determined" (Polanyi 1957, 158). The model of the moral economy initially broached by E. P. Thompson, further developed by James C. Scott, and harking back to Aristotle's notion of the "just price," emphasizes the social and cultural embeddedness of economic life, and partakes of this view (Thompson 1971; Scott 1976, 1985). Lukacs and Sahlins have stressed the relative absence in such societies of a differentiation between the realms of economic and other forms of behavior. An example of such a fusion that I have already invoked (and will again) would be the family, and its discursive form the ideology of familism.

Let me now pass briefly to a discussion of the methodological aspects that economic history and cultural history (or if one prefers, positivistic and hermeneutic approaches) share with one another. First, there is the technique of upstreaming; that is, the practice of applying systematized contemporary experience, transformed into theoretical formulations, to decipher questions or ambiguities imposed by the separation of object and observer in time, and by the decay or loss of information about the past. One of the points that Polanyi, Lukacs, and other writers make about this technique, of course, is that it may lead to anachronism in interpretation. Second, there is quantification, obvious in economic and other sorts of more positivistic approaches, but less so in cultural history. Cultural history, like its progenitor discipline (history without modifiers), would claim to be a science of the particular. Normally we think of cultural history, probably, as looking at the idiopathic phenomenon, of which the most extreme form would be biography in a cultural context. But in fact, to make statements of any wider applicability at all, which almost all historians try to do, cultural history generally relies on repetition and frequency, and in this regard a small N (number of observations) may be criticized as much in cultural as in economic history.[28]

---

28. One example drawn from the twentieth-century historiography rather than that of the colonial period would be the work on popular *cardenismo* in Michoacán in the 1930s by Marjorie Becker (1995). While this book has a great deal to recommend it, including very evocative writing and an extremely insightful discussion of gender and politics in the

Cultural historians also use a vocabulary with dynamic terms implying change of velocity and quantity over time, among them *more, less, frequently, increasing, overwhelming majority, acceleration,* and so forth. Third, the two approaches share a probative structure in which tests of reasonableness and realness bend back upon interpretation; that is, in which tests of common sense are applied. In the case of cultural history this common sense criterion is typically based upon a long process of learning something about the culture that one is studying, something that anthropologists do all the time.[29] During this process of studying the cultural context of behavior, especially in the symbolic realm, information accumulates in layers, producing a textured and saturated image, much like the technique of impasto in painting. Fourth, cultural and economic history share something of symmetry in their evolution, albeit in opposite directions: while economic history has demonstrated a tendency to move from the local to the institutional (particularly in its Northian variant, to be discussed in a moment), cultural history has tended to move from the institutional to the local (especially in its Geertzian mode).

Now, let us turn to some differences between the two. A growing divergence in the study of what we may call cultural behaviors and economic behaviors can be noted in the evolution of the human sciences over the last two centuries and more. I have not inquired deeply enough into this genealogy to reconstruct its long-term movement with any precision, but we can see a pretty clear distinction developing from the time of Adam Smith between "sentiment" (which may for some purposes be taken as a proxy for culture) and political economy.[30] From that period in the late

---

Michoacán countryside, the size of the "sample" upon which its conclusions are based—as nearly as I can determine, about seven oral informants—is not one of them.

29. There are a number of ways in which the influence of anthropology in general, and ethnographic method in particular, have set cultural historians up for disappointment, since cultural historians often ask anthropologists' questions without having recourse to their tools, as I have suggested above. A striking illustration of how the *form* of symbolic behavior may be readily observable but its *content* remain incomprehensible without a knowledge of cultural context is provided by the well-known case of Temple Grandin, the American academic who has struggled with autism all her life and become in recent years the poster child for positive adaptations to the condition. She has written movingly that her disability so distances her from an empathic understanding of emotional interaction among other human beings that often, when she sees two people interacting, she feels "like an anthropologist on Mars," the title essay describing her life in a collection of case studies by the famous neuropsychologist Oliver W. Sacks (1995).

30. It is nonetheless interesting to note the proximity of Smith to other figures of the Scottish Enlightenment such as David Hume, who were less overtly concerned with principles of economy than with human affective states and symbolic activities. Smith himself wrote a major work on the role of "sympathy" (what today we would call empathy) in human civility, something much closer to the notion of culture being explored here than his

eighteenth century we have the invention of the *homo economicus*, of which the apotheosis is today's rational choice theory. This distinction has obviously hardened since at least the Enlightenment, and can be seen in a number of differences between cultural and economic history; let me cite three of them here. First, as I mentioned above, cultural history is what might be called an ironic project. Economic history would attempt to clear away this irony as obfuscating the "real" story. Cultural historians, by contrast, would revel in it and the attendant slippages between the accounts of different actors, not only as eye-witnesses with different angles of perception (the so-called "Rashomon effect"), but as bearers of culture and personal histories. Second, as suggested in an earlier chapter, the advent of cultural history has to some degree displaced the scalar or unilinear model of social development, substituting for it more relativist and internalist models of behavior. Fully reconstructing intracranial events or symbolic expressions is difficult, of course, and represents one of the dangers of this genre of history writing: that while its methods may be hermeneutic, its outcomes may be hermetic: speculative—clothed in impenetrable language, and unfalsifiable. In keeping with its mentalist/localist approach, cultural history has tended to look more intensely at internalist explanations of behavior, including individual motivations mediated by webs of socially shared and reproduced symbolic systems. With economic history, we have just the opposite: cultural, social, and political change tends to be seen as the reflexive responses to externalities such as markets, external capital flows, or resource endowment. Finally, in economic or other sorts of quantitative or "objectivist" history we tend to see a subject (the historian-observer) and an object (an economic transaction of some sort), and generally assume that the former is unbiased and the latter stable and knowable.[31] In cultural history, on the other hand, we have at least two subjects—one of them the interpreting observer, the other a subject observed (which may be evasive, duplicitous, unstable, and so forth)—or even three if the maker of the source-text is distinct from the actors being observed through the medium of written language.

These differences are not necessarily to be seen as irreconcilable, although they may appear as such when the epistemological and methodological brickbats come out. Let us leave these questions aside, however, and look to at least one of the potential points of contact between cul-

---

later ideas on political economy; Adam Smith, *The Theory of Moral Sentiments* (1754). On the Scottish Enlightenment, see James Buchan (2003).

31. I generally prefer a term such as *objectivist* to the more loaded *positivist*, with its pejorative connotations, although I would personally be perfectly happy to use *positivist* as a neutral descriptor.

tural history and economic, quantitative, or objectivist historical approaches (I will concentrate here on economic history as a genre of the objectivist variety). It is possible to detect a bifurcation in the field of economic history, one branch tending toward increasing technification, model building, and macroeconomic approaches, the other toward studies of socially embedded economic activity that blurs at the margins into forms of social and cultural history. This "softer," less technified study of economic behaviors over time can meet the emphasis on culture on the field of institutional history. The institutional approach can mediate in large measure between "pure" economic life and culture; it shows ways in which some roads are taken and others not because of the constraints and opportunities offered by institutions in facing situations of historical change ("path dependency"). The approach developed by Douglass North and his disciples to the institutional practices and structures that condition economic choices is less mechanical, its advocates insist, than a rigid reliance on strict neoclassical market principles. But it does tend to beg the question, as I understand it, of where institutions originate, and to take institutional complexes as initiating conditions from which causal arrows move forward in time, but not necessarily from the past to the historical present. Nonetheless, what has been called the "new institutional history" reinjects history into economic history by reducing the abstraction of the latter. The invisible hand, in other words, becomes all too visible. It goes without saying that many of the sources through which cultural history is studied (perhaps most of them) originate in institutional complexes. The documents used by cultural historians bear the strong traces of the formal, institutionalized structures of property systems, judicial and administrative arrangements, kinship relations, and so forth, and more particularly are generated at the points where individual lives bump up against the state, leaving records, truncated though these may be. Moreover, the institutional approach convincingly contests the notion, inherited from neoclassical economics, that the workings of the market economy are frictionless aside from strictly economic factors intrinsic to the maximal allocation of resources; that is, the "friction of distance" of the geographers produced by distance, transport/production bottlenecks, inadequacy of information systems, and so on.

Since I have already offered a brief definition of culture, let me here offer one of institutions, paraphrasing various authors. Institutions are sets of rules and procedures that ideally govern interactions between individuals and or corporate bodies in society. Lest this seem excessively formalistic and dessicated, let me add another element: that institutions are also made up of more or less stable social roles in which those interactions are instantiated. Hard economic history tends to treat institutions retrospectively, as I have suggested, as antecedent and shaping frameworks within which economic behavior occurs, and the softer economic history treats them (or at least may treat them) prospectively, as effects of the culturally determined decisions of large groups of social actors over time—states, for example. Institutional history seems to explain a considerable amount about why the Latin American economies never operated the way Adam Smith said they should, or the way in which nineteenth-century liberals hoped they would. But where do institutions come from? One view, which we might call the functionalist approach, would be that they are generated, through politics both formal and informal, by an economic mode/system to ensure its own reproduction; another view, more properly a historical approach, would be that they arise over time from the substrates of cultural norms in a given social order, crystalized from ideas about "The Good."

There are a number of examples of this "middle ground" on which the cultural approach may meet the economic approach, whether of the harder or softer variety. One of these would be in institutional history in the narrow sense of the term, such as credit and lending practices in a prebanking society, commercial systems, or arrangements relating to property rights. To take the first example, credit relationships in such an economy are very likely to be linked to kinship and community membership, notions of masculine honor, and social status that are not in themselves reducible to economic factors. Yet another good illustration would be the history of power groups, which typically act to gain as much economic leverage, status, or intangible goods as they can—that is, social influence, access to divine forces, and political power. The history of family groups—elites, it is fair to say—in Latin America, especially during the colonial period, has almost become a distinct subgenre of the economic, social, and cultural historiography, but the same considerations would also theoretically apply to common people, where the documentation is weaker. Such groups might act simultaneously to optimize their position vis-à-vis the market, but to express cultural norms (perhaps even unconsciously) as they did so. In a preindustrial economy, such as that of Mexico for most of its history, the conflation in the extended family of place of work and place of residence, site of wealth accumulation, center of affective life, and important locus of personal identity, looks quite different from the splitting and differentiated roles of modern life.

Let me cite another example here of the ways in which cultural and economic behaviors may be intertwined. As we know well, during much of Mexican history, at least up until the Reforma period in the mid-nineteenth century, elite families sent many of their sons and daughters into the Church. Was this action taken in the mundane money economy, or the otherworldly spiritual economy, or both? Sending children into the priesthood or monastic life certainly produced a connection to the Church that might eventuate in more access to credit through borrowing the principals of chaplaincies, taking loans from confraternities, or even having an inside track on tithe farming. It also helped elite families to avoid the dispersion of family wealth through inheritance fragmentation (most especially in the case of female marriage dowries). But it is also the case that a habit of religious piety formed the channel down which a family's spiritual investments were made. Which was the primary motive here, then: leverage in the worldly economy, or in the otherworldly economy? Moreover, does trying to pry these behaviors apart perhaps undermine the usefulness of an explanation derived from their interaction?

The connection between family and economy, furthermore, is a close one even on etymological grounds, since the very word *economy* derives from the Latin form *oeconomus* and an even earlier Greek word. It is the designation of one who managed a house, especially a steward, through a combination of the word for *house* itself and the word for *management* or *control*. For a long time the word *economy* thus invoked the art or science of managing a household. In this way political, economic, and cultural history are hard to disentangle in the behavior of elite families. The kin-based household economy engaged in action in which the key element was not necessarily the gaining of economic leverage in the marketplace, but the preservation and even exaltation of a cultural value antecedent to economic organization and even resistant to changes in that organization. Elite family structure, practice, and familistic ideology were certainly discernible aspects of a single institution that molded economic behavior, but were themselves cultural constructs compounded of many elements. Among these were historical traditions of Iberian and native worlds, religious belief and normative prescription, changing demographic regimes, conceptions of gender roles, structures of property and citizenship rights, the presence or absence of economic opportunities for women outside the home, and so forth.

We need to ask ourselves the question, then, whether the abstraction of economic behavior from its cultural context, and the posing of questions about it in terms of an abstract, maximizing rationality is necessarily a good idea. Well, for certain purposes yes, for others no. This increased porosity between cultural and economic realms is reflected in recent disciplinary changes. For all its postmodern tone and overheated rhetoric, postcolonial theory as employed by historians and anthropologists in a sense demonstrates the ascendancy of cultural analysis over the pure economic rationality of colonialism as an explanation for the shape of colonial life, as dependency theory was earlier the reification of that rationality, even its apotheosis. The emphasis in postcolonial studies on representational practices from the formerly colonized periphery (including Mexico) is the detritus of the emphasis on economic exploitation of periphery by metropolis (e.g., Thurner and Guerrero 2003). In any case, the putative tension between culturalist and materialist explanations is a salutary one, since it helps us denaturalize familiar explanatory schemes. Doing so may create a certain amount of confusion, but it also can throw some light on complicated historical questions.

CONCLUSION

I close these observations with a return to the dilemma posed by the two epigraphs with which I opened, one transposed to cultural history from fiction, the other from anthropology. They are the eloquent views, respectively, of the novelist Henry James glorifying particularity, the "social mystery, the lurking human secret," and by implication the insight, empathy, and imagination required to penetrate them; and of the anthropologist Melford Spiro, a Cassandra warning against a research strategy of excessive granularity, and decrying the mutation of anthropology from a scientific into a hermeneutic discipline. I have no solution to offer to this dilemma. It does seem to be true that in Mexican cultural history we are well into a pendulum swing away from the confident generalizing of structuralist explanations, and toward the hermeneutic systems of symbols and meanings. This should not be an exclusive stance, however, since the usefulness of the approach depends upon what sources one has at hand, what question one is asking, and in what realm of experience one is likely to find the answer. The test of the explicatory power of an interpretation is still likely to be parsimony, replicability, and breadth. A Polonian moderation (some would call it fence-sitting) and reasonableness are easier to recommend than to achieve. Although I have in this essay been mainly critical of work in the field, and may have offered a somewhat more reserved than unalloyedly positive view of the possibilities for working on the cultural history of colonial Mexico, in the final analysis these are caveats, not objections. The cultural approach is rich in potential and accomplishment to date, and promises more in the future. In the end I think its strategy should be to subsume rather than supplant other traditional genres of historical inquiry on the imperialist assumption that all history is cultural history.

Bibliography

Adams, David B. 1991. *Las colonias tlaxcaltecas de Coahuila y Nuevo León en la Nueva España*. Saltillo: Archivo Municipal de Saltillo.
Adams, Richard Newbold. 1975. *Energy and Structure: A Theory of Social Power*. Austin: University of Texas Press.
Adas, Michael. 1979. *Prophets of Rebellion: Millenarian Protest Movements against the European Colonial Order*. Chapel Hill: University of North Carolina Press.
Adelman, Jeremy. 1994. *Frontier Development: Land, Labour, and Capital on the Wheatlands of Argentina and Canada, 1890–1914*. Oxford: Clarendon Press.
———. 1999. *Republic of Capital: Buenos Aires and the Legal Transformation of the Atlantic World*. Stanford, CA: Stanford University Press.
———. 2006. *Sovereignty and Revolution in the Iberian Atlantic*. Princeton, NJ: Princeton University Press.
Adorno, Rolena. 1986. *Guamán Poma: Writing and Resistance in Colonial Peru*. Austin: University of Texas Press.
Aguirre, Carlos. 2005. *Breve historia de la esclavitud en el Perú: Una herida que no deja de sangrar*. Lima: Fondo Editorial del Congreso del Perú.
Aguirre Beltrán, Gonzalo. 1946. *La población negra de México, 1519–1810: Estudio etnohistórico*. Mexico City: Ediciones Fuente Cultural.
———. 1953. *Formas de gobierno indígena*. Mexico City: Impr. Universitario.
———. 1963. *Medicina y magia*. Mexico City: Instituto Nacional Indigenista.
———. 1992. *Pobladores del Papaloapan: Biografía de una hoya*. Mexico City: Centro de Investigación y Estudios Superiores en Antropología Social.
Alamán, Lucas. 1942. *Obras de d. Lucas Alamán*. Edited by Rafael Aguayo Spencer. 12 vols. Mexico City: Editorial Jus.
———. 1968. *Historia de Méjico desde los primeros movimientos que prepararon su independencia en el año de 1808 hasta la época presente*. 5 vols. Mexico City: Editorial Jus. (Orig. pub. 1849–1852.)
Alberro, Solange. 1988. *Inquisition et société au Mexique, 1571–1700*. Mexico City: Centre d'Etudes Mexicaines et Centraméricaines.
Alexander, Rani, ed. 2003. "Beyond the Hacienda: Agrarian Relations and Socioeconomic Change in Rural Mesoamerica." Special issue of *Ethnohistory* 50 (Winter).

Almada, Francisco R. 1952. *Diccionario de historia, geografía y biografía sonorenses*. Chihuahua City: n.p.
———. 1955. *Resúmen de historia del estado de Chihuahua*. Mexico City: Libros Mexicanos.
Alperovich, M. S. 1967. *Historia de la independencia de México (1810–1824)*. Mexico City: Grijalbo.
Alvarado Gómez, Antonio Armando. 1995. *Comercio interno en la Nueva España. El abasto en la ciudad de Guanajuato, 1777–1810*. Mexico City: Instituto Nacional de Antropología e Historia.
Amaral, Samuel. 1998. *The Rise of Capitalism on the Pampas: The Estancias of Buenos Aires, 1785–1870*. Cambridge: Cambridge University Press.
Amaya Topete, Jesús. 1951. *Ameca, protofundación mexicana*. Mexico City: Editorial Lumen.
Amith, Jonathan D. 2005. *The Möbius Strip: A Spatial History of Colonial Society in Guerrero, Mexico*. Stanford, CA: Stanford University Press.
Anderson, Arthur J. O., and Susan Schroeder, eds. and trans. 1997–. *Codex Chimalpahin: Society and Politics in Mexico Tenochtitlan, Tlatelolco, Culhuacan, and Other Nahua Altepetl in Central Mexico: The Nahuatl and Spanish Annals and Accounts Collected and Recorded by don Domingo de San Antón Muñón Chimalpahin Cuauhtlehuanitzin*. Norman: University of Oklahoma Press.
Anderson, Benedict. 1991. *Imagined Communities: Reflections on the Origins and Spread of Nationalism*, revised. London: Verso.
Andrien, Kenneth J., and Lyman L. Johnson, eds. 1994. *The Political Economy of Spanish America in the Age of Revolution, 1750–1850*. Albuquerque: University of New Mexico Press.
Anna, Timothy. 1978. *The Fall of the Royal Government in Mexico City*. Lincoln: University of Nebraska Press.
———. 1983. *Spain and the Loss of America*. Lincoln: University of Nebraska Press.
———. 1990. *The Mexican Empire of Iturbide*. Lincoln: University of Nebraska Press.
———. 1998. *Forging Mexico, 1821–1835*. Lincoln: University of Nebraska Press.
Annino, Antonio, et al. 1995a. *El águila bifronte: Poder y liberalismo en México*. Mexico City: Instituto Nacional de Antropología e Historia.
———, ed. 1995b. *Historia de las elecciones en Iberoamérica, siglo XIX: De la formación del espacio político nacional*. Buenos Aires: Fondo de Cultura Económica.
Appadurai, Arjun, ed. 1986. *The Social Life of Things: Commodities in Cultural Perspective*. Cambridge: Cambridge University Press.
Appleby, Gordon. 1976. "Export Monoculture and Regional Social Structure in Puno, Peru." In Smith, *Regional Analysis*, 2:291–307.
Appleby, Joyce, Lynn Hunt, and Margaret Jacob. 1994. *Telling the Truth about History*. New York: Norton.
Archer, Christon I. 1977. *The Army in Bourbon Mexico, 1760–1810*. Albuquerque: University of New Mexico Press.

———, ed. 2000. *The Wars of Independence in Spanish America*. Wilmington, DE: Scholarly Resources.
———, ed. 2003. *The Birth of Modern Mexico, 1780–1824*. Wilmington, DE: Scholarly Resources.
Arnold, Linda J. 1988. *Bureaucracy and Bureaucrats in Mexico City, 1742–1835*. Tucson: University of Arizona Press.
Arrom, Silvia M. 1985. *The Women of Mexico City, 1790–1857*. Stanford, CA: Stanford University Press.
———. 2000. *Containing the Poor: The Mexico City Poor House, 1774–1871*. Durham, NC: Duke University Press.
Artís Espriu, Gloria, et al. 1992. *Trabajo y sociedad en la historia de México, siglos XVI–XVII*. Mexico City: Centro de Investigaciones y Estudios Superiores en Antropología Social.
Assadourian, Carlos Sempat. 1982. *El sistema de la economía colonial: Mercado interno, regiones y espacio económico*. Lima: Instituto de Estudios Peruanos.
Assadourian, Carlos Sempat, et al. 1980. *Minería y espacio económico en los Andes, siglos XVI–XX*. Lima: Instituto de Estudios Peruanos.
Aston, T. H., and C.H.E. Philpin, eds. 1987. *The Brenner Debate: Agrarian Class Structure and Economic Development in Pre-Industrial Europe*. Cambridge: Cambridge University Press.
Ávila, Alfredo. 2002. *En nombre de la nación: La formación del gobierno representativo en México, 1808–1824*. Mexico City: Centro de Información y Docencia Económica/Taurus.
———. 2004. "De las independencias a la modernidad: Notas sobre un cambio historiográfico." In *Conceptuar lo que se ve: François-Xavier Guerra, historiador: Homenaje*, edited by Erika Pani and Alicia Salmerón, 76–112. Mexico City: Instituto de Investigaciones Dr. José María Luis Mora.
———, Virginia Guedea, and Christon I. Archer, eds. 2007. *La independencia de México: Temas e interpretaciones recientes*. Mexico City: Universidad Nacional Autónoma de México.
Ávila Palafox, Ricardo, Carlos Martínez Assad, and Jean Meyer, eds. 1992. *Las formas y las políticas del dominio agrario: Homenaje a F. Chevalier*. Guadalajara: Universidad de Guadalajara.
Axel, Brian Keith, ed. 2002. *From the Margins: Historical Anthropology and Its Futures*. Durham, NC: Duke University Press.
Bacigalupo, Marvyn Helen. 1981. *A Changing Perspective: Attitudes toward Creole Society in New Spain (1521–1610)*. London: Tamesis.
Bakewell, Peter J. 1971. *Silver Mining and Society in Colonial Mexico: Zacatecas 1546–1700*. Cambridge: Cambridge University Press.
———. 1984. *Miners of the Red Mountain: Indian Labor in Potosí, 1545–1650*. Albuquerque: University of New Mexico Press.
Balmori, Diana, Stuart F. Voss, and Miles Wortman, eds. 1984. *Notable Family Networks in Latin America*. Chicago: University of Chicago Press.
Banfield, Edward C. 1965. *The Moral Basis of a Backward Society*. Glencoe, IL: Free Press.

Barabas, Alicia M. 1989. *Utopías indias: Movimientos sociorreligiosos en México*. Mexico City: Editorial Grijalbo.

Barham, Bradford L., and Oliver T. Coomes. 1996. *Prosperity's Promise: The Amazon Rubber Boom and Distorted Economic Development*. Boulder, CO: Westview Press.

Barickman, Bert J. 1998. *A Bahian Counterpoint: Sugar, Tobacco, Cassava, and Slavery in the Recôncavo, 1780–1860*. Stanford, CA: Stanford University Press.

Barkin, David, and Timothy King. 1970. *Regional Economic Development: The River Basin Approach in Mexico*. Cambridge: Cambridge University Press.

Barragán López, Esteban, ed. 1994. *Rancheros y sociedades rancheras*. Zamora: El Colegio de Michoacán.

Barrett, Elinore M. 1987. *The Mexican Colonial Copper Industry*. Albuquerque: University of New Mexico Press.

Barrett, Ward. 1970. *The Sugar Hacienda of the Marqueses del Valle*. Minneapolis: University of Minnesota Press.

Barsky, Osvaldo, ed. 2003–2005. *Historia del capitalismo agrario pampeano*, vol. 1, *La expansión ganadera hasta 1895*, by Osvaldo Barsky and Julio Djenderedjian; vol. 2, *La vanguardia ganadera bonaerense, 1856–1900*, by Carmen Sesto. Buenos Aires: Universidad de Belgrano/Siglo Veintiuno Editores Argentina.

Baskes, Jeremy. 2000. *Indians, Merchants, and Markets: A Reinterpretation of the Repartimiento and Spanish-Indian Economic Relations in Colonial Oaxaca, 1750–1821*. Stanford, CA: Stanford University Press.

Bassols Batalla, Angel. 1967. *La división económica regional de México*. Mexico City: Universidad Nacional Autónoma de México.

———. 1979. *México: Formación de regiones económicas. Influencias, factores y sistemas*. Mexico City: Universidad Nacional Autónoma de México.

———. 1984. *Geografía económica de México: Teoría, fenómenos generales, análisis regional*. Mexico City: Trillas.

Bataillon, Claude. 1982. *Las regiones geográficas de México*, 6th ed. Mexico City: Siglo Veintiuno.

Bauer, Arnold J. 1975. *Chilean Rural Society from the Spanish Conquest to 1930*. Cambridge: Cambridge University Press.

———. 1979. "Rural Workers in Spanish America: Problems of Peonage and Oppression." *Hispanic American Historical Review* 59:34–63.

———. 1998. "Modernizing Landlords and Conservative Peasants in the Mexican Countryside." *Mexican Studies/Estudios Mexicanos* 14 (Winter): 191–212.

———. 2001. *Goods, Power, History: Latin America's Material Culture*. Cambridge: Cambridge University Press.

Bazant, Jan. 1971. *Los bienes de la iglesia en México (1856–1875): Aspectos económicos de la revolución liberal*. Mexico City: El Colegio de México.

———. 1975. *Cinco haciendas mexicanas: Tres siglos de vida rural en San Luis Potosí (1600–1910)*. Mexico City: El Colegio de México.

Beals, Carleton. 1932. *Porfirio Diaz, Dictator of Mexico*. Philadelphia and London: J. B. Lippincott.

Becker, Marjorie. 1995. *Setting the Virgin on Fire: Lázaro Cárdenas, Michoacán*

Peasants, and the Redemption of the Mexican Revolution. Berkeley: University of California Press.
Beezley, William H., and David Lorey, eds. 2001. *¡Viva México! ¡Viva la Independencia! Celebrations of September 16*. Wilmington, DE: Scholarly Resources.
Beezley, William H., Cheryl E. Martin, and William E. French, eds. 1994. *Rituals of Rule, Rituals of Resistance: Public Celebrations and Popular Culture in Mexico*. Wilmington, DE: Scholarly Resources.
Behar, Ruth. 1993. *Translated Woman: Crossing the Border with Esperanza's Story*. Boston: Beacon Press.
Belaúnde Guinassi, Manuel. 1945. *La encomienda en el Perú*. Lima: Ediciones Mercurio Peruano.
Benjamin, Thomas, and Mark Wasserman, eds. 1990. *Provinces of the Revolution: Essays on Regional Mexican History, 1910-1929*. Albuquerque: University of New Mexico Press.
Bennett, Herman L. 2003. *Africans in Colonial Mexico: Absolutism, Christianity, and Afro-Creole Consciousness, 1570-1640*. Bloomington: Indiana University Press.
Benson, Nettie Lee, ed. 1966. *Mexico and the Spanish Cortes, 1810-1822: Eight Essays*. Austin: Institute of Latin American Studies, University of Texas.
———. 1992. *The Provincial Deputation in Mexico: Harbinger of Provincial Autonomy*. Austin: University of Texas Press.
Bergad, Laird W. 1983. *Coffee and the Growth of Agrarian Capitalism in Nineteenth-Century Puerto Rico*. Princeton, NJ: Princeton University Press.
———. 1990. *Cuban Rural Society in the Nineteenth Century: The Social and Economic History of Monoculture in Matanzas*. Princeton, NJ: Princeton University Press.
———. 1999. *Slavery and the Demographic and Economic History of Minas Gerais, Brazil, 1720-1888*. Cambridge: Cambridge University Press.
Berkhofer, Robert F., Jr. 1995. *Beyond the Great Story: History as Text and Discourse*. Cambridge, MA: Harvard University Press.
Bernstein Harry. 1967. "Regionalism in the Natural History of Mexico." In *Latin American History: Essays on Its Study and Teaching*, vol. 1, edited by Howard Cline, 389-94. Austin: University of Texas Press.
Berry, Brian J. L. 1967. *Geography of Market Centers and Retail Distribution*. Englewood Cliffs, NJ: Prentice-Hall.
Bethell, Leslie, ed. 1984. The *Cambridge History of Latin America*, 2 vols. Cambridge: Cambridge University Press.
Bitrán Goren, Yael. 1997. "Servando Teresa de Mier." In Guedea, *El surgimiento de la historiografía nacional*, 65-91.
Blanchard, Peter. 1992. *Slavery and Abolition in Early Republican Peru*. Wilmington, DE: Scholarly Resources.
Bloch, Marc. 1961. *Feudal Society*. Translated by L. A. Manyon, Foreword by M. M. Postan. Chicago: University of Chicago Press. (Orig. pub. 1939-40.)
———. 1966. *French Rural History: An Essay on Its Basic Characteristics*. Translated by Janet Sondheimer. Foreword by Bryce Lyon. Berkeley: University of California Press. (Orig. pub. 1931.)

———. 1992. *The Historian's Craft*. Manchester, UK: Manchester University Press.
Bonnell, Victoria E., and Lynn Hunt, eds. 1999. *Beyond the Cultural Turn: New Directions in the Study of Society and Culture*. Berkeley: University of California Press.
Booker, Jackie R. 1993. *Veracruz Merchants, 1770–1829: A Merchant Elite in Late Bourbon and Early Independent Mexico*. Boulder, CO: Westview Press.
Borah, Woodrow W. 1983. *Justice by Insurance: The General Indian Court of New Spain and the Legal Aides of the Half-Real*. Berkeley: University of California Press.
Borde, Jean, and Mario Góngora. 1956. *Evolución de la propiedad rural en el Valle del Puangue*, 2 vols. Santiago, Chile: Editorial Universitaria, S.A.
Bowser, Frederick P. 1974. *The African Slave in Colonial Peru, 1524–1650*. Stanford, CA: Stanford University Press.
Boyer, Richard E. 1995. *Lives of the Bigamists: Marriage, Family, and Community in Late Colonial Mexico*. Albuquerque: University of New Mexico Press.
———. 1997. *Cast [sic] and Identity in Colonial Mexico: A Proposal and an Example*. Storrs, CT: Center for Latin American and Caribbean Studies, University of Connecticut.
Bracamonte y Sosa, Pedro. 1993. *Amos y sirvientes: Las haciendas de Yucatán, 1789–1860*. Mérida: Universidad Autónoma de Yucatán.
———. 1994. *La memoria enclaustrada: Historia indígena de Yucatán*. Mexico City: Centro de Investigaciones y Estudios Superiores en Antropología Social.
Brading, David A. 1971. *Miners and Merchants in Bourbon Mexico, 1763–1810*. Cambridge: Cambridge University Press.
———. 1978. *Haciendas and Ranchos in the Mexican Bajío: León, 1700–1860*. Cambridge: Cambridge University Press.
———, ed. 1980. *Caudillo and Peasant in the Mexican Revolution*. Cambridge: Cambridge University Press.
———. 1984a. "Bourbon Spain and Its American Empire." In Bethell, *Cambridge History of Latin America*, 1:389–439.
———. 1984b. *Prophecy and Myth in Mexican History*. Cambridge: Centre of Latin-American Studies, Cambridge University.
———. 1985. *The Origins of Mexican Nationalism*. Cambridge: Cambridge University Press.
———. 1991. *The First America: The Spanish Monarchy, Creole Patriots, and the Liberal State, 1492–1867*. Cambridge: Cambridge University Press.
———. 1994. *Church and State in Bourbon Mexico: The Diocese of Michoacán, 1749–1810*. Cambridge: Cambridge University Press.
———. 2001. *Mexican Phoenix: Our Lady of Guadalupe. Image and Tradition across Five Centuries*. Cambridge: Cambridge University Press.
———. 2007. "A Recusant Abroad." In Deans-Smith and Van Young, *Mexican Soundings*, 13–37.
Bricker, Victoria Reifler. 1981. *The Indian Christ, the Indian King: The Historical Substrate of Maya Myth and Ritual*. Austin: University of Texas Press.
Brinton, Crane. 1965. *The Anatomy of Revolution*. New York: Vintage Books.

Brown, Jonathan C. 1979. *A Socioeconomic History of Argentina, 1776–1860*. Cambridge: Cambridge University Press.
Buchan, James. 2003. *Crowded with Genius. The Scottish Enlightenment: Edinburgh's Moment of the Mind*. New York: Perennial.
Bulmer-Thomas, Victor, John H. Coatsworth, and Roberto Cortés Conde, eds. 2006. *The Cambridge Economic History of Latin America*: I. *The Colonial Era and the Short Nineteenth Century*. Cambridge: Cambridge University Press.
Burke, Michael. 1980. "Peasant Responses to the Hidalgo Revolt in Central Mexico, 1810–1813." Unpublished manuscript.
Burkhart, Louise M. 1989. *The Slippery Earth: Nahua-Christian Moral Dialogue in Sixteenth-Century Mexico*. Tucson: University of Arizona Press.
———. 1996. *Before Guadalupe: The Virgin Mary in Early Colonial Mexico*. Philadelphia: University of Pennsylvania Press.
———. 2001. *Holy Wednesday: A Nahua Drama from Early Colonial Mexico*. Albany, NY: Institute for Mesoamerican Studies, University at Albany.
Bustamante, Carlos María de. 1961. *Cuadro histórico de la revolución mexicana, iniciada el 15 de septiembre de 1810 por el C. Miguel Hidalgo y Costilla, cura del pueblo de Dolores en el obispado de Michoacán*. 3 vols. Mexico City: Ediciones de la Comisión Nacional Para la Celebración del Sesquicentenario de la Proclamación de la Independencia Nacional y del Cincuentenario de la Revolución Mexicana. (Orig. pub. 1823–1832.)
Buttimer, Anne, and David Seamon, eds. 1980. *The Human Experience of Space and Place*. London: Croon Helm.
Buve, Raymond, ed. 1984. *Haciendas in Central Mexico from Late Colonial Times to the Revolution: Labour Conditions, Hacienda Management, and Its Relation to the State*. Amsterdam: Center for Latin American Research and Documentation.
Cahill, David, and Blanca Tovías, eds. 2006. *New World, First Nations: Native Peoples of Mesoamerica and the Andes under Colonial Rule*. Brighton, UK: Sussex Academic Press.
Calderón, Francisco R. 1988. *Historia económica de la Nueva España en tiempo de los Austrias*. Mexico City: Fondo de Cultura Económica.
Calero, Luis Fernando. 1997. *Chiefdoms Under Siege: Spain's Rule and Native Adaptation in the Southern Colombian Andes, 1535–1700*. Albuquerque: University of New Mexico Press.
Calvo, Thomas. 1989. *La Nueva Galicia en los siglos XVI y XVII*. Guadalajara: El Colegio de Jalisco.
———. 1992. *Guadalajara y su región en el siglo XVII: Población y economía*. Guadalajara: Universidad de Guadalajara.
Cambrezy, Luc, and Yves Marchal. 1992. *Crónicas de un territorio fraccionado: De la hacienda al ejido (Centro de Veracruz)*. Mexico City: Larousse.
Cañizares-Esguerra, Jorge. 2001. *How to Write the History of the New World: Historiographies, Epistemologies, and Identities in the Eighteenth-Century Atlantic World*. Stanford, CA: Stanford University Press.
Cannadine, David. 2001. *Ornamentalism: How the British Saw Their Empire*. Oxford: Oxford University Press.

Cardoso, Ciro F. S. 1982. "Regional History," *Bibliotheca Americana* 1:2–3.
Cardoso, Ciro F. S., and Héctor Pérez Brignoli. 1984. *Historia económica de América Latina*, 2 vols. Barcelona: Crítica.
Cardoso, Gerald. 1983. *Negro Slavery in the Sugar Plantations of Veracruz and Pernambuco, 1550–1680*. Washington, DC: University Press of America.
Carmagnani, Marcello. 1973. *Les mecanismes de la vie économique dans une société coloniale: le Chili, 1680–1830*. Paris: S.E.V.P.E.N.
———. 1976. *Formación y crisis de un sistema feudal: América Latina del siglo XVI a nuestros días*. Mexico City: Siglo Veintiuno Editores.
———. 1983. "Finanzas y estado en México, 1820–1880." *Ibero-Americanisches Archiv* 9:277–317.
———. 2001. *Los mecanismos de la vida económica en una sociedad colonial: Chile, 1680–1830*. Santiago, Chile: Ediciones de la Dirección de Bibliotecas, Archivos y Museos: Centro de Investigaciones Diego Barros Arana.
Carr, Barry. 1973. "Las peculiaridades del norte mexicano, 1880–1927: Ensayo de interpretación." *Historia Mexicana* 22:320–46.
Carroll, Patrick J. 2001. *Blacks in Colonial Veracruz: Race, Ethnicity, and Regional Development*, 2nd ed. Austin: University of Texas Press. (Orig. pub. 1991.)
Caruso, John Anthony. 1954. *The Liberators of Mexico*. Gloucester, MA: P. Smith.
Castañeda, Carmen. 1989. *Violación, estupro y sexualidad: Nueva Galicia, 1790–1821*. Guadalajara: Editorial Hexágono.
Castel, Robert. 1988. *The Regulation of Madness: The Origins of Incarceration in France*. Translated by W. D. Halls. Berkeley: University of California Press.
Castleman, Bruce A. 2005. *Building the King's Highway: Labor, Society, and Family on Mexico's Caminos Reales, 1757–1804*. Tucson: University of Arizona Press.
Castro Gutiérrez, Felipe. 1996. *La rebelión de los indios y la paz de los españoles*. Mexico City: Centro de Investigaciones y Estudios Superiores en Antropología Social.
Cerutti, Mario. 1992. "Monterrey and Its *Ambito Regional*, 1850–1910: Historical Context and Methodological Recommendations." In Van Young, *Mexico's Regions*, 145–65.
Cervantes, Fernando. 1994. *The Devil in the New World: The Impact of Diabolism in New Spain*. New Haven, CT: Yale University Press.
Chalarca, José. 1998. *Vida y hechos del café en Colombia*. Bogotá: Común Presencia Editores.
Chance, John K. 1978. *Race and Class in Colonial Oaxaca*. Stanford, CA: Stanford University Press.
———. 1989. *Conquest of the Sierra: Spaniards and Indians in Colonial Oaxaca*. Norman: University of Oklahoma Press.
Chandler, D. S. 1991. *Social Assistance and Bureaucratic Politics: The Montepios of Colonial Mexico, 1767–1821*. Albuquerque: University of New Mexico Press.
Chang-Rodríguez, Raquel. 1992. "Foreword." *Colonial Latin American Review* 1(1–2): 1–2.
Chartier, Roger. 1982. "Intellectual History or Sociocultural History? The French

Trajectories." In *Modern European Intellectual History: Reappraisals and New Perspectives*, edited by Dominick LaCapra and Steven L. Kaplan, 13–46. Ithaca, NY: Cornell University Press.

———. 1988. *Cultural History: Between Practices and Representations*. Translated by Lydia G. Cochrane. Cambridge: Polity Press.

Chayanov, A. V. 1986. *The Theory of Peasant Economy*. Edited by Daniel Thorner, Basil Kerblay, and R.E.F. Smith. Foreword by Teodor Shanin. Madison: University of Wisconsin Press.

Chevalier, François. 1952. *La formation des grands domaines au Méxique: Terre et société aux XVIe–XVIIe siécles*. Paris: Université de Paris, Institut d'Ethnologie.

———. 1956. *La formación de los grandes latifundios en México (Tierra y sociedad en los siglos XVI y XVII)*. Translated by Antonio Alatorre. Problemas agrícolas e industriales de México 8. Mexico City: n.p.

———. 1966. *Land and Society in Colonial Mexico: The Great Hacienda*. Edited by Leslie B. Simpson. Translated by Alvin Eustis. Berkeley: University of California Press.

———. 1999. *La formación de los latifundios en México. Haciendas y sociedad en los siglos XVI, XVII y XVIII*. 3rd edition, corrected and enlarged. Mexico City: Fondo de Cultura Económica.

Chust Calero, Manuel. 1993. "La cuestión nacional americana en las Cortes de Cádiz (1808-1814)." PhD diss., Universidad de Valencia.

———, ed. 2001. *La independencia de México y el proceso autonomista novohispano, 1808–1824*. Mexico City: Universidad Nacional Autónoma de México/ Instituto de Investigaciones Doctor José María Luis Mora.

Clarence-Smith, William Gervase, and Steven C. Topik, eds. 2003. *The Global Coffee Economy in Africa, Asia and Latin America, 1500–1989*. Cambridge: Cambridge University Press (electronic book).

Clendinnen, Inga. 1987. *Ambivalent Conquests: Maya and Spaniard in Yucatan, 1517–1570*. Cambridge: Cambridge University Press.

———. 1991. *Aztecs: An Interpretation*. Cambridge: Cambridge University Press.

Clifford, James. 1986. "On Ethnographic Allegory." In Clifford and Marcus, *Writing Culture*, 98–121.

Clifford, James, and George E. Marcus, eds. 1986. *Writing Culture: The Poetics and Politics of Ethnography*. Berkeley: University of California Press.

Cline, Howard F. 1947–48. "The Sugar Episode in Yucatán, 1815–1850," *Inter-American Economic Affairs* 1:79–100.

Cline, S. L. 1986. *Colonial Culhuacán: A Social History of an Aztec Town*. Albuquerque: University of New Mexico Press.

———, ed. and trans. 1993. *The Book of Tributes: Early Sixteenth-Century Nahuatl Censuses from Morelos*. Los Angeles: University of California, Los Angeles, Latin American Center Publications.

Cline, S. L., and Miguel León-Portilla, eds. 1984. *The Testaments of Culhuacán*. Los Angeles: University of California, Los Angeles, Latin American Center Publications.

Coatsworth, John H. 1981. *Growth Against Development: The Economic Impact of Railroads in Porfirian Mexico.* DeKalb: University of Northern Illinois Press.

———. 1987. "Estimating Mexico's Gross Domestic Product, 1800–1877." Unpublished manuscript.

———. 1990. *Los orígenes del atraso: Nueve ensayos de historia económica de México en los siglos XVIII y XIX.* Mexico City: Alianza Editorial.

Cohen, Paul A. 1997. *History in Three Keys: The Boxers as Event, Experience, and Myth.* New York: Columbia University Press.

Colmenares, Germán. 1980. *Cali, terratenientes, mineros y comerciantes, siglo XVIII.* Bogotá: Carlos Valencia Editores.

Compact Oxford English Dictionary. 1991. 2nd ed. Oxford: Clarendon Press.

Conference on Latin American History. 2004. *Membership Directory.*

Connaughton, Brian F. 2003. *Clerical Ideology in a Revolutionary Age: The Guadalajara Church and the Idea of the Mexican Nation, 1788–1853.* Translated by Mark Alan Healey. Calgary: University of Calgary Press.

Cook, Sherburne F. 1949. *The Historical Demography and Ecology of the Teotlalpan.* Berkeley: University of California Press.

———. 1970. "Las migraciones en la historia de la población mexicana: Datos modelo del occidente del centro de México." In *Historia y sociedad en el mundo de habla española; homenaje a José Miranda,* edited by Bernardo García Martínez, 355–78. Mexico City: Colegio de Mexico.

Cook, Sherburne F., and Woodrow W. Borah. 1974–1980. *Essays in Population History: Mexico and the Caribbean.* 3 vols. Berkeley: University of California Press.

———. 1980. "Indian Food Production and Consumption in Central Mexico Before and After the Conquest." In Cook and Borah, *Essays in Population History,* 3:129–76.

Cope, Douglas R. 1994. *The Limits of Racial Domination: Plebeian Society in Colonial Mexico City, 1660–1720.* Madison: University of Wisconsin Press.

Costeloe, Michael P. 1986. *Response to Revolution: Imperial Spain and the Spanish American Revolutions, 1810–1840.* Cambridge: Cambridge University Press.

———. 1993. *The Central Republic in Mexico: "Hombres de bien" in the Age of Santa Anna.* Cambridge: Cambridge University Press.

Countryman, Edward, and Susan Deans-Smith. 1983. "Independence and Revolution in the Americas: A Project for Comparative Study." *Radical History Review* 27:144–71.

Couturier, Edith B. 1976. *La Hacienda de Hueyapan, 1550–1936.* Mexico City: Secretaría de Educación Pública.

———. 2003. *The Silver King: Remarkable Life of the Count of Regla in Colonial Mexico.* Albuquerque: University of New Mexico Press.

Crapanzano, Vincent. 1986. "Hermes' Dilemma: The Making of Subversion in Ethnographic Description." In Clifford and Marcus, *Writing Culture,* 51–76.

Crespo, Horacio. 1984a. "El azúcar en el mercado de la ciudad de México, 1885–1910." In Crespo, *Morelos,* 165–222, passim.

———., ed. 1984b. *Morelos: Cinco siglos de la historia regional.* Mexico City:

Centro de Estudios Históricos de Agrarismo en México/Universidad Autónoma del Estado de Morelos.
Crespo, Horacio, et al. 1988–1990. *Historia del azúcar en México*, 2 vols. Mexico City: Fondo de Cultura Económica.
Crosby, Alfred W. 1997. *The Measure of Reality: Quantification and Western Society, 1250–1600*. Cambridge: Cambridge University Press.
Cross, Harry. 1978. "Living Standards in Rural Nineteenth-Century Mexico: Zacatecas, 1820–1880." *Journal of Latin American Studies* 10:1–19.
Cuello, José. 1990. *El norte, el noreste y Saltillo en la historia colonial de México*. Saltillo: Archivo Municipal de Saltillo.
Curcio-Nagy, Linda. 1996. "Introduction: Spectacle in Colonial Mexico." *The Americas* 52:275–81.
Curtin, Philip D. 1998. *The Rise and Fall of the Plantation Complex: Essays in Atlantic History*. Cambridge: Cambridge University Press.
Cushner, Nicholas P. 1980. *Lords of the Land: Sugar, Wine and Jesuit Estates of Coastal Peru, 1600–1767*. Albany: State University of New York Press.
———. 1982. *Farm and Factory: The Jesuits and the Development of Agrarian Capitalism in Colonial Quito, 1600–1767*. Albany: State University of New York Press.
———. 1983. *Jesuit Ranches and the Agrarian Development of Colonial Argentina, 1650–1767*. Albany: State University of New York Press.
Cutter, Charles R. 1995. *The Legal Culture of Northern New Spain, 1700–1810*. Albuquerque: University of New Mexico Press.
Darnton, Robert. 1984. *The Great Cat Massacre and Other Episodes in French Cultural History*. New York: Basic Books.
Davies, Keith A. 1984. *Landowners in Colonial Peru*. Austin: University of Texas Press.
Davis, Natalie Zemon. 1987. *Fiction in the Archives: Pardon Tales and Their Tellers in Sixteenth-Century France*. Stanford, CA: Stanford University Press.
de Certeau, Michel. 1983. "History: Ethics, Science, and Fiction." In *Social Science as Moral Inquiry*, edited by Norma Hahn, Robert Bellah, Paul Rabinow, and William Sullivan, 173–209. New York: Columbia University Press.
de la Peña, Guillermo. 1981a. "Los estudios regionales y la antropología social en México," *Relaciones* 8:43–93.
———. 1981b. *A Legacy of Promises: Agriculture, Politics, and Ritual in the Morelos Highlands of Mexico*. Austin: University of Texas Press.
de la Peña, José F. 1983. *Oligarquía y propiedad en Nueva España, 1550–1624*. Mexico City: Fondo de Cultura Económica.
Dean, Warren. 1976. *Rio Claro: A Brazilian Plantation System, 1820–1920*. Stanford, CA: Stanford University Press.
———. 1987. *Brazil and the Struggle for Rubber: A Study in Environmental History*. Cambridge: Cambridge University Press.
———. 1995. *With Broadax and Firebrand: The Destruction of the Brazilian Atlantic Forest*. Berkeley: University of California Press.
Deans-Smith, Susan. 1992. *Bureaucrats, Planters, and Workers: The Making of the Tobacco Monopoly in Bourbon Mexico*. Austin: University of Texas Press.

———. 1998. "Culture, Power, and Society in Colonial Mexico." *Latin American Research Review* 33:257–77.
Deans-Smith, Susan, and Gilbert M. Joseph, eds. 1999. "Mexico's New Cultural History: ¿Una lucha libre?" Special issue of *Hispanic American Historical Review* 79:203–8.
Deans-Smith, Susan, and Eric Van Young, eds. 2007. *Mexican Soundings: Essays in Honour of David A. Brading*. London: Institute for the Study of the Americas, University of London.
Deeds, Susan M. 2003. *Defiance and Deference in Mexico's Colonial North: Indians under Spanish Rule in Nueva Vizcaya*. Austin: University of Texas Press.
Deerr, Noel. 1949–50. *The History of Sugar*, 2 vols. London: Chapman and Hall.
Degler, Carl N. 1986. *Neither Black nor White: Slavery and Race Relations in Brazil and the United States*, revised. Madison: University of Wisconsin Press.
Dehouve, Danièle. 1994. *Entre el caimán y el jaguar: Los pueblos indios de Guerrero*. Mexico City: Centro de Investigaciones y Estudios Superiores en Antropología Social.
del Río, Ignacio. 1989. "De la pertinencia del enfoque regional en la investigación histórica sobre México." *Históricas* 27:21–32.
Delpar, Helen. 1992. *The Enormous Vogue of Things Mexican: Cultural Relations Between the United States and Mexico, 1920–1935*. Tuscaloosa: University of Alabama Press.
De Vos, Jan. 1994. *Vivir en frontera: La experiencia de los indios de Chiapas*. Mexico City: Centro de Investigaciones y Estudios Superiores en Antropología Social.
Domínguez, Jorge I. 1980. *Insurrection or Loyalty: The Breakdown of the Spanish American Empire*. Cambridge, MA: Harvard University Press.
Domínguez Michael, Christopher. 2004. *Vida de Fray Servando*. Mexico City: Ediciones Era/Consejo Nacional para la Cultura y las Artes-Instituto Nacional de Antropología e Historia.
Doyle, Don H., and Marco Antonio Pamplona, eds. 2006. *Nationalism in the New World*. Athens: University of Georgia Press.
Ducey, Michael T. 2004. *A Nation of Villages: Riot and Rebellion in the Mexican Huasteca, 1750–1850*. Tucson: University of Arizona Press.
Duhau, Emilio. 1988. *Mercado interno y urbanización en el México colonial*. Mexico City: Universidad Autónoma Metropolitana/Gernika.
Duncan, Kenneth, and Ian Rutledge, eds. 1977. *Land and Labour in Latin America: Essays on the Development of Agrarian Capitalism in the Nineteenth and Twentieth Centuries*. With the collaboration of Colin Harding. Cambridge: Cambridge University Press.
Dunn, Richard S. 1973. *Sugar and Slaves: The Rise of the Planter Class in the English West Indies, 1624–1713*. New York: Norton.
Duverger, Christian. 1993. *La conversión de los indios de Nueva España: Con el texto de los "Coloquios de los doce" de Bernardino de Sahagún (1564)*. Translated by María Dolores de la Peña. Mexico City: Fondo de Cultura Económica.
Eagleton, Terry. 1983. *Literary Theory: An Introduction*. Minneapolis: University of Minnesota Press.

Edelman, Marc. 1992. *The Logic of the Latifundio: The Large Estates of Northwestern Costa Rica since the Late Nineteenth Century.* Stanford, CA: Stanford University Press.

Eisenberg, Peter L. 1974. *The Sugar Industry in Pernambuco: Modernization Without Change, 1840–1910.* Berkeley: University of California Press.

Ellis, John M. 1989. *Against Deconstruction.* Princeton, NJ: Princeton University Press.

Entrikin, Nicholas. 1991. *The Betweenness of Place: Towards a Geography of Modernity.* Baltimore, MD: Johns Hopkins University Pres.

Escobar Ohmstede, Antonio. 1998. *De la costa a la sierra: Los pueblos indios de las Huastecas, 1750–1900.* Mexico City: Centro de Investigaciones y Estudios Superiores en Antropología Social.

Ewald, Ursula. 1977. "The von Thünen Principle and Agricultural Zonation in Colonial Mexico," *Journal of Historical Geography* 3:123–33.

Fagoaga Hernández, Ricardo. 2004. "Circuitos mercantiles de la Huasteca potosina, 1743–1812." Tésis de maestría en historia, Colegio de San Luis Potosí.

Fajardo, Darío. 1983. *Haciendas, campesinos y políticas agrarias en Colombia, 1920–1980.* Bogotá: Editorial Oveja Negra.

———. 1993. *Espacio y sociedad: Formación de las regiones agrarias en Colombia.* Bogotá: Corporación Colombiana para la Amazonia-Araracuara.

Falcón, Romana. 1984. *Revolución y caciquismo: San Luis Potosí, 1910–1938.* Mexico City: El Colegio de México.

Farriss, Nancy M. 1968. *Crown and Clergy in Colonial Mexico, 1759–1821: The Crisis of Ecclesiastical Privilege.* London: Athlone Press.

———. 1984. *Maya Society under Spanish Colonial Rule: The Collective Enterprise of Survival.* Princeton, NJ: Princeton University Press.

Fernández, Rodolfo. 1994. *Latifundios y grupos dominantes en la historia de la Provincia de Ávalos.* Guadalajara: Instituto Nacional de Antropología e Historia/Editorial Agata.

———. 1999. *Mucha tierra y pocos dueños: Estancias, haciendas y latifundios avaleños.* Mexico City: Instituto Nacional de Antropología e Historia.

———. 2003. *La gran propiedad en Cocula de Ávalos 1539–1700.* Mexico City: Instituto Nacional de Antropología e Historia.

Ferrer, Aldo. 1967. *The Argentine Economy.* Berkeley: University of California Press.

Ferry, Robert J. 1989. *The Colonial Elite of Early Caracas: Formation and Crisis, 1567–1767.* Berkeley: University of California Press.

Fisher, Andrew. 2002. "Worlds in Flux, Identities in Motion: A History of the Tierra Caliente of Guerrero, Mexico, 1521–1821." PhD diss., University of California, San Diego.

Fisher, Lillian E. 1955. *Champion of Reform: Manuel Abad y Queipo.* New York: Library Publishers.

Florescano, Enrique. 1969. *Precios del maíz y crisis agrícolas en México (1708–1810).* Mexico City: Colegio de México.

———. 1971. *Estructuras y problemas agrarios de México (1500–1821).* Mexico City: Secretaría de Educación Pública.

———, ed. 1979. *Ensayos sobre el desarrollo económico de México y América Latina*. Mexico City: Fondo de Cultura Económica.
———. 1984. "The Formation and Economic Structure of the Hacienda in New Spain." In Bethell, *Cambridge History of Latin America*, 2:153–88.
———. 1991. *El nuevo pasado mexicano*. Mexico City: Cal y Arena.
———. 1994. *Memory, Myth, and Time in Mexico: From the Aztecs to Independence*. Translated by Albert G. Bork, with the assistance of Kathryn R. Bork. Austin: Univeristy of Texas Press.
———. 1997. *Etnia, estado y nación: Ensayo sobre las identidades colectivas en México*. Mexico City: Aguilar.
———. 1998. *La bandera mexicana: Breve historia de su formación y simbolismo*. Mexico City: Fondo de Cultura Económica.
———. 1999. *The Myth of Quetzalcoatl*. Translated by Lysa Hochroth. Baltimore, MD: Johns Hopkins University Press.
———. 2002. *Historia de las historias de la nación mexicana*. Mexico City: Taurus.
———. 2006. *National Narratives in Mexico: A History*. Translated by Nancy Hancock. Norman: University of Oklahoma Press.
Florescano, Enrique, and Isabel Gil Sánchez. 1974. *1750–1808: La época de las reformas borbónicas y del crecimiento económico*. Mexico City: Cuadernos de Trabajo del Departamento de Investigaciones Históricas, Instituto Nacional de Antropología e Historia.
———, eds. 1977. *Descripciones económicas regionales de Nueva España. Provincias del Centro, Sureste, y Sur, 1766–1827*. Mexico City: Instituto Nacional de Antropología e Historia.
Font, Mauricio A., and Alfonso W. Quiroz, eds. 2005. *Cuban Counterpoints: The Legacy of Fernando Ortiz*. Lanham, MD: Lexington Books.
Forment, Carlos A. 2003. *Democracy in Latin America, 1760–1900*, vol. 1, *Civic Selfhood and Public Life in Mexico and Peru*. Chicago: University of Chicago Press.
Fradkin, Raúl. 1993. "La historia agraria y los estudios de establecimientos productivos en Hispanoamérica colonial: Una mirada desde el Río de la Plata." In *La historia agraria del Río de la Plata colonial: Los establecimientos productivos*, 2 vols., edited by Raúl Fradkin, 1:7–44. Buenos Aires: Centro Editorial de América Latina.
Fradkin, Raúl, and Juan Carlos Garavaglia, eds. 2004. *En busca de un tiempo perdido: La economía de Buenos Aires en el país de la abundancia 1750–1865*. Buenos Aires: Prometeo.
Fradkin, Raúl, and Jorge Gelman. 2004. "Recorridos y dasafíos de una historiografía. Escalas de observación y fuentes en la historia rural rioplatense." In *Microanálisis: Ensayos de historiografía argentina*, edited by Beatriz Bragoni, 31–54. Buenos Aires: Prometeo.
Frank, André Gunder. 1967. *Capitalism and Underdevelopment in Latin America: Historical Studies of Chile and Brazil*. New York: Monthly Review Press.
———. 1975. *On Capitalist Underdevelopment*. Bombay and New York: Oxford University Press.

———. 1979. *Mexican Agriculture, 1521–1630: Transformation of the Mode of Production.* Cambridge: Cambridge University Press.
Freeman, Joanne B. 2001. *Affairs of Honor: National Politics in the New Republic.* New Haven, CT: Yale University Press.
French, William E. 1999. "Imagining and the Cultural History of Nineteenth-Century Mexico." *Hispanic American Historical Review* 79:249–268.
Freud, Sigmund, and William C. Bullitt. 1967. *Thomas Woodrow Wilson, Twenty-Eighth President of the United States: A Psychological Study.* Boston: Houghton Mifflin.
Freyre, Gilberto. 1946. *The Masters and the Slaves: A Study in the Development of Brazilian Civilization.* Translated by Samuel Putnam. New York: Knopf. (Orig. pub. 1933.)
Friedmann, John, Nathan Gardels, and Adrian Pennink. 1980. "The Politics of Space: Five Centuries of Regional Development in Mexico." *International Journal of Urban and Regional Research* 4:319–49.
Friedrich, Paul. 1986. *The Princes of Naranja: An Essay in Anthrohistorical Method.* Austin: University of Texas Press.
Frye, David L. 1996. *Indians into Mexicans: History and Identity in a Mexican Town.* Austin: University of Texas Press.
Furtado, Celso. 1965. *The Economic Growth of Brazil: A Survey from Colonial to Modern Times.* Berkeley: University of California Press.
Garavaglia, Juan Carlos. 1983. *Mercado interno y economía colonial.* Mexico City: Editorial Grijalbo.
———. 1987. *Economía, sociedad y regiones.* Buenos Aires: Ediciones de la Flor.
———. 1999. *Pastores y labradores de Buenos Aires: Una historia agraria de la campaña bonaerense 1700–1830.* Buenos Aires: Ediciones de la Flor.
Garavaglia, Juan Carlos, and Jorge D. Gelman. 1995. "Rural History of the Río de la Plata, 1600–1850: Results of a Historiographical Renaissance." *Latin American Research Review* 30:75–105.
Garavaglia, Juan Carlos, and Juan Carlos Grosso. 1994. *Puebla desde una perspectiva microhistórica: La villa de Tepeaca y su entorno agrario: población, producción e intercambio (1740–1870).* Mexico City: Editorial Claves Latinoamericanas/Universidad Autónoma de Puebla.
García Acosta, Virginia. 1988. *Los precios del trigo en la historia colonial de México.* Mexico City: Centro de Investigaciones y Estudios Superiores en Antropología Social.
———. 1989. *Las panaderías, sus dueños y trabajadores: Ciudad de México, siglo XVIII.* Mexico City: Centro de Investigaciones y Estudios Superiores en Antropología Social.
———, ed. 1995. *Los precios de alimentos y manufacturas novohispanos.* Mexico City: Instituto de Investigaciones Dr. José María Luis Mora/Centro de Investigaciones y Estudios Superiores en Antropología Social.
García de León, Antonio. 1985. *Resistencia y utopía: Memorial de agravios y crónica de revueltas y profecías acaecidas en la provincia de Chiapas durante los últimos 500 años.* 2 vols. Mexico City: Era.
García de León, Antonio, Enrique Semo, and Ricardo Gamboa Ramírez. 1988.

Historia de la cuestión agraria mexicana, vol. 1, *El siglo de la hacienda, 1800–1900*. Mexico City: Siglo Veintiuno Editores.
García Martínez, Bernardo. 1987. *Los pueblos de la sierra: El poder y el espacio entre los indios del norte de Puebla hasta 1700*. Mexico City: El Colegio de México.
García Martínez, Bernardo, and Alba González Jácome, eds. 1999. *Estudios sobre historia y ambiente en América Latina*, vol. 1, *Argentina, Bolivia, México, Paraguay*. Mexico City: El Colegio de México.
García Ugarte, Marta Eugenia. 1992. *Hacendados y rancheros queretanos (1780–1920)*. Mexico City: Consejo Nacional para la Cultura y las Artes.
García Ugarte, Marta Eugenia, and José Manuel Rivero Torres. 1991. *Esplendor y poderío de las haciendas queretanas*. Querétaro: Dirección de Patrimonio Cultural, Gobierno del Estado de Querétaro.
Garner, Richard L., and Spiro E. Stefanou. 1993. *Economic Growth and Change in Bourbon Mexico*. Gainesville: University Press of Florida.
Gasco, Janine. 1994. "Recent Trends in Ethnohistoric Research on Postclassic and Colonial Central Mexico." *Latin American Research Review* 29:132–42.
Geertz, Clifford. 1973. "Thick Description: Toward an Interpretive Theory of Culture." In Clifford Geertz, *The Interpretation of Cultures*, 3–33. New York: Basic Books.
———. 1973a. "Deep Play: Notes on the Balinese Cockfight." In *The Interpretation of Cultures*, edited by Clifford Geertz, 412–53. New York: Basic Books.
———. 1983a. "Blurred Genres: The Refiguration of Social Thought." In Geertz, *Local Knowledge*, 19–35.
———. 1983b. *Local Knowledge: Further Essays in Interpretive Anthropology*. New York: Basic Books.
Gelman, Jorge D. 1996. *De mercachifle a gran comerciante: Los caminos del ascenso en el Río de la Plata colonial*. Huelva: Universidad Internacional de Andalucía.
———. 1998. *Campesinos y estancieros: Una región del Río de la Plata a fines de la época colonial*. Buenos Aires: Editorial los Libros del Riel.
———. 2005. *Rosas, estanciero: Gobierno y expansión ganadera*. Buenos Aires: Capital Intelectual.
Gerhard, Peter. 1972. *A Guide to the Historical Geography of New Spain*. Cambridge: Cambridge University Press.
———. 1979. *The Southeast Frontier of New Spain*. Princeton, NJ: Princeton University Press.
———. 1982. *The North Frontier of New Spain*. Princeton, NJ: Princeton University Press.
Giberti, Horacio. 1981. *Historia económica de la ganadería argentina*. Buenos Aires: Ediciones Solar;. (Revised and expanded editions 1961, 1970; orig. pub. 1954).
Gibson, Charles. 1964. *The Aztecs under Spanish Rule: A History of the Indians of the Valley of Mexico, 1519–1810*. Stanford, CA: Stanford University Press.
Gilbert, Anne. 1988. "The New Regional Geography in English and French-speaking Countries." *Progress in Human Geography* 12:208–28.

Ginzburg, Carlo. 1980. *The Cheese and the Worms: The Cosmos of a Sixteenth-Century Miller*. Translated by John and Anne Tedeschi. Baltimore, MD: Johns Hopkins University Press.
Goldstone, Jack A. 1991. *Revolution and Rebellion in the Early Modern World*. Berkeley: University of California Press.
Golte, Jürgen. 1980. *Repartos y rebeliones: Túpac Amaru y las contradicciones de la economía colonial*. Lima: Instituto de Estudios Peruanos.
Góngora, Mario. 1971. *Encomenderos y estancieros: Estudios acerca de la constitución social aristocrática de Chile después de la conquista, 1580–1660*. Santiago de Chile: Editorial Universitaria.
Gonzales, Michael J. 1985. *Plantation Agriculture and Social Control in Northern Peru, 1875–1933*. Austin: University of Texas Press.
González, Luis. 1968. *Pueblo en vilo. Microhistoria de San José de Gracia*. Mexico City: El Colegio de México.
———. 1973. "El arte de la microhistoria." In *Invitación a la microhistoria*, by Luis González, 8–53. Mexico City: Secretaría de Educación Pública.
———. 1982. "El Oeste Mexicano." In *La Querencia*, by Luis González, 11–41. Mexico City: Clio.
González Angulo Aguirre, Jorge. 1983. *Artesanado y ciudad a finales del siglo XVIII*. Mexico City: Instituto Nacional de Antropología e Historia.
Gore, Charles. 1984. *Regions in Question: Space, Development Theory, and Regional Policy*. London: Methuen.
Gorender, Jacob. 1988. *O escravismo colonial*, 5th ed., revised and enlarged. São Paulo: Editora Atica.
Gosner, Kevin. 1992. *Soldiers of the Virgin: The Moral Economy of a Colonial Maya Rebellion*. Tucson: University of Arizona Press.
Goubert, Pierre. 1960. *Beauvais et le Beauvaisis de 1600 à 1730, contribution à l'histoire sociale de la France au XVIIe siècle*. Paris: S.E.V.P.E.N.
———. 1971. "Local History." *Daedelus* 100:113–14.
Goveia, Elsa. 1965. *Slave Society in the British Leeward Islands at the End of the Eighteenth Century*. New Haven, CT: Yale University Press.
Grafton, Anthony. 1997. *The Footnote: A Curious History*. Cambridge, MA: Harvard University Press.
Graham, Richard. 1994. *Independence in Latin America: A Comparative Approach*, 2nd ed. New York: McGraw-Hill.
Green, Donald P., and Ian Shapiro. 1994. *Pathologies of Rational Choice Theory: A Critique of Applications in Political Science*. New Haven, CT: Yale University Press.
Green, Stanley C. 1987. *The Mexican Republic: The First Decade, 1823–1832*. Pittsburgh, PA: University of Pittsburgh Press.
Greenblatt, Stephen Jay. 1991. *Marvelous Possessions: The Wonder of the New World*. Chicago: University of Chicago Press.
Greenow, Linda. 1983. *Credit and Socioeconomic Change in Colonial Mexico: Loans and Mortgages in Guadalajara, 1720–1820*. Boulder, CO: Westview Press.

Grigg, David. 1967. "Regions, Models, and Classes." In *Models in Geography*, edited by Richard J. Chorley and Peter Haggett, 461–509. London: Methuen.

Grob, Gerald N. 1994. *The Mad Among Us: A History of the Care of America's Mentally Ill*. Cambridge, MA: Harvard University Press.

Grosso, Juan Carlos, and Juan Carlos Garavaglia. 1995. *Circuitos mercantiles y mercados en Latinoamérica, siglos XVIII–XIX*. Mexico City: Instituto de Investigaciones Dr. José María Luis Mora/Universidad Nacional Autónoma de México.

———. 1996. *La región de Puebla y la economía novohispana: Las alcabalas en la Nueva España, 1776–1821*. Mexico City: Instituto de Investigaciones Dr. José María Luis Mora/Universidad Autónoma de Puebla.

Grunstein, Arturo. 1994. "Railroads and Sovereignty: Policymaking in Porfirian Mexico." PhD diss., University of California, Los Angeles.

Gruzinski, Serge. 1989. *Man-Gods in the Mexican Highlands: Indian Power and Colonial Society, 1520–1800*. Translated by Eileen Corrigan. Stanford, CA: Stanford University Press.

———. 1993. *The Conquest of Mexico: The Incorporation of Indian Societies in the Western World, 16th–18th Centuries*, revised. Translated by Eileen Corrigan. Stanford, CA: Stanford University Press.

———. 2001. *Images at War: Mexico from Columbus to Blade Runner*, revised. Translated by Heather MacLean. Durham, NC: Duke University Press.

———. 2002. *The Mestizo Mind: The Intellectual Dynamics of Colonization and Globalization*. Translated by Deke Dusinberre. New York: Routledge.

Guardino, Peter F. 1996. *Peasants, Politics, and the Formation of Mexico's National State: Guerrero, 1800–1857*. Stanford, CA: Stanford University Press.

———. 2005. *The Time of Liberty: Popular Political Culture in Oaxaca, 1750–1850*. Durham, NC: Duke University Press.

Guarisco, Claudia. 2003. *Los indios de valle de México y la construcción de una nueva sociabilidad política, 1770–1835*. Mexico City: El Colegio Mexiquense.

Gudmundson, Lowell. 1983. *Hacendados, políticos y precaristas: La ganadería y el latifundio guanacasteco*. San José, Costa Rica: Editorial Costa Rica.

———. 1986. *Costa Rica Before Coffee: Society and Economy on the Eve of the Export Boom*. Baton Rouge: Louisiana State University Press.

Guedea, Virginia. 1992. *En busca de un gobierno alterno: Los Guadalupes de México*. Mexico City: Instituto de Investigaciones Históricas, Universidad Nacional Autónoma de México.

———. 1995. *Prontuario de los insurgentes*. Mexico City: Instituto de Investigaciones Dr. José María Luis Mora.

———. 1996. *La insurgencia en el Departamento del Norte: Los Llanos de Apan y la Sierra de Puebla, 1810–1816*. Mexico City: Instituto de Investigaciones Históricas, Universidad Nacional Autónoma de México.

———, ed. 1997. *Historiografía mexicana*, vol. 3, *El surgimiento de la historiografía nacional*. Mexico City: Universidad Nacional Autónoma de México.

Guerra, François-Xavier. 1993. *Modernidad e independencias: ensayos sobre las revoluciones hispánicas*, 2nd ed. Madrid: Editorial MAPFRE; Mexico City: Fondo de Cultura Económica.

Guerrero, Andrés. 1980. *Los oligarcas del cacao: Ensayo sobre la acumulación originaria en el Ecuador: Hacendados cacaoteros, banqueros, exportadores y comerciantes en Guayaquil (1890)*. Quito: Editorial El Conejo.

———. 1991a. *De la economía a las mentalidades*. Quito: Editorial El Conejo.

———. 1991b. *La semántica de la dominación: El concertaje de indios*. Quito: Ediciones Libri Mundi/Enrique Grosse-Luemern.

Guha, Ranajit. 1983. *Elementary Aspects of Peasant Insurgency in Colonial India*. Delhi: Oxford University Press.

Gutiérrez Brockington, Lolita. 1989. *The Leverage of Labor: Managing the Cortés Haciendas in Tehuantepec, 1588–1688*. Durham, NC: Duke University Press.

Guzmán Pérez, Moisés. 1994. *La junta de Zitácuaro, 1811–1813*. Morelia: Universidad Michoacana de San Nicolás de Hidalgo.

———. 1996. *Miguel Hidalgo y el gobierno insurgente en Valladolid*. Morelia: Universidad Michoacana de San Nicolás de Hidalgo.

Haber, Stephen, ed. 1997a. "Economic Growth and Latin American Economic Historiography." In Haber, *How Latin America Fell Behind*, 1–33.

———. 1997b. *How Latin America Fell Behind: Essays on the Economic History of Brazil and Mexico, 1800–1914*. Stanford, CA: Stanford University Press.

———. 1997c. "The Worst of Both Worlds: The New Cultural History of Mexico." *Mexican Studies/Estudios Mexicanos* 13:363–83.

———. 1999. "Anything Goes: Mexico's 'New' Cultural History." *Hispanic American Historical Review* 79:309–30.

Hale, Charles A. 1968. *Mexican Liberalism in the Age of Mora, 1821–1853*. New Haven, CT: Yale University Press.

Halperín Donghi, Tulio. 1973. *The Aftermath of Revolution in Latin America*. Translated by Josephine de Bunsen. New York: Harper and Row.

Hamill, Hugh M., Jr. 1966. *The Hidalgo Revolt: Prelude to Mexican Independence*. Gainesville: University of Florida Press.

Hamnett, Brian R. 1971. *Politics and Trade in Southern Mexico, 1750–1821*. Cambridge: Cambridge University Press.

———. 1985. *La política española en una época revolucionaria, 1790–1820*. Mexico City: Fondo de Cultura Económica.

———. 1986. *Roots of Insurgency: Mexican Regions, 1750–1824*. Cambridge: Cambridge University Press.

———. 1999. *A Concise History of Mexico*. Cambridge: Cambridge University Press.

Handler, Jerome S., and Frederick W. Lange. 1978. *Plantation Slavery in Barbados: An Archaeological and Historical Investigation*. Cambridge, MA: Harvard University Press.

Hardoy, Jorge E., and Carmen Aranovich. 1978. "The Scale and Functions of Spanish American Cities Around 1600: An Essay on Methodology." In *Urbanization in the Americas from Its Beginnings to the Present*, edited by Richard B. Schaedel, Jorge E. Hardoy, and Nora Scott Kinzer, 63–97. The Hague: Mouton.

Harland, Richard. 1987. *Superstructuralism: The Philosophy of Structuralism and Post-structuralism*. London: Methuen.
Harris, Charles H., III. 1975. *A Mexican Family Empire: The Latifundio of the Sáncehz Navarros, 1765–1867*. Austin: University of Texas Press.
Harris, Marvin. 1964. *Patterns of Race in the Americas*. New York: Norton.
Hart, Paul. 2005. *Bitter Harvest: The Social Transformation of Morelos, Mexico, and the Origins of the Zapatista Revolution, 1840–1910*. Albuquerque: University of New Mexico Press.
Haskett, Robert. 1991. *Indigenous Rulers: An Ethnohistory of Town Government in Colonial Cuernavaca*. Albuquerque: University of New Mexico Press.
Haslip-Viera, Gabriel. 1999. *Crime and Punishment in Late Colonial Mexico City, 1692–1810*. Albuquerque: University of New Mexico Press.
Hassig, Ross. 1985. *Trade, Tribute, and Transportation: The Sixteenth-Century Political Economy of the Valley of Mexico*. Norman: University of Oklahoma Press.
Hawking, Stephen W. 1988. *A Brief History of Time: From the Big Bang to Black Holes*. New York: Bantam Books.
Hernández Sáenz, Luz María. 1997. *Learning to Heal: The Medical Profession in Colonial Mexico, 1767–1831*. New York: Peter Lang.
Hernández y Dávalos, Juan E. 1968. *Colección de documentos para la historia de la guerra de independencia de México de 1808 a 1821, coleccionados por J. E. Hernández y Dávalos*, 6 vols. Liechtenstein: Kraus Reprint. (Orig. pub. 1880.)
Herrejón Peredo, Carlos, ed. 1984. *Morelos: Vida preinsurgente y lecturas*. Zamora: El Colegio de Michoacán.
———, ed. 1985. *Los procesos de Morelos: Estudio y compilación de Carlos Herrejón Peredo*. Zamora: El Colegio de Michoacán.
———. 2003. *Del sermón al discurso cívico: México, 1760–1834*. Mexico City: El Colegio de México.
Herrera, Robinson. 2003. *Natives, Europeans, and Africans in Sixteenth-Century Santiago de Guatemala*. Austin: University of Texas Press.
Herrera Canales, Inés, ed. 1998. *La minería mexicana: De la colonia al siglo XIX*. Mexico City: Instituto de Investigaciones Dr. José María Luis Mora.
Herrero Bervera, Carlos. 2001. *Revuelta, rebelión y revolución en 1810: Historia social y estudios de caso*. Mexico City: M.A. Porrúa Grupo Editorial.
Himmelfarb, Gertrude. 1987. *The New History and the Old*. Cambridge, MA: Harvard University Press.
Himmerich y Valencia, Robert. 1991. *The Encomenderos of New Spain, 1521–1555*. Austin: University of Texas Press.
Hoberman, Louisa Schell. 1991. *Mexico's Merchant Elite, 1590–1660*. Durham, NC: Duke University Press.
Hoberman, Louisa Schell, and Susan Migden Socolow, eds. 1996. *The Countryside in Colonial Latin America*. Albuquerque: University of New Mexico Press.
Hobsbawm, Eric J. 2002. *Interesting Times: A Twentieth-Century Life*. New York: Pantheon Books.
Hoekstra, Rik. 1993. *Two Worlds Merging: The Transformation of Society in the*

Valley of Puebla, 1570–1640. Amsterdam: Center for Latin American Research and Documentation.
Horn, Rebecca. 1997. *Postconquest Coyoacán: Nahua-Spanish Relations in Central Mexico, 1519–1650*. Stanford, CA: Stanford University Press.
Hu-DeHart, Evelyn. 1981. *Missionaries, Miners, and Indians: Spanish Contact with the Yaqui Nation of Northwestern New Spain, 1533–1820*. Tucson: University of Arizona Press.
———. 1995. *Adaptación y resistencia en el Yaquimi: Los yaquis durante la colonia*. Mexico City: Centro de Investigaciones y Estudios Superiores en Antropología Social.
Hugo, Victor. 1987. *Les Misérables*. New York: Signet. (Orig. pub. 1862.)
Hulme, Peter. 1986. *Colonial Encounters: Europe and the Native Caribbean, 1492–1797*. London: Methuen.
Hunt, Lynn, 1989a. "Introduction: History, Culture, and Text." In Hunt, *The New Cultural History*, 1–22.
———, ed. 1989b. *The New Cultural History*. Berkeley: University of California Press.
Ibargüengoitia, Jorge. 1982. *Los pasos de López*. Mexico City: Ediciones Océano.
Ibarra, Ana Carolina. 1996. *Clero y política en Oaxaca: Biografía del Doctor José de San Martín*. Mexico City: Universidad Nacional Autónoma de México.
Ibarra Romero, Antonio. 1995. "Masa, rebelión y vida privada: Los infidentes novohispanos, 1809–1815." *Anuario de Estudios Americanos* 52:99–120.
———. 2000a. "Crímenes y castigos políticos en la Nueva España, 1809–1816: Una aproximación cuantitativa al perfil social de la disidencia política colonial." *Ibero-Amerikanisches Archiv* 26:163–90.
———. 2000b. *La organización regional del mercado interno novohispano: La economía colonial de Guadalajara, 1770–1804*. Mexico City: Universidad Nacional Autónoma de México.
———. 2002. "Crímenes y castigos políticos en la Nueva España borbónica: Patrones de obediencia y disidencia política, 1809–1816." In *Las guerras de independencia en la América Española*, edited by José Antonio Serrano Ortega and Martha Terán, 255–72. Mexico City: El Colegio de Michoacán/Instituto Nacional de Antropología e Historia.
———. 2003a. "La persecución institucional de la disidencia novohispana: Patrones de inculpación y temores políticos de una época." In *Disidencias y disidentes en la historia de México*, edited by Felipe Castro and Marcela Terrazas, 117–37. Mexico City: Instituto de Investigaciones Históricas, Universidad Nacional Autónoma de México.
———. 2003b. "A modo de presentación: La historia económica mexicana de los noventa, una apreciación general." Special number of *Historia Mexicana* dedicated to Ruggiero Romano. *Historia Mexicana* 52:613–47.
Iglesias, Esther. 1984. *Las haciendas de Yucatán a mediados del siglo XIX*. Mexico City: Instituto de Investigaciones Económicas, Universidad Nacional Autónoma de México.
Ilhui Pacheco Chávez, María Antonieta. 1996. "Juan Evaristo Hernández y

Dávalos." In *Historiografía mexicana*, vol. 4, *En busca de un discurso integrador de la nación, 1848–1884*, edited by Antonia Pi-Suñer Llorens, 407–24. Mexico City: Universidad Nacional Autónoma de México.

Isard, Walter. 1956. *Location and the Space-Economy: A General Theory Relating to Industrial Location, Market Areas, Land Use, Trade, and Urban Structure*. Cambridge, MA: Harvard University Press.

———. 1975. *Introduction to Regional Science*. Englewood Cliffs, NJ: Prentice-Hall.

Jackson, Robert H. 1994. *Regional Markets and Agrarian Transformation in Bolivia: Cochabamba, 1539–1960*. Albuquerque: University of New Mexico Press.

Jacobs, Ian. 1982. *Ranchero Revolt: The Mexican Revolution in Guerrero*. Austin: University of Texas Press.

Jacobsen, Nils. 1993. *Mirages of Transition: The Peruvian Altiplano, 1780–1930*. Berkeley: University of California Press.

———, and Hans-Jürgen Puhle, eds. 1986. *The Economies of Mexico and Peru during the Late Colonial Period, 1760–1810*. Berlin: Colloquium Verlag.

Jaffary, Nora. 2000. "Deviant Orthodoxy: A Social and Cultural History of Ilusos and Alumbrados in Colonial Mexico." PhD diss., Columbia University.

James, Henry. 1917. *The Sense of the Past*. New York: Scribner's.

Jara, Alvaro. 1981. *Guerra y sociedad en Chile: La transformación de la guerra de Arauco y la esclavitud de los indios*. Santiago de Chile: Editorial Universitaria.

Jarquín Ortega, María T., et al. 1990. *Origen y evolución de la hacienda en México, siglos XVI al XX: Memorias del simposio realizado del 27 al 30 de septiembre de 1989*. Zinacantepec: El Colegio Mexiquense.

Jiménez Pelayo, Agueda. 1989. *Haciendas y comunidades indígenas en el sur de Zacatecas*. Mexico City: Instituto Nacional de Antropología e Historia.

Johnson, Lyman L., and Enrique Tandeter, eds. 1990. *Essays on the Price History of Eighteenth-Century Latin America*. Albuquerque: University of New Mexico Press.

Jones, Gareth Stedman. 1982. *Languages of Class: Studies in English Working Class History, 1832–1982*. Cambridge: Cambridge University Press.

Jones, Grant D. 1989. *Maya Resistance to Spanish Rule: Time and History on a Colonial Frontier*. Norman: University of Oklahoma Press.

Joseph, Gilbert M. 1992. "On the Trail of Latin American Bandits: A Reexamination of Peasant Resistance." In *Patterns of Contention in Mexican History*, edited by Jaime E. Rodríguez O., 293–336. Wilmington, DE: Scholarly Resources.

———, ed. 2001. *Reclaiming the Political in Latin American History: Essays from the North*. Durham, NC: Duke University Press.

Kanigel, Robert. 1997. *The One Best Way: Frederick Winslow Taylor and the Enigma of Efficiency*. New York: Viking.

Kartunnen, Frances, and James Lockhart, eds. 1976. *Nahuatl in the Middle Years: Language Contact Phenomena in Texts of the Colonial Period*. Berkeley: University of California Press.

Katz, Friedrich, ed. 1984. *La servidumbre agraria en México en la época porfiriana*. Mexico City: Ediciones Era.

———, ed. 1988. *Riot, Rebellion, and Revolution: Rural Social Conflict in Mexico*. Princeton, NJ: Princeton University Press.
Katzew, Ilona, and Susan Deans-Smith, eds. 2009. *Race and Classification: The Case of Mexican America*. Stanford, CA: Stanford University Press.
Kay, Cristóbal. 1980. *El sistema señorial europeo y la hacienda latinoamericana*. Mexico City: Ediciones Era.
Keen, Benjamin. 1985. "Main Currents in United States Writings on Colonial Spanish America." *Hispanic American Historical Review* 65:657–82.
Keith, Robert G. 1976. *Conquest and Agrarian Change: The Emergence of the Hacienda System on the Peruvian Coast*. Cambridge, MA: Harvard University Press.
Kellogg, Susan. 1995. *Law and the Transformation of Aztec Culture, 1500–1700*. Norman: University of Oklahoma Press.
———, and Matthew Restall, eds. 1998. *Dead Giveaways: Indigenous Testaments of Colonial Mesoamerica and the Andes*. Salt Lake City: University of Utah Press.
Kicza, John E. 1983. *Colonial Entrepreneurs: Families and Business in Bourbon Mexico City*. Albuquerque: University of New Mexico Press.
———. 1995. "Recent Books on Ethnohistory and Ethnic Relations in Colonial Mexico." *Latin American Research Review* 30:239–53.
Kinsbruner, Jay. 1994. *Independence in Spanish America: Civil Wars, Revolutions, and Underdevelopment*. Albuquerque: University of New Mexico Press.
Klarén, Peter F. 1973. *Modernization, Dislocation, and Aprismo: Origins of the Peruvian Aprista Party, 1870–1932*. Austin: University of Texas Press.
Klein, Herbert S. 1978. *The Middle Passage: Comparative Studies in the Atlantic Slave Trade*. Princeton, NJ: Princeton University Press.
———. 1986. *African Slavery in Latin America and the Caribbean*. New York: Oxford University Press.
———. 1993. *Haciendas and 'Ayllus': Rural Society in the Bolivian Andes in the Eighteenth and Nineteenth Centuries*. Stanford, CA: Stanford University Press.
———. 1999. *The Atlantic Slave Trade*. Cambridge: Cambridge University Press.
———, and Ben Vinson, III. 2007. *African Slavery in Latin America and the Caribbean*, 2nd ed., revised. New York: Oxford University Press.
Klor de Alva, J. Jorge. 1992. "Sin and Confession among the Colonial Nahuas: The Confessional as a Tool for Domination." In *La ciudad y el campo en la historia de México*, 2 vols., edited by Ricardo Sánchez, Eric Van Young, and Gisela von Wobeser, 1:91–102. Mexico City: Universidad Nacional Autónoma de México.
Knight, Alan. 1986. *The Mexican Revolution*, 2 vols. Cambridge: Cambridge University Press.
———. 2002a. *Mexico: From the Beginning to the Spanish Conquest*. Cambridge: Cambridge University Press.
———. 2002b. *Mexico: The Colonial Era*. Cambridge: Cambridge University Press.
———. 2002c. "Subalterns, Signifiers, and Statistics: Perspectives on Mexican Historiography." *Latin American Research Review* 37:136–58.

———. 2004. "Eric Van Young, *The Other Rebellion* y la historiografía mexicana." *Historia Mexicana* 54:445–515.
Knight, Franklin W. 1970. *Slave Society in Cuba during the Nineteenth Century.* Madison: University of Wisconsin Press.
Konrad, Herman W. 1980. *A Jesuit Hacienda in Colonial Mexico: Santa Lucia, 1576–1767.* Stanford, CA: Stanford University Press.
Korth, Eugene H. 1968. *Spanish Policy in Colonial Chile: The Struggle for Social Justice, 1535–1700.* Stanford, CA: Stanford University Press.
Kramer, Wendy. 1994. *Encomienda Politics in Early Colonial Guatemala, 1524–1544: Dividing the Spoils.* Boulder, CO: Westview Press.
Krippner-Martínez, James. 2000. *Rereading the Conquest: Power, Politics, and the History of Early Colonial Michoacan, Mexico, 1521–1565.* University Park: Pennsylvania State University Press.
Kroeber, Clifton L. 1985. *Man, Land, and Water: Mexico's Farmlands Irrigation Policies, 1885–1911.* Berkeley: University of California Press.
Kuhn, Thomas S. 1970. *The Structure of Scientific Revolutions,* 2nd ed. Chicago: University of Chicago Press.
Kuntz Ficker, Sandra. 1995. *Empresa extranjera y mercado interno: El Ferrocarril Central Mexicano, 1870–1929.* Mexico City: El Colegio de México.
———. 2004. "Sobre el ruido y las nueces: Comentarios al artículo de Pedro L. San Miguel." *Historia Mexicana* 53 (211): 959–88.
Kuntz Ficker, Sandra, and Priscilla Connolly, eds. 1999. *Ferrocarriles y obras públicas.* Mexico City: Instituto Mora/El Colegio de Michoacán/Instituto de Investigaciones Históricas, Universidad Nacional Autónoma de México.
Kuntz Ficker, Sandra, and Paolo Riguzzi, eds. 1996. *Ferrocarriles y vida económica en México, 1850–1950: Del surgimiento tardío al decaimiento precoz.* Mexico City: El Colegio Mexiquense/Ferrocarriles Nacionales de México/Universidad Autónoma de México-Xochimilco.
Ladd, Doris M. 1976. *The Mexican Nobility at Independence, 1780–1826.* Austin: University of Texas Press.
———. 1989. *The Making of a Strike: Mexican Workers' Struggles in the Real del Monte, 1766–1775.* Lincoln: University of Nebraska Press.
Lafaye, Jacques. 1976. *Quetzalcóatl and Guadalupe: The Formation of Mexican National Consciousness, 1531–1813.* Translated by Benjamin Keen. Chicago: University of Chicago Press.
Landázuri Benítez, Gisela, and Verónica Vázquez Mantecón. 1988. *Azúcar y estado (1750–1880).* Mexico City: Fondo de Cultura Económica.
Langley, Lester D. 1996. *The Americas in the Age of Revolution, 1750–1850.* New Haven, CT: Yale University Press.
Langue, Frédérique. 1992. *Mines, Terres et Société a Zacatecas (Méxique) de la Fin du XVIIe Siècle a l'Independence.* Paris: Publications de la Sorbonne.
———. 1998. "La historiografía mexicanista y la hacienda colonial: Balances y perspectivas." *Secuencia* 42:65–116.
Lara, Silvia H. 1988. *Campos da violencia: Esclavos e senhores na Capitania do Rio de Janeiro, 1750–1808.* Rio de Janeiro: Paz e Terra.

Larson, Brooke. 1998. *Cochabamba, 1550–1900: Colonialism and Agrarian Transformation in Bolivia,* revised. Durham, NC: Duke University Press.
Laslett, Peter. 1965. *The World We Have Lost: England Before the Industrial Age.* New York: Scribner's.
Laviada, Iñigo. 1984. *Vida y muerte de un latifundio.* Mexico City: Editorial Porrua.
Lavrin, Asunción, ed. 1989. *Sexuality and Marriage in Colonial Latin America.* Lincoln: University of Nebraska Press.
Leal, Juan Felipe, and Mario Huacuja Rountree. 1982. *Economía y sistema de haciendas en México: La hacienda pulquera en el cambio, siglos XVIII, XIX y XX.* Mexico City: Ediciones Era.
Lefebvre, Henri. 1991. *The Production of Space.* Oxford: Blackwell.
Le Grand, Catherine. 1986. *Frontier Expansion and Peasant Protest in Colombia, 1850–1936.* Albuquerque: University of New Mexico Press.
Lemoine Villicaña, Ernesto. 1965. *Morelos: Su vida revolucionaria a través de sus escritos y de otros testimonios de la época.* Mexico City: Universidad Nacional Autónoma de México.
Le Roy Ladurie, Emmanuel. 1966. *Les paysans de Languedoc.* 2 vols. Paris: S.E.V.P.E.N.
———. 1978. *Montaillou, the Promised Land of Error.* New York: George Braziller.
Levene, Ricardo. 1927–28. *Investigaciones acerca de la historia económica del Virreinato de la Plata.* Buenos Aires: Universidad Nacional de la Plata.
Lewis, Laura A. 2003. *Hall of Mirrors: Power, Witchcraft, and Caste in Colonial Mexico.* Durham, NC: Duke University Press.
Licate, Jack. 1981. *Creation of a Mexican Landscape: Territorial Organization and Settlement in the Eastern Puebla Basin, 1520–1605.* Chicago: Department of Geography, University of Chicago.
Lindley, Richard B. 1983. *Haciendas and Economic Development: Guadalajara, Mexico, at Independence.* Austin: University of Texas Press.
Lindo Fuentes, Héctor. 1980. "La utilidad de los diezmos como fuente para la historia económica." *Historia Mexicana* 30:273–89.
Lipsett-Rivera, Sonya. 1999. *To Defend Our Water with the Blood of Our Veins: The Struggle for Resources in Colonial Puebla.* Albuquerque: University of New Mexico Press.
Liss, Peggy K. 1983. *Atlantic Empires: The Network of Trade and Revolution, 1713–1826.* Baltimore, MD: Johns Hopkins University Press.
Liverman, Diana, and Altha Cravey. 1992. "Geographic Perspectives on Mexican Regions." In Van Young, *Mexico's Regions,* 39–57.
Lockhart, James. 1986. "Social Organization and Social Change in Colonial Spanish America." In Bethell, *Cambridge History of Latin America,* 2:265–319.
———. 1991a. "Charles Gibson and the Ethnohistory of Postconquest Central Mexico." In Lockhart, *Nahuas and Spaniards,* 159–82.
———. 1991b. *Nahuas and Spaniards: Postconquest Central Mexican History and Philology.* Stanford, CA: Stanford University Press.
———. 1992. *The Nahuas after the Conquest: A Social and Cultural History of*

the Indians of Central Mexico, Sixteenth through Eighteenth Centuries. Stanford, CA: Stanford University Press.

———. 1993. *We People Here: Nahuatl Accounts of the Conquest of Mexico.* Berkeley: University of California Press.

———. 2000. *Of Things of the Indies: Essays Old and New in Early Latin American History.* Stanford, CA: Stanford University Press.

———. 2001a. *Grammar of the Mexican Language, with an Explanation of Its Adverbs, by Horacio Carochi, S.J.* Stanford, CA: Stanford University Press.

———. 2001b. *Nahuatl as Written: Lessons in Older Written Nahuatl, with Copious Examples and Texts.* Stanford, CA: Stanford University Press.

———, Frances Berdan, and Arthur J. O. Anderson. 1986. *The Tlaxcalan Actas: A Compendium of the Records of the Cabildo of Tlaxcala (1545–1627).* Salt Lake City: University of Utah Press.

Loera, Margarita. 1981. *Economía campesina indígena en la colonia.* Mexico City: Instituto Nacional Indígena.

Lomnitz, Larissa Adler, and Marisol Pérez Lizaur. 1987. *A Mexican Elite Family, 1820–1980: Kinship, Class, and Culture.* Translated by Cinna Lomnitz. Princeton, NJ: Princeton University Press.

Lomnitz-Adler, Claudio. 1992. "Concepts for the Study of Regional Culture." In Van Young, *Mexico's Regions*, 59–89.

———. 2001. *Deep Mexico, Silent Mexico: An Anthropology of Nationalism.* Minneapolis: University of Minnesota Press.

López de Albornoz, Cristina. 2003. *Los dueños de la tierra. Economía, sociedad y poder: Tucumán, 1770–1820.* Tucumán: Universidad Nacional de Tucumán.

Love, Joseph. 1978. "An Approach to Regionalism," in Richard Graham and Peter H. Smith, eds., *New Approaches to Latin American History,* pp. 137–55. Austin: University of Texas Press.

Lozano Armendares, Teresa. 1987. *La criminalidad en la ciudad de México, 1800–1821.* Mexico City: Universidad Nacional Autónoma de México.

———. 1997. "Lorenzo de Zavala." In Guedea, *El surgimiento de la historigrafía nacional,* 213–40.

Lukacs, Georg. 1971. *History and Class Consciousness.* Cambridge, MA: Harvard University Press.

Lynch, John. 1981. *Argentine Dictador: Juan Manuel de Rosas, 1829–1852.* Oxford: Oxford University Press.

———. 1986. *The Spanish American Revolutions, 1808–1821,* 2nd ed. New York: Norton.

———. 1999. "Spanish American Independence in Recent Historiography." In *Independence and Revolution in Spanish America: Perspectives and Problems,* edited by Anthony McFarlane and Eduardo Posada-Carbó, 13–42. London: Institute of Latin American Studies, University of London.

———, ed. 1994. *Latin American Revolutions, 1808–1826: Old and New World Origins.* Norman: University of Oklahoma Press.

MacLachlan, Colin E. 1974. *Criminal Justice in Eighteenth-Century Mexico: A Study of the Tribunal of the Acordada.* Berkeley: University of California Press.

MacLeod, Murdo J. 1973. *Spanish Central America: A Socio-Economic History, 1520–1720.* Berkeley: University of California Press.

———. 2000. "Mesoamerica since the Spanish Invasion: An Overview." In *The Cambridge History of the Native Peoples of the Americas,* vol. 2, *Mesoamerica,* edited by Richard E. W. Adams and Murdo J. MacLeod, 2:1–43. Cambridge: Cambridge University Press.

Mallon, Florencia E. 1994. *Peasant and Nation: The Making of Postcolonial Mexico and Peru.* Berkeley: University of California Press.

Mandrini, Raúl, and Andrea Reguera. 1993. *Huellas en la tierra: Indios, agricultores y hacendados en la pampa bonaerense.* Tandil: Instituto de Estudios Histórico-Sociales.

Maniquis, Robert M., Oscar R. Martí, and Joseph Pérez, eds. 1989. *La revolución francesa y el mundo ibérico.* Madrid: Sociedad Estatal Quinto Centenario.

Marcus, George E., and Michael M. J. Fischer, eds. 1986. *Anthropology as Cultural Critique: An Experimental Moment in the Human Sciences.* Chicago: University of Chicago Press.

Markusen, Ann R. 1987. *Regions: The Economics and Politics of Territory.* Totowa, NJ: Rowman and Littlefield.

Marrero, Leví. 1972–. *Cuba, economía y sociedad,* 15 vols. Rio Piedras, Puerto Rico: Editorial San Juan.

Martin, Cheryl E. 1985. *Rural Society in Colonial Morelos.* Albuquerque: University of New Mexico Press.

———. 1996. *Governance and Society in Colonial Mexico: Chihuahua in the Eighteenth Century.* Stanford, CA: Stanford University Press.

Martínez Rosales, Alfonso. 1991. *Documentos de la Hacienda de la Tenería.* San Luis Potosí, Mexico: Archivo Histórico de San Luis Potosí.

Mata de López, Sara. 2000. *Tierra y poder en Salta: El noroeste argentino en vísperas de la independencia.* Seville: Diputación de Sevilla.

Mayo, Carlos. 1995. *Estancia y sociedad en la pampa (1740–1820).* Buenos Aires: Editorial Biblos.

McBride, George McCutcheon. 1923. *The Land Systems of Mexico.* New York: American Geographical Society.

McCreery, David. 1994. *Rural Guatemala, 1760–1940.* Stanford, CA: Stanford University Press.

McFarlane, Anthony, and Eduardo Posada-Carbó, eds. 1999. *Independence and Revolution in Spanish America: Perspectives and Problems.* London: Institute of Latin American Studies, University of London.

McGreevey, William P. 1971a. *An Economic History of Colombia, 1845–1930.* Cambridge: Cambridge University Press.

———. 1971b. "A Statistical Analysis of Primacy and Lognormality in the Size Distribution of Latin American Cities, 1750–1960." In *The Urban Development of Latin America, 1750–1920,* edited by Richard M. Morse, 116–29. Stanford, CA: Stanford University Press.

McWatters, David Lorne. 1979. "The Royal Tobacco Monopoly in Bourbon Mexico, 1764–1810." PhD diss., University of Florida.

Medina Rubio, Arístides. 1983. *La iglesia y la producción agrícola en Puebla, 1540–1795*. Mexico City: El Colegio de México.

Megged, Amos. 1996. *Exporting the Catholic Reformation: Local Religion in Early-Colonial Mexico*. New York: E.J. Brill.

Melville, Elinor G. K. 1994. *A Plague of Sheep: Environmental Consequences of the Conquest of Mexico*. Cambridge: Cambridge University Press.

Méndez G., Cecilia. 2005. *The Plebeian Republic: The Huanta Rebellion and the Making of the Peruvian State, 1820–1850*. Durham, NC: Duke University Press.

Menegus Bornemann, Margarita. 1991. *Del señorío a la república de indios: El caso de Toluca, 1500–1600*. Madrid: Ministerio de Agricultura, Pesca y Alimentación, Secretaría General Técnica.

———. 1995. *Problemas agrarios y propiedad en México, siglos XVIII y XIX*. Mexico City: El Colegio de México.

———, and Alejandro Tortolero Villaseñor, eds. 1999. *Agricultura mexicana: Crecimiento e innovaciones*. Mexico City: Instituto de Investigaciones Dr. José María Luis Mora.

Mentz, Brígida von. 1988. *Pueblos de indios, mulatos y mestizos, 1770–1870: Los campesinos y las transformaciones protoindustriales de Morelos*. Mexico City: Centro de Investigaciones y Estudios Superiores en Antropología Social.

———. 1999. *Trabajo, sujeción y libertad en el centro de la Nueva España*. Mexico City: Editorial Porrua/Centro de Investigaciones y Estudios Superiores en Antropología Social.

———, et al. 1997. *Haciendas de Morelos*. Mexico City: Editorial Porrua/Consejo Nacional para la Cultura y las Artes/Instituto de Cultura de Morelos.

Metcalf, Alida C. 1992. *Family and Frontier in Colonial Brazil: Santana de Parnaíba, 1580–1822*. Berkeley: University of California Press.

Meyer, Jean. 1973. *Problemas campesinas y revueltas agrarias (1821–1910)*. Mexico City: Secretaría de Educación Pública.

———. 1989. *A la voz del rey: Una historia verídica*. Mexico City: Cal y Arena.

Meyer, Michael C. 1984. *Water in the Hispanic Southwest: A Social and Legal History, 1550–1850*. Tucson: University of Arizona Press.

———, and William H. Beezley, eds. 2000. *The Oxford History of Mexico*. Oxford: Oxford University Press.

Meyer Cosío, Rosa María, ed. 1999. *Identidad y prácticas de los grupos de poder en México, siglos XVII–XIX*. Mexico City: Instituto Nacional de Antropología e Historia.

Mier Noriega y Guerra, José Servando Teresa de. 1920. *Historia de la revolución de Nueva España: Antiguamente Anáhuac, ó verdadero origen y causas de él; escribíala Dn. José Guerra*. 2 vols. Mexico City: Cámara de Diputados. (Orig. pub. 1813.)

Mignolo, Walter D. 1995. *The Darker Side of the Renaissance: Literacy, Territoriality, and Colonization*. Ann Arbor: University of Michigan Press.

Miller, Simon. 1995. *Landlords and Haciendas in Modernizing Mexico: Essays in Radical Reappraisal*. Amsterdam: CEDLA.

Miño Grijalva, Manuel. 1990. *Obrajes y tejedores de Nueva España, 1700–1810*. Madrid: Instituto de Cooperación Iberoamericana, Quinto Centenario.

———, ed. 1991. *Haciendas, pueblos y comunidades: Los valles de México y Toluca entre 1530 y 1916*. Mexico City: Consejo Nacional para la Cultura y las Artes.

———. 1993. *La protoindustria colonial hispanoamericana*. Mexico City: El Colegio de México.

———. 2001. *El mundo novohispano: Población, ciudades y economía, siglos XVII y XVIII*. Mexico City: El Colegio de México.

Mintz, Sidney. 1986. *Sweetness and Power: The Place of Sugar in Modern History*. New York: Penguin Books.

Miranda, José. 1965. *La función económica del encomendero en los origines del régimen colonial (Nueva España, 1525–1531)*. Mexico City: Instituto de Investigaciones Históricas, Universidad Nacional Autónoma de México.

Molina Enríquez, Andrés. 1909. *Los grandes problemas nacionales*. Mexico City: A. Carranza e Hijos.

Monsiváis, Carlos. 1992. "'Just Over that Hill': Notes on Centralism and Regional Cultures." In Van Young, *Mexico's Regions*, 247–54.

Montoya, Alfredo. 1956. *Historia de los saladeros argentinos*. Buenos Aires: Raigal.

Moore, Barrington, Jr. 1966. *Social Origins of Dictatorship and Democracy: Lord and Peasant in the Making of the Modern World*. Boston: Beacon Press.

———. 1978. *Injustice: The Social Bases of Obedience and Revolt*. New York: M.E. Sharpe.

Mora, José María Luis. 1965. *México y sus revoluciones*. 3 vols. Mexico City: Porrúa. (Orig. pub. 1836.)

Morán Leyva, Paola. 2002. *Lucas Alamán*. Mexico City: Editorial Planeta DeAgostini.

Moreno Cebrián, Alfredo. 1977. *El corregidor de indios y la economía peruana del siglo XVIII: Los repartos forzosos de mercancías*. Madrid: Consejo Superior de Investigaciones Científicas, Instituto G. Fernández de Oviedo.

Moreno Fraginals, Manuel. 2001. *El ingenio*. 3 vols. Barcelona: Crítica. (Orig. pub. 1964.)

Moreno García, Heriberto. 1982. *Guaracha: Tiempos viejos, tiempos nuevos*. Mexico City: El Colegio de Michoacán.

———. 1989. *Haciendas de tierra y agua en la antigua Ciénega de Chapala*. Guadalajara: El Colegio de Michoacán.

Moreno Toscano, Alejandra. 1978. "México." In *Las ciudades latinoamericanas*, vol. 2, *Desarrollo histórico*, edited by Richard M. Morse, 172–96. Mexico City: Secretaría de Educación Pública.

———, and Enrique Florescano. 1977. *El sector externo y la organización espacial y regional de México (1521–1910)*. Puebla: Instituto Nacional de Antropología e Historia.

Morin, Claude. 1979. *Michoacán en la Nueva España del siglo XVII: Crecimiento y desigualdad en una economía colonial*. Mexico City: Fondo de Cultura Económica.

Mörner, Magnus. 1973. "The Spanish American Hacienda: A Survey of Recent Research and Debate." *Hispanic American Historical Review* 53:183–216.

Morse, Richard M. 1986. "The Urban Development of Colonial Spanish America." In Bethell, *Cambridge History of Latin America*, 2:67–104.
Moulaert, Frank. 1983. "The Theories and Methods of Regional Science and Regional Political Economy Compared." In *Regional Analysis and the New International Division of Labor*, edited by Frank Moulaert and Patricia Salinas, 15–19. Boston: Kluwer-Nijhoff.
———, and Patricia Salinas, eds. 1983. *Regional Analysis and the New International Division of Labor*. Boston: Kluwer-Nijhoff.
Mundy, Barbara E. 1996. *The Mapping of New Spain: Indigenous Cartography and the Maps of the Relaciones Geográficas*. Chicago: University of Chicago Press.
Murphy, Arthur D., and Alex Stepick. 1993. *Social Inequality in Oaxaca: A History of Resistance and Change*. Philadelphia: Temple University Press.
Murphy, Michael E. 1986. *Irrigation in the Bajío Region of Colonial Mexico*. Boulder, CO: Westview Press.
Murra, John V. 1980. *The Economic Organization of the Inca State*. Greenwich, CT: JAI Press. (Orig. pub. 1956.)
Myers, Kathleen, and Amanda Powell, eds. and trans. 1999. *A Wild Country Out in the Garden: The Spiritual Journals of a Colonial Mexican Nun*. Bloomington: Indiana University Press.
Namala, Doris M. 2002. "Chimalpahin in His Time: An Analysis of the Writings of a Nahua Annalist of Seventeenth-Century Mexico Concerning His Own Lifetime." PhD diss., University of California, Los Angeles.
Naro, Nancy P. 2000. *A Slave's Place, a Master's World: Fashioning Dependency in Rural Brazil*. London: Continuum.
Naveda Chávez-Hita, Adriana. 1987. *Esclavos negros en las haciendas azucareras de Córdoba, Veracruz, 1690–1830*. Xalapa: Universidad Veracruzana, Centro de Investigaciones Históricas.
Nickel, Herbert. 1984. "The Food Supply of Hacienda Laborers in Puebla-Tlaxcala During the Porfiriato: A First Approximation." In *Haciendas in Central Mexico from Late Colonial Times to the Revolution*, edited by Raymond Buve, 118–59. Amsterdam: CEDLA.
———. 1987. *Relaciones de trabajo en las haciendas de Puebla y Tlaxcala (1740–1914): Cuatro análisis sobre reclutamiento, peonaje y remuneración*. Mexico City: Universidad Iberoamericana.
———. 1988. *Morfología social de la hacienda mexicana*. Mexico City: Fondo de Cultura Económica.
———, ed. 1989. *Paternalismo y economía moral en las haciendas mexicanas del porfiriato*. Mexico City: Universidad Iberoamericana.
———. 1997. *El peonaje en las haciendas mexicanas: Interpretaciones, fuentes, hallazgos*. Mexico City: Universidad Iberoamericana.
———, and María Eugenia Ponce Alcocer, eds. 1996. *Hacendados y trabajadores agrícolas ante las autoridades: Conflictos laborales a fines de la época colonial documentados en el Archivo General de Indias*. Mexico City: Universidad Iberoamericana.

Nunn, Charles F. 1979. *Foreign Immigrants in Early Bourbon Mexico, 1700–1760*. Cambridge: Cambridge University Press.
Obeyesekere, Gananath. 1992. *The Apotheosis of Captain Cook: European Mythmaking in the Pacific*. Princeton, NJ: Princeton University Press.
Ocampo, José Antonio. 1984. *Colombia y la economía mundial, 1830–1910*. Mexico City: Siglo Veintiuno Editores.
Oddone, Jacinto. 1975. *La burguesía terrateniente argentina: Buenos Aires Colonial, Capital Federal, Provincia de Buenos Aires, Provincia de Entre Ríos, Territorios Nacionales*, 2nd ed. Buenos Aires: Ediciones Libera. (Orig. pub. 1936.)
Offutt, Leslie S. 1993. *Una sociedad urbana y rural en el norte de México: Saltillo a fines de la época colonial*. Saltillo: Archivo Municipal de Saltillo.
———. 2001. *Saltillo, 1770–1810: Town and Region in the Mexican North*. Tucson: University of Arizona Press.
O'Hara, Matthew. 1997. "Ascent into Discord: Theory and Latin America's 'New Cultural History.'" Unpublished manuscript.
———. 2001. "Politics and Piety: The Church in Colonial and Nineteenth-Century Mexico." *Mexican Studies/Estudios Mexicanos* 17:213–31.
Ohnuki-Tierney, Emiko, ed. 1990. *Culture through Time: Anthropological Approaches*. Stanford, CA: Stanford University Press.
Orellana, Sandra. 1995. *Ethnohistory of the Pacific Coast: Prehispanic and Colonial Life in Guatemala and Mexico*. Lancaster, CA: Labyrinthos.
Ortega, Sergio, ed. 1986. *De la santidad a la perversión: O de porque no se cumplía la ley de Dios en la sociedad novohispana*. Mexico City: Editorial Grijalba.
Ortiz, Fernando. 1947. *Cuban Counterpoint: Tobacco and Sugar*. Translated by Harriet de Onís. New York: Knopf. (Orig. pub. 1940.)
Ortiz de la Tabla Ducasse, Javier. 1993. *Los encomenderos de Quito, 1534–1660: Origen y evolución de una elite colonial*. Seville: Escuela de Estudios Hispano-Americanos.
Ortiz Escamilla, Juan. 1997. *Guerra y gobierno: Los pueblos y la independencia de México*. Seville: Universidad de Sevilla/El Colegio de México.
Ortiz Monasterio, José. 2004. *México eternamente: Vicente Riva Palacio ante la escritura de la historia*. Mexico City: Fondo de Cultura Económica/Instituto de Investigaciones Dr. José María Luis Mora.
Ouweneel, Arij. 1996. *Shadows over Anáhuac: An Ecological Interpretation of Crisis and Development in Central Mexico, 1730–1800*. Albuquerque: University of New Mexico Press.
———, and Cristina Torales Pacheco, eds. 1992. *Empresarios, indios y estado: Perfil de la economía mexicana (siglo XVIII)*. Amsterdam: Center for Latin American Research and Documentation.
Ouweneel, Arij, and Simon Miller, eds. 1990. *The Indian Community of Colonial Mexico: Fifteen Essays on Land Tenure, Corporate Organizations, and Village Politics*. Amsterdam: Center for Latin American Research and Documentation.
Palacios, Marco. 2002. *El café en Colombia, 1850–1970: Una historia económica, social y política*, 3rd ed., corrected and revised. Bogotá: Planeta.
Palma, Gabriel. 1978. "Dependency: A Formal Theory of Underdevelopment or

a Methodology for the Analysis of Concrete Situations of Underdevelopment?" *World Development* 6:881–924.
Palmer, Bryan. 1990. *Descent into Discourse: The Reification of Language and the Writing of Social History.* Philadelphia: Temple University Press.
Palmer, Colin A. 1975. *Slaves of the White God: Blacks in Mexico, 1570–1650.* Cambridge, MA: Harvard University Press.
Pares, Richard. 1968. *A West-India Fortune.* Hamden, CT: Archon Books. (Orig. pub. 1950.)
Pastor, Rodolfo. 1987. *Campesinos y reformas: La Mixteca, 1700–1856.* Mexico City: El Colegio de México.
Patch, Robert W. 1985. "Agrarian Change in Eighteenth-Century Yucatán." *Hispanic American Historical Review* 65:21–49.
———. 1993. *Maya and Spaniard in Yucatan, 1648–1812.* Stanford, CA: Stanford University Press.
Patterson, Orlando. 1967. *The Sociology of Slavery: An Analysis of the Origins, Development and Structure of Negro Slave Society in Jamaica.* London: MacGibbon and Kee.
Pérez Brignoli, Héctor, and Mario Samper Kutschbach, eds. 1994. *Tierra, café y sociedad: Ensayos sobre la historia agraria centroamericana.* San José, Costa Rica: Programa Costa Rica, FLACSO.
Pérez Herrero, Pedro. 1989. "El crecimiento económico novohispano durante el siglo xviii: Una revisión." *Revista de Historia Económica* 7:69–110.
———. 1990. "Centralización versus regionalización: México (1786–1857)." Unpublished manuscript.
———. 1992a. "El México borbónico: ¿Un éxito fracasado?" In *Interpretaciones del siglo XVIII mexicano*, edited by Josefina Zoraida Vázquez, 109–52. Mexico City: Nueva Imagen.
———. 1992b. "Regional Conformation in Mexico, 1700–1850: Models and Hypotheses." In Van Young, *Mexico's Regions*, 117–44.
———, ed. 1991. *Región e historia en México (1750–1850). Métodos de análisis regional.* Mexico City: Instituto Dr. José María Luis Mora and Universidad Autónoma Metropolitana.
Pérez Verdía, Luis. 1951. *Historia particular del estado de Jalisco*, 3 vols., 2nd ed. Guadalajara: Gráfica.
Peterson, Jeanette Favrot. 1993. *The Paradise Garden Murals of Malinalco: Utopia and Empire in Sixteenth-Century Mexico.* Austin: University of Texas Press.
Piccato, Pablo. "Conversación con los difuntos: Una perspectiva mexicana ante el debate sobre la historia cultural." *Signos históricos: Revista semestral* 8:13–41.
Piel, Jean. 1975. *Capitalisme agraire au Pérou*, vol. 1, *Originalité de la société agraire péruvienne au XIXe siécle.* Paris: Éditions Anthropos.
Piqueras, José A. 2002. *Azúcar y esclavitud en el final del trabajo forzado: Homenaje a M. Moreno Fraginals.* Madrid: Fondo de Cultura Económica.
Pi-Suñer Llorens, Antonia, ed. 1996. *Historiografía mexicana*, vol. 4, *En busca de un discurso integrador de la nación, 1848–1884.* Mexico City: Universidad Nacional Autónoma de México.

Plant, Roger. 1987. *Sugar and Modern Slavery: A Tale of Two Countries*. London: Zed Books.
Poinsett, Joel Roberts. 1824. *Notes on Mexico, Made in the Autumn of 1822; Accompanied by an Historical Sketch of the Revolution, by a Citizen of the United States*. Philadelphia: H. C. Carey and I. Lea.
Polanyi, Karl. 1957. *The Great Transformation: The Political and Economic Origins of Our Time*. Boston: Beacon Press.
Poole, Stafford, C.M. 1987. *Pedro Moya de Contreras: Catholic Reform and Royal Power in New Spain, 1571–1591*. Berkeley: University of California Press.
———. 1995. *Our Lady of Guadalupe: The Origins and Sources of a Mexican National Symbol, 1531–1797*. Tucson: University of Arizona Press.
Popkin, Jeremy D. 2005. *History, Historians, and Autobiography*. Chicago: University of Chicago Press.
Porter, Roy. 1987. *Mind-Forg'd Manacles: A History of Madness in England from the Reformation to the Regency*. Cambridge, MA: Harvard University Press.
Prados de la Escosura, Leandro, and Samuel Amaral, eds. 1993. *La Independencia americana: Consecuencias económicas*. Madrid: Alianza Editorial.
Prem, Hans J. 1989. *Milpa y hacienda: Tenencia de la tierra indígena y española en la cuenca del Alto Atoyac, Puebla, México, 1520–1650*. Mexico City: Centro de Investigación y Estudios Superiores en Antropología Social.
Prescott, William Hickling. 1961. *The Literary Memoranda of William Hickling Prescott*, 2 vols. Edited and with an introduction by C. Harvey Gardiner. Norman: University of Oklahoma Press.
———. 1970. *The Correspondence of William Hickling Prescott, 1833–1847*. Transcribed and edited by Roger Wolcott. New York: Da Capo Press. (Orig. pub. 1925.)
Puente Brunke, José de la. 1992. *Encomienda y encomenderos en el Perú: Estudio social y político de una institución colonial*. Seville: Excma. Diputación de Sevilla.
Queirós Mattoso, Katia M. de. 1986. *To Be a Slave in Brazil, 1550–1888*, revised. New Brunswick, NJ: Rutgers University Press.
Quiroz, Enriqueta. 2000. "La carne entre el lujo y la subsistencia: Mercado, abastecimiento y precios en la Ciudad de México, 1750–1812." PhD diss., El Colegio de México.
Rabell, Cecilia. 1986. *Los diezmos de San Luis de la Paz: Economía de una región del Bajío en el siglo XVIII*. Mexico City: Instituto de Investigaciones Sociales, Universidad Nacional Autónoma de México.
Radding, Cynthia. 1995. *Entre el desierto y la sierra: Las naciones O'odham y Tegûima de Sonora, 1530–1840*. Mexico City: Centro de Investigaciones y Estudios Superiores en Antropología Social.
———. 1997. *Wandering Peoples: Colonialism, Ethnic Spaces, and Ecological Frontiers in Northwestern Mexico, 1700–1850*. Durham, NC: Duke University Press.
———. 1998. "Cultural Dialogues: Recent Trends in Mesoamerican Ethnohistory." *Latin American Research Review* 33:193–211.
Ragatz, Lowell J. 1971. *The Fall of the Planter Class in the British Caribbean*,

1763–1833: A Study in Social and Economic History. New York: Octagon Books. (Orig. pub. 1928.)

Ramírez Bacca, Renzo. 2001. *Colonización del Líbano: De la distribución de baldíos a la consolidación de una región cafetera, Tolima, Colombia 1849–1907*. Bogotá: Universidad Nacional de Colombia.

———. 2004. *Formación y transformación de la cultura laboral cafetera en el siglo XX*. Medellín: Carreta Editores.

Ramírez Rancaño, Mario. 1990. *El sistema de haciendas de Tlaxcala*. Mexico City: Consejo Nacional para la Cultura y las Artes.

Randolph, Jorge. 1966. *Las guerras de Arauco y la esclavitud*. Santiago de Chile: Sociedad Impresora "Horizonte."

Redfield, Robert. 1960. *The Little Community and Peasant Society and Culture*. Chicago: University of Chicago Press.

———. 1968. *The Folk Culture of Yucatan*. Chicago: University of Chicago Press.

Reff, Daniel T. 1991. *Disease, Depopulation, and Culture Change in Northwestern New Spain, 1518–1764*. Salt Lake City: University of Utah Press.

Reina Aoyama, Leticia. 1980. *Las rebeliones campesinas en México (1819–1906)*. Mexico City: Siglo Veintiuno.

———, and Elisa Servín, eds. 2002. *Crisis, reforma y revolución—México: Historias de fin de siglo*. Mexico City: Taurus/Consejo Nacional para la Cultura y las Artes/Instituto Nacional de Antropología e Historia.

Reis, João José, and Herbert S. Klein. 2011. "Slavery in Brazil." In *Handbook of Latin American History*, edited by José Moya, 181–211. New York: Oxford University Press.

Reis, João José, and Eduardo Silva. 1989. *Negociação e conflito: A resistencia negra no Brasil escravista*. São Paulo: Companhia das Letras.

Relph, E. C. 1976. *Place and Placelessness*. London: Pion.

———. 1981. *Rational Landscapes and Humanistic Geography*. Totowa, NJ: Barnes and Noble.

Rendón Garcini, Ricardo. 1990. *Dos haciendas pulqueras en Tlaxcala, 1857–1884*. Tlaxcala: Gobierno del Estado de Tlaxcala/Universidad Iberoamericana.

———. 1994. *Haciendas de México*. Mexico City: Fomento Cultural Banamex.

Restall, Matthew. 1995. *Life and Death in a Maya Community: The Ixil Testaments of the 1760s*. Lancaster, CA: Labyrinthos.

———. 1997. *The Maya World: Yucatec Culture and Society, 1550–1850*. Stanford, CA: Stanford University Press.

———. 2003. "A History of the New Philology and the New Philology in History." *Latin American Research Review* 38:113–34.

Reygadas, Fermín de. 1811. *Discurso contra el fanatismo y la impostura de los rebeldes de Nueva España . . .* Mexico City: Casa de Arizpe.

Reyna, María del Carmen. 1991. *Formación y desintegración de la Hacienda de San Francisco de Borja*. Mexico City: Instituto Nacional de Antropología e Historia.

Ricard, Robert. 1966. *The Spiritual Conquest of Mexico: An Essay on the Apostolate and the Evangelizing Methods of the Mendicant Orders in New Spain*,

1523–1572. Translated by Lesly B. Simpson. Berkeley: University of California Press. (Orig. pub. 1933.)

Richards, Thomas. 1990. *The Commodity Culture of Victorian England: Advertising and Spectacle, 1851–1914*. Stanford, CA: Stanford University Press.

Richardson, Henry Ward. 1978. *Regional Economics*. Urbana: University of Illinois Press.

Ricouer, Paul. 1981. *Hermeneutics and the Human Sciences: Essays on Language, Action, and Interpretation*. Edited and translated by John B. Thompson. Cambridge: Cambridge University Press.

Riva Palacio, Vicente, et. al. 1887–89. *México a través de los siglos: Historia general y completa del desenvolvimiento social, político, religioso, militar, artístico, científico y literario de México desde la antigüedad más remota hasta la época actual*. 6 vols. Barcelona: España y Compañía.

Roberts, Bryan. 1992. "The Place of Regions in Mexico." In Van Young, *Mexico's Regions*, 227–45.

Robertson, William Spence. 1952. *Iturbide of Mexico*. Durham, NC: Duke University Press.

Robinson, David J. 1989. "The Language and Significance of Place in Latin America." In *The Power of Place: Bringing Together Geographical and Sociological Imaginations*, edited by John A. Agnew and James S. Duncan, 157–84. Boston: Unwin Hyman.

Rodríguez Baquero, Luis Enrique. 1995. *Encomienda y vida diaria entre los indios de Muzo, 1550–1620*. Bogotá: Instituto Colombiano de Cultura Hispánica.

Rodríguez Gómez, María Guadalupe. 1984. *Jalpa y San Juan de los Otates, dos haciendas en el Bajío colonial*. León: El Colegio del Bajío.

Rodríguez O., Jaime E. 1980. *Down from Colonialism: Mexico's Nineteenth-Century Crisis*. Distinguished Faculty Lecture, University of California, Irvine.

———, ed. 1989. *The Independence of Mexico and the Creation of the New Nation*. Los Angeles: Center for Latin American Studies, University of California, Los Angeles.

———, ed. 1992. *Patterns of Contention in Mexican History*. Wilmington, DE: Scholarly Resources.

———, ed. 1994. *Mexico in the Age of Democratic Revolutions, 1750–1850*. Boulder, CO: Lynne Rienner.

———. 1998. *The Independence of Spanish America*. Cambridge: Cambridge University Press.

Rojas, Teresa, ed. 1990. *La agricultura en tierras mexicanas desde sus orígenes hasta nuestros días*. Mexico City: Grijalbo/Consejo Nacional para la Cultura y las Artes.

Romano, Ruggiero. 1993. *Coyunturas opuestas: La crisis del siglo XVII en Europa e Hispanoamérica*. Mexico City: El Colegio de México.

Romero Frizzi, María de los Angeles. 1996. *El sol y la cruz: Los pueblos indios de Oaxaca colonial*. Mexico City: Centro de Investigaciones y Estudios Superiores en Antropología Social.

Rosaldo, Renato. 1986. "From the Door of His Tent: The Fieldworker and the Inquisitor." In Clifford and Marcus, *Writing Culture*, 77–97.

Roseberry, William. 1983. *Coffee and Capitalism in the Venezuelan Andes.* Austin: University of Texas Press.

———. 1989. *Anthropologies and Histories: Essays in Culture, History, and Political Economy.* New Brunswick, NJ: Rutgers University Press.

———, Lowell Gudmundson, and Mario Samper Kutschbach. 1995. *Coffee, Society, and Power in Latin America.* Baltimore, MD: Johns Hopkins University Press.

Rugeley, Terry. 1996. *Yucatán's Maya Peasantry and the Origins of the Caste War.* Austin: University of Texas Press.

———. 2001. *Of Wonders and Wise Men: Religion and Popular Cultures in Southeast Mexico, 1800–1876.* Austin: University of Texas Press.

Ruiz Abreu, Carlos E. 1994. *Señores de la tierra y el agua: Propiedad, comercio y trabajo en el Tabasco colonial.* Villahermosa, Tabasco: Universidad Juárez Autónoma de Tabasco.

———. 2001. *Tabasco en la época de los Borbones: Comercio y mercados, 1777–1811.* Villahermosa, Tabasco: Universidad Juárez Autónoma de Tabasco.

Rutledge, Ian. 1987. *Cambio agrario e integración: El desarrollo del capitalismo en Jujuy, 1550–1960.* Buenos Aires: Centro de Investigaciones en Ciencias Sociales.

Ruz, Mario Humberto. 1994. *Un rostro encubierto: Los indios del Tabasco colonial.* Mexico City: Centro de Investigaciones y Estudios Superiores en Antropología Social.

Sabato, Hilda. 1990. *Agrarian Capitalism and the World Market: Buenos Aires in the Pastoral Age, 1840–1890.* Albuquerque: University of New Mexico Press.

Sabean, David W. 1990. *Property, Production, and Family in Neckerhausen, 1700–1870.* Cambridge: Cambridge University Press.

Sacks, Oliver W. 1995. *An Anthropologist on Mars: Seven Paradoxical Tales.* New York: Knopf.

Saco, José Antonio. 1875–1877. *Historia de la esclavitud desde los tiempos mas remotos hasta nuestros días.* Paris: Tipografía Lahure.

Sacristán, María Cristina. 1992. *Locura e Inquisición en Nueva España, 1571–1700.* Mexico City: Fondo de Cultura Económica.

———. 1994. *Locura y disidencia en el México ilustrado, 1760–1810.* Zamora: El Colegio de Michoacán.

Sahlins, Marshall. 1976. *Culture and Practical Reason.* Chicago: University of Chicago Press.

———. 1987. *Islands of History.* Chicago: University of Chicago Press.

———. 1995. *How "Natives" Think: About Captain Cook, for Example.* Chicago: University of Chicago Press.

Said, Edward. 1978. *Orientalism.* New York: Pantheon Books.

Salamini, Heather Fowler. 1978. *Agrarian Revolution in Veracruz, 1920–1938.* Lincoln: University of Nebraska Press.

Salmerón, Roberto M. 1991. *Indian Revolts in Northern New Spain: A Synthesis of Resistance (1680–1786).* Lanham, MD: University Press of America.

Salvatore, Ricardo D. 2003. *Wandering Paysanos: State Order and Subaltern Experience in Buenos Aires during the Rosas Era.* Durham, NC: Duke University Press.

Salvucci, Richard J. 1987. *Textiles and Capitalism in Mexico: An Economic History of the Obrajes, 1539–1840*. Princeton, NJ: Princeton University Press.
San Miguel, Pedro L. 2004. "La representación del atraso: México en la historiografía estadounidense." *Historia Mexicana* 53(211): 745–96.
Sánchez Maldonado, María Isabel. 1994. *Diezmos y crédito eclesiástico: El diezmatorio de Acámbaro, 1724–1771*. Zamora: El Colegio de Michoacán.
Sánchez Santiró, Ernest. 2001. *Azúcar y poder: Estructura socioeconómica de las alcaldías mayores de Cuernavaca y Cuautla de Amilpas, 1730–1821*. Mexico City: Editorial Praxis.
Sánchez Silva, Carlos. 1998. *Indios, comerciantes y burocracia en la Oaxaca poscolonial, 1786–1860*. Oaxaca: Instituto Oaxaqueño de las Culturas/Fondo Estatal para la Cultura y las Artes/Universidad Autónoma Benito Juárez de Oaxaca.
Sauer, Carl Ortwin. 1963. *Land and Life: A Selection from the Writings of Carl Ortwin Sauer*. John Leighly, ed. Berkeley: University of California Press.
Scarano, Francisco A. 1984. *Sugar and Slavery in Puerto Rico: The Plantation Economy of Ponce, 1800–1850*. Madison: University of Wisconsin Press.
Scardaville, Michael. 1977. "Crime and the Urban Poor: Mexico City in the Late Colonial Period." PhD diss., University of Florida.
Schama, Simon. 1991. *Dead Certainties (Unwarranted Speculations)*. New York: Knopf.
Scharrer Tamm, Beatriz. 1997. *Azúcar y trabajo: Tecnología de los siglos XVII y XVIII en el actual Estado de Morelos*. Mexico City: Centro de Investigaciones y Estudios Superiores en Antropología Social.
Schell, William, Jr. 1986. *Medieval Iberian Tradition and the Development of the Mexican Hacienda*. Syracuse, NY: Maxwell School of Citizenship and Public Affairs, Syracuse University.
Schlesinger, Arthur M. 2000. *A Life in the Twentieth Century*. Boston: Houghton Mifflin.
Schmit, Roberto. 2004. *Ruina y resurrección en tiempos de guerra: Sociedad, economía y poder en el Oriente entrerriano posrevolucionario, 1810–1852*. Buenos Aires: Prometeo Libros.
Schroeder, Susan. 1991. *Chimalpahin and the Kingdoms of Chalco*. Tucson: University of Arizona Press.
———, ed. 1998. *The "Pax Colonial" and Native Resistance in New Spain*. Lincoln: University of Nebraska Press.
Schroeder, Susan, Stephanie Wood, and Robert Haskett, eds. 1997. *Indian Women of Early Mexico*. Norman: University of Oklahoma Press.
Schryer, Frans J. 1990. *Ethnicity and Class Conflict in Rural Mexico*. Princeton, NJ: Princeton University Press.
Schwaller, John Frederick. 1987. *The Church and Clergy in Sixteenth-Century Mexico*. Albuquerque: University of New Mexico Press.
Schwartz, Stuart B. 1984. "Colonial Brazil, 1750–1808." In Bethell, *Cambridge History of Latin America*, 2:423–500, 601–60.
———. 1985. *Sugar Plantations in the Formation of Brazilian Society: Bahia, 1550–1835*. Cambridge: Cambridge University Press.

———. 1992. *Slaves, Peasants, and Rebels: Reconsidering Brazilian Slavery*. Urbana: University of Illinois Press.
Scobie, James R. 1964. *Revolution on the Pampas: A Social History of Argentine Wheat, 1860–1910*. Austin: University of Texas Press.
Scott, James C. 1976. *The Moral Economy of the Peasant: Rebellion and Subsistence in Southeast Asia*. New Haven, CT: Yale University Press.
———. 1985. *Weapons of the Weak: Everyday Forms of Peasant Resistance*. New Haven, CT: Yale University Press.
———. 1990. *Domination and the Arts of Resistance: Hidden Transcripts*. New Haven, CT: Yale University Press.
Scull, Andrew T. 1989. *Social Order/Mental Disorder: Anglo-American Psychiatry in Historical Perspective*. Berkeley: University of California Press.
Seed, Patricia. 1988. *To Love, Honor, and Obey in Colonial Mexico: Conflicts over Marriage Choice, 1574–1821*. Stanford, CA: Stanford University Press.
———, Hernán Vidal, Walter Mignolo, and Rolena Adorno. 1993. Exchanges on "postcolonial discourses." *Latin American Research Review* 28:113–52.
Semo, Enrique. 1993. *The History of Capitalism in Mexico: Its Origins, 1521–1763*. Translated by Lidia Lozano. Austin: University of Texas Press. (Orig. pub. 1973.)
———, ed. 1977. *Siete ensayos sobre la hacienda mexicana, 1780–1880*. Mexico City: Instituto Nacional de Antropología e Historia.
Serrano Ortega, José Antonio. 2001. *Jerarquía territorial y transición política: Guanajuato, 1790–1836*. Zamora: El Colegio de Michoacán/Instituto de Investigaciones Dr. José María Luis Mora.
Serrera Contreras, Ramón María. 1977. *Guadalajara ganadera: Estudio regional novohispano, 1760–1805*. Seville: Consejo Superior de Investigaciones Científicas.
Service, Elman R. 1971. *Spanish-Guaraní Relations in Early Colonial Paraguay*. Westport, CT: Greenwood Press. (Orig. pub. 1954.)
Shadle, Stanley F. 1994. *Andrés Molina Enríquez: Mexican Land Reformer of the Revolutionary Era*. Tucson: University of Arizona Press.
Shanin, Teodor. "Chayanov's Message: Illuminations, Miscomprehensions, and the Contemporary 'Development Theory.'" In Chayanov, *The Theory of Peasant Economy*, 1–24.
Sheridan, Thomas E., ed. 1999. *Empire of Sand: The Seri Indians and the Struggle for Spanish Sonora, 1645–1803*. Tucson: University of Arizona Press.
Sherman, William L. 1979. *Forced Native Labor in Sixteenth-Century Central America*. Lincoln: University of Nebraska Press.
Sierra Méndez, Justo. 1940. *Evolución política del pueblo mexicano*. Mexico City: Ediciones de la Casa de España.
Sigal, Pete. 2000. *From Moon Goddess to Virgins: The Colonization of Yucatecan Sexual Desire*. Austin: University of Texas Press.
Silva Riquer, Jorge. 1997. "Producción agropecuaria y mercados regionales en Michoacán, siglo XVIII." PhD diss., El Colegio de México.
———. 2008. *Mercado regional y mercado urbano en Michoacán y Valladolid, 1778–1809*. Mexico City: El Colegio de México.

Silva Riquer, Jorge, and Antonio Escobar Ohmstede, eds. 2000. *Mercados indígenas en México, Chile y Argentina, siglos XVIII–XIX*. Mexico City: Instituto de Investigaciones Dr. José María Luis Mora/Centro de Investigación y Estudios Superiores en Antropología Social.

Silva Riquer, Jorge, Juan Carlos Grosso, and Carmen Yuste, eds. 1995. *Circuitos mercantiles y mercados en Latinoamérica, siglos XVIII–XIX*. Mexico City: Instituto de Investigaciones Dr. José María Luis Mora.

Silva Riquer, Jorge, and Jesús López Martínez, eds. 1998. *Mercado interno en México: siglos XVIII–XIX*. Mexico City: Instituto de Investigaciones Dr. José María Luis Mora/El Colegio de Michoacán/El Colegio de México/Instituto de Investigaciones Históricas, Universidad Nacional Autónoma de México.

Silva Riquer, Jorge, et al. 2003. *Los mercados regionales de México en los siglos XVIII y XIX*. Mexico City: Instituto de Investigaciones Dr. José María Luis Mora/Consejo Nacional para la Cultura y las Artes.

Simpson, Lesley Byrd. 1938. *Studies in the Administration of the Indians in New Spain: III. The Repartimiento System of Native Labor in New Spain and Guatemala*. Berkeley: University of California Press.

———. 1949. *Exploitation of Land in Central Mexico in the Sixteenth Century*. Berkeley: University of California Press.

———. 1982. *The Encomienda in New Spain: The Beginning of Spanish Mexico*. Revised and enlarged edition. Berkeley: University of California Press. (Orig. pub. 1950.)

Skinner, G. William. 1967. "Marketing and Social Structure in Rural China (Part 1)." In *Peasant Society: A Reader*, edited by Jack M. Potter, May N. Diaz, and George M. Poster, 63–97. Boston: Little, Brown.

Skocpol, Theda. 1979. *States and Social Revolutions: A Comparative Analysis of France, Russia, and China*. Cambridge: Cambridge University Press.

Slatta, Richard W. 1983. *Gauchos and the Vanishing Frontier*. Lincoln: University of Nebraska Press.

Slicher Van Bath, Bernhard H. 1963. *The Agrarian History of Western Europe, A.D. 500–1850*. Translated by Olive Ordish. London: Edward Arnold.

Smith, Adam. 1979. *The Theory of the Moral Sentiments*. Oxford: Oxford University Press. (Orig. pub. 1754.)

Smith, Carol A. 1975. "Examining Stratification Systems through Peasant Marketing Arrangements: An Application of Some Models from Economic Geography." *Man* (New Series) 10:95–122.

———, ed. 1976a. *Regional Analysis*, 2 vols. New York: Academic Press.

———. 1976b. "Regional Economic Structures: Linking Geographical Models and Socioeconomic Problems." In Smith, *Regional Analysis*, 1:3–63.

———. 1976c. "Exchange Systems and the Spatial Distribution of Elites: The Organization of Stratification in Agrarian Societies." In Smith, *Regional Analysis*, 2:309–74, passim.

———. 1977. "How Marketing Systems Affect Economic Opportunity in Agrarian Societies." In *Peasant Livelihood: Studies in Economic Anthropology and Cultural Ecology*, edited by Rhoda Halperin and James Dow, 117–46. New York: St. Martin's Press.

Smith-Kleiner, Felicia. 2003. "The Re/formation of the Female Body: Gender, Law, and Culture in Colonial New England and New Spain." PhD diss., New York University.

Solberg, Carl E. 1987. *The Prairies and the Pampas: Agrarian Policy in Canada and Argentina, 1880–1930.* Stanford, CA: Stanford University Press.

Souldre-La France, Renée. 2004. *Región e imperio: El Tolima Grande y las reformas borbónicas en el siglo XVIII.* Bogotá: Instituto Colombiano de Antropología e Historia.

Sousa, Lisa, Stafford Poole, C.M., and James Lockhart, eds. and trans. 1998. *The Story of Guadalupe: Luis Laso de la Vega's Huei tlamahuiçoltica of 1649.* Stanford, CA: Stanford University Press.

Spicer, Edward H. 1963. *Cycles of Conquest: The Impact of Spain, Mexico, and the United States on the Indians of the Southwest, 1533–1960.* Tucson: University of Arizona Press.

Spiro, Melford. 1982. *Oedipus in the Trobriands.* Chicago: University of Chicago Press.

———. 1986. "Cultural Relativism and the Future of Anthropology." *Cultural Anthropology* 1(3): 259–86.

Spores, Ronald. 1984. *The Mixtecs in Ancient and Colonial Times.* Norman: University of Oklahoma Press.

Stein, Stanley J. 1976. *Vassouras: A Brazilian Coffee County, 1850–1900.* New York: Atheneum. (Orig. pub. 1957.)

Stein, Stanley J., and Barbara H. Stein. 1970. *The Colonial Heritage of Latin America: Essays on Economic Dependence in Historical Perspective.* New York: Oxford University Press.

Stern, Claudio. 1973. *Las regiones de México y sus niveles de desarrollo socioeconómico.* Mexico City: El Colegio de México.

Stern, Steve J. 1982. *Peru's Indian Peoples and the Challenge of Spanish Conquest: Huamanga to 1640.* Madison: University of Wisconsin Press.

———. 1987a. *Resistance, Rebellion, and Consciousness in the Andean Peasant World, 18th to 20th Centuries.* Madison: University of Wisconsin Press.

———. 1987b. "New Approaches to the Study of Peasant Rebellion and Consciousness: Implications of the Andean Experience." In Stern, *Resistance, Rebellion, and Consciousness,* 3–25.

———. 1988. "Feudalism, Capitalism, and the World-System in the Perspective of Latin America and the Caribbean." *American Historical Review* 93:829–72.

———. 1995. *The Secret History of Gender: Women, Men, and Power in Late Colonial Mexico.* Chapel Hill: University of North Carolina Press.

———. 1998. *Remembering Pinochet's Chile: On the Eve of London, 1998* (vol. 1 of *The Memory Box of Pinochet's Chile*). Durham: University of North Carolina Press.

Stone, Lawrence. 1965. *The Crisis of the Aristocracy, 1558–1641.* Oxford: Clarendon Press.

Strickon, Arnold. 1965. "Hacienda and Plantation in Yucatán: An Historical-Ecological Consideration of the Folk-Urban Continuum in Yucatán." *América Indígena* 25:35–63.

Suárez Arguello, Clara Elena. 1997. *Camino real y carrera larga: La arriería en la Nueva España durante el siglo XVIII*. Mexico City: Centro de Investigación y Estudios Superiores en Antropología Social.
Super, John C. 1988. *Food, Conquest, and Colonization in Sixteenth-Century Spanish America*. Albuquerque: University of New Mexico Press.
Swann, Michal M. 1982. *Tierra Adentro: Settlement and Society in Colonial Durango*. Boulder, CO: Westview Press.
Tannenbaum, Frank. 1933. *The Mexican Agrarian Revolution*. Washington, DC: The Brookings Institution.
Tarrow, Sidney. 1994. *Power in Movement: Social Movements, Collective Action and Politics*. Cambridge: Cambridge University Press.
Taussig, Michael T. 1991. *Shamanism, Colonialism, and the Wild Man: A Study in Terror and Healing*. Chicago: University of Chicago Press.
Tawney, R. H. 1967. *The Agrarian Problem in the Sixteenth Century*. Reprinted, with an introduction by Lawrence Stone. New York: Harper and Row. (Orig. pub. 1912.)
Taylor, William B. 1972. *Landlord and Peasant in Colonial Oaxaca*. Stanford, CA: Stanford University Press.
———. 1979. *Drinking, Homicide, and Rebellion in Colonial Mexican Villages*. Stanford, CA: Stanford University Press.
———. 1985. "Between Global Process and Local Knowledge: An Inquiry into Early Latin American Social History, 1500–1900." In *Reliving the Past: The Worlds of Social History*, edited by Olivier Zunz, 115–90. Chapel Hill: University of North Carolina Press.
———. 1996. *Magistrates of the Sacred: Priests and Parishioners in Eighteenth-Century Mexico*. Stanford, CA: Stanford University Press.
Teja, Jesús F. de la. 1995. *San Antonio de Béxar: A Community on New Spain's Northern Frontier*. Albuquerque: University of New Mexico Press.
Terán, Marta. 2004. "Atando cabos en la historiografía del siglo XX sobre Miguel Hidalgo." *Históricas* 59:23–44.
Terán, Marta, and Norma Páez, eds. 2004. *Miguel Hidalgo: Ensayos sobre el mito y el hombre (1953–2003) / selección de textos, historiografía y bibliografía*. Mexico City: Instituto Nacional de Antropología e Historia.
Terraciano, Kevin. 2001. *The Mixtecs of Colonial Oaxaca: Ñudzahui History, Sixteenth through Eighteenth Centuries*. Stanford, CA: Stanford University Press.
Thomas, Hugh. 1997. *The Slave Trade: The Story of the Atlantic Slave Trade, 1440–1870*. New York: Simon and Schuster.
Thompson, Edward P. 1963. *The Making of the English Working Class*. New York: Pantheon.
———. 1967. "Time, Work-Discipline, and Industrial Capitalism." *Past and Present* 38:56–97.
———. 1971. "The Moral Economy of the English Crowd in the Eighteenth Century." *Past and Present* 50:76–136.
Thomson, Guy. 1989. *Puebla de los Angeles: Industry and Society in a Mexican City, 1700–1850*. Boulder, CO: Westview Press.

Thorner, Daniel. 1986. "Chayanov's Concept of Peasant Economy." In Chayanov, *The Theory of Peasant Economy*, xi–xxiii.

Thurner, Mark. 1997. *From Two Republics to One Divided: Contradictions of Postcolonial Nationmaking in Andean Peru*. Durham, NC: Duke University Press.

Thurner, Mark, and Andrés Guerrero, eds. 2003. *After Spanish Rule: Postcolonial Predicaments of the Americas*. Durham, NC: Duke University Press.

Timmons, Wilbert H. 1970. *Morelos: Priest, Soldier, Statesman of Mexico*. El Paso: Texas Western College Press.

Todorov, Tzvetan. 1984. *The Conquest of America: The Question of the Other*. Translated by Richard Howard. New York: Harper and Row.

Topik, Steven C., and Allen Wells, eds. 1998. *The Second Conquest of Latin America: Coffee, Henequen, and Oil During the Export Boom, 1850–1930*. Austin: University of Texas Press.

Tord Nicolini, Javier. 1981. *Hacienda, comercio y luchas sociales (Perú colonial)*. Lima: Biblioteca Peruana de Historia, Economía y Sociedad.

Torre Villar, Ernesto de la. 1964. *La constitución de Apatzingán y los creadores del estado mexicano*. Mexico City: Universidad Nacional Autónoma de México.

———. 1982. *La independencia mexicana*. Mexico City: Fondo de Cultura Económica.

Torres Sánchez, Jaime. 2002. *Haciendas y posesiones de la Compañía de Jesús en Venezuela: El Colegio de Caracas en el siglo XVIII*. Seville: Universidad de Sevilla.

Tortolero Villaseñor, Alejandro. 1995. *De la coa a la máquina de vapor: Actividad agrícola e innovación tecnológica en las haciendas mexicanas, 1880–1914*. Mexico City: El Colegio Mexiquense/Siglo Veintiuno.

———, ed. 1997. *Tierra, agua y bosques: Historia y medio ambiente en el México central*. Mexico City: Centro de Investigación y Estudios Superiores en Antropología Social.

Tovar Pinzón, Hermes. 1971–. *Fuentes para el estudio de las actividades socio-económicos de la Compañía de Jesús y otras misiones religiosas*. Bogotá: Universidad Nacional de Colombia, Facultad de Ciencias Humanas.

———. 1980. *Grandes empresas agrícolas y ganaderas: Su desarrollo en el siglo XVIII*. Bogotá: Universidad Nacional de Colombia, Ediciones CIEC.

———. 1988. *Hacienda colonial y formación social*. Barcelona: Sendai Ediciones.

Trabulse, Elías, ed. 1979. *Fluctuaciones económicas en Oaxaca durante el siglo XVIII*. Mexico City: El Colegio de México.

Trautmann, Wolfgang. 1981. *Las transformaciones en el paisaje cultural de Tlaxcala durante la época colonial: Una contribución a la historia de México bajo especial consideración de aspectos geográfico-económicos y sociales*. Wiesbaden: F. Steiner.

Trelles Aréstegui, Efraín. 1982. *Lucas Martínez Vegazo: Funcionamiento de una encomienda peruana inicial*. Lima: Fondo Editorial, Pontificia Universidad Católica del Perú.

Trexler, Richard C. 1984. "We Think, They Act: Clerical Readings of Missionary Theatre in Sixteenth-Century New Spain." In *Understanding Popular Culture:*

Europe from the Middle Ages to the Nineteenth Century, edited by Stephen L. Kaplan, 189–227. Berlin: Mouton.
———. 1988. "Dressing and Undressing the Saints in the Old World and the New." Bronowski Renaissance Symposium dedicated to the memory of Michel de Certeau, University of California, San Diego, November.
———. 1995. *Sex and Conquest: Gendered Violence, Political Order, and the European Conquest of the Americas*. Ithaca, NY: Cornell University Press.
Tuan, Yi Fu. 1974. *Topophilia*. Englewood Cliffs, NJ: Prentice-Hall.
———. 1977. *Space and Place: The Perspective of Experience*. Minneapolis: University of Minnesota Press.
Tudela, Elisa Sampson Vera. 2000. *Colonial Angels: Narratives of Gender and Spirituality in Mexico, 1580–1750*. Austin: University of Texas Press.
Turner, Victor W. 1969. *The Ritual Process: Structure and Anti-Structure*. Chicago: Aldine.
———. 1974. *Dramas, Fields, and Metaphors: Symbolic Action in Human Society*. Ithaca, NY: Cornell University Press.
Tutino, John. 1976. "Spanish Elites, Haciendas, and Indian Towns, 1750–1810." PhD diss., University of Texas at Austin.
———. 1986. *From Insurrection to Revolution in Mexico: Social Bases of Agrarian Violence, 1750–1940*. Princeton, NJ: Princeton University Press.
Uribe-Urán, Victor M., ed. 2001. *State and Society in Spanish America during the Age of Revolution*. Wilmington, DE: SR Books.
Valadés, José C. 1938. *Alamán, estadista y historiador*. Mexico City: Antigua Librería Robredo, J. Porrúa de hijos.
Valdés, Dennis Nodin. 1978. "The Decline of the Sociedad de Castas in Mexico City." PhD diss., University of Michigan.
Valdés Dávila, Carlos Manuel. 1995a. *Aux marges de l'empire: société e deliquence à Saltillo à l'epoque coloniale*. Perpignan: Université de Perpignan.
———. 1995b. *La gente del mezquite: Los nómadas del noreste en la colonia*. Mexico City: Centro de Investigaciones y Estudios Superiores en Antropología Social.
Vallecilla Gordillo, Jaime. 2001. *Café y crecimiento económico regional: El Antiguo Caldas, 1870–1970*. Manizales, Colombia: Universidad de Caldas.
Van Young, Eric. 1970. "The Cortés Ingenio at Tuxtla: A Study in Economic Decline." Unpublished manuscript.
———. 1978. "Rural Life in Eighteenth-Century Mexico: The Guadalajara Region, 1675–1820," 2 vols. PhD diss., University of California, Berkeley.
———. 1979. "Regional Agrarian Structures and Foreign Commerce in Nineteenth-Century Latin America: A Comment." American Historical Association annual meeting, New York.
———. 1981. *Hacienda and Market in Eighteenth-Century Mexico: The Rural Economy of the Guadalajara Region, 1680–1820*. Berkeley: University of California Press.
———. 1982. "Rural Middlemen in Bourbon Mexico: The Guadalajara Countryside in the Eighteenth Century." Paper presented at the American Historical Association annual meeting, Washington, DC (unpublished).

———. 1983. "Mexican Rural History since Chevalier: The Historiography of the Colonial Hacienda." *Latin American Research Review* 18:5–62.
———. 1984. "On Regions: A Comment." Address at the Conference on Regional Aspects of US-Mexican Integration, Center for US-Mexican Studies, University of California, San Diego.
———. 1985. "Recent Anglophone Scholarship on Mexico and Central America in the Age of Revolution (1750–1850)." *Hispanic American Historical Review* 65:725–43.
———. 1986a. "The Age of Paradox: Mexican Agriculture at the End of the Colonial Period, 1750–1810." In *The Economies of Mexico and Peru in the Late Colonial Period, 1769–1820*, edited by Nils Jacobsen and Hans-Jürgen Puhle, 64–90. Berlin: Colloquium Verlag.
———. 1986b. "Millennium on the Northern Marches: The Mad Messiah of Durango and Popular Rebellion in Mexico, 1800–1815." *Comparative Studies in Society and History* 28:385–413.
———. 1987. "L'enigma dei re: Messianismo e rivolta populare in Messico, 1800–1815." *Rivista Storica Italiana* 99:754–86.
———. 1989a. "Quetzalcóatl, King Ferdinand, and Ignacio Allende Go to the Seashore; Or, Messianism and Mystical Kingship in Mexico, 1800–1821." In *The Independence of Mexico and the Creation of the Federal Republic*, edited by Jaime E. Rodríguez O., 109–27. Los Angeles: Center for Latin American Studies, University of California, Los Angeles.
———. 1989b. "The Raw and the Cooked: Elite and Popular Ideology in Mexico, 1800–1821." In *The Middle Period in Latin American History: Values and Attitudes in the 17th–19th Centuries*, edited by Mark D. Szuchman, 75–102. Boulder, CO: Lynne Rienner.
———. 1990. "To See Someone Not Seeing: Historical Studies of Peasants and Politics in Mexico." *Mexican Studies/Estudios Mexicanos* 6:133–59.
———. 1992a. "Haciendo historia regional: Consideraciones metodológicas y teóricas." In Van Young, *La crisis del orden colonial*, 429–51.
———. 1992b. "Introduction: Are Regions Good to Think?" In Van Young, ed., *Mexico's Regions*, pp. 1–36.
———. 1992c. *La crisis del orden colonial: Estructura agraria y rebeliones populares de la Nueva España, 1750–1821*. Mexico City: Editorial Alianza.
———, ed. 1992d. *Mexico's Regions: Comparative History and Development*. La Jolla, CA: Center for U.S.-Mexican Studies, University of California, San Diego.
———. 1993. "The Cuautla Lazarus: Double Subjectives in Reading Texts on Popular Collective Action." *Colonial Latin American Review* 2:3–26.
———. 1994a. "Conclusion: The State as Vampire—Hegemonic Projects, Public Ritual, and Popular Culture in Mexico, 1600–1990." In Beezley, Martin, and French, eds., *Rituals of Rule*, 343–74.
———. 1994b. "Doing Regional History: Methodological and Theoretical Considerations." *Conference of Latin Americanist Geographers Yearbook, 1994* 20:21–34.
———. 1994c. "Material Life." In *The Countryside in Colonial Latin America*,

edited by Louisa Schell Hoberman and Susan Migden Socolow, 49–74. Albuquerque: University of New Mexico Press.

———. 1995a. "El Lázaro de Cuautla: Dobles subjetivos al leer textos sobre la acción popular colectiva." *Historia y Grafía* 5:165–94.

———. 1995b. "Paisaje de ensueños con figuras y vallados: Disputa y discurso cultural en el campo mexicano de fines de la colonia." In *Paisajes rebeldes: Una larga noche de rebelión indígena*, edited by Jane-Dale Lloyd and Laura Pérez Rosales, 149–79. Mexico City: Universidad Iberoamericana.

———. 1996. "Dreamscape with Figures and Fences: Cultural Contention and Discourse in the Late Colonial Mexican Countryside." In *Le Nouveau Monde—Mondes Nouveaux: L'expérience américaine*, edited by Nathan Wachtel and Serge Gruzinski, 137–59. Paris: Ecole des Hautes Etudes en Sciences Sociales.

———. 1999. "The 'New Cultural History' Comes to Old Mexico." *Hispanic American Historical Review* 79:211–48.

———. 2001a. "Conclusion—Was There an Age of Revolution in Spanish America?" In Uribe-Urán, ed., *State and Society in Spanish America*, pp. 219–46.

———. 2001b. "Estudio introductorio: Ascenso y caída de una loca utopia." *Secuencia: Revista de historia y ciencias sociales* 51:11–29.

———. 2001c. *The Other Rebellion: Popular Violence, Ideology, and the Mexican Struggle for Independence, 1810–1821*. Stanford, CA: Stanford University Press.

———. 2002. "Confesión, interioridad y subjetividad: Sujeto, acción y narración en los inicios del siglo XIX en México." *Signos históricos: Revista semestral* 8:43–59.

———. 2003a. "Beyond the Hacienda: Agrarian Relations and Socioeconomic Change in Rural Mesoamerica—A Comment." *Ethnohistory* 50:231–45.

———. 2003b. "In the Gloomy Caverns of Paganism: Popular Culture, the Bourbon State, and Rebellion in Mexico, 1800–1815." In *The Birth of Modern Mexico, 1780–1824*, edited by Christon I. Archer, 41–65. Wilmington, DE: Scholarly Resources.

———. 2003c. "La pareja dispareja: Algunos comentarios sobre la relación entre la historia cultural e historia económica." *Historia Mexicana* 52:831–70.

———. 2004a. "De aves y estatuas: Respuesta a Alan Knight." *Historia Mexicana*, 54:517–73.

———. 2004b. "Two Decades of Anglophone Historical Writing on Colonial Mexico: Continuity and Change since 1980." *Mexican Studies/Estudios Mexicanos* 20:275–326.

———. 2005. "Ascenso y caída de una loca utopia: El Manicomio General en la Ciudad de México a comienzos del siglo XX." In *Avatares de la medicalización en América Latina (1870–1970)*, edited by Diego Armus, 229–52. Buenos Aires: Lugar Editorial.

———. 2006a. *Hacienda and Market in Eighteenth-Century Mexico: The Rural Economy of the Guadalajara Region, 1675–1820*, 2nd ed., revised. Lanham, MD: Rowman and Littlefield.

———. 2006b. "A Nationalist Movement without Nationalism: The Limits of Imagined Communities in Mexico, 1810–1821." In *New World, First Nations:*

Native Peoples of Mesoamerica and the Andes under Colonial Rule, edited by David Cahill and Blanca Tovías, 218–51. Brighton, UK: Sussex Academic Press.

———. 2006c. *La otra rebelión: La lucha por la independencia de México, 1810–1821*. Mexico City: Fondo de Cultura Económica.

———. 2007a. "Brading's Century: Some Reflections on David A. Brading's Work and the Historiography of Mexico, 1750–1850." In Deans-Smith and Van Young, *Mexican Soundings*, 32–64.

———. 2007b. "De razones y regiones." In *Historia regional. El centro occidente de México: siglos XVI al XX*, edited by Gladys Lizama Silva, 13–33. Guadalajara: Universidad de Guadalajara.

———. 2009a. "Etnia, política local e insurgencia en México, 1810–1821." In *Los colores de las independencias iberoamericanas: Liberalismo, etnia y raza*, edited by Manuel Chust and Ivana Frasquet, 143–69. Madrid: Consejo Superior de Investigaciones Científicas.

———. 2009b. "El lugar de encuentro entre la historia cultural y la historia económica." In *Relaciones intra e interregionales en el occidente de México: Memorias del VI Coloquio Internacional de Occidentalistas*, edited by Daniel Barragán Trejo and José Rafael Martínez Gómez, 15–39. Guadalajara: Universidad de Guadalajara.

———, and Alan Knight. 2007. *En torno a La otra rebelión*. Mexico City: El Colegio de México.

Vanderwood, Paul J. 1987. "Building Blocks but Yet No Building: Regional History and the Mexican Revolution." *Mexican Studies/Estudios Mexicanos* 3:421–32.

———. 1992. *Disorder and Progress: Bandits, Police, and Mexican Development*. Wilmington, DE: Scholarly Resources.

———. 1994. "Using the Present to Study the Past: Religious Movements in Mexico and Uganda a Century Apart." *Mexican Studies/Estudios Mexicanos* 10 (1994), pp. 99–134.

———. 1998. *The Power of God Against the Guns of Government: Religious Upheaval in Mexico at the Turn of the Nineteenth Century*. Stanford, CA: Stanford University Press.

Vargas, Otto. 1983. *Sobre el modo de producción dominante en el Virreinato del Río de la Plata*. Buenos Aires: Editorial Agora.

Vargas-Lobsinger, María. 1984. *La Hacienda de "La Concha": Una empresa algodonera de la Laguna, 1883–1917*. Mexico City: Universidad Nacional Autónoma de México.

———. 1992. *Formación y decadencia de una fortuna: Los mayorazgos de San Miguel de Aguayo y de San Pedro del Álamo, 1583–1929*. Mexico City: Universidad Nacional Autónoma de México.

Vaughan, Mary Kay. 1999. "Cultural Approaches to Peasant Politics in the Mexican Revolution." *Hispanic American Historical Review* 79:269–308.

Velásquez, María del Carmen. 1988. *Hacienda del Señor San José Deminyó, 1780–1784*. Mexico City: El Colegio de México.

Vérastique, Bernardino. 2000. *Michoacán and Eden: Vasco de Quiroga and the Evangelization of Western Mexico*. Austin: University of Texas Press.

Vidal Luna, Francisco, and Herbert S. Klein. 2003. *Slavery and the Economy of São Paulo, 1750–1850.* Stanford, CA: Stanford University Press.
Vilar, Pierre. 1976. *Crecimiento y desarrollo: Economía e historia—reflexiones sobre el caso español,* 3rd ed. Madrid: Ariel.
Villalpando César, José Manuel. 2000. *Mi gobierno será detestado: Novela: Las memorias que nunca escribió Félix María Calleja, Virrey de la Nueva España y frustrado libertador de México.* Mexico City: Planeta.
Villamarin, Juan A., and Judith E. Villamarin. 1975. *Indian Labor in Mainland Colonial Spanish America.* Newark: Latin American Studies Program, University of Delaware.
Villoro, Luis. 1983. *El proceso ideológico de la revolución de independencia.* Mexico City: Universidad Nacional Autónoma de México. (Orig. pub. 1953.)
Vincent, Theodore G. 2001. *The Legacy of Vicente Guerrero: Mexico's First Black Indian President.* Gainesville: University of Florida Press.
Vinson, Ben, III. 2001. *Bearing Arms for His Majesty: The Free-Coloured Militia in Colonial Mexico.* Stanford, CA: Stanford University Press.
Viqueira Albán, Juan Pedro. 1987. *¿Relajados o reprimidos? Diversiones públicas y vida social en la Ciudad de México durante el Siglo de las Luces.* Mexico City: Fondo de Cultura Económica.
———. 1999. *Propriety and Permissiveness in Bourbon Mexico,* revised. Translated by Sonya Lipsett-Rivera and Sergio Rivera Ayala. Wilmington, DE: Scholarly Resources.
Voekel, Pamela. 2002. *Alone Before God: The Religious Origins of Modernity in Mexico.* Durham, NC: Duke University Press.
von Thünen, J. H. 1966. *Von Thünen's Isolated State.* Peter Hall, ed. London: Pergamon Press. (Orig. pub. 1826.)
Voss, Stuart F. 2002. *Latin America in the Middle Period, 1750–1929.* Wilmington, DE: Scholarly Resources.
Wachtel, Nathan. 1977. *The Vision of the Vanquished.* Translated by Ben Reynolds and Sian Reynolds. New York: Barnes and Noble.
Walker, Charles F. 1999. *Smoldering Ashes: Cuzco and the Creation of Republican Peru, 178–1840.* Durham, NC: Duke University Press.
Warman, Arturo. 1981. *We Come to Object: The Peasants of Morelos and the National State.* Baltimore, MD: Johns Hopkins University Press.
Warren, Fintan B. 1963. *Vasco de Quiroga and His Pueblo-Hospitals of Santa Fe.* Washington, DC: American Academy of Franciscan History.
Warren, J. Benedict. 1985. *The Conquest of Michoacán: The Spanish Domination of the Tarascan Kingdom in Western Mexico, 1521–1530.* Norman: University of Oklahoma Press.
Warren, Richard A. 2001. *Vagrants and Citizens: Politics and the Masses in Mexico City from Colony to Republic.* Wilmington, DE: SR Books.
Wasserman, Mark. 1984. *Capitalists, Caciques, and Revolution: The Native Elite and Foreign Enterprise in Chihuahua, Mexico, 1854–1911.* Chapel Hill: University of North Carolina Press.
Wasserstrom, Robert. 1983. *Class and Society in Central Chiapas.* Berkeley: University of California Press.

Weber, David J. 1992. *The Spanish Frontier in North America*. New Haven, CT: Yale University Press.
Weinstein, Barbara. 1983. *The Amazon Rubber Boom, 1850–1920*. Stanford, CA: Stanford University Press.
Wells, Allen. 1985. *Yucatán's Gilded Age: Haciendas, Henequen, and International Harvester, 1860–1915*. Albuquerque: University of New Mexico Press.
Wells, Allen, and Gilbert M. Joseph. 1996. *Summer of Discontent, Seasons of Upheaval: Elite Politics and Rural Insurgency in Yucatán, 1876–1915*. Stanford, CA: Stanford University Press.
White, Hayden. 1987. *The Content of the Form: Narrative Discourse and Historical Representation*. Baltimore, MD: Johns Hopkins University Press.
White, Richard. 1991. *The Middle Ground: Indians, Empires, and Republics in the Great Lakes Region, 1650–1815*. Cambridge: Cambridge University Press.
———. 1992. "Far West: See Also *Frontier*: The 'New Western History,' Textbooks, and the U.S. History Survey Course." *Perspectives* (Newsletter of the American Historical Association) 30:10–12.
Whitmore, Thomas M. 1992. *Disease and Death in Early Colonial Mexico: Simulating Amerindian Depopulation*. Boulder, CO: Westview Press.
Wibel, John, and Jesse de la Cruz. 1971. "Mexico." In *The Urban Development of Latin America*, edited by Richard Morse, 98. Stanford, CA: Center for Latin American Studies, Stanford University.
Wilkie, James W. 1967. *The Mexican Revolution: Federal Expenditure and Social Change since 1910*. Berkeley: University of California Press.
Williams, Eric. 1966. *Capitalism and Slavery*. New York: Capricorn Books. (Orig. pub. 1944.)
Withrow, G. J. 1988. *Time in History: The Evolution of Our General Awareness of Time and Temporal Perspective*. Oxford: Oxford University Press.
Wobeser, Gisela von. 1980. *San Carlos Borromeo: Endeudamiento de una hacienda colonial (1608–1728)*. Mexico City: Universidad Nacional Autónoma de México.
———. 1983. *La formación de la hacienda en la época colonial: El uso de la tierra y el agua*. Mexico City: Universidad Nacional Autónoma de México.
———. 1984. "Las haciendas azucareras de Cuernavaca y Cuautla en la época colonial." In Crespo, *Morelos*, 107–13.
———. 1988. *La hacienda azucarera en la época colonial*. Mexico City: Secretaría de Educación Pública.
———. 1994. *El crédito eclesiástico en la Nueva España, siglo XVIII*. Mexico City: Universidad Nacional Autónoma de México.
Wolf, Eric R. 1966. *Peasants*. Englewood Cliffs, NJ: Prentice-Hall.
———. 1969. *Peasant Wars of the Twentieth Century*. New York: Harper.
———. 1983. *Europe and the People Without History*. Berkeley: University of California Press.
———, and Sidney W. Mintz. 1957. "Haciendas and Plantations in Middle America and the Antilles." *Social and Economic Studies* 6:380–412.
Womack, John. 1969. *Zapata and the Mexican Revolution*. New York: Knopf.
Zavala, Lorenzo de. 1985. *Ensayo histórico de las revoluciones de México desde*

1808 hasta 1830. Mexico City: Fondo de Cultura Económica. (Orig. pub. 1831–32.)

Zavala, Silvio A. 1967. *Contribución a la historia de las instituciones coloniales en Guatemala.* Guatemala City: Universidad de San Carlos de Guatemala.

———. 1978. *El servicio personal de los indios en el Perú: Extractos del Siglo XVI.* Mexico City: El Colegio de México.

———. 1984–. *El servicio personal de los indios en la Nueva España, 1521–1550.* Mexico City: El Colegio de México.

———. 1988. *Estudios acerca de la historia del trabajo en México: Homenaje del Centro de Estudios Históricos a Silvio Zavala.* Mexico City: El Colegio de México.

———. 1992. *La encomienda indiana*, 3rd ed., rev. Mexico City: Editorial Porrúa. (Orig. pub. 1935.)

———. 1994. *Los esclavos indios en Nueva España.* 3rd ed., revised. Mexico City: Colegio Nacional.

Zavala, Silvio A., et al. 1987. *Peones, conciertos y arrendamientos en América Latina.* Bogotá: Centro Editorial, Universidad Nacional de Colombia.

Zermeño, Guillermo. 1993. "Presentación." *Historia y Grafía* 1:3–4.

Index

Abad y Queipo, Manuel, 114
Abascal, José Fernando de, 189–90, 190n, 192n
Acordada, 111
Adams, David B., 240n
Adams, Henry, 161
Adams, Richard Newbold, 195
Adas, Michael, 206n8
Adelman, Jeremy, 69, 158, 160n
Adorno, Rolena, 213
African slavery, 53, 56, 61, 63, 71, 98; abolition of, 74, 75; in Brazil, 57, 68n, 74–80, 181n15; and coffee production, 55; in Mexico, 23, 37, 38n, 48, 74, 78–79, 107–8; and sugar production, 23, 37, 38n, 48, 68n, 74, 78–79, 181n15
Afro-Mestizos, 107–8
agency: in cultural history, 9, 87–88, 107, 214–15, 250, 250n; hyper-agentialism, 200, 214–15, 250n; relationship to culture, 244–46; of subalterns, 25, 51, 71, 87–88, 107, 108, 124, 149, 156, 158, 244–46, 250
Age of Revolution periodization (1750–1850): and Argentina, 70–71; and Brading, 90n12, 94, 147–48; and Mexico, 89–90, 90n12, 92, 94, 106, 147, 149, 155–56, 162. *See also* colonial/national divide
Aguayo Spencer, Rafael, 7n

Aguirre, Carlos, 78
Aguirre Beltrán, Gonzalo, 56n3, 64, 78, 231
Alamán, Lucas, 137, 151n; autobiographical writings, 4nn4,5, 5–6, 7; biographies of, 1, 4n5, 5, 13, 16; vs. Bulnes, 131n; vs. Bustamante, 128, 129, 136, 147; on Hidalgo, 139n11; *Historia de México*, 4n6, 6–7, 6n11, 127–28, 127n; as historian, 1–2, 3–5, 4n6; as letter writer, 4–5, 4n6, 7, 7n; on memoirs and autobiographies, 3–4; "Memorias de D. Lucas Alamán," 3–4, 4nn4,5, 5–7, 6n11; on Mexican independence movement, 1–2, 127–28, 130, 131, 132, 133, 135, 136, 139n11, 141, 151; vs. Mier, 147; vs. Mora, 135, 138; relationship with Bustamante, 129n2, 135; relationship with Mier, 134; on task of historian, 5–6; vs. Zarate, 138; vs. Lorenzo de Zavala, 134, 135, 136
Alberro, Solange, 238
alcabala, 46–47, 188n31
Alexander, Rani, 24n5, 43, 44n
Alhóndiga de Granaditas, 128
Allende, Ignacio, 210
Almada, Francisco R., 175
Almonte, Juan N., 205n6
Alperovich, M. S., 141n14
Altamirano, Ignacio Manuel, 137
altepetl, 124

316 Index

Alvarado, Pedro, 128n
Alvarado Gómez, Antonio Armando, 47
Amaral, Samuel, 67, 69
Amaya Topete, Jesús, 57n
Ameca Valley, 57n
American Revolution, 131, 159n24, 161
Americas, The, 93, 242n19
Amith, Jonathan, 38, 62
anachronisms, 235–36, 257
Andean region, 55, 60–61, 69, 145n; Andean verticality, 62; encomiendas in, 64; labor systems in, 57; *reparto/repartimiento de mercancías* in, 65; sugar production in, 74. See also Bolivia; Chile; Peru
Anderson, Arthur J. O., 124n51, 125n
Anderson, Benedict: *Imagined Communities*, 150n, 156n20, 176; on print capitalism, 143
Andrien, Kenneth J., 239
Anglophone historians: attitudes regarding Mexico among, 83–85, 84nn2,3, 145–46; and colonial/national divide, 89–90, 90n12, 91n15, 108–9, 146–47; vs. Hispanophone historians, 13, 16, 26–27, 32–33, 55, 60, 86, 90n13, 92n18, 99, 103n, 125, 130, 140, 144, 145, 148, 150, 161–63
Anna, Timothy, 91n15, 148, 151–52, 151n, 153, 155, 157n, 159
Annales-school historians, 89, 142, 175, 247
Annino, Antonio, 141, 143, 158
Antequera, 171, 178n10
anthropology: and cultural history, 24, 24nn4,5, 25, 26, 38, 39, 50, 61, 83, 89, 100–101, 103, 109, 125, 169n2, 171, 226, 227–28, 234, 237, 239, 253, 258, 258n29, 263; ethnography, 200, 200n, 202–3, 204, 211–13, 227–28, 234, 237, 258n29; Spiro on, 223
Appadurai, Arjun, 71

Appleby, Joyce, 107n, 184n20, 186n27, 228n4
Aranovich, Carmen, 182n16
Archer, Christon I., 91n15, 112, 157n; *The Army in Bourbon Mexico*, 152
Archivo General de la Nación, 151, 151n
Archivo Municipal de Saltillo, 240n
Argentina, 59, 59n7, 62, 64, 184n21; agrarian capitalism in, 69; agricultural labor force in, 53–54; Buenos Aires province, 68, 69, 71; export economy of, 55, 66–71, 183; gauchos, 68, 71; Jujuy province, 69; landownership in, 68–70; livestock industry, 68, 69, 183; vs. Mexico, 69, 70, 79; pampas, 37, 55, 57, 59n7, 68, 69, 71; as Río de la Plata region, 61, 68, 69, 70, 72n; Salta province, 71; sheep industry in, 69–70; Tucumán province, 71; wheat production in, 69, 183
Armendares, Teresa Locano, 132n5
Arnold, Linda, 106, 148, 246
Arrom, Silvia, 89, 108, 111, 238
Artís Espriu, Gloria, 48
Asociación Mexicana de Historia Económica, 87n
Assadourian, Carlos Sempat, 62, 70, 177, 194
Aston, T. H., 29
Australia, 145
Ávila, Alfredo, 132n5, 140–41, 140n12, 141n13, 143, 158
Ávila Palafox, Ricardo, 39
Axel, Brian Keith, 24n4, 110n, 136n, 253
Aztecs, 36, 103, 118, 128, 136, 138, 235, 236; Gibson's *Aztecs under Spanish Rule*, 120, 121–22, 124, 231, 239

Bacigalupo, Marvyn Helen, 108n41
Bajío, the, 35, 49, 154, 168, 171–72, 188n31, 189; Brading's *Haciendas and Ranchos in the Mexican Bajío*,

21n, 27, 33, 40, 41, 60, 90n12, 98, 114; during independence movement, 195
Bakewell, Peter J., 65, 103n
Balmori, Diana, 42
Balsas River Depression, 38, 108n40
bananas, 67
Bancroft, H. H., 146
Banda Oriental, 71
banditry, 23, 153, 212n
Banfield, Edward C., 255
Barabas, Alicia M., 242n18
Barham, Bradford, 72
Barickman, Bert, 75
Barkin, David, 196
Barragán López, Esteban, 43
Barrett, Elinor M., 103n
Barrett, Ward, 34, 78–79, 184n22
Barsky, Osvaldo, 69
Baskes, Jeremy, 28, 33, 47, 65, 103–4
Bassols Batalla, Angel, 175
Bataillon, Claude, 175, 180n, 182n16
Bauer, Arnold J., 47, 49, 55, 60, 63, 66n14; on history of rural Mexico, 24n6, 50–51
Bazant, Jan, 43, 60
Beals, Carleton, 138
Beard, Charles, 161
Becker, Marjorie, 228n5, 257n
Beezley, William H., 102n35, 107, 132n6, 148, 230, 234, 242n19
Behar, Ruth, 226
Belaúnde Guinassi, Manuel, 64
Benjamin, Thomas, 175
Bennett, Herman, 108
Benson, Nettie Lee, 143, 148
Berdan, Frances, 125n
Bergad, Laird W., 73, 75, 77
Berkhofer, Robert F., Jr., 228n4
Bernstein, Harry, 168n, 170n
Berry, Brian J. L., 169n2, 172n, 178, 178n9; on markets, 182
biases, cultural, 200
biographies, 130, 143, 149, 150–51, 155, 239, 249; of Alamán, 1–2, 4n5, 5, 13, 16; autobiographies, 3–4, 4nn4,5, 5, 5n9, 109n; as out of fashion, 96, 106n, 114, 125, 145
Bitrán Goren, Yael, 132n5
Blanchard, Peter, 78
Bloch, Marc, 11, 29, 35, 57, 58; *Feudal Society*, 30n; *French Rural History*, 30n; *The Historian's Craft*, 5n8
Bolívar, Simón, 127, 127n, 136
Bolivia: agriculture in, 61n9; silver mining in, 64–65, 70
Bolton-Johnson Prize, 94n21
Bonnell, Victora E., 88n8
Booker, Jackie, 106
Book of Tributes, The, 123
Borah, Woodrow W., 43, 94n22, 105, 191n33; *Essays in Population History*, 104; on General Indian Court, 110, 239
Borde, Jean, 57n
Boserup, Ester, 33
Bourdieu, Pierre, 232
Bowser, Frederick P., 78
Boyer, Richard, 108n41, 109, 238
Bracamonte y Sosa, Pedro, 45, 239
Brading, David A., 5n9, 26, 27n, 35, 36, 99, 103n, 133, 135, 171, 172, 191n34, 196, 249; and Age of Revolution periodization (1750–1850), 90n12, 94, 147–48; *Church and State in Bourbon Mexico*, 114, 115; on Creole patriotism, 147; *The First America*, 115, 116n, 119, 241; *Haciendas and Ranchos in the Mexican Bajío*, 21n, 27, 33, 40, 41, 60, 90n12, 98, 114; on Mexican independence, 147–48, 159n24; *Mexican Phoenix*, 115–16, 119; *Miners and Merchants*, 106, 114; *Origins of Mexican Nationalism*, 115; on Virgin of Guadalupe, 27, 115–16, 119
Braudel, Fernand, 60, 71
Brazil, 53, 54, 69n, 145; Bahia region, 75; coffee production in, 55, 57, 73, 75, 76, 77, 183; export economy

in, 75–76, 183; independence of, 66, 67; Pernambuco region, 75; São Paulo region, 76; slavery in, 57, 68n, 74–80, 181n15; sugar production in, 55, 57, 68n15, 74, 75, 181n15, 183, 184n21
Breña, Roberto, 158
Bricker, Victoria, 231
Brinton, Crane, 151
Brown, Jonathan, 68
Brungardt, Maurice, 205n6
Buffon, Comte de, 134
Bullit, William, 236
Bulmer-Thomas, Victor, 67
Bulnes, Francisco, 131n
Burke, Edmund, 136
Burke, Michael, 151n
Burkhart, Louise, 116, 241
Bustamante, Carlos María de, 137, 138, 151n; vs. Alamán, 128, 129, 136, 147; on Mexican independence, 128–29, 130, 133, 135, 136; on Mexican national identity, 134, 137; vs. Mier, 134, 136; relationship with Alamán, 4, 129n2; vs. Lorenzo de Zavala, 133, 135
Buttimer, Anne, 177
Buve, Raymond, 39

cacao production, 72
Cahill, David, 157n
Calderón, battle of, 210, 215
Calderón, Francisco R., 32
Calero, Luis Fernando, 64
Calleja, Félix María, 204
Calvo, Thomas, 37
Cambrezy, Luc, 36
Campeche, 66
Canada, 69, 84, 145
Cañizares-Esguerra, Jorge, 95n22; *How to Write the History of the New World*, 116n
Cannadine, David, 84n2
capitalism, 29, 76, 102, 103, 143, 154, 177, 181n15, 197, 251; capitalist model of haciendas, 21–23,

22n, 34, 47, 55, 58–66, 58n6, 69, 97–98, 97n28, 254–55, 254n26
Cardoso, Ciro F. S., 60, 169n3, 171n5
Cardoso, Gerald, 108
Carmagnani, Marcello, 59, 60, 196
Carr, Barry, 170n
Carranza, Venustiano, 21n
Carroll, Patrick, 48, 78, 98, 108
Caruso, John A., 150
Castañeda, Carmen, 239
Castel, Robert, 238
Castleman, Bruce A., 48, 179
Castro Gutiérrez, Felipe, 242n18
Catholic Church, 113–14, 115n, 131n, 143, 159n24; Counter-Reformation, 117; Dominicans, 117; and elites, 261–62; Franciscans, 117; Inquisition procedures, 208, 212, 238; *juzgados de capellanías*, 255–56; land ownership by, 54; Sacrament of confession, 211n; as source of credit, 45–46, 262; wealth of, 255–56. *See also* Jesuits; religion
Caudillo and Peasant in the Mexican Revolution, 27n
Central America, 67, 73, 74, 79, 92, 185n24
central-place theory: dendritic type of marketing system in, 181, 181n14; and regionality, 34, 62, 168, 169n2, 172, 172n, 173, 173n, 177, 178, 178n9, 181, 181n14, 182, 193; solar type of marketing system in, 181, 181n14
Centro de Investigaciones y Estudios Superiores en Antropología Social (CIESAS), 240
Certeau, Michel de, 202, 232
Cerutti, Mario, 196
Cervantes, Fernando, 117, 241–42
Chalarca, José, 73
Chalco, 123
Chance, John, 44n, 100n33, 171; on Oaxaca, 38, 100, 107, 111, 178n10
Chandler, D. S., 111n43, 246

Chang-Rodríguez, Raquel, 231n11
Chartier, Roger, 202n, 247
Chayanov, A. V., 224n2
Chevalier, François: on colonial haciendas, 21n, 24, 29, 29nn11,12, 34–35, 35, 39, 40, 58–59, 58n6, 100n31, 254; *La formación de los latifundios en México*, 29, 29nn11,12, 58n5; *La formation des grands domains au Méxique*, 29nn11,12, 34, 58–59, 58nn5,6, 60
Chiapas, 117, 240; debt peonage in, 66; Zapatista uprising in, 54
Chihuahua, 27, 39, 101, 112, 113, 168n, 245
Chile, 26n8, 53, 64, 184n21; copper mining in, 67; Santiago, 60; Valle del Puangue, 57n; wheat production in, 60
Chimalpahin, 123–24, 123n, 239
Chust Calero, Manuel, 143, 158
Clarence-Smith, William Gervase, 73
class, social, 15, 25, 38, 64, 100, 136, 140n12, 147, 177, 214, 235–36; cross-class alliances, 51, 153, 155, 156, 157, 158; and independence movement, 141–42, 141n14, 153, 158; in Marxism, 141, 141n14, 149, 176, 250; relationship to action, 10, 11, 227; relationship to race, 25, 101, 107, 107n, 149, 229–30; relationship to regionality, 178–79, 179n, 181, 183, 184, 184n23, 186, 186n26, 189, 194–95, 196, 197. *See also* elites; hegemony; wealth
Clendinnen, Inga, 116–17, 235, 235n
Clifford, James, 203, 212; *Writing Culture*, 200
Cline, Howard, 185
Cline, Sarah L., 123–24, 240
Coatsworth, John, 33, 67, 85n, 159n24, 162, 191n33; on Mexican economic development, 31–32, 179, 193
cochineal, 28, 47, 65, 103–4

coffee production: in Brazil, 55, 57, 73, 75, 76, 77, 183; in Colombia, 73; in Mexico, 73
Cohen, Paul A., 234n
Colegio de México, El, 144n
Collección de documentos para la Guerra de Independencia de México, 137n
Colmenares, Germán, 78
Colombia, 61n10, 64, 66, 72, 73, 184n21
Colonial Latin American Review, 93, 225n, 231, 232
colonial/national divide, 89–90, 90n12, 91n15, 108–9, 146–47, 179, 192–93
Conference on Latin American History, 94n21, 145n
Connaughton, Brian, 89–90, 115n, 143, 159n24
Connolly, Priscilla, 179
Constitution of 1824, Mexican: Charter of 1824, 157n
Constitution of 1917, Mexican: Article 27, 21n
Constitution of Cádiz, 141, 143, 156, 156n21, 157n, 159
context of domination, 209–10, 212
Contreras, Pedro Moya de, 114
Cook, Sherburne F., 69n, 105, 171, 191n33; *Essays in Population History*, 104
Coomes, Oliver, 72
Cope, R. Douglas, 108
copper mining, 67
Cortés, Fernando, 4, 48, 128n, 135, 167
Cortés Conde, Roberto, 67
Costeloe, Michael, 148, 159
Countryman, Edward, 160n
Couturier, Edith B., 59n8, 106n
Coyoacán, 123
Crapanzano, Vincent, 212–13
Cravey, Altha, 182n17
credit, 45–46, 261, 262
Crespo, Horacio, 37, 78, 184n21

crisis del orden colonial, La, 8–10, 8n15
Crosby, Alfred W., 224n1
Cross, Harry, 191n33
Cuautla, 78, 183
Cuautla Lazarus. *See* Rodríguez, José Marcelino Pedro
Cuba, 184n21; slavery in, 56, 77; sugar production in, 77
Cuban revolution, 54, 67
Cuello, José, 240n
Cuernavaca region, 11, 37, 49, 78, 123
Culhuacán, 123
cultural history, 26–28, 55, 77, 85–88, 86n5, 88n8, 94, 94n21, 99, 110, 114–15, 116–19, 121, 124–25; agency in, 9, 87–88, 107, 214–15, 250, 250n; anachronism in, 235–36; and anthropology, 24, 24nn4,5, 25, 26, 38, 39, 50, 61, 83, 89, 100–101, 103, 109, 125, 169n2, 171, 226, 227–28, 234, 237, 239, 253, 258, 258n29, 263; characteristics of new cultural history, 229; culturalist vs. materialist interpretation of history, 8–16, 247–48, 248n, 263; definition of, 14–16, 226, 252–53; definition of culture, 242–43, 252–53; vs. fiction, 201–3, 228, 228n5; and independence movement, 145, 148, 149, 157–58, 227; in journals, 93, 225n, 231–33, 233n; localist approach of, 15, 253, 258, 259; of madness, 238; and meaning, 14–15, 85–86; mentalities in, 2, 10, 14–15, 85–86, 229, 241, 252–53, 258, 259; vs. political history, 239; reification of culture in, 242–43; relationship to colonial state, 237–39, 237n, 244, 246; relationship to dependency theory, 86n5, 228, 228n6; relationship to economic history, 8, 13–16, 17–18, 24n5, 55n1, 224–25, 227, 244, 244n, 247–63; relationship to ethnohistory, 120, 120n, 239–42; relationship to political history, 14, 225, 229, 233n, 246, 250, 262; relationship to postmodernism, 86, 87, 226, 228, 240, 253; relationship to subaltern history, 87–88, 117, 229–30, 244–46; vs. social history, 2, 86, 115, 120, 229, 231, 233n; terminology in, 231, 233; texts as sources in, 95–96, 117–18, 120, 227–28, 229, 234–38, 241, 242, 259. *See also* ethnicity; ethnohistory; gender; hermeneutic approach to history; religion
Curcio-Nagy, Linda, 242n19
Curtin, Philip D., 56n3, 74
Cushner, Nicholas, 61, 69
Cutter, Charles, 110, 239

Darnton, Robert, 202n, 234, 243
Davies, Keith A., 60
Davis, Natalie Zemon, 211n
Dean, Warren, 69n, 72, 76
Deans-Smith, Susan, 38n, 73, 86n5, 103, 160n, 225n, 242n18, 246; *Bureaucrats, Planters, and Workers*, 94n21
debt peonage, 50, 51, 65–66
deconstruction, 213, 213n, 217
Deeds, Susan M., 44, 111, 112; *Defiance and Deference*, 121
Deerr, Noel, 74
Degler, Carl N., 76
Dehouve, Danièle, 240, 249
de la Cruz, Jesse, 188n31
de la Peña, Guillermo, 42, 169n2, 171n6, 178n11, 185n23; on Morelos, 183n19, 184, 184n23, 186n27
Delpar, Helen, 84n3
del Río, Ignacio, 196; on regions, 173
De Pauw, Cornelius, 134
dependency theory, 11, 16, 59, 85, 98, 98n29, 177, 183n18, 226, 263; relationship to cultural history, 86n5, 228, 228n6
deprivation theory, 153
Derrida, Jacques: on interpretation as misinterpretation, 199

De Vos, Jan, 240
De Vos, Paula, 116n
Díaz, Porfirio, 37, 56, 94, 137, 179
dissertations, 38, 91, 91n16, 94–96, 94n22, 95n23, 96nn24,25, 108, 111n43, 116n, 150
Domínguez Michael, Christopher, 133, 160n
Dominican Republic: sugar production in, 66
Doyle, Don H., 157n
drinking behaviors, 110
Ducey, Michael, 25, 50, 144, 155, 156–57, 156n20, 157n
Duhau, Emilio, 47
Duncan, Kenneth, 66n13, 181n15, 183n18
Dunn, Richard, 77
Durango, 38, 112
Durkheim, Émile, 163
Duverger, Christian, 241

Eagleton, Terry, 200n
Eakin, Marshall, 83n
economic history, 53–55, 55n2, 77, 85n, 87n, 91, 94n21, 101–6, 102n34, 140, 145, 233n; decline in, 13, 89, 92–93, 92n18, 94, 96; feudalism/capitalism debate, 21–23, 22n, 34, 55, 58–66, 58n6, 69, 97–98, 97n28, 254–55, 254n26; and neoclassical economics, 15–16, 85, 86–87, 98; price history, 46, 66, 192, 192n; and regionality, 33, 172–73, 175; relationship to cultural history, 8, 13–16, 17–18, 24n5, 55n1, 224–25, 227, 244, 244n, 247–63; vs. social history, 2, 11, 27–28, 94, 99n, 105–6, 260
Ecuador, 61
Edelman, Marc, 73
Eisenberg, Peter, 75
ejidos, 21n
elites, 54, 105–7, 114, 117, 134, 143, 155, 156, 176, 194, 197, 229, 242, 249, 250; and Catholic Church, 261–62; *hacendados*, 34, 45, 49, 79, 186n26, 232; during independence movement, 153–54, 156; indigenous elites, 44, 64, 120, 235, 235n, 239, 240–41; as landowners, 24, 34, 41–42, 42, 45, 49, 51, 79, 186n26, 232; social reproduction of, 72, 106, 251, 255, 262
Ellis, John M., 200n, 213n
encomiendas, 63–64, 106
Enlightenment, the, 140, 141, 238, 258n30
En torno a La otra rebelión, 9n17
Entrikin, Nicholas, 177
environmental history, 28, 69n, 80, 98, 104–5, 121, 249
Epazoyuca, 216
Escobar Ohmstede, Antonio, 192n, 239
estancias, 68, 69, 70, 71, 79
ethnicity, 13, 24, 38, 85, 107, 107n, 122, 148, 178, 194; cross-ethnic alliances, 51, 153, 158; differentiation based on, 11, 110, 116, 149, 156, 229–30, 236; ethnic identity, 8, 9, 28, 96, 108, 108n40, 109, 121, 158, 211, 230, 231, 239; of *hacendados*, 45; and independence movement, 1, 9, 11–13, 158; relationship to social class, 25, 101, 107, 107n, 149, 229–30. *See also* ethnohistory; indigenous people; subaltern history
ethnohistory, 74n, 77, 91, 93, 94, 105, 110, 112, 113, 116, 226, 231, 240n, 242n18, 249; dissertations on, 96n25; emergence of, 25, 107, 119–25; native-language-based studies, 44, 86, 86nn5,6, 87, 119–20, 120n, 121–24, 122n, 240; northern branch vs. central/southern branch, 120–21; relationship to cultural history, 120, 120n, 239–42; texts as sources for, 119–20, 121–22, 123–24. *See also* rural resistance and rebellion; subaltern history

Ethnohistory, 24n5, 44n
Europe, 111, 125, 190n; agrarian history of, 11, 29–30, 33, 35, 40, 55n2, 57, 102; medieval and early modern history of, 29, 35, 40, 88, 89, 97, 106, 114, 179, 254; migration to Latin America from, 53
Ewald, Ursula, 182n16
exports: boom-and-bust cycles, 49, 53, 55, 59, 68, 69n, 72, 73, 183, 183n18; vs. domestic products, 21–22, 23, 73, 74, 180, 181, 181n15, 183, 184n21; export economies, 66–73, 75, 80; funnel/dendritic type regions, 180–81, 181n14, 183–86, 183n19, 185n24

Fagoaga Hernández, Ricardo, 47
Fajardo, Darío, 73
Falcón, Romana, 175
familism, 255, 257, 262
Farriss, Nancy M., 36, 159n24, 185n24, 231; *Maya Society under Colonial Rule*, 122, 123
federalism, 154
Ferdinand VII, 159, 215, 216, 217
Fernández, Rodolfo, 25–26, 37, 59n8; *Latifundios y grupos dominantes*, 42
Ferrer, Aldo, 68
Ferry, Robert, 71–72
feudalism, 29, 102; feudal model of haciendas, 21–23, 21n, 22n, 28, 34, 40, 55, 58–66, 58n6, 69, 70, 97–98, 97n28, 99, 254–55, 254n26
Feyerabend, Paul, 87
Fischer, Michael M. J., 200n
Fisher, Andrew, 38, 108n40, 229n7
Fisher, Lillian E., 114
Florescano, Enrique, 1, 25n, 27, 46, 66, 99, 99n, 132n5, 170, 177, 189, 190n, 241; *Memory, Myth, and Time in Mexico*, 118, 119; on Mexican historians, 90n13, 131–32, 144n, 226n; *National Narratives in Mexico*, 4n6; *El nuevo pasado mexicano*, 231; on Riva Palacio, 138
Font, Mauricio A., 56n4
Forment, Carlos, 143, 158, 160n; *Democracy in Latin America*, 90n12
Fortes, Meyer, 248n
Foucault, Michel, 202; on governmentality, 101; on regions, 177
Fournier, Jacques, 212
Fradkin, Raúl, 68, 71
Frank, André Gunder, 59, 98
Freeman, Joanne, 131
French, William E., 86n5, 107, 148, 226n, 230, 234, 242n19, 246
French Intervention, 132, 137, 146
French Revolution, 132, 137, 141, 142, 232
Freud, Sigmund, 236
Freyre, Gilberto, 57, 75, 76; *The Masters and the Slaves*, 56
friction of distance, 174, 177, 180, 195, 196, 260
Friedmann, John, 196
Friedrich, Carl, 153
Friedrich, Paul, 226
Frye, David, 239
Furet, François, 243; *Modernidad e independencias*, 142–43
Furtado, Celso, 181n15

Gamboa Ramírez, Ricardo, 39
Garavaglia, Juan Carlos, 36, 47, 62, 68n, 70, 71, 72n, 73
García Acosta, Virginia, 46, 48
García de León, Antonio, 39, 44, 242n18
García Mantínez, Bernardo, 44, 49, 172, 240n
García Ugarte, Marta Eugenia, 35, 59n8
Gardels, Nathan, 196
Garner, Richard L., 32, 62, 102, 103n, 159n24
Gasco, Janine, 225n
Geertz, Clifford, 15, 97, 234, 243, 248n; on local knowledge, 39,

100–101, 253, 258; on thick description, 39, 201
Gelman, Jorge D., 68n, 69, 70, 71, 72n
gender, 14, 15, 26n8, 55, 85, 94, 107, 109n, 148, 149, 233, 254, 257n; dissertations on, 96, 96n25, 108; gender roles, 108–9, 225, 262; Stern on, 109, 226, 230, 238, 245, 246; violence against women, 109, 226
Gerhard, Peter, 105n
Giberti, Horacio, 68
Gibson, Charles, 123; *The Aztecs under Spanish Rule,* 34, 65–66, 105, 120, 121–22, 124, 231, 239
Gilbert, Anne, 172
Gil Sánchez, Isabel, 189, 190n
Ginzburg, Carlo, 88
gold mining, 75
Goldstone, Jack, 149
Golte, Jürgen, 65
Gómez Farías, Valentín, 134
Góngora, Mario, 57n, 63, 64
Gonzales, Michael, 66
González, Luis, 38–39, 100, 152, 168n, 170n, 171n5
González Angulo Aguirre, Jorge, 194
González Jácome, Alba, 49
Gore, Charles, 177
Gorender, Jacob, 75
Gosner, Kevin, 112, 113n, 242n18
Goubert, Pierre, 11, 30, 57, 179; on localities, 170–71, 171n5
Goveia, Elsa, 77
Grafton, Anthony, 228n5
Graham, Richard, 149–50
grain production, 40, 41, 49, 58, 62, 72; maize, 21, 46, 185n25, 186, 189–90, 190n, 191n33, 192; wheat, 21, 48, 60, 67, 68, 69, 183, 191n33
Gramsci, Antonio: on hegemony, 214, 243, 246
Gran Colombia, 67
Grandin, Temple, 258n29
Great Britain, 84, 84n2, 145, 146, 149, 161
Green, Donald P., 245n

Green, Stanley, 148
Greenblatt, Stephen J., 213
Greenow, Linda, 46, 103n
Green Revolution, 68
Grigg, David, 174, 175
Grob, Gerald N., 238
Grosso, Juan Carlos, 36, 47, 192n
Grunstein, Arturo, 179
Gruzinski, Serge, 207n, 230, 248, 253; *The Conquest of Mexico,* 118–19; on conquest of the imaginary, 91, 118, 241; *Images at War,* 119; *Man-Gods in the Mexican Highlands,* 112, 113
Guadalajara region, 47, 90, 99n, 168, 171, 181n15, 194; agrarian history of, 8, 10–11, 28, 29, 36–37, 62; Battle of Calderón, 210, 215; during colonial period, 1, 2, 10–11, 32, 34, 36–37, 62n, 249; exports from, 189–91, 190n; haciendas of, 11, 23–24, 27–28, 34, 36–37, 51, 62, 248; during independence movement, 1, 2, 28, 152–53, 154, 215; indigenous people in, 28, 248; as pressure cooker/solar type, 183, 183n19, 187, 188–92, 188nn31,32, 192n; sugar production in, 78
Guanajuato region, 35, 37, 47, 128, 143, 153, 171
guano mining, 60, 67
Guardino, Peter, 25, 50, 91n15, 144, 155–56, 156n20, 157n
Guarisco, Claudia, 144
Guatemala, 44n, 64, 73, 112, 186n27
Gudmundson, Lowell, 73
Guedea, Virginia, 132n5, 141, 141n13, 144, 158, 206n7
Guerra, François-Xavier, 141, 142–43, 159
Guerrero (state), 44n2, 155–56, 240, 249
Guerrero, Andrés, 64, 65, 72, 157n, 263
Guerrero, Vicente, 129n, 132n5, 135, 138

Guha, Ranajit, 212
Gutiérrez Brockington, Lolita, 40, 48, 66, 98
Guzmán Pérez, Moisés, 143

Haber, Stephen, 24n5, 85n, 86n5, 98n29, 226, 226n, 229n8
Hacienda and Market in Eighteenth-Century Mexico, 17
Hacienda de Guaracha, 41
haciendas, 17, 24nn5,6, 26n7, 79, 125, 187n30; capitalist model of, 21–23, 22n, 34, 47, 55, 58–66, 58n6, 69, 97–98, 97n28, 254–55, 254n26; during colonial period, 22, 22n, 24, 25n, 29, 29nn11,12, 31–39, 40, 41–45, 44n, 47–49, 50–51, 59, 59n8, 61–62, 99, 254; after colonial period, 22, 31n, 39, 40–41, 44n, 45, 47, 49, 50, 59n8, 61–62, 97–101; credit sources, 45–46; feudal model of, 21–23, 21n, 22n, 28, 34, 40, 55, 58–66, 58n6, 69, 70, 97–98, 97n28, 99, 254–55, 254n26; generalizing approach to, 33, 39–40; of Guadalajara region, 11, 23–24, 27–28, 34, 36–37, 51, 62, 248; *hacendados,* 34, 45, 49, 79, 186n26, 232; of Jesuits, 40, 41, 54, 61; labor sources, 23, 26, 31, 33, 34, 35, 42, 43, 44, 45, 47–49, 50, 51, 60, 78; and regions, 33–39, 51, 62; relationship to location, 33–39; relationship to markets, 21–23, 28, 32, 33, 34–35, 40, 41, 42, 45, 46, 47, 48–49, 51, 57, 58–66, 97n28, 254–55; relationship to mining, 31, 35–36, 58; relationship to other production units, 42–45; relations with indigenous communities, 23, 25, 37, 40, 42, 44–45, 50, 54, 61, 65–66, 78, 79, 248; single-estate approach to, 35, 39–40, 41, 51; sources regarding, 25, 29, 36, 37, 41–43, 48, 49, 51, 61, 61n10, 99; technology utilized by, 26, 37, 40, 41, 48–49

Haiti, 67
Hale, Charles, 148
Halperín Donghi, Tulio, 67
Hamill, Hugh M., Jr.: *The Hidalgo Revolt,* 91n15, 150–51, 155
Hamnett, Brian, 12, 50, 65, 91n15, 102n35, 103–4, 159, 204n; *Roots of Insurgency,* 152–53, 154, 157; vs. Tutino, 154
Handler, Jerome, 77
Hardoy, Jorge E., 182n16
Harland, Richard, 200n
Harris, Charles, III, 66n13, 98, 249
Harris, Marvin, 76
Hart, Paul, 79
Haskett, Robert, 109, 123, 240
Haslip-Viera, Gabriel, 111
Hassig, Ross, 62, 103, 180, 187n30, 191n33
Hawaii, 237
health/medicine, 96, 116n
hegemony, 216–17, 244–45; Gramsci on, 214, 243, 246
henequen production, 66, 67, 168n, 183, 185–86, 185n24; Wells on, 68n, 72, 183n19, 185, 186nn26,27
hermeneutic approach to history, 199, 226, 247–48, 250, 251, 257, 259, 263. *See also* cultural history
Hernández Sáenz, Luz María, 116n
Hernández y Dávalos, Juan E., 137n
Herrejón Peredo, Carlos, 142, 143
Herrera, Robinson, 64
Herrera Canales, Inés, 103n
Herrero Bervera, Carlos, 12, 141, 144
Hidalgo (state), 156
Hidalgo y Costilla, Miguel, 136, 137, 141, 150, 207; attitudes of historians regarding, 128, 132, 134–35, 151, 152; during independence movement, 128, 134–35, 139–40, 142, 143, 151, 152, 206; physical appearance, 139n11
Hilario, Pablo, 216
Himmelfarb, Gertrude, 228n4
Himmerich y Valencia, Robert, 64, 106

Hispanic American Historical Review (HAHR), 92n19, 93n20, 226n; colonial Mexico in, 92–93, 94n21; cultural history in, 9, 86n5, 94, 94n21, 233, 233n, 246; economic history in, 13, 92, 93, 94, 94n21
histoire événementielle, 155
histoire totale approach, 38, 54, 100
historia de bronce, 155, 160, 161
Historia de los pueblos indígenas de México, 240, 240n
Historia Mexicana, 9n17, 87n, 92n18
Historia y Grafía, 225n, 231–32, 231n11
historical demography, 104
historical geography, 100, 104, 105n
history as craft, 5–6, 7–8, 84n2, 137–38. *See also* dissertations
history of ideas, 116n, 142–43
history of medicine, 116n
history of science, 116n, 230
Hoberman, Louisa Schell, 49, 53, 106, 229, 249
Hobsbawm, Eric J., 5n9, 153, 229
Hoekstra, Rik, 38, 100, 240n
Horn, Rebecca, 123–24, 240
Huacuja Rountree, Mario, 36, 59n8
Huasteca, the, 11, 47, 156–57, 168, 172
Hu-DeHart, Evelyn, 38, 100, 112, 240
Hugo, Victor, 209n
Hulme, Peter, 213
Humboldt, Alexander von, 133
Hume, David, 258n30
Hunt, Lynn, 24n4, 88n8, 107n, 228n4, 243, 247
hyperagentialism, 200, 214–15, 215, 250n

Ibargüengoitia, Jorge, 139
Ibarra, Ana Carolina, 143
Ibarra Romero, Antonio, 46, 62, 87n, 92n18, 144; on Guadalajara region, 32, 33, 47, 62n, 192n
identity, personal and collective, 14, 85, 228, 254, 261; ethnic identity, 8, 9, 28, 96, 108, 108n40, 109, 121, 158, 211, 230, 231, 239; localist identity, 8, 100–101, 170–71, 230, 239; Mexican national identity, 27, 134, 135, 138–39, 196
Iglesias, Esther, 36
Iguala Valley, 38
Ilhui Pacheco Chávez, María Antonieta, 137n
imports, 193; import substitution industrialization, 68, 72
Incas, 236
Independence day celebrations, 132n6
independence movement, 84, 91, 91n15, 92, 99, 110, 114, 146–47, 159n24; Alamán on, 1–2, 127–28, 130, 131, 132, 133, 135, 136, 139n11, 141, 151; vs. American Revolution, 131, 159n24; Bustamante on, 128–29, 130, 133, 135, 136; and cultural history, 145, 148, 149, 157–58, 227; historiography of, 12, 12n, 16; indigenous people during, 1, 9, 11–13, 144, 158; materialist vs. culturalist interpretation of, 8–9; messianic expectation during, 205, 206, 207, 207n, 215; middle-class professionals in, 142; motivation of insurgents during, 8–9, 153–54, 156, 199, 212, 213, 217, 218, 227; origins of, 11–13, 23, 31, 107n, 128–29, 130, 133–34, 139–42, 150–51, 152–54, 156, 158–59, 195, 217, 227; and political culture, 148–49, 155, 156, 161, 162; and political history, 140–41, 140n12, 142–43, 144, 148, 155–59, 161, 162; and regionality, 152–54; siege of Cuautla, 204; and social class, 141–42, 141n14, 153, 158; and social history, 91n15, 143–44, 145, 148, 149, 150, 151; sources regarding, 199; and subaltern politics, 155–59, 162
Indian Women of Early Mexico, 109

indigenous people, 93, 112, 121, 136, 231, 249; attitudes regarding monarchism among, 215–17, 218; collective memory among, 110, 118; and colonial legal system, 110; elites among, 44, 64, 120, 235, 235n, 239, 240–41; General Indian Court, 110, 239; during independence movement, 1, 9, 11–13, 144, 158; and Mexican national identity, 134, 135, 137, 138–39; native imaginary, 51, 110, 118, 241; population decline, 65–66, 103, 104, 105; relations with *encomenderos*, 63–64, 64n, 65; relations with haciendas, 23, 25, 37, 40, 42, 44–45, 50, 54, 61, 65–66, 78, 79, 248; and religion, 54, 91, 113–14, 115–19, 122, 241–42; slavery of, 63, 64n
inductivism, 229
inequality, social and economic, 54, 110
Inquisition procedures, 208, 212, 238
institutional history, 13, 113–14, 115n; definition of institutions, 260–61; and Douglass North, 14, 15–16, 69, 103, 103n, 258, 260
Instituto Nacional Indigenista, 240
intellectual history, 86, 99, 117, 119, 233n, 241
Iriarte, Rafael, 131
irony, 230, 230n10
irrigation, 40, 49, 196
Irving, Washington, 146
Isard, Walter, 169n2, 170, 176
Isthmus of Tehuantepec, 48
Iturbide, Agustín de, 131, 132, 132n6, 135, 150, 151n
Iturrigaray, José de, 133

Jackson, Robert H., 61n9
Jacob, Margaret, 107n, 228n4
Jacobs, Ian, 175
Jacobsen, Nils, 32, 72, 102n34, 159n24

Jaffary, Nora, 96n24
Jalisco (state), 112, 137n
James, Henry, 85, 223, 263
Jansenism, 114
Jara, Alvaro, 63
Jarquín Ortega, María T., 39
Jesuits, 70, 232; landownership by, 40, 41, 54, 61, 61n10
Jiménez Pelayo, Agueda, 45, 598
Johnson, Lyman, 46, 66, 239
Jones, Gareth Stedman, 248n
Jones, Grant, 112, 242n18
Joseph, Gilbert M., 23n, 25, 45, 86nn5,6, 156n20, 186n26, 212n, 237
Journal of Latin American Studies, 93
Joyce, Arthur, 44n
Juana Inés de la Cruz, Sor, 232
Juan Diego, St., 115
Juárez, Benito, 137, 139
Juchipila, 215

Kanigel, Robert, 224n1
Kartunnen, Frances, 125n
Katz, Friedrich, 66n13, 230
Kay, Cristóbal, 59
Keen, Benjamin, 92n17
Keith, Robert G., 60
Kellogg, Susan, 110, 122n, 239
Kicza, John, 41–42, 106, 225n, 229, 249
King, Timothy, 196
Kinsbruner, Jay, 150
kinship, 24, 64, 236, 260, 261, 262
Klarén, Peter, 66, 76, 185n23
Klein, Herbert S., 62, 74, 74n, 76, 77
Klor de Alva, J. Jorge, 211n
Knight, Alan, 9n17, 22n, 24n5, 59, 89n11, 97n28, 102, 155, 157, 246; on the colonial hacienda, 32, 33, 254n26; on cultural history, 86n5; *The Mexican Revolution*, 153; "Subalterns, Signifiers, and Statistics," 86n5
Knight, Franklin, 77
Konrad, Herman W., 61, 95n22, 98

Korth, Eugene H., 63
Kramer, Wendy, 64
Krippner-Martínez, James, 119; *Rereading the Conquest*, 117–18
Kroeber, Clifton L., 196
Kuhn, Thomas, 230
Kuntz Ficker, Sandra, 85n, 179
Kyle, Chris, 44n

La Barca, 188
labor: as coerced, 23, 34, 35, 45, 47–48, 59, 63–66, 103; corvée labor, 63, 64–65; debt peonage, 50, 51, 65–66; *enganche* system, 66; as free wage-labor, 34, 35, 43, 47–48, 61, 63, 65, 79, 108; indigenous slavery, 63, 64n; labor tribute, 63–64, 65; percentage of labor force in agriculture, 53–54; social division of, 180, 193, 194; wages, 66, 225, 251, 253–54. *See also* African slavery
Ladd, Doris, 41, 103, 106, 159n24, 229, 235–36, 249
Lafaye, Jacques, 115, 242n18
Lake Chapala, 112
Lake Chapala basin, 1, 28, 37, 57n
Landázuri Benítez, Gisela, 37, 78
land ownership, 54
land sales, small-scale, 251, 252–53
land suits, 14–15
Lange, Frederick, 77
Langley, Lester, 150, 160n
language: instability of meaning in, 200, 204, 217, 218; linguistic turn in social sciences, 26, 86, 118, 122, 124, 125, 200, 212–13, 228; multivocality of, 203, 217; native-language-based ethnohistory, 44, 86, 86nn5,6, 87, 119–20, 120n, 121–24, 122n, 240; relationship to power, 241; relationship to reality, 87, 203–4, 212, 216–18, 219; vocabulary change, 13, 92, 93–94, 95–96, 253
Langue, Frédérique, 21n, 31n, 35–36, 59n8

Lara, Silvia H., 77
Larson, Brooke, 61n9
Laslett, Peter, 197
Latin American Research Review, 93
Laviada, Iñigo, 40
Lavrin, Asunción, 108, 238
Lazarus of Cuautla. *See* Rodríguez, José Marcelino Pedro
Leal, Juan Felipe, 36, 59n8
Lefebvre, Henri, 177
Le Grand, Catherine, 73
Lemoine Villicaña, Ernesto, 142
León-Portilla, Miguel, 123
Le Roy Ladurie, Emmanuel, 11, 30, 35, 57, 248; *Montaillou*, 211
letter writing, 2–3, 4–5
Levene, Ricardo, 68
Lévy-Strauss, Claude, 169
Lewis, Laura, 95n22, 109
liberalism, 134, 135, 138, 139, 139n10, 141, 147, 152; liberal reforms, 56, 57, 132, 137, 146, 261
Licate, Jack, 36, 104
Lindley, Richard, 37, 59n8, 98, 249
Lindo Fuentes, Héctor, 192, 192n
Lipsett-Rivera, Sonya, 28, 36, 59n8, 98
Liss, Peggy, 149–50
Liverman, Diana, 182n17
livestock production, 21, 22, 43, 58, 61, 62, 62n, 65, 67, 73, 80, 185n24, 190n; in Argentina, 68, 69–70, 183; sheep, 28, 69–70, 69n, 94n21, 98, 105, 249
Llanos de Apan, 144
localities, 27, 35, 38–39, 152, 153, 176; Goubert on, 170–71, 171n5; local history, 56n4, 100–101, 109, 137n, 141, 167, 168n, 171n5, 174–75, 253; localist approach of cultural history, 15, 87, 253, 258, 259; localist identities, 8, 100–101, 170–71, 230, 239; local knowledge, 39, 87, 100–101, 253; local politics, 156, 157, 158
location theory, 169n2, 182n16

Lockhart, James, 44, 105, 115, 120n, 122, 124n52, 125n, 191n34; influence of, 121, 123, 240–41; *Nahuas after the Conquest*, 124–25
Loera, Margarita, 44
Lomnitz, Larissa Adler, 249
Lomnitz-Adler, Claudio, 86n5, 102n35, 150n, 170n
longue durée approach, 239
López de Albornoz, Cristina, 71
López Martínez, Jesús, 47, 192n
López Rayón brothers, 131
Lorey, David, 132n6
Love, Joseph, 168n
Lozano Armendares, Teresa, 239
Lukacs, George, 256, 257; *History and Class Consciousness*, 251n
Lynch, John, 69, 132n5, 149–50, 157n

MacLachlan, Colin, 111
MacLeod, Murdo, 44n, 112, 120n, 185n24
Madero, Francisco I., 21n, 139
maize, 21, 46, 185n25, 186, 189–90, 190n, 191n33, 192
Malinowski, Bronislaw, 237
Mallon, Florencia E., 50, 86n5, 156n20
Mandrini, Raúl, 71
Maniquis, Robert M., 141
Marchal, Yves, 36
Marcus, George: *Writing Culture*, 200
María de San José, 109n
markets, 103, 146, 196, 260; and central-place theory, 181, 181n14, 182; and indigenous peasants, 46–47; market periodicity, 187–88, 187n30; and regions, 175; relationship to haciendas, 21–23, 28, 32, 33, 34–35, 40, 41, 42, 45, 46, 47, 48–49, 51, 57, 58–66, 60, 61–62, 97n28, 254–55; and urbanization, 62, 62n. *See also* exports; neoclassical economics
Markusen, Ann R., 176, 196

Marrero, Leví, 77
marriage, 15, 109
Marroquín, Agustín, 131
Martí, Oscar R., 141
Martin, Cheryl, 103n, 107, 148, 172, 183n19, 230, 234, 242n19; on Chihuahua, 39, 101, 245; on colonial Morelos sugar industry, 37, 78, 98, 101, 108, 184, 184n23; scholarly trajectory, 26, 27, 101
Martínez Assad, Carlos, 39
Martínez Rosales, Alfonso, 40
Martínez Vegazo, Lucas, 64
Marxism, 16, 23, 59, 75, 85, 85n, 133, 139, 161, 200n, 256; capitalism in, 63; and regionalism, 196; social class in, 141, 141n14, 149, 176, 250
Mata de López, Sara, 71
materialist interpretation of history, 32, 113, 124–25, 158, 226, 227, 250, 256; vs. culturalist interpretation of history, 8–16, 247–48, 248n, 263
Maya: language, 121, 122; Restall's *Life and Death in a Maya Community*, 122n; in Yucatán, 111, 112, 113n, 116–17, 119, 122, 235
Mayo, Carlos, 70
mayorazgos, 255
McBride, George McCutcheon, 42
McCreery, David, 73
McFarlane, Anthony, 157n
McGreevey, William P., 73, 184n21
McWatters, David Lorne, 38n
Mead, Margaret, 237
Medina Rubio, Arístides, 36, 59n8
"Meeting of Economic and Cultural History, The," 17–18
Megged, Amos, 117
Melville, Elinor, 49, 69n, 95n22, 104, 105; *A Plague of Sheep*, 28, 94n21, 98, 249
memoirs: Alamán on, 3–4; "Memorias de D. Lucas Alamán," 3–4, 4nn4,5, 5–7, 6n11

memory, collective, 110, 118, 144, 160
Méndez G., Cecilia, 156n20
Menegus Bornemann, Margarita, 40, 49, 240n
mentalities, 229, 241, 252–53, 258, 259. *See also* motivation
Mentz, Brígida von, 37, 48
mercantilism, 67
merchants, 106
mestizos, 138–39, 158
Metcalf, Alida, 75–76
Mexican-American War, 94, 127, 129, 157
Mexican Creoles, 115, 133, 134, 141, 147, 151, 152, 159
Mexican museums, 232
Mexican national identity, 27, 134, 135, 138–39, 196
Mexican nationalism, 115, 118, 196, 242n18
Mexican psychiatry, 2
"Mexican Rural History since Chevalier," 17, 30
Mexican Studies/Estudios Mexicanos, 89, 89n10, 93, 232–33
Mexico City, 47, 62n11, 91, 106, 107, 108, 151, 152, 157n, 171n5, 193, 244n; class relations in, 194–95; crime in, 111, 111n43; Los Guadalupes, 144; as market for Morelos sugar, 183–84, 184n21; Poor House, 89, 111; public entertainments in, 238; San Francisco de Borja, 41. *See also* Valley of Mexico
Mexico (state), 156
Meyer, Jean, 39, 50, 139
Meyer, Michael C., 102n35, 104, 105
Meyer Cosío, Rosa María, 42
Meyers, Kathleen, 109n
Mezquital Valley, 28, 69n, 98, 104, 105, 249
Michoacán region, 37, 47, 78, 117, 153, 168n, 189; cotton production in, 187n29; diocese of Michoacán, 114; popular *cardenismo* in, 257n; as pressure cooker/solar type, 183, 183n19, 187–88, 192n; and salt trade, 187n29
Mier Noriega y Guerra, Servando Teresa de, 130, 132, 132n5, 137, 147, 151n; vs. Alamán, 134; vs. Bustamante, 134, 136; *Historia de la Revolución de Nueva España,* 133–34
Mier y Terán, Manuel, 4
Mignolo, Walter, 241, 248; *Darker Side of the Renaissance,* 119
migration patterns, 171
Miller, Simon, 21n, 25, 40, 44, 62
Miño Grijalva, Manuel, 32, 33, 44, 46, 62, 192n, 244n
Mintz, Sidney, 26n7, 33, 61–62, 74
Miranda, José, 64
mita, 64–65
Mixtec, 119, 121, 122
modernity, 149; modernization, 142–43; modernization theory, 85
Molina Enríquez, Andrés, 57; *Los grandes problemas nacionales,* 56; on haciendas, 21–22, 58; during Revolution, 21n
Monaghan, John, 44n
Monsiváis, Carlos, 182n17
Montoya, Alfredo, 68
Moore, Barrington, Jr., 149; *Injustice,* 153; *Social Origins of Dictatorship and Democracy,* 153
Mora, José María Luis, 130, 137; vs. Alamán, 135, 138; *México y sus revoluciones,* 133, 134–35
moral topography, 176, 177
Morán Leyva, Paola, 4n5
Morelos (state), 108; as funnel/dendritic region, 183–84, 183n19, 184n23; lowlands in, 23, 154, 183, 184n23, 186n27; sugar production in, 23, 27, 37, 78–79, 98, 101, 168, 183–84, 183n19, 184n23, 185
Morelos y Pavón, José María, 12, 132, 135, 142, 150; and Cuautla Lazarus, 199, 204, 205, 205n6, 206–8, 218

Moreno, Pedro, 131
Moreno Cebrián, Alfredo, 65
Moreno Fraginals, Manuel, 77
Moreno García, Heriberto, 37, 39, 41, 59n8
Moreno Toscano, Alejandra, 170, 177, 188n31
Morin, Claude, 168n, 183n19, 187, 187n30, 188, 192n
Mörner, Magnus, 61, 181n15
Morse, Richard M., 188n31, 191n34
motivation, 219, 251, 259; and cultural history, 229; economic vs. noneconomic, 254, 255, 256–57, 262; of insurgents, 8–9, 142n, 153–54, 156, 199, 212, 213, 217, 218, 227; and overdetermination, 225, 262
Moulaert, Frank, 176, 177
mule transport, 48
Mundy, Barbara, 105
Murphy, Arthur D., 100n33
Murphy, Michael E., 49, 59n8, 98n30
Murra, John V., 62

Nahuatl, 115, 119, 121, 122, 122n, 123, 124, 240
Namala, Doris M., 96n24
Napoleon I, 133
Naro, Nancy, 77
Nash, Gary, 161
Naveda Chávez-Hita, Adriana, 48, 78
neoclassical economics, 251, 260; and economic history, 15–16, 85, 86, 98; and regionality, 174, 177
neoliberalism, 21n, 72
New Philology, 119n, 122n
Nicaraguan revolution, 67
Nickel, Herbert, 21n, 25–26, 48, 66n13, 191n33; *Morfología social de la hacienda mexicana*, 39–40, 58n6
nonlognormality, 183, 184n21, 188, 188n31, 195
normative values, 14, 16, 136, 225, 252, 254, 257, 262

North, Douglass, 14, 15–16, 69, 103, 103n, 258, 260
Nueva Vizcaya, 112
Núñez, Jacinto, 215, 215n
Nunn, Charles, 106
Nuño de Guzmán, Beltrán, 117

Oaxaca, 27, 36, 44n, 107, 143, 156, 240; cochineal production in, 28, 47, 65, 103–4; colonial Mixtecs of, 122; race relations in, 38, 100; Sierra Zapoteca, 111
Obeyesekere, Gananath, 237
objectivity, 135–36, 138, 144n, 202, 203, 212, 219, 259–60
obrajes, 103
Ocampo, José Antonio, 73
Oddone, Jacinto, 68
Offutt, Leslie, 39, 101, 240n
O'Hara, Matthew, 96n26, 115n, 228n7, 229
Ohnuki-Tierney, Emiko, 24n4
Olsen, Stephen M., 178n11
Ortega, Sergio, 238
Ortiz, Fernando, 57; *Cuban Counterpoint*, 56, 56n4
Ortiz de la Tabla Ducasse, Javier, 64
Ortiz Escamilla, Juan, 141, 143–44
Ortiz Monasterio, José, 132n5, 138, 138n
Osorno, Francisco, 131
Other Rebellion, The, 2, 6n16, 8, 10–13, 17
outcomism, 160–61
Ouweneel, Arij, 32, 33, 44, 62, 102, 159n24, 244n, 249
overdetermination, 219, 225, 237, 254, 256, 262

Pachuca silver mines, 235–36
Paéz, Norma, 140n11
Palacios, Marco, 73
Palm, Gabriel, 60
Palmer, Bryan D., 88n8, 200n, 228n4
Palmer, Colin: *Slaves of the White God*, 78, 108

Pamplona, Marco Antonio, 157n
Paraguay, 64, 70; *yerba mate* industry in, 73
Pares, Richard, 77
Parkman, Francis, 200
Parkman, George, 200, 201
Pastor, Rodolfo, 36, 172
Patch, Robert W., 113n; on Yucatán, 36, 59n8, 98, 112, 183n19, 185, 185n24
Patterson, Orlando, 77
Pátzcuaro, 187
Pennick, Adrian, 196
Pérez, Joseph, 141
Pérez, Luciano, 209
Pérez Brignoli, Héctor, 60, 73
Pérez Herrero, Pedro, 32, 34, 62n, 173, 177, 182n17, 195
Pérez Lizaur, Marisol, 249
Pérez Verdía, Luis, 175
periodization. *See* Age of Revolution periodization; colonial/national divide
Pernambuco, 108
Peru, 26n8, 58n6, 76, 156n20; Arequipa region, 60; guano export industry, 60, 67, 183; Jesuits in, 61; land reform in, 67; vs. Mexico, 193–94; silver mining in, 53, 60, 67; slavery abolished in, 74; sugar production in, 61, 66, 74, 183, 185n23; wine production in, 61; wool exports, 72, 184n20
Peterson, Jeanette, 241
petroleum, 183
Philpin, C. H. E., 29
Piccato, Pablo, 3n
Piel, Jean, 58n6, 60, 61, 69
Piqueras, José A., 77
Pizarro, Francisco, 129n2
Plan of Texcoco, 21n
Plant, Roger, 66
Poinsett, Joel R., 135, 146
Polanyi, Karl: on economic vs. emotional motives, 256–57; *The Great Transformation*, 256–57
political economy, 177, 182n17, 228n6, 248n, 258–59, 258n30. *See also* Marxism
political history, 13, 40, 86, 86n6, 102, 103, 168n, 239; and independence movement, 140–41, 140n12, 142–43, 144, 148, 155–59, 161, 162; political culture in, 89, 90n12, 91n15, 93, 96, 141, 143, 144, 148–49, 155, 156, 156n21, 161; relationship to cultural history, 14, 225, 229, 233n, 246, 250, 262
Polk, James K., 83
Ponce Alcocer, María Eugenia, 48
Poole, Stafford, 114, 115, 116, 242n18
Popkin, Jeremy D., 5n9
population: decline in indigenous people, 65–66, 103, 104, 105; distribution of, 73, 172n, 178; growth in, 11, 42, 66, 185n24
Porfiriato, 37, 56, 137, 139, 179
Porter, Roy, 238
Posada-Carbó, Eduardo, 157n
positivism, 133, 138, 139, 139n10, 203, 250, 257, 259
postcolonial studies, 84n2, 87–88, 94, 107n, 125, 253, 262–63
postmodernism, 199, 202–3, 225n; relationship to cultural history, 86, 87, 226, 228, 240, 253
poststructuralism, 200n, 228
Potosí, 64–65, 70
Powell, Amanda, 109n
power projects, 196
Prados de la Escosura, Leandro, 67
pre-Columbian Mexico, 32, 118, 134, 217
Prem, Hans J., 36
Prescott, William H., 4, 5, 83, 83n, 146
price history, 46, 66, 192, 192n
prosopography, 86, 106, 249
Provincia de Ávalos, 42
psychoanalysis, 213, 236
public ceremonies/rituals, 107, 148, 157n, 160, 242n19, 253

Puebla region, 28, 36, 38, 40, 44n, 47, 48, 98, 100, 104, 152–53, 168
Puente Brunke, José de la, 64
Puerto Rico: coffee production in, 73; slavery in, 78; sugar production in, 77
Puhle, Hans-Jürgen, 32, 102n34, 159n24
pulque, 36
Putumayo, 66, 72

quantitative techniques, 33, 102, 103, 250, 251, 257–58, 259, 260
Queirós Mattoso, Katia M. de, 76–77
Querétaro, 35
Quiroz, Alfonso W., 56n4
Quiroz, Enriqueta, 47

Rabell, Cecilia, 35
race relations, 54, 56, 57, 76–77, 107–8, 109; in Oaxaca, 38, 100; relationship to class, 25, 101, 107, 107n, 149, 229–30. *See also* African slavery; indigenous people
Radding, Cynthia, 25, 44, 112, 225n, 239, 240; *Wandering Peoples*, 121, 249
Ragatz, Lowell, 77
railroads, 62, 179–80, 183, 193
Ramírez, Ignacio, 137
Ramírez Bacca, Renzo, 73
Ramírez Rancaño, Mario, 36
ranchos, 23, 38n, 41, 43–44, 70, 79
Randolph, Jorge, 63
rational choice theory, 214, 245, 245n, 259
Raynal, Abbé, 134
Real del Monte, 103, 236
Redfield, Robert: on folk-urban continuum, 171
Reff, Daniel, 104, 105
Reform period, 132, 137, 146, 261
regionalism, 18, 168n, 169, 175–76; vs. regionality, 170
regionality, 11, 18, 137n, 143; and central-place theory, 34, 62, 168, 169n2, 172, 172n, 173, 173n, 177, 178, 178n9, 181, 181n14, 182, 193; definition of regions, 29, 62n, 99–100, 100n32, 167–70, 168n, 172–74, 180, 180n, 182, 186n27; and disarticulation, 179n, 193–97; and economic history, 33, 172–73, 175; finalist approach to, 171–72; formal/homogeneous regions vs. nodal/functional regions, 173–74, 173n, 180–82, 180n; and friction of distance, 174, 177, 180, 195, 196, 260; funnel/dendritic type regions, 180–81, 181n14, 183–86, 183n19, 185n24; and haciendas, 33–39, 51, 62; historicity of regions, 172, 174–76; instrumentalist approach to, 171–72; levels of regional analysis, 173; and Mexican independence movement, 152–54; and neoclassical economics, 174, 177; new regional history, 28–29, 99–100, 152; and precapitalist societies, 174; pressure cooker/solar type regions, 180–81, 181n14, 183, 185, 187–92, 187n30, 192n; processualist approach to, 171–72; regional exceptionalism, 36; vs. regionalism, 170; regional science theory, 172, 176, 177, 193; regions as good to think, 169, 170–72, 176–77, 197; regions vs. political/administrative entities, 168n, 169, 173; relationship to energy extraction, 195–97; relationship to mode of production, 177, 182n17; relationship to social class, 178–79, 179n, 181, 183, 184, 184n23, 186, 186n26, 189, 194–95, 196; relationship to the state, 194, 195–97; and traditional economic theory, 169n2; typology of Mexican regions, 179, 180–92, 181n14
Regla, Conde de, 106n, 236
Reguera, Andrea, 71
Reina Aoyama, Leticia, 50, 90n12

Reis, João José, 74n, 77
relaciones geográficas, 105
religion, 93, 109, 110, 113–19; as cultural history, 14, 15, 85, 96, 96n25, 122, 148, 233, 253, 254; the Devil, 117, 241–42; evangelization process, 116–18; and indigenous people, 54, 91, 113–14, 115–19, 122, 205–7, 205n5, 241–42; messianic figures, 112, 135, 206n6, 217, 218; and overdetermination, 225, 262; Virgin of Guadalupe, 11–12, 27, 115–16, 119, 153, 158, 206, 216, 242n18. *See also* Catholic Church
Relph, E. C., 177
Rendón Garcini, Ricardo, 40, 41, 59n8
repartimiento, 47, 64–65, 104
reparto/repartimiento de mercancías, 65, 104
Restall, Matthew, 86nn5,6, 119, 119n, 122, 240; *Life and Death in a Maya Community,* 122n
revolutionary mythology, 160–61
Revolution of 1910, 84, 132, 139, 146; as agrarian upheaval, 22, 42, 43, 78; Molina Enríquez during, 21n; origins of, 22, 23, 31, 37, 41, 42, 43, 54, 56, 57, 67, 78, 79, 186n26; Zapata during, 37, 78, 79
Reygadas, Fermín de, 206n7
Reyna, María del Carmen, 41
Ricard, Robert, 113, 115, 230
Ricardo, David, 69
Richards, Thomas, 175
Richardson, Henry Ward, 172, 174, 194
Ricouer, Paul, 232, 234
Riguzzi, Paolo, 179
Riva Palacio, Vicente, 138n; *México a través de los siglos,* 137–38, 139n10
Rivero Torres, José Manuel, 35
Roberts, Bryan, 177, 182n17
Robertson, William, 134

Robertson, William Spence, 150
Robinson, David, 175–76, 196
Rodríguez, José Marcelino Pedro, 12, 199, 204–11, 205n6, 213, 215, 218–19
Rodríguez Gómez, María Guadalupe, 40, 59n
Rodríquez Baquero, Luis Enrique, 64
Rodríquez O., Jaime E., 90n12, 102n34, 148, 150, 157n, 158–59, 163, 239
Rojas Rabiela, Teresa, 49, 240
Romano, Ruggiero, 66, 87n
Romero, José Ignacio Luciano, 215
Romero Frizzi, María de los Angeles, 240
Rosaldo, Renato, 211–12
Rosas, Juan Manuel de, 68–69, 71
Roseberry, William, 73, 248n
rubber production, 66, 72
Rugeley, Terry, 50, 113n
Ruiz Abreu, Carlos E., 36, 47
rural resistance and rebellion, 49–51, 98–99, 110–13, 111n44, 125, 153–54, 155–59, 230, 242n18, 244–46; role of religion in, 113, 205n5; sources regarding, 200. *See also* independence movement
Russell, Bertrand, 9, 9n18, 91n15
Rutledge, Ian, 66n13, 69, 181n15, 183n18
Ruz, Mario Humberto, 240

Sabato, Hilda, 69–70
Sabean, David, 248–49
Sacks, Oliver W., 258n29
Saco, José Antonio, 56, 57, 77
Sacristán, María Christina, 238
Sahlins, Marshall, 237, 253; on culture, 247–48, 248n, 256, 257; *Culture and Practical Reason,* 247–48
Said, Edward: *Orientalism,* 84n3
Saint Domingue, 77
Salamini, Heather Fowler, 175
Salinas, Patricia, 176, 177

Salmerón, Roberto, 112
Saltillo, 39, 101
Salvatore, Ricardo, 71
Salvucci, Richard J., 33, 103
Samper Kutschbach, Mario, 73
San Antonio de Béxar, 39, 101
Sánchez Maldonado, María Isabel, 46
Sánchez Navarro family, 249
Sánchez Santiró, Ernest, 37, 48, 78
Sánchez Silva, Carlos, 47, 65
San Francisco de Borja, 41
San Luis Potosí, 154, 156
San Miguel, Pedro L., 85n
Santa Anna, Antonio López de, 3, 4, 129
Sauer, Carl, 104, 176
Scarano, Francisco, 77
Scardaville, Michael, 111n43
Schama, Simon: *Dead Certainties*, 200, 201–2, 218; on death of James Wolf, 200, 202; on murder of George Parkman, 200, 201
Scharrer Tamm, Beatriz, 49, 78
Schell, William, Jr., 40, 59, 98n28
Schlesinger, Arthur M., 5n9
Schmit, Roberto, 67
Schroeder, Susan, 25, 109, 111, 112, 124n51, 230, 240; on Chimalpahin, 123–24, 123n, 239
Schryer, Frans J., 25
Schwaller, John, 113–14, 229, 249
Schwartz, Stuart B., 75, 76, 181n15
Scobie, James, 69
Scott, James C., 99, 205n5, 230n9, 257; *Domination and the Arts of Resistance*, 200, 213, 214–19; on hidden transcripts of resentment and resistance, 209, 214–15, 216–17, 218; on public transcripts of domination and subordination, 210, 211, 214, 216, 217; *Weapons of the Weak*, 214
Scott, Ridley: *Blade Runner*, 119
Scull, Andrew T., 238
Seamon, David, 177
Seed, Patricia, 109, 238, 246

Semo, Enrique, 39, 45, 60, 85n; *History of Capitalism in Mexico*, 102
serial history, 46
Serrano Ortega, José Antonio, 143
Serrera Contreras, Ramón María, 33, 62
Service, Elman R., 64
Servín, Elisa, 90n12
Shadle, Stanley F., 21n
Shanin, Teodor, 224n2
Shapiro, Ian, 245n
sheep: in Argentina, 69–70; Melville's *A Plague of Sheep*, 28, 94n21, 98, 249
Sheridan, Thomas E., 121
Sherman, William L., 63
Sierra Gorda, 154
Sierra Méndez, Justo: *Evolución política del pueblo mexicano*, 139n10
Sigel, Pete, 117
Silva, Eduardo, 77
Silva Riquer, Jorge, 47, 192n
silver mining: in Bolivia, 64–65, 70; in Mexico, 27, 31, 32, 35, 36, 38, 41, 45, 53, 58, 60, 67, 100, 102, 103n, 106n, 128, 143, 181n15, 183, 193, 235–36, 249; in Peru, 60, 67
Simpson, Lesley Byrd, 64, 65, 104, 105, 110
Sinaloa (state), 112
sisal, 66, 67
sistema de castas, 38, 100, 107n, 108
skepticism, 199, 200–201
Skinner, G. William, 187n30
Skipp, Victor, 33
Skocpol, Theda, 149, 154
Slatta, Richard W., 71
slavery: abolition of, 74, 78, 79; in Brazil, 57, 68n, 74–80; of indigenous people, 63, 64n; in Mexico, 63, 64n, 74, 78–79. *See also* African slavery
Slicher Van Bath, Bernhard, 30, 33, 57, 194
Smith, Adam, 258, 258n30, 261

Smith, Carol, 169n2, 178n10, 181n14; on definition of regions, 180n; on dendritic regional systems, 184n20, 186, 186n27; on marketing structures, 187n30; on regional analysis, 171, 172n, 178, 178n11, 182n17; *Regional Analysis,* 187n30; on solar regional systems, 188n32, 192n; on surplus and exchange, 182n17
Smith-Kleiner, Felicia, 96n24
social history, 13, 87, 94n21, 101, 103, 120n, 140; vs. cultural history, 2, 86, 115, 120, 229, 231, 233n; vs. economic history, 2, 11, 27–28, 94, 99n, 105–6, 260; and independence movement, 91n15, 143–44, 145, 148, 149, 150, 151. *See also* subaltern history
social mobility, 108, 178
Socolow, Susan Migden, 49, 53, 86n5
Solberg, Carl, 69
Sonora (state), 240
Soulodre-La France, Renée, 73
sources, historical, 58, 135, 157, 234–42; *alcabala* data, 46–47, 188n31; as ambiguous, 15, 16, 109, 204–19; archival sources, 10–11, 12, 28, 37, 41–42, 45, 51, 70, 88, 99, 102, 140, 144, 151, 151n; and context of domination, 209–10, 212; criminal records, 70, 88, 109, 151n, 199, 207, 238–39; cultural history and texts, 95–96, 117–18, 229, 234–38, 241, 259; estate account books, 25, 29, 40, 43, 61, 65, 70; ethnohistory and texts, 119–20, 121–22, 123–24; explicit vs. implicit forms of evidence, 201–2; regarding free labor, 65; regarding haciendas, 25, 29, 36, 37, 41–43, 48, 49, 51, 61, 61n10, 99; lack of, 65, 113, 116, 120, 155; letters as, 3–5; in native languages, 119–20, 121–22, 123–24; newspapers, 3; notary records, 25, 37, 41, 51, 70, 106, 211; parish records, 25, 45, 65, 70; popular collective action and texts, 199–219; relationship to colonial state, 237–39, 237n, 244, 246, 260; regarding slavery, 79–80; regarding subaltern groups, 107
Sousa, Lisa, 115
Spanish Caribbean islands, 74, 74n, 75, 77–78
Spanish conquest, 36, 84, 103, 116, 128n, 146, 179–80, 228–30, 235, 235n; Bustamante on, 128–29; Mier on, 133–34; Trexler on, 236; Zarate on, 138
Spanish crown: Bourbon Reforms, 11, 65, 91, 104, 106, 111, 114, 142, 157; and encomiendas, 63; relations with conquistadores, 133–34; relations with Jesuits, 41
Spicer, Edward H.: *Cycles of Conquest,* 120–21
Spiro, Melford, 175, 248; on anthropology, 223, 233, 263
Spores, Ronald, 44n, 112
Stefanou, Spiro E., 32, 62, 102, 103n, 159n24
Stein, Barbara H., 67
Stein, Stanley J., 67, 76, 181n15
Stepick, Alex, 100n33
Stern, Claudio, 174, 175
Stern, Steve, 63; on adaptive resistance, 88; on gender relations, 109, 226, 230, 238, 245, 246; scholarly trajectory of, 26n8
Stevens, Donald, 205n6
Stone, Lawrence, 106
Strickon, Arnold, 183n19, 185nn24,25, 186, 186n27
structuralism, 39, 101, 120, 122, 125, 155, 263
Suárez Arguello, Clara Elena, 48
subaltern history, 89, 106–7, 109, 120, 228; emergence of, 50, 85–86, 145; relationship to cultural history, 87–88, 117, 229–30,

244–46; subaltern agency, 25, 51, 71, 87–88, 107, 108, 124, 149, 156, 158, 244–46, 250; subaltern politics, 155–59, 162; subaltern studies, 25, 50–51, 72n, 76–77, 140, 145
sugar production: and African slavery, 23, 37, 38n, 48, 68n, 74, 78–79; in Andean region, 57; in Brazil, 55, 57, 68n15, 74, 75, 181n15, 183, 184n21; in Dominican Republic, 66; for export, 37, 57, 67, 68n, 74, 184, 184n21, 187; in Mexico, 23, 37, 38n, 48, 49, 51, 74, 78–79, 98, 101, 183–84, 183n19, 184n21, 185, 185n25; in Peru, 61, 66
Super, John C., 49
Swann, Michael, 38, 100

Tabasco region, 36, 47, 66, 240
Tandeter, Enrique, 46, 66
Tangancícuaro, 187
Tannenbaum, Frank, 42
Tarascans, 112, 117
Tarrow, Sidney, 149
Taussig, Michael, 72
Tawney, R. H., 11, 30, 57
Taxco, 38
Taylor, Frederick Winslow, 224, 224n1
Taylor, William B., 34, 50, 59n8, 98, 99, 148, 159n24, 230; on drinking, homicide and rebellion, 110–11; on Oaxaca, 47; on parish priests, 114, 115, 115n, 238; scholarly trajectory of, 26–27
Teja, Jesús F. de la, 39, 101
Tenenbaum, Barbara, 205n6
Tepeaca, 36
Terán, General, 4
Terán, Marta, 132n5, 139, 139n11, 141
Terraciano, Kevin, 122, 240
Terranova y Monteleone, Duque de, 4
Testaments of Culhuacán, The, 123
Texas Republic, 135
textile production, 103, 244n

thick description, 39, 87, 100–101, 109, 201
Third World economic development, 145
Thirsk, Joan, 11, 57
Thomas, Hugh, 74
Thomism, 117
Thompson, Edward P., 175, 215, 224, 229; on class, 176, 236; on modernity, 224n1; on moral economy, 257
Thomson, Guy, 36
Thorner, Daniel, 224n2
Thurner, Mark, 156n20, 157n, 263
Timmons, Wilbert H., 150
títulos primordiales, 119
Tlaxcala, 36, 40, 48
Tlayacapan, 184n23
tobacco production, Mexican, 37n, 73, 78, 103, 244n
Todorov, Tzvetan, 213
Tomóchic episode, 113
Topik, Steven C., 67, 73
topography, 167–68, 169
Torales Pacheco, Cristina, 44
Tord Nicolini, Javier, 64n
Torres Sánchez, Jaime, 72
Torre Villar, Ernesto de la, 141
Tortolero Villaseñor, Alejandro, 49
Tovar Pinzón, Hermes, 61n10
Tovías, Blanca, 157n
Trabulse, Elías, 66
Trautmann, Wolfgang, 36
Trelles Aréstegui, Efraín, 64
Trevelyan, George, 148
Trexler, Richard, 109n, 236n; *Sex and Conquest*, 236, 241
Tuan, Yi Fu, 176
Tudela, Elisa Sampson Vera, 109n
Turner, Victor, 153, 234
Tutino, John, 12, 42, 44, 50, 91n15, 98–99, 249; *From Insurrection to Revolution in Mexico*, 153–54, 155, 157; vs. Hamnett, 154
two republics (dos repúblicas), 43
Tzeltal Indians: evangelization of, 117; Rebellion of, 112

United States: academic specialization on Mexico, 84n3, 89n10, 93, 125, 144n, 145–46, 145n; economic history in, 24, 57, 66, 92n18, 96; vs. Mexico, 13, 16, 83–85, 109; Oregon and Britain, 83, 83n; relations with Mexico, 94, 121, 127, 129, 136, 157, 193; slavery in, 76; social and cultural history in, 107–8, 107n, 125, 145, 149, 253; University of California system, 89n10; University of Chicago, 89n10; University of Texas-Austin, 89n10, 150; Vietnam War, 50, 72n, 111, 145. See also Anglophone historians
Universidad Nacional Autónoma de México, 144n
University of California Consortium on Mexico and the United States (UC MEXUS), 89n10
upstreaming, 58, 235, 236, 257
urbanization, 53, 62
Uribe-Urán, Victor M., 90n12, 157n, 162, 239
Uruguay, 53, 71

Valadés, José C., 4n5
Valdés, Dennis Nodin, 108n41
Valdés Dávila, Carlos Manuel, 239, 240, 240n
Valladolid/Morelia, 143, 187
Vallecilla Gordillo, Jaime, 73
Valley of Mexico, 103, 104, 105, 121, 249; Gibson on, 34, 124; Guarisco on, 144; Hassig on, 179–80; vs. regions, 28, 99
Vanderwood, Paul, 50, 179, 196, 206n8; on bandits, 23n; on Cuautla Lazarus, 205n6; on Tomóchic rebels, 113, 225
Vargas, Otto, 64
Vargas-Lobsinger, María, 42, 59n8
Vasco de Quiroga, 114, 117
Vásquez Mantecón, Verónica, 37
Vaughan, Mary Kay, 86n5, 226n, 246
Vázquez Mantecón, Verónica, 78

Veblen, Thorstein, 251
Vega, Luis Laso de la: *Huey tlamahuiçoltica/Nican mopuhua*, 115
Velásquez, María del Carmen, 40
Venezuela: Caracas, 71–72, 184n21; coffee production in, 73; export economy in, 72
Veracruz region, 36, 48, 78, 98, 106, 108, 156
Vérastique, Bernardino: *Michoacán and Eden*, 117
Victoria, Guadalupe, 130
Vidal de la Blache, Paul, 175
Vidal Luna, Francisco, 76, 77
Vietnam War, 50, 72n, 111, 145
Vilar, Pierre, 174
Villagrán family, 131
Villalpando César, José Manuel, 139
Villamarin, Juan A. and Judith E., 64n
Villaseñor Tortolero, Alejandro, 31n
Villoro, Luis, 141–42
Vinson, Ben, III, 74n, 107n, 108
Viqueira Albán, Juan Pedro, 106–7, 110, 114, 238
Virgin of Guadalupe, 153, 242n18; Brading on, 27, 115–16, 119; and independence movement, 12, 158, 206, 216
vocabulary change, 13, 92, 93–94, 95–96, 253
Voekel, Pamela, 119; *Alone Before God*, 114–15
von Thünen, J. H., 169n2, 182n16
Voss, Stuart F., 22n, 42, 97n28

Wachtel, Nathan, 235
wages, 66, 225, 251, 253–54
Walker, Charles E., 156n20
Warman, Arturo, 184n22
Warren, Fintan B., 114
Warren, J. Benedict, 112
Warren, Richard A., 90n12, 91n15, 148; *Vagrants and Citizens*, 157n
Wasserman, Mark, 168n, 175
Wasserstrom, Robert, 25
water resources, 36, 37, 41, 98, 104

wealth, 35, 38, 42, 100, 251, 252, 253–54; of Catholic Church, 255–56; distribution of, 67, 68, 178; preservation of, 41, 106, 262
Weber, David, 121
Weber, Max, 153, 163, 251
Webster, James, 200, 202
Weinstein, Barbara, 72
Wells, Allen, 41, 45, 67, 156n20, 185n25, 237; on henequen industry, 72, 168n, 183n19, 185, 186nn26,27
West, Benjamin, 202
wheat, 21, 48, 60, 67, 68, 69, 183, 191n33
White, Hayden, 218
White, Richard, 113, 168n
Whitmore, Thomas, 104
Wibel, John, 188n31
Wilde, Oscar: on the cynic, 254n25
Wilkie, James W., 175
Williams, Eric, 77
Withrow, G. J., 224n1
Wobeser, Gisela von, 25, 37, 40, 46, 78, 184n21
Wolf, Eric, 39, 50, 101, 122, 154; *Europe and the People Without History*, 248n; on haciendas, 26n7, 33, 61–62
Wolf, James, 200, 202
Womack, John, 184n22
women, 94, 108–9, 148, 226, 245, 262. *See also* gender

Wood, Gordon, 161
Wood, Stephanie, 109
wool production, 57, 67, 72, 184n20
world-systems theory, 149, 177
Wortman, Miles, 42

Yaquis, 38, 100, 240
Yautepec, 183
Yucatán, 44n, 45, 180; as funnel/dendritic region, 183, 183n19, 185–86, 185n24; henequen production in, 66, 67, 72, 168n, 183, 183n19, 185–86, 185n24, 186nn26,27; Maya in, 111, 112, 113n, 116–17, 119, 122, 235; Patch on, 36, 59n8, 98, 112, 183n19, 185, 185n24; sugar production in, 185, 185n25
Yuste, Carmen, 47, 192n

Zacatecas, 35–36; Los Cañones, 45
Zamora, 187
Zapata, Emiliano, 37, 78, 79
Zapotec, 121
Zarate, Julio, 138–39
Zavala, Lorenzo de, 130, 132, 132n5, 136n, 137, 138; vs. Alamán, 134, 135, 136; vs. Bustamonte, 133, 135; *Ensayo histórico de las revoluciones de México*, 135–36; on objectivity, 135–36
Zavala, Silvio, 63, 64, 64n
Zermeño, Guillermo, 231n11
Zitácuaro, 143

The authorized representative in the EU for product safety and compliance is:
Mare Nostrum Group
B.V Doelen 72
4831 GR Breda
The Netherlands

www.ingramcontent.com/pod-product-compliance
Lightning Source LLC
Chambersburg PA
CBHW030333240426
43661CB00052B/1617